JOURNAL FOR THE STUDY OF THE NEW TESTAMENT
SUPPLEMENT SERIES
203

Executive Editor
Stanley E. Porter

Sheffield Academic Press

Matthew, Poet of the Beatitudes

H. Benedict Green, CR

Journal for the Study of the New Testament
Supplement Series 203

For Peter Walker, ἐπίσκοπος φιλόμουσος
and in grateful memory of
Frederick William Dillistone

Published by Sheffield Academic Press Ltd
Mansion House
19 Kingfield Road
Sheffield S11 9AS
England

www.SheffieldAcademicPress.com

Printed on acid-free paper in Great Britain
by MPG Books Ltd
Bodmin, Cornwall

British Library Cataloguing-in-Publication Data

A catalogue record for this book is available
from the British Library

ISBN 1-84127-165-9

CONTENTS

PREFACE

Twenty-five years ago I published a small commentary on the Gospel of Matthew in the New Clarendon series. If anyone is curious to turn up what is said there about the Beatitudes, they will find a conventional treatment of the source material combined with a more original account of the formal characteristics of the Matthaean composition. Doubts about the compatibility of these two approaches arose in my mind very soon after publication, but for some years I was not free to explore the question systematically.

The present study thus began as unfinished business. I am grateful to my Community for relieving me of responsibility for its theological college in 1984 and thus giving me freedom to pursue this and related New Testament studies. The research required has necessarily involved extended visits to libraries at a distance from where I live. This has been made possible by the generous hospitality of friends, to whom I gratefully acknowledge a great debt: in particular to Rowan and Jane Williams, Pamela Paul, David and Jayne Conner, Nicholas Cranfield, Andrew and Virginia Greany, the Franciscans of St Francis' House, Cambridge, the Dominicans of Blackfriars, Oxford, and the Benedictines of the Abbey of St Matthias, Trier.

David Ravens (who has also shared the proofreading), Hugh Pyper and David Lane read the original draft and encouraged me with their comments. Philip Alexander gave prompt bibliographical assistance at points when it was urgently needed. Other friends with a feeling for poetry have sustained the project by their patient interest over a number of years. To two of them in particular the book is dedicated.

ACKNOWLEDGMENTS

The substance of Chapter 4 §4 was previously published in fuller form as 'Matthew 11.7-15: Redaction or Self-Redaction?' in C. Focant (ed.), *The Synoptic Gospels: Source Criticism and the New Literary Criticism* (BETL, 110; Leuven: Leuven University Press/Peeters, 1993), pp. 459-66, and appears here in an abridged version by permission of Leuven University Press.

I thank Professor emeritus Birger Gerhardsson for permission to reproduce on p. 238-39 a paragraph from *The Testing of God's Son* (ConBNT 2.1; Lund: C.W.K. Gleerup, 1966).

The passages on pp. 42 and 125 from *The Art of Biblical Poetry*, copyright ©1985 Robert Alter, and that on p. 20 from *The World of Biblical Literature*, copyright © 1992 Robert Alter, are reprinted by permission of Georges Borchardt, Inc. All rights reserved.

The extract from the Qumran Community Rule on p. 197 is quoted from the version of Geza Vermes, *The Dead Sea Scrolls in English* (Penguin Books, 4th edn, 1995, copyright © G. Vermes 1995). Reproduced by permission of the author and of Penguin Books Ltd.

Quotations from the LXX follow (with minor orthographical adjustments) the edition of A. Rahlfs, *Septuaginta* (Stuttgart: Württembergische Bibelanstalt, 6th edn, 1954).

Finally I must thank the editorial staff of the Sheffield Academic Press for the skill and patience with which they transformed an unwieldy typescript into a presentable book, and in particular Frances Mawer, whose handling of the final stages was as author-friendly as it was vigilant. For any remaining blemishes I alone am responsible.

ABBREVIATIONS

AB	Anchor Bible
AnBib	Analecta biblica
ANTJ	Arbeiten zum Neuen Testament und Judentum
AV	Authorized Version
BAGD	Walter Bauer, William F. Arndt, F. William Gingrich and Frederick W. Danker, *A Greek–English Lexicon of the New Testament and Other Early Christian Literature* (Chicago: University of Chicago Press, 2nd edn, 1958)
BBB	Bonner biblische Beiträge
BDB	Francis Brown, S.R. Driver and Charles A. Briggs, *A Hebrew and English Lexicon of the Old Testament* (Oxford: Clarendon Press, 1907)
BETL	Bibliotheca epheridum theologicarum lovaniensium
BibInt	*Biblical Interpretation: A Journal of Contemporary Approaches*
Bib	*Biblica*
BJ	Bible de Jérusalem
BJRL	*Bulletin of the John Rylands University Library of Manchester*
BJS	Brown Judaic Studies
BNTC	Black's New Testament Commentaries
BTB	*Biblical Theology Bulletin*
BU	Biblische Untersuchungen
BWANT	Beiträge zur Wissenschaft vom Alten und Neuen Testament
BZ	*Biblische Zeitschrift* [NF = Neue Folge]
BZNW	Beihefte zur *ZNW*
CBC	Cambridge Bible Commentaries
CBQ	*Catholic Biblical Quarterly*
CBQMS	*Catholic Biblical Quarterly*, Monograph Series
CHB	P.R. Ackroyd and C.F. Evans (eds.), *Cambridge History of the Bible*, I (Cambridge: Cambridge University Press, 1970)
ConBNT	Coniectanea Biblica, New Testament
CSJCA	Centre for the Study of Judaism and Christianity in Antiquity
EDNT	*Exegetical Dictionary of the New Testament*
EKKNT	Evangelischer-katholischer Kommentar zum Neuen Testament
EstE	*Estudios eclesiásticos*

ETL	*Ephemerides theologicae lovanienses*
EvT	*Evangelische Theologie*
FB	Forschung zur Bibel
FRLANT	Forschungen zur Religion und Literatur des Alten und Neuen Testaments
GP	Gospel Perspectives (Oxford: Clarendon Press, 1897)
H-R	E. Hatch and H.A. Redpath, *Concordance to the Septuagint*
HTKNT	Herders theologischer Kommentar zum Neuen Testament
HTR	*Harvard Theological Review*
ICC	International Critical Commentary
JB	Jerusalem Bible
JBL	*Journal of Biblical Literature*
JR	*Journal of Religion*
JSNT	*Journal for the Study of the New Testament*
JSNTSup	*Journal for the Study of the New Testament*, Supplement Series
JSOTSup	*Journal for the Study of the Old Testament*, Supplement Series
JTS	*Journal of Theological Studies*
KEKNT	Kritisch-exegetischer Kommentar über das Neue Testament
LD	Lectio divina
LSJ	H.G. Liddell, Robert Scott and H. Stuart Jones, *The Greek–English Lexicon* (Oxford: Clarendon Press, 9th edn, 1968)
LkR	Lukan redaction
LumV	*Lumen Vitae*
M-M	J.H. Moulton and G. Milligan, *Vocabulary of the Greek Testament* (London: Hodder & Stoughton, 1930)
MkR	Markan redaction
MtR	Matthaean redaction
N-A	Nestle-Aland, *Novum Testamentum Graece*
NEB	*New English Bible*
NIV	New International Version
NJB	*New Jerusalem Bible*
NovT	*Novum Testamentum*
NovTSup	*Novum Testamentum*, Supplements
NRSV	New Revised Standard Version
NTAbh	Neutestamentliche Abhandlungen
NTD	Das Neue Testament Deutsch
NTS	*New Testament Studies*
OBO	Orbis biblicus et orientalis
PS	*Palästina-Studien* (Vienna)
RB	*Revue biblique*
REB	Revised English Bible
RHPR	*Revue d'histoire et de philosophie religieuses*
RSV	Revised Standard Version
RTL	*Revue théologique de Louvain*

RV	Revised Version
S-B	H.L. Strack/P. Billerbeck, *Kommentar zum New Testament aus Talmud und Midrasch* (7 vols., Munich: Beck, 1922–61)
SBG	Studies in Biblical Greek
SBL	Society of Biblical Literature
SBLDS	SBL Dissertation Series
SBLSCS	SBL Septuagint and Cognate Studies
SBS	Stuttgarter Bibelstudien
SBT	Studies in Biblical Theology
ScrB	*Scripture Bulletin*
SE	*Studia Evangelica*
SJLA	Studies in Judaism in Late Antiquity
SJT	*Scottish Journal of Theology*
SNTSMS	Society for New Testament Studies Monograph Series
SNTU(L)	*Studien zum Neuen Testament und seiner Umwelt* (Linz)
ST	*Studia theologica*
TDNT	Gerhard Kittel and Gerhard Friedrich (eds.), *Theological Dictionary of the New Testament* (trans. Geoffrey W. Bromiley; 10 vols.; Grand Rapids: Eerdmans, 1964–)
TRu	*Theologische Rundschau*
ThV	*Theologische Versuche*
TPI	Trinity Press International New Testament Commentaries
TSS	Toronto Semitic Studies
TU	Texte und Untersuchungen
UBS	United Bible Societies (and the edition of the Greek New Testament published by them)
VT	*Vetus Testamentum*
WBC	Word Bible Commentary
WMANT	Wissenschaftliche Monographien zum Alten und Neuen Testament
WUNT	Wissenschaftliche Untersuchungen zum Neuen Testament
ZNW	*Zeitschrift für die neutestamentliche Wissenschaft*
ZTK	*Zeitschrift für Theologie und Kirche*

Part I
THE BEATITUDES AS POETRY

Chapter 1

PRIORITIES IN THE STUDY OF A TEXT

'All the modern literature', in the words of a contemporary challenge to it, 'attempts to trace the formation of the Beatitudes tradition into its present forms by form-critical and redactional techniques, and commonly urges an original Aramaic form'.[1] The method first establishes, by comparison of Matthew with Luke, a common underlying text assumed to have been transmitted as part of the hypothetical source Q; it then distinguishes, within this text, between elements that can only reflect the experience of the post-resurrection Church and elements that could (and therefore presumably do) go back to the preaching of Jesus himself, and finally, with the assistance of Old Testament texts reflected in the material, it seeks to identify a *Sitz im Leben Jesu* for the latter. With that object achieved it is free to return to the texts of the two

1.   M.D. Goulder, *Midrash and Lection in Matthew* (London: SPCK, 1974, p. 273. A recent exception to this reading of the evidence is the account proposed by H.D. Betz, *The Sermon on the Mount* (Hermeneia; Minneapolis: Fortress Press, 1995) (see the Introduction, pp. 43-44, for his conclusions, and cf. his *Essays on the Sermon on the Mount* [Philadelphia: Fortress Press, 1985], pp. 17-22). Betz will not entertain any questioning of the Q hypothesis (for his tradition of scholarship not so much a hypothesis as a *datum*), but he recognizes the presence of formal literary composition in the Sermon on the Mount (and Sermon on the Plain), not least in the Beatitudes and Lord's Prayer, and sees that it is not adequately understood as the redactional accumulation of small units. His alternative is a complete sermon composed (in Greek) very early and afterwards incorporated in the version of Q known to Matthew (Q^{Mt}), who took it over into his Gospel virtually as it stood (a parallel process is posited for Luke and the Sermon on the Plain). I concur with his observations concerning composition and Greek language origin; my quarrel is with his insistence (which his source-critical assumptions have forced upon him) on keeping the Evangelist out of the picture. (For previous criticisms of his position see C.E. Carlston, 'Betz on the Sermon on the Mount', *CBQ* 50 [1988], pp. 47-57; G.N. Stanton, *A Gospel for a New People: Studies in Matthew* [Edinburgh: T. & T. Clark 1992], pp. 309-25.)

Gospels and discuss the stages by which they reached their present form, the background in the tradition of the additional beatitudes found in Matthew (and the woes in Luke), and the part played by the Evangelists in their final arrangement.

The completion in 1973, after nearly twenty years' work, of Dom Jacques Dupont's three-volume study *Les Béatitudes*[2] left an abiding monument to this approach, and probably took it as far as it can ever be taken, while the comprehensiveness of its documentation will make it a required work of reference as long as the subject is studied. Yet neither the sheer weight of the author's erudition nor the general acuteness of his critical judgement should blind the reader to a certain oddness about its arrangement, particularly in that part of the huge final volume which is devoted to the Matthaean version, where the two beatitudes that speak of righteousness (IV, VIII) are taken first; next I, II and III (the two remaining 'original' beatitudes and a newly formulated parallel to one of them); and finally the 'new' beatitudes (V, VI and VII).[3] Is this really the way to read the Matthaean Beatitudes as a composition, and does such an uneasy blend of pre-history and literary form do justice to the Evangelist as an author with a message to convey?

There are two questions behind that uncertainty: the priority given to the genetic method, with its concentration on antecedent sources, in the exegetical process as applied to a particular text; and the validity of the Two Document hypothesis (2DH) as the solution to the synoptic problem with which Dupont, in common with the vast majority of contemporary scholars, approaches the genesis of this one. The first of those questions is the more fundamental, and I therefore take it first. But the second is highly relevant to any examination of this text in the light of others that may be taken as evidence of the Evangelist's authorial hand, and we shall return to it (see §2 below).

1. *Literary Analysis Prior to Source Analysis*

The analysis of a literary composition (as opposed to a chronicle, or a mere pastiche of extracts from earlier writings) does not ordinarily (reserving one exception) begin with the identification of its sources; the primary task is the examination of the text.[4] To discover what a

2.   J. Dupont, *Les Béatitudes* (3 vols.; Paris: Gabalda, I-II 1969, III 1973).
3.   Dupont, *Béatitudes*, III, pp. 307-67.
4.   See D.B. Howell, *Matthew's Inclusive Story* (JSNTSup, 42; Sheffield: JSOT

document is saying, and to analyse the literary means by which it does so, is methodologically prior to discussion of its authority for saying it. The latter is (i) an aspect of the relationship of a document to the wider literary (and pre-literary) tradition in which it stands;[5] (ii) part of the assessment of its historical or factual reliability and the proximity (or otherwise) of the author to the persons, events or sayings that he or she records,[6] and these two functions are not always carefully distinguished; only the former belongs to the strictly literary analysis, and even as such must not be anticipated. Our reserved case (see above) is that of a work (usually narrative) which takes up that of a predecessor and seeks to enhance or to correct it; a well-known example is the books of Chronicles (the English title is a misnomer here);[7] the char-

Press, 1990), p. 36: 'the insight of formalist literary theory that the text itself is the proper focus of literary study should be retained by the biblical literary critic'. Howell's whole introduction (pp. 18-53) offers an admirably balanced account of the literary dimension to Gospel study as it has developed in the past two decades, and its proper relation to the historical and theological dimensions, which he rightly argues should not be kept in separate compartments. 'The intention of the author and the historical situation in which the text was produced are...not a matter of indifference for the biblical literary critic. These must be primarily inferred, however, on the basis of the literary genre and the conventions utilized in the text.' (*Story*, p. 50).

5.   The genetic approach to the Gospels has been over-influenced by the methods and the success of Pentateuchal criticism (Wellhausen was a pioneer in both). But that success could be, and often was, achieved at the cost of literary appreciation of the texts as they now stand. See R. Alter, *The World of Biblical Literature* (New York: Basic Books; London: SPCK, 1992), pp. 68-72, 136-52, 205-10. In any case the process of bringing the deposit of centuries of oral tradition to literary form, as in the older parts of the Pentateuch, is an imperfect model for understanding the development of the 'Jesus tradition' in the course of fifty years or less.

6.   This has clearly been the motivation for much of the source analysis of the Gospels in the past two centuries, to which there is no objection on its own terms. But the validity of historical inferences based on a specific text will depend on correct exegesis of that text in relation to its literary context.

7.   On these see G. von Rad, *Old Testament Theology* (trans. D.M.G. Stalker; Edinburgh: Oliver & Boyd, 1962), I, pp. 347-54; M. Noth, *The Chronicler's History* (JSOTSup, 50; Sheffield, JSOT Press, 1987), esp. pp. 29-50, 75-81, and H.G.M. Williamson's introduction to the English edition, pp. 11-25; S. Japhet, *The Ideology of the Book of Chronicles and its Place in Biblical Thought* (Frankfurt: Lang,

acter of these and the literary method of their author cannot be properly understood without reference to the earlier historical books of the Old Testament out of which he made a fresh literary creation. These are not simply a 'source' in the sense of a quarry for materials with which to construct a fuller account; they are the earlier story to which the Chronicler offers a revised and purposely alternative version. The intertextual[8] relationship is built into his venture from the start, and recognition of this is basic to the literary analysis of his work. But no conclusions are to be drawn from this as to the derivation of the remaining items included by the Chronicler; the primary question to be put to these, as concerns literary analysis, is not where they came from but what they are saying and what part they play in his story.

The initial impetus for the development of redaction criticism of the Synoptic Gospels[9] came from the recognition that Matthew (to say nothing of Luke) occupies the same kind of position in relation to Mark as I have claimed for the Chronicler in relation to the earlier historical books of the Old Testament.[10] His expansion and redaction of Mark is so central to his purpose in writing that his Gospel, especially in its narrative sections, cannot fully speak for itself as a literary document in its own right if that dimension is ignored.[11] But no other *literary* sources are extant as such, and if they were they could hardly be seen as other than subsidiary; they do not therefore fall within the scope of our reserved case. At this point redaction criticism, if it is to be true to

1987), pp. 2-3; P.R. Ackroyd, *The Chronicler and his Age* (JSOTSup, 101; Sheffield: JSOT Press, 1991). Goulder makes his own contribution to the subject in *Midrash*, pp. 203-21.

8.   See n. 24 below.

9.   W. Marxsen's study of Mark (*Mark the Evangelist* [trans. R.A. Harrisville *et al.*; Nashville: Abingdon Press, 1969]) which, as originally published (1956), antedated the earliest work on Matthew (though not Conzelmann's on Luke) is no exception to this. Its aim throughout is to recover Mark's own meaning by distinguishing it from that imposed on his text by the later Evangelists (and their readers).

10.   H. Frankemölle, *Jahwebund und Kirche Christi* (NTAbh NS, 10; Münster: Aschendorff, 1973), pp. 314-17, implies, and Goulder, *Midrash*, pp. 3-4, 28-34, 43-44, 227-33, explicitly maintains that Matthew consciously adopted Chronicles as a model. Though this may well be the case, it is more than I am claiming for the position of the earlier redaction critics.

11.   See my review of B. Bauer, *The Structure of Matthew's Gospel* (JSNTSup, 31; Sheffielu: JSOT Press, 1988), in *JTS* NS 41 (1990), pp. 175-78.

itself, needs to move into composition criticism: the units of added material must be examined first as literary texts in themselves, and secondly in their relation to the total composition that is the Gospel. Where this priority is not observed redaction criticism has a tendency to fall back on the two methods which preceded it: on form criticism by a concentration on the smallest possible units of tradition,[12] which has an atomizing effect on the material and fails to allow for the possibility of greater complexity and sophistication in its original forms; and on a thinly veiled source criticism by the use of (often somewhat superficial) observation of an Evangelist's redactional habits to establish the content of a conjectural source text.[13] In either case the tendency to assume the presence of both 'tradition' and 'redaction' in any significant pericope, however short, has meant that where evidence of a redactor's hand is detected, his responsibility is confined to the sentence or clause in question, often without consideration of the possibility that the pericope is a literary unity and he the author of the whole of it.[14]

12.   This can be illustrated from numerous treatments of the redaction history of the so-called 'secondary' beatitudes in Matthew; e.g. I. Broer, *Die Seligpreisungen der Bergpredigt* (BBB, 61; Bonn: Peter Hanstein, 1985), pp. 59-63; G. Strecker, 'Die Makarismen der Bergpredigt', *NTS* 17 (1971), pp. 255-75: 259-60; *idem*, *The Sermon on the Mount* (trans. O.C. Dean; Edinburgh: T. & T. Clark, 1989), p. 30; U. Luz, *Matthew 1–7* (trans. W.C. Linss; Edinburgh: T. & T. Clark, 1989), pp. 226-29 (criticized by Betz, *Sermon on the Mount*, p. 109).

13.   Contrast D.E. Orton's account (*The Understanding Scribe* [JSNTSup, 25; Sheffield: JSOT Press, 1989], pp. 141-42) of Matthew's authorial use of the expression διὰ τοῦτο (see n. 108 to Chapter 7, below) with M.E. Boring's attempt to show that he owed it in the first place to the influence of (synoptic) sources ('The Beelzebul Pericope', in F. Van Segbroeck *et al.* [eds.], *The Four Gospels 1992* [Festschrift F. Neirynck; BETL, 100; Leuven: Peeters, 1993], pp. 587-619 [613-14]).

14.   E.g. Stanton's argument for a 'traditional' core to 11.28-30 (*Gospel*, pp. 364-77), and J.P. Meier's for a similar analysis of 28.16-20 ('Two Disputed Questions in Matthew 28.16-20', *JBL* 96 [1977], pp. 407-24): a considered rejection of proposals for a unitary understanding of the text. See, respectively, nn. 123 and 311 to Chapter 4. Contrast Alter, *World*, p. 70: 'If literary analysis...is in one way or another a response to the esemplastic activity of the literary imagination, it will not be surprising that the new literary criticism of the Bible has tended to uncover unities where previous scholars, following the hidden imperative *the more atomistic, the more scientific*, found discontinuities, duplications, fissures' (his emphasis). Cf. Howell, *Story*, pp. 20-22.

a. *Analysing a Poem*

The Matthaean Beatitudes are a text in which these questions are particularly at issue, because, as is coming to be increasingly recognized, their formal structure is that of a poem. They are printed as such in a growing number both of editions and translations of the Greek text[15] (if sometimes with an imperfect understanding of the boundaries of the poetic composition[16]); a number of scholars (including, with qualifications, Dupont[17]) accept a 2×4 arrangement of the lines, and one at least is cautiously prepared to allow this insight some weight in his interpretation of the text.[18] But, for the reasons noted above, its full implications for exegesis have yet to be faced.

What is true of the analysis of any literary composition is true *par excellence* when the subject is a poem. It does not start from identification of possible sources, but from the words themselves, in the full range of connotations that they can carry,[19] and in their formal relation to one another as this is conveyed by meaning, sound and position within the overall composition. According to the influential structuralist critic Roman Jakobson,[20] 'the distinctive feature of poetry lies in the

15. E.g. N-A, 25th edn (1963), 26th edn (1979), 27th edn (1993); UBS (1958, 1966, 1973, 1994); JB, NEB, NIV, NJB, REB.

16. K. Aland in particular has been guilty of this; in addition to his shared responsibility for N-A, 26th and 27th edns, see his *Synopsis Quattuor Evangeliorum* (Stuttgart: Württemburgischer Bibelanstalt, 2nd edn, 1979), p. 75.

17. *Béatitudes*, III, pp. 310-12.

18. H. Frankemölle, 'Die Makarismen (Mt 5,1-12; Lk 6,20-23): Motive und Umfang der redaktionelle Komposition', *BZ* NS 15 (1971), pp. 52-75. Betz, *Sermon on the Mount*, pp. 59, 108, 143, though he does not go so far as to speak of poetry, gives priority in his treatment to the form of the composition; the neglect of this in much Q research has clearly influenced his hypothesis of a pre-Q origin for the Sermon on the Mount in its entirety.

19. See following notes. English-speaking biblical scholarship (with the partial exception of Johannine studies) has tended to share the conventional British resistance to punning, an attitude at variance with those of almost all literary cultures, including the Hebraic. See J. Culler (ed.), *On Puns* (Oxford: Basil Blackwell, 1973). D.C. Allison rightly maintains that 'religious speech for [Matthew] was polysemous and heavily connotative'; see *The New Moses: A Matthean Typology* (Edinburgh: T. & T. Clark, 1993), p. 285.

20. Jakobson's work forms a bridge between the poetics of the Russian Formalist school of the early post-Revolution years and the later structuralism of the West; hence its central importance (see T. Hawkes, *Structuralism and Semiotics* [London: Methuen, 1977], pp. 59-64, 70-87). For an extended statement of his position see

fact that a word is perceived as a word and not merely a proxy for the denoted object or an outburst of an emotion, that words and their arrangement, their meaning, their outward and inward form, acquire weight and value of their own'.[21] In other words, form and content are inseparable in poetry;[22] as the poet Louis MacNeice said, 'in any poet's poem the shape is half the meaning'.[23] The shape has therefore to be attended to first, as it is disclosed by such formal devices as rhythm, metre, stress, rhyme and alliteration, and by the structure, where discernible, of the whole piece. It is only when this primary examination has been completed that the further question of the text's relationship to other texts, its intertextuality,[24] can be allowed to surface, and the investigation of this can point in three directions.

(1) Vertically, it will look for contacts between the wording (and the structure) of the poem and the literary tradition in which both the author and his or her implied readership certainly or presumably stood; these will be primarily verbal echoes of texts forming part of that tradition. While it is not assumed that readers will have been equipped and ready to pick up every resonance of these texts at a first reading,[25] a

his 'Closing Statement: Linguistics and Poetics', in T.A. Sebeok (ed.), *Style in Language* (Cambridge, MA: MIT Press, 1960), pp. 350-77. Its relevance to biblical poetry is explored by A. Berlin, *The Dynamics of Hebrew Parallelism* (Bloomington, IN: University of Indiana Press, 1985), pp. 7-17.

21. Quoted by Hawkes, *Structuralism*, p. 64, from V. Erlich, *Russian Formalism* (The Hague: Mouton, 2nd edn, 1965), p. 183.

22. See E. Stankiewicz, 'Linguistics and the Study of Poetic Language', in Sebeok (ed.), *Style in Language*, pp. 69-87 (71). Jakobson's own technical contribution was to take up de Saussure's distinction between 'signifier' and 'signified' (see his *Course in General Linguistics* [trans. Wade Baskin; New York: Philosophical Library, 1959], p. 16), and to show that in poetry they are, paradoxically, identified; see 'Closing Statement', pp. 371-72, and cf. A. Easthope, *Poetry as Discourse* (London: Methuen, 1983), p. 15.

23. Quoted by P. Fussell, *Poetic Metre and Poetic Form* (New York: Random House, 1965), p. 133.

24. This coinage of Julia Kristeva (Σημειωτική: *Recherches pour une sémanalyse* [Paris: Seuil, 1962], pp. 146, 213), for all that it may be said to dramatize the obvious, is now in general use. Cf. Easthope, *Poetry*, p. 85: 'Every text is intertextual...' For the application to scripture see S. Draisma (ed.), *Intertextuality in Biblical Writings* (Festschrift B.M.F. van Iersel; Kampen: Kok, 1989).

25. Here the restrictive assumptions of some forms of reader-response criticism cannot be allowed the last word. Cf. V. Erlich, 'Roman Jakobson: Grammar of Poetry and Poetry of Grammar', in S. Chatman (ed.), *Approaches to Poetics* (New

readership without access of any kind to the inspirational sources of the author is hardly thinkable, since poetry is essentially a social activity.[26]

In the present instance the primary tradition behind the poem will of course be the Old Testament, and since the Matthaean community was evidently Greek-speaking, the LXX Greek version which was its Bible should be taken as that tradition's presenting point.[27] However, the totality of tradition available to be drawn on was wider than this, and a strong, though not uncontested, case can be made for the Evangelist's familiarity with the Hebrew original.[28] Possible contacts with or influences from the Aramaic Targums and other post-canonical Jewish texts (including those of Qumran) can be considered on their merits, and the same goes for the nascent Christian tradition in so far as that had already attained literary form. Hypothetical source documents of which

York: Columbia University Press, 1973), pp. 1-27 (25): 'It is an elementary psychological fact that not everything that on closer inspection turns out to occur in the poem can be apprehended by the most alert reader'; also F. Landy, 'In Defence of Jakobson', *JBL* 111 (1992), pp. 105-13 (111): 'It is a fallacy to hold that an unsophisticated audience implies an unsophisticated author or authors and excludes complexity'. Allison, *New Moses*, p. 286, allows the possibility of 'a conscious hermeneutical gap between the author of Mt. and some of his readers'. The hymns of Charles Wesley (1707–88) offer a striking literary and historical parallel. Written for use, both public and private, by a largely unlettered readership, they are nevertheless the work of a 'classicist and skilled linguist who has a feel for words, and particularly for the resonance of meaning and allusion that can be created by a word with the right associations' (Frank Baker, *Charles Wesley's Verse* (London: Epworth Press, 1989), p. 36. His range of allusion covers not only the whole of scripture, but on occasion patristic and classical writings as well: e.g. Plutarch's report of the death of Pan (*God of unexampled grace*: see F. Baker, *Representative Verse of Charles Wesley* [London: Epworth Press, 1962], No. 54, l. 34). We cannot presume that his actual readership could have recognized the allusion. In Matthew's case Howell, *Story*, p. 39, resolves the difficulty by positing an 'implied reader' who could, and 'which the text invites the actual reader to become'.

26. See Hawkes, *Structuralism*, pp. 80-83. The scope and variety of this aspect is sensitively explored by Seamus Heaney, *The Redress of Poetry* (London: Faber, 1995).

27. By the first century CE a number of variants from the LXX which afterwards found their way into the later versions of Aq., Thdt. or Sym. seem to have been already in independent circulation (see Chapter 3, §4), and there are places where acquaintance with these seems the most natural explanation of Matthew's text. Cf. nn. 29, 63 to Chapter 3.

28. So W.D. Davies and D.C. Allison, *Matthew* (ICC; Edinburgh: T. & T. Clark, I, 1988; II, 1991; III, 1997), pp. 32-58.

the wording can only be conjectured are another matter; and while echoes of sayings orally transmitted are admissible in principle if well known to the readership, it is difficult to see how a structured poem could result from simply piecing these together.[29]

(2) Horizontally, it will seek to correlate its findings with evidence from other known writings of the poem's presumed author. Here it will look for evidence of formal verse composition in general rather than parallels to a particular form, and be concerned less with words than with meanings, and thus not so much with verbal correspondences as with convergences with what is said elsewhere in other words. In a poem, as we have seen, words have priority, so that its full meaning cannot be conveyed without remainder by using different ones[30] (hence the problems inherent in the translation of poetry). It is in this that its uniqueness lies. But comparison with other writings of the author[31] can still help to elucidate his or her meaning and to corroborate the results of the internal examination of the poem. In the present case they will all be found within the covers (to speak anachronistically for a moment) of one book, in which it is reasonable to presume (unless good reason can be shown to the contrary) a coherence of outlook and consistency of treatment even when the Evangelist is redacting the work of other writers.

(3) The vertical relationship can of course work in the other direction: later writings in their turn can carry allusions to the earlier one, and these will provide evidence of how their authors understood it, even if it cannot be simply assumed that their understanding of it was present, even unconsciously, to the mind of its own author. While there is in principle no temporal limit to this process, the post-biblical Christian hermeneutic of the Beatitudes (an immense subject in itself[32]) is at best only obliquely relevant to the purpose of this study, which is to

29. See n. 12 above.

30. Cleanth Brooks' essay 'The Heresy of Paraphrase', in *The Well-Wrought Urn* (New York: Reynal & Hitchcock, 1947), p. 182 (quoted by Howell, *Story*, p. 35) speaks of 'the temptation to mistake certain remarks which we make *about* the poem...for the essential core of the poem itself'.

31. On Betz's view (*Sermon on the Mount*, pp. 43-44) these would be restricted to the Sermon on the Mount itself, and offer little clue to the character of the readership. Chapters 3–4 below argue to the contrary.

32. Cf. Dupont, *Béatitudes*, III, pp. 399-418; Luz, *Matthew*, I, pp. 229-30, 234-35, 239-41, 244-46; Betz, *Sermon on the Mount*, pp. 105-108.

recover an aspect of their original resonance which was lost to sight in the later tradition. It therefore confines itself to writings within the canon of the New Testament.

The range of possible influences on a text from other texts in category (1) is far wider than source and redaction critics of the Gospels have generally allowed. These have tended to think of older texts simply as sources for a writer to draw on for his content, usually by incorporating them, whether substantially as they stand, or paraphrased, or deliberately emended, in his own work, as, for example, Josephus does on the Old Testament,[33] and Matthew, by general consensus, on Mark. But while this process is common enough in prose narrative, it is in the nature of things very rare in poetry, and for the result to be a poem in its own right is even rarer. There can however be a wide range of contact short of this, from the half-conscious reminiscences of a mind soaked in the earlier literature[34] to pointed allusion to one or more texts for purposes of comparison or questioning.[35] An earlier text can be taken as the model for a new one, either materially[36] or formally[37] or both; though even in the latter case total correspondence will be exceptional.[38] The 'sources' of a poem will thus be inspirational rather than

33. See, e.g., F.G. Downing, 'Redaction Criticism: Josephus' *Antiquities* and the Synoptic Gospels', *JSNT* 8 (1980), pp. 46-65 (= I); 9 (1981), pp. 29-48 (= II).

34. Charles Wesley's hymns (n. 25 above) exemplify this too. An exuberant mind steeped in the scriptures can 'switch on' biblical wording without conscious intention to make a point with it.

35. Thus Ps. 8 with reference to Gen. 1.26-28. For a post-biblical example cf. Hopkins' sonnet 'Thou art indeed just, Lord, if I contend' (*Gerard Manley Hopkins* [ed. Catherine Phillips; The Oxford Authors; Oxford: Oxford University Press, 1986], p. 183), a dialogue with the Lord starting from (and quoting) Jer. 12.1-2.

36. As is, e.g., the Song of Hannah (1 Sam. 2.1-10) for the Magnificat (Lk. 1.46-55).

37. See below in Chapter 2, for the relationship suggested between Ps. 119 and the Beatitudes. Post-biblical examples might include the hymns composed by St Thomas Aquinas for the Breviary offices for the feast of Corpus Christi, using the opening lines of older Latin hymns, and Wesley's *Love divine, all loves excelling*, which begins as a devout parody of an undistinguished piece of libretto verse by Dryden (on which it signally improves). In all these the motive was probably musical. But there can be other reasons for presenting the unfamiliar in the guise of the familiar.

38. The stock example from English literature, Pope's rewriting of two of Donne's satires (see *The Poems of Alexander Pope* [ed. J. Butt; Oxford Paperbacks;

material, and in view of the dominance of the latter connotation of the word in New Testament studies it is probably better in this connection to speak of influences, or (looking in the other direction) of allusions.[39]

The complexity of this question is no reason to duck it, but it is also not to be anticipated; to embark on it prematurely is liable to have a distorting effect on what should be the primary study. An example of this is provided by Dupont himself in his own examination of the structure of the Matthaean version of the Beatitudes to which I have already alluded.[40] He recognizes that the *inclusio* in Mt. 5.10 marks the end of the formal composition,[41] so that vv. 11-12 fall outside it (though he continues to speak, a little confusingly, of *nine* beatitudes in Matthew,[42] while admitting in practice that the structured composition consists of eight), and that the repetition of δικαιοσύνη in vv. 6, 10 divides it in two, indicating a 2 × 4 structure for it.[43] But when he comes to consider further subdivision of the two quatrains, he begins by importing into the discussion considerations derived from source and redaction criticism. Because, according to him, v. 5 has been formulated by Matthew as a doublet of v. 3,[44] and v. 10 of vv. 11–12,[45] each quatrain consists of three 'traditional' beatitudes and a fourth, 'redac-

London: Oxford University Press, 1965], pp. 676-87) assumed a limited and highly sophisticated readership.

39. Cf. Allison, *New Moses*, pp. 284-87.

40. See §1.a above.

41. *Béatitudes*, III, p. 309.

42. *Béatitudes*, III, pp. 308, 316; cf. Betz, *Sermon on the Mount*, pp. 108-109, 142.

43. *Béatitudes*, III, pp. 309-12; cf. 312-13 for details of scholars who have favoured an alternative 3 × 3 arrangement. To these must now be added Davies and Allison, *Matthew*, I, pp. 430-31, who argue that '5.10 has been inserted in order to bring the total number of beatitudes to a multiple of 3'. They ignore both the *inclusio* between 5.10 and 5.3 and the oddness of a triad consisting of VII, VIII and 5.11-12. Equally strange is Betz's reading (following Delitzsch and [unacknowledged] B.W. Bacon, *Studies in Matthew* [London: Constable, 1930], p. 174) of 5.11-12 as *two* beatitudes, making the total count ten (*Sermon on the Mount*, pp. 105-109, 151; cf. *Essays*, pp. 23-25), especially as he rejects Delitzsch's analogy with the Decalogue in its position as heading for the Torah in Exod. 20 (see Chapter 10 [with n. 1] below). 5.11-12 are more like the protasis and apodosis of one beatitude (note the position of ὅτι in v. 12), though still discontinuous with the preceding eight.

44. *Béatitudes*, III, p. 474.

45. *Béatitudes*, III, p. 352.

tional' one.[46] This, even if it were unassailable as redaction criticism, would still be structurally irrelevant, since the two supposedly redactional beatitudes stand in quite different relations to their respective quatrains, with one of them 'doubling' a beatitude inside the composition, the other the so-called 'ninth' beatitude outside it.

Dupont thus leaves the structural analysis of the composition half finished, to fall back on a discipline which for him is methodologically prior. For the method outlined above it is not prior, and some almost equally obvious formal characteristics remain to be identified. This task will be taken up in the following chapter. But attention must first be given to the extent to which the source hypothesis adopted for the Gospel will affect the handling of the 'horizontal' aspect of its intertextuality. What, for this, is to count as Matthaean?[47]

2. Matthew and his Sources

A major problem with the 2DH lies in the equal weight that it gives to two 'documents', the status and attestation of which are totally different. The Gospel of Mark is extant, and the marked difference of its spurious ending is convincing testimony to the integrity of the remainder.[48] It can be laid alongside the parts of Matthew and Luke which are parallel to it for objective comparison. Q on the other hand is essentially no more than an inference from the existence of parallels between Matthew and Luke which have no counterpart in Mark; it offers from

46. *Béatitudes*, III, p. 314.
47. Assuming his involvement as author; contra Betz (n. 31 above).
48. W.R. Farmer, *The Last Twelve Verses of Mark* (SNTSMS, 25; Cambridge: Cambridge University Press, 1974), fails to make out a case dictated *a priori* by his position on sources. E. Linnemann, 'Der (wiedergefundene) Markusschluss', *ZTK* 66 (1969), pp. 255-87, argues unimpressively for Mk 16.15-18 as embodying the original ending. M. Smith, *Clement of Alexandria and a Secret Gospel of Mark* (Cambridge, MA: Harvard University Press, 1973) (cf. *idem*, *The Secret Gospel* [London: Gollancz, 1974]) has not convincingly established his case that the 'Gospel' examined by him is the original form of Mark, rather than a version enhanced with material derived from or inspired by John. See C.A. Evans, 'Jesus in the Agrapha and Apocryphal Gospels', in B.D. Chilton and C.A. Evans (eds.), *Studying the Historical Jesus* (Leiden: E.J. Brill, 1994), pp. 526-32; contra M.W. Meyer, 'The Youth in Secret Mark and the Beloved Disciple in John', in J.E. Goehing *et al.* (eds.), *Gospel Origins and Christian Beginnings* (Festschrift J.M. Robinson; Sonoma, CA: Polebridge Press, 1990), pp. 94-105.

internal evidence an explanation of the manner of composition of two closely related documents, that is, of two connected events in literary history. *That* they were composed—that the historical events of their respective composition actually happened—is a *datum*, self-evidently true but for that very reason uninteresting. *How* it happened is a question which, in the absence of contemporary external attestation, can only be answered hypothetically, and no answer will be susceptible of demonstrative proof; the most that can be expected even from the most rigorous testing is a high degree of probability. Q is simply that hypothesis (out of several that have been proposed, as we shall see) which has commended itself to the majority of scholars working in this field as the best available explanation of the evidence before them, and like any such hypothesis it must always remain open to revision—or to supersession by another which explains the evidence better. The fact of majority support, while a warning to the dissenter to be sure of his or her ground, does not by itself settle anything; studies of the part played by 'paradigms' in the sociology (and, it must be faced, the group psychology) of knowledge have revealed how often a breakthrough in the development of scientific understanding comes from the fringes of the scientific establishment and in the teeth of the resistance of the majority.[49] Nor does the internal coherence of results arrived at on the prior assumption of Q confirm the soundness of the assumption rather than the observant eye and dialectical skill of the scholar. Reconstruction of the supposed content[50] of the source or of its 'original' order,[51] let alone

49. See T.S. Kuhn, *The Structure of Scientific Revolutions* (Chicago: University of Chicago Press, 2nd edn, 1970). A.D. Jacobson, 'The Literary Unity of Q', *JBL* 101 (1982), pp. 365-89: 366-69, has questioned the applicability of the paradigm model to historical hypotheses which have 'no predictive power'. The point is well taken, but does not dispose of the subjective component in the response of a professional establishment to fundamentally new developments in its field.

50. E.g. A.P. Polag, *Fragmenta Q: Textheft zur Logienquelle* (Neukirchen: Neukirchener Verlag, 1979); and the current international project sponsored by Claremont University, under the direction of James M. Robinson, to establish 'the definitive text of Q'.

51. A topic much canvassed since the studies of Vincent Taylor: 'The Order of Q', *JTS* NS 4 (1953), pp. 27-31; 'The Original Order of Q', in A.J.B. Higgins (ed.), *New Testament Essays (in memoriam T.W. Manson)* (Manchester: Manchester University Press, 1959), pp. 240-69. Taylor's methodology is flawed by his insistence on treating the Five Discourses as the only significant collections of sayings material in Matthew. But see further S. Schulz, *Q: Die Spruchquelle der Evan-*

theorizing about the community that produced it or the theology with which they were working,[52] adds nothing to the initial plausibility of the hypothesis; the chain of inference is no stronger than its weakest link.

When the protagonists of Q are asked to justify their postulation of a hypothetical source in preference to the more economical solution of a known one (that is, dependence of one of the two Gospels on the other), their bottom line is almost invariably the alleged inconceivability of any writer, let alone Luke as we know him, proceeding in the way that the latter hypothesis requires that he did.[53] Whether we know comprehensively enough what Luke was about to be able to say with conviction (and not from merely subjective impression, or from following the herd) what in the way of omission or transposition was not possible for him as an author is a question on which a little less confidence would not be misplaced. We shall return to this shortly; but, first, a glance at the alternatives.

gelisten (Zürich: Theologischer Verlag, 1972); J.S. Kloppenborg, *The Formation of Q* (Philadelphia: Fortress Press, 1987), pp. 64-80; A.D. Jacobson, *The First Gospel: An Introduction to Q* (Sonoma, CA: Polebridge Press, 1992); D.R. Catchpole, *The Quest for Q* (Edinburgh: T. & T. Clark, 1993), pp. 60-80; C.M. Tuckett, *Q and the History of Early Christianity* (Edinburgh: T. & T. Clark, 1996), pp. 34-39.

52. This line of study has become a growth industry; for successive overviews of it see Schulz, *Q*; M. Devisch, 'Le document Q, source de Matthieu: Problématique actuelle', in M. Didier (ed,), *L'Evangile selon Matthieu: Redaction et théologie* (BETL, 29; Gembloux: Ducoulot, 1972), pp. 71-97; R.D. Worden, 'Redaction Criticism of Q', *JBL* 94 (1975), pp. 532-46; R.A. Edwards, *A Theology of Q* (Philadelphia: Fortress Press, 1976); Kloppenborg, *Formation*; Tuckett, *Q*, pp. 1-106. The research has produced contributions of distinction, including W.D. Davies, *The Setting of the Sermon on the Mount* (Cambridge: Cambridge University Press, 1963); see esp. pp. 366-87; D. Lührmann, *Die Redaktion der Logienquelle* (WMANT, 3; Neukirchen–Vluyn: Neukirchener Verlag, 1969); P. Hoffmann, *Studien zur Theologie der Logienquelle* (NTAbh NS, 8; Münster: Aschendorff, 1972). But not a little of it justifies the comment of E.P. Sanders: 'This work is mostly of curiosity value, since it shows how far a hypothesis can be pushed despite its lack of fundamental support' (E.P. Sanders and M. Davies, *Studying the Synoptic Gospels* [London: SCM Press, 1992], p. 116).

53. Thus B.H. Streeter, *The Four Gospels* (London: Macmillan, 1924), esp. pp. 182-91; W.G. Kümmel, *Introduction to the New Testament* (London: SCM Press, 1975), pp. 63-64; for a different form of the argument, see Downing, 'Redaction Criticism', I, pp. 61-63; II, pp. 43-44.

There are actually three versions of the hypothesis that Luke used Matthew. Two of them dispense with Markan priority as well as with Q, and may thus be said to commit the error of the 2DH in an inverted form: that is, they dispense with the extant document as a source as well as with the hypothetical one, as if the two still stood or fell together. All three are open to challenge on the further ground that they do not leave room for an adequate account of the composition of one or more of the Gospels. The 'Augustinian' account, last defended systematically by the late Bishop Christopher Butler,[54] makes Mark dependent on Matthew, and Luke on both (with Mark his primary source). This (to dispensers with Q) is satisfactory so far as Luke is concerned; but, apart from the well-known objections (of common sense, rather than logic, where Butler scored some palpable hits[55]—as he also did on Q) to the case for Matthaean priority in individual passages, it is virtually impossible to explain how Mark, whose account marches closely with Matthew's from ch. 6, could have arrived at the arrangement of his earlier chapters on the basis of what (on this hypothesis) he had before him in Matthew; whereas Matthew's assembly of healing and other miracles is fully understandable as a systematic (and thematic) reorganization of the material he found in Mark.

The revived Griesbachian hypothesis (GH), which has found favour with a minority in recent years mainly in the United States,[56] makes

54. B.C. Butler, *The Originality of St Matthew* (Cambridge: Cambridge University Press, 1951). J.W. Wenham, *Redating Matthew, Mark and Luke* (London: Hodder & Stoughton, 1991), adhered to this position.

55. The best post-Butler account of these is still probably that of G.M. Styler, 'The Priority of Mark', Excursus IV to C.F.D. Moule, *The Birth of the New Testament* (London: A. & C. Black, 1962), pp. 225-32.

56. See W.R. Farmer, *The Synoptic Problem* (London: Collier-Macmillan, 1964); *idem*, 'The Statement of the [Two Gospel] Hypothesis', in D.L. Dungan (ed.), *The Interrelations of the Gospels* (BETL, 95; Leuven: Peeters, 1990), pp. 125-56; D.L. Dungan, 'Mark: The Abridgement of Matthew and Luke', in D.G. Buttrick (ed.), *Jesus and Man's Hope* (Pittsburgh: Pittsburgh Theological Seminary, 1970), pp. 51-77; O.L. Cope, *Matthew: A Scribe Trained for the Kingdom of Heaven* (CBQMS, 5; Washington: Catholic Biblical Association, 1976); for further literature, C.M. Tuckett, *The Revival of the Griesbach Hypothesis* (SNTSMS, 44; Cambridge: Cambridge University Press, 1983); Dungan (ed.), *Interrelations*; J.S. Kloppenborg, 'Theological Stakes in the Synoptic Problem', in Van Segbroeck *et al.* (eds.), *Four Gospels 1992*, pp. 93-120: 94 n. 5. The hypothesis has gained some currency in Britain also, mainly through the advocacy of J.B. Orchard; see his *Matthew, Luke and Mark* (Manchester: Koinonia, 1976), and *A Synopsis of the*

Luke dependent on Matthew alone, and reduces Mark to a verse-by-verse conflation of material from the other two. The account that this gives of Luke suffers from the same drawbacks as the Augustinian account of Mark, while the Griesbachian account of Mark 'would appear', in the words of A.D. Jacobson,[57] 'to deny theological intentionality' (to say nothing of literary creativity) to the Evangelist. The theological and the literary work done on this Gospel in the past century, from Wrede to Kermode, conspire to deny conviction to a patchwork theory such as this.

GH may thus be said to incur double jeopardy. Its unsatisfactoriness, it would not be unfair to say, has tended to divert the attention of scholars from the serious shortcomings of the 2DH, and until very recently (at any rate outside Britain) from the very existence of a real alternative, namely that Mark is a source for Matthew, and both Mark and Matthew for Luke. Partly anticipated by E. Simons as far back as 1880,[58] this was first proposed in its full form (though not worked out systematically or in detail) by James Hardy Ropes of Harvard in 1934;[59] but it is generally associated with the case argued for it, mainly against the objections of B.H. Streeter,[60] by Austin Farrer in 1955,[61] and

Four Gospels Arranged according to the Two Gospel Hypothesis (Edinburgh: T. & T. Clark, 1988). But support for it in Britain is less strong, both numerically and in academic weight, than for the FGH (see below), being largely confined to those without other research interests.

57. Jacobson, 'Literary Unity', p. 368 n. 11.

58. E. Simons, *Hat der dritte Evangelist den kanonischen Matthäus benutzt?* (Bonn: Strauss, 1880). Simons argued for Lukan knowledge of Matthew without relinquishing a sayings source shared by the two; his true inheritors at the present time are thus R. Morgenthaler, *Statistische Synopse* (Zürich: Gotthelf, 1971), p. 303; W. Wilken, 'Zur Frage der literarische Beziehung zwischen Matthäus und Lukas', *NovT* 8 (1966), pp. 48-57; and R.H. Gundry, *Matthew: A Commentary on his Literary and Theological Art* (Grand Rapids: Eerdmans, 1982), p. 5.

59. J.H. Ropes, *The Synoptic Gospels* (Oxford: Blackwell, 2nd edn, 1963 [1934]), p. 93; followed by his former student M.S. Enslin, *Christian Beginnings* (New York: Charles Scribner's Sons, 1938), pp. 431-36.

60. Note 53 above; on this M.D. Goulder, 'The Order of a Crank', in C.M. Tuckett (ed.), *Synoptic Studies* (JSNTSup, 7; Sheffield: JSOT Press, 1985), pp. 111-30; Sanders and Davies, *Studying*, p. 114.

61. A.M. Farrer, 'On Dispensing with Q', in D.E. Nineham (ed.), *Studies in the Gospels (In Memoriam R.H. Lightfoot)* (Oxford: Basil Blackwell, 1955), pp. 55-86. On this M.D. Goulder, 'Farrer on Q', *Theology* 88 (1980), pp. 190-95; Klop-

maintained and refined by Michael Goulder in a succession of publications over the past thirty years.[62] It is now becoming customary to refer to it as the Farrer–Goulder hypothesis (FGH).[63]

FGH, like its two rivals, remains exposed to the charge of offering an implausible account of the genesis of one of the Gospels, in this case Luke, though unlike them it offers no further hostage of this sort to fortune. Goulder's recent commentary on the latter[64] is the most sustained attempt to date to swing the debate on purely literary (as opposed to more historical) grounds; to readers prepared to entertain, even provisionally, its basic assumption of Luke's knowledge and use of Matthew it offers a generally plausible account of how the material derived by Luke from his two predecessors could have reached its final form in his Gospel. While one can continue to argue over details, his overall case will not quickly be improved on. But the sledge-hammer indictment in the introduction that precedes it of the inconsequences of the historical process through which the Q hypothesis became dominant, and of the shortcomings, both logical and factual, of the arguments with which it is still commonly defended,[65] has so far, to judge by the literature, done little to shake the confidence of the mainstream. Though pressure of the dominant paradigm has surely played its part, it would be unwise (not to say complacent) to blame the negative response exclusively on this. The question it raises is whether the assumptions of Goulder's 'new paradigm',[66] as regards composition from sources, have been sufficiently distanced from those of his opponents for the real reasons for preferring it to emerge.

Goulder's Luke is thought of as close in time to Matthew, and the process of composition of his new Gospel as comparable to the 2DH account of both Matthew and Luke: the combination, harmonization

penborg, 'Theological Stakes', pp. 115-16, 117-18. H.B. Green, 'The Credibility of Luke's Transformation of Matthew', in Tuckett (ed.), *Synoptic Studies*, pp. 138-57, is a critical updating of the argument.

62. See Bibliography. On the Beatitudes see his Reply (pp. 207-15) to C.M. Tuckett, 'The Beatitudes: A Source-Critical Study', *NovT* 25 (1983), pp. 193-207.

63. So Kloppenborg, 'Theological Stakes', pp. 93-94; Boring, 'Beelzebul Pericope', p. 588 n. 4.

64. *Luke: A New Paradigm* (JSNTSup, 20; Sheffield: JSOT Press, 1989).

65. *Luke*, pp. 3-71.

66. See *Luke*, pp. 22-23. While I am in general agreement with the content of this, I would date Matthew slightly, and Luke significantly, later.

and reconciliation[67] of two or more written sources which he has before him in the scriptorium; apparently all redactional decisions are made there in the course of writing.[68] The prior motives, especially non-literary ones, that Luke might have had for deciding to proceed in the way that, on the FGH, he did are insufficiently investigated.[69] Though Luke's handling of Mark is in certain respects freer than is always recognized,[70] it is hardly to be compared with the drastic redistribution of the material that, on this view, he took from Matthew; and though the latter is partly explicable on the reasonable assumption that he knew Mark first and made it the original basis for his own project, but only encountered Matthew when that was far advanced,[71] yet even so it is pertinent to ask what prompted him to go to such trouble with a source discovered so late in the day.

In his recent study of the formation of the New Testament canon, John Barton writes: 'Whatever the motive of Mark or even Matthew, the purpose of the third Gospel as stated in its prologue does seem to envisage a supersession of other Gospels: "Luke" is providing the definitive version of the story, to replace earlier and more imperfect versions'.[72] There is an ambivalence about that word 'imperfect' with which its author may not have been fully complicit. Luke has indeed written a revised and enlarged version of Mark, to replace the original with something more complete. At a certain stage, however, it will have transpired that he was not the first; Matthew, from a rather different standpoint, had already done the same. But Luke did not then write a

---

67. All words used by Goulder of Luke's literary activity; cf. 'Order of a Crank', p. 112; *Luke*, pp. 201-202, 382 etc. There is apparently no thought of systematic preference for one source over another.

68. This seems to be implied at, e.g., 'Order of a Crank', p. 113; *Luke*, pp. 291, 346, 410, and has prompted the objection of F.G. Downing, 'A Paradigm Perplex: Luke, Matthew and Mark', *NTS* 38 (1992), pp. 15-36, that the procedures posited for the FGH Luke are anachronistic. The details of Downing's attack are not always fair, but on his own presuppositions he has the better of the argument.

69. Goulder's reply to Downing, 'Luke's Compositional Options', *NTS* 39 (1993), pp. 150-52, though it scores valid points, has finally to admit that Luke's method with multiple sources is quite different from, e.g., Josephus', and then offers no serious explanation of the discrepancy.

70. See Green, 'Credibility', pp. 134-35; E. Franklin, *Luke, Interpreter of Paul, Critic of Matthew* (JSNTSup, 92; Sheffield: JSOT Press, 1993), pp. 288-97, 369-70.

71. So Green, 'Credibility', p. 133 and n. 17; Franklin, *Luke*, pp. 313-15.

72. J. Barton, *The Spirit and the Letter* (London: SPCK, 1997), p. 46.

revised or enlarged version of Matthew once he had discovered it; indeed he could not have done so without abandoning his original project and starting again. If he chose not to take Matthew's comprehensive content as the basis for a final authoritative account, but instead to raid it for material to be included piecemeal in his updated Mark (and for features which he preferred to present in a different idiom[73]), that would imply that he saw it not as incomplete but as in some way flawed: that there were aspects, whether of its historical construction or of its theological stance, to which he was unsympathetic, and therefore he aimed not to supplement but to supplant it.

As regards the history, Luke was in a position (as his Theophilus possibly was not) to compare Matthew with Mark, and thus to recognize that the assembly of miracle stories in Matthew 8–9 was derived from Mark, and that their arrangement there was both artificial and incompatible with their order in the Markan narrative. As the wording of his preface shows, narrative order was a high priority for Luke;[74] it imposed a choice on him, and an option to follow Mark was necessarily an option against Matthew. The possibility that Luke had also theological (more strictly, ideological) difficulties with Matthew was briefly anticipated by me in connection with the infancy narrative.[75] Two more recent studies, written in complete independence of one another, have now taken it up on a broader front: Eric Franklin's *Luke, Follower of Paul, Critic of Matthew*,[76] and David Ravens' *Luke and the Restoration of Israel*.[77] Both authors see Luke as balancing a qualified approval of Paul with a questioning of Matthew. But whereas for Franklin Luke is a one-time personal follower of Paul[78] who softened certain aspects of his teaching in interpreting him for a later generation, for Ravens he has

73. E.g. the infancy narrative (see n. 75 below), the genealogy of Jesus (3.23-38), and the expansion of the resurrection narrative; also (following Goulder) certain parables.

74. Lk. 1.3; cf. Goulder, *Luke*, pp. 199, 203-204. L.C.A. Alexander, *The Preface to Luke's Gospel* (SNTSMS, 78; Cambridge: Cambridge University Press, 1993), pp. 131-32, 135, prefers a less specific interpretation of Luke's καθεξῆς, but her argument does not allow for the possibility that the predecessors that he was reviewing included Matthew as well as Mark.

75. 'Credibility', pp. 143-44.

76. Especially pp. 280-388.

77. JSNTSup, 119; Sheffield: Sheffield Academic Press, 1995. A postscript on pp. 256-57 summarizes his points of dissent from Franklin.

78. Franklin, *Luke*, pp. 152-54.

first-hand knowledge of him only through the medium of certain of his letters, and what he invites approval for is a plainly revisionist account of Paul's story and teaching.[79] Franklin's Luke, who sides with Paul over the question of the supersession of the law as a way to salvation,[80] objects to Matthew's 'new law' because it is law;[81] Ravens' Luke, whose ulterior aim is the reintegration of Jews and Christians in a single (not 'new') Israel,[82] objects to it because it is new.[83] They are nevertheless united in rejecting Matthew's seemingly radical exclusion of the old Israel from a share in the final kingdom.[84]

I offer no premature resolution to an incipient debate. But it is a reminder of how little we can still take for granted about the objects, character and provenance of Luke's writing. Given their shared assumptions, either position will make a significant contribution to the credibility of the FGH Luke, which will allow of realistic comparison with that of the 2DH Matthew—who is a systematic redactor, organizer, conflator and redistributor of 'traditional' texts, but the original author of very few of them.[85] There is a family likeness about the sayings material in Matthew which cuts across conventional source attributions, yet cannot be put down simply to Matthaean redaction of the tradition, since in many cases the Lukan version is either (a) virtually identical or (b) itself the one that shows evidence of redaction.[86] The achievement of Goulder's earlier book *Midrash and Lection in Matthew*, despite its wilder flights of fancy, was that it conveyed to the reader with ears to hear a vivid impression of this family likeness. The present study builds on that impression and aims to carry it further, with

---

79. Ravens, *Luke*, pp. 158-211.
80. Franklin, *Luke*, pp. 65-66, 198-212, 370-71.
81. Franklin, *Luke*, pp. 309, 311, 321-23.
82. Ravens, *Luke*, pp. 250-52.
83. Ravens, *Luke*, pp. 220-21, 246, 251-52.
84. Franklin, *Luke*, pp. 312, 360, 371; Ravens, *Luke*, pp. 216-19.
85. The attractive recent presentation of this by Stanton, *Gospel*, which speaks of Matthew as 'a creative interpreter of the sayings of Jesus' (esp. pp. 328-40) too readily assumes the ubiquity of the process of redacting tradition in the formation of this Gospel. See n. 14 above, and cf. my review, *NovT* 37 (1995), pp. 95-97.
86. Relatively uncontroversial examples are: (a) 3.7-10//Lk. 3.7b-9; 7.3-5//Lk. 6.41-42; 11.5-6//Lk. 7.22; (b) 6.19-21//Lk. 12.33-34; 7.7-11//Lk. 11.9-13; 7.24-27//Lk. 6.47-49; 8.19-22//Lk. 9.57-60; 10.34-35//Lk. 12.51-53.

special reference to those texts which combine formal verse characteristics comparable to those that I shall shortly identify in the Beatitudes with intensive and usually multiple reminiscence of the Old
Testament. It makes no apology for ignoring the claims of Q to be a
distinct source for part of this material. If Q is finally upheld, then my
thesis fails. But, conversely, if the thesis should be found to carry conviction, then the case for Q will need to be re-examined. There is no
other way to break through the *impasse* to which the dominance of a
particular hypothesis has brought us than to decline to assume it and
then to observe how the evidence looks without it.[87] From its adherents
I ask nothing more exacting than a suspension of judgment.

87. This has previously been attempted by J. Drury, *Tradition and Design in
Luke's Gospel* (London: Darton, Longman & Todd, 1976); *idem, The Parables of
the Gospels* (London: SPCK, 1985); and by myself in 'Matthew 12.22-50: An
Alternative to Matthaean Conflation', in Tuckett (ed.), *Synoptic Studies*, pp. 157-76;
in 'Matthew, Clement and Luke', *JTS* NS 40 (1989), pp. 1-25; and in 'Matthew
11.7-15: Redaction or Self-Redaction?', in C. Focant (ed.), *The Synoptic Gospels:
Source Criticism and the New Literary Criticism* (BETL, 110; Leuven: Peeters,
1993), pp. 459-66.

Chapter 2

THE BEATITUDES: EVIDENCES OF POETIC STRUCTURE

| I | Μακάριοι οἱ πτωχοὶ τῷ πνεύματι· |
| | ὅτι αὐτῶν ἐστιν ἡ βασιλεία τῶν οὐρανῶν. |

| II* | μακάριοι οἱ πενθοῦντες· |
| | ὅτι αὐτοὶ παρακληθήσονται. |

| III* | μακάριοι οἱ πραεῖς· |
| | ὅτι αὐτοὶ κληρονομήσουσιν τὴν γῆν. |

| IV | μακάριοι οἱ πεινῶντες καὶ διψῶντες τὴν δικαιοσύνην· |
| | ὅτι αὐτοὶ χορτασθήσονται. |

| V | μακάριοι οἱ ἐλεήμονες· |
| | ὅτι αὐτοὶ ἐλεηθήσονται. |

| VI | μακάριοι οἱ καθαροὶ τῇ καρδίᾳ· |
| | ὅτι αὐτοὶ τὸν θεὸν ὄψονται. |

| VII | μακάριοι οἱ εἰρηνοποιοί· |
| | ὅτι αὐτοὶ** υἱοὶ θεοῦ κληθήσονται. |

| VIII | μακάριοι οἱ δεδιωγμένοι ἕνεκεν δικαιοσύνης· |
| | ὅτι αὐτῶν ἐστιν ἡ βασιλεία τῶν οὐρανῶν. |

*II and III transposed: D 33 b f q vg sy[e] bo[ma]: Cl Or Eus Hil Eph [Chr] Bas GrNy Hier Aph

**om. αὐτοὶ: C D f13 pc: Did

1. *Further Defining Characteristics of the Composition*

Mention was made in the previous chapter of other formal characteristics of the Beatitudes' composition which remain to be noted. The first of these is the pattern running through the apodoses of the respective beatitudes, in which the rhyming future passive (in circumlocution for the action of God) alternates with an active verbal form. These are actually arranged chiastically, XYXYYXYX, a device which makes possible the *inclusio* between I and VIII. It need not follow from this that the Beatitudes themselves are also chiastic (other features are in fact against that, in particular the repetition of δικαιοσύνη in IV and VIII); but the pattern indicated is, at any rate, an alternating arrangement of pairs within the quatrains, the lines not in simple juxtaposition but dovetailed, ABABABAB.[1]

Prima facie this is supported by the meaning of the words; the mourners and the hungry both represent, in some sense, privation followed by relief; the merciful and the peacemakers practise parallel forms of beneficence, while the correspondence between the poor in spirit and the meek was sufficiently recognized in the early Church for the MS order of the Beatitudes to be affected by it once its original rationale (as suggested here) had been lost to sight.[2] But the correspondences between the pairs extend to sound as well as meaning: πτωχοὶ...πραεῖς (dissyllables, alliterated, same quantitative scansion); πενθοῦντες... πεινῶντες (trisyllabic participles, alliterated, same quantitative scansion, near-rhyming); ἐλεήμονες...εἰρηνοποιοί (pentesyllables, assonant,[3] converse correspondence of scansion); καθαροὶ τῇ καρδίᾳ

---

1.   For precedents for this see J.T. Willes, 'Alternating A B A' B' Parallelism in Old Testament Psalms and Prophetic Literature', in E.R. Follis (ed.), *Directions in Biblical Hebrew Poetry* (JSOTSup, 40; Sheffield: JSOT Press, 1987), pp. 49-76, which examines a sample from a total of 199 instances (including three from Ps. 119 [see below]). On 'distant parallelism' generally cf. Berlin, *Dynamics*, pp. 3, 141.

2.   For ancient witnesses to this order see above; for modern supporters of it down to 1972, see Dupont, *Béatitudes*, III, p. 473 n. 2. To these must now be added C. Michaelis, 'Die π-Alliteration der Subjectsworte der ersten 4 Seligpreisungen in Mt. v 3-6 und ihre Bedeutung für den Aufbau der Seligpreisungen bei Mt., Lk. und in Q', *NovT* 10 (1968), pp. 148-61; S. Légasse, *Les Pauvres en Esprit* (LD, 78; Paris: Cerf, 1974), p. 26; R.A. Guelich, 'The Matthean Beatitudes: "Entrance Requirements" or "Eschatological Blessings"?', *JBL* 95 (1976). pp. 415-34: 424-26; NJB (1985); A.A. Di Lella, 'The Structure and Composition of the Matthean Beatitudes', in M.P. Horgan and P.J. Kobielski (eds.), *To Touch the Text* (Festschrift J.A. Fitzmyer; New York: Crossroad, 1989), pp. 237-42; E. Puech, '4Q525 et la pericope des Béatitudes en Ben-Sira et Matthieu', *RB* 98 (1991), pp. 80-106. For the latter's presentation of Di Lella's chiastic arrangement based on the transposition of the two Beatitudes see n. 9 below.

3.   I speak of assonance rather than alliteration here. In Greek (as opposed, for obvious reasons, to Hebrew) initial vowels can play a part in alliteration; but here

(trisyllables, alliterated); δεδιωγμένοι ἕνεκεν δικαιοσύνης (pentesyllables, alliterated, inverse correspondence of scansion).[4] The π-alliteration, previously pointed out by C. Michaelis,[5] has the further function of defining the first quatrain, while the addition to it in IV of the alliterated διψῶντες τὴν δικαιοσύνην matches the duplicated δ-alliteration in VIII and thus holds the two quatrains together. The duplicated κ in VI may serve to relate it to VIII with its duplicated δ (the only pair of which I have not given some account), but its real affinities are with I. πτωχοὶ τῷ πνεύματι and καθαροὶ τῇ καρδίᾳ are analogous in grammatical form as well as rhythmically akin,[6] and the special link between the two beatitudes to which this correspondence points will be elucidated in due course.

There are too many of these details for it to be plausible to dismiss them either as merely subjective impressions or as sheer coincidences, especially when they are read in the context of the uniform characteristics of the composition. Every line (more strictly distich or bicolon) begins with the same word μακάριοι. The closest parallel to this (which has in fact been proposed as a literary model for Matthew's Beatitudes[7]) is the acrostic Psalm 119 (LXX 118), every section of which consists of eight distichs each beginning with the same initial letter. In addition, although the individual beatitudes are somewhat uneven in length, each of the quatrains, as Schniewind[8] pointed out many years

---

(1) no consonants are involved; (2) the vowel sounds are kindred rather than identical.

    4.   To clarify an unavoidably arbitrary use of terms: *converse* indicates that short syllables are substituted for long, and vice versa; *inverse* that the arrangement of short and long syllables in the second member of the comparison is related either chiastically (as here) or mirror-wise (as suggested in n. 6) to that in the first.

    5.   Michaelis, 'π-Alliteration'. Michaelis predictably rushes into speculation about a supposed Aramaic source before asking herself whether other, comparable patterns are discernible in Matthew's Greek text, or elsewhere in the Gospel.

    6.   καθαροὶ τῇ καρδίᾳ could be scanned either as the rhythmical equivalent of πτωχοὶ τῷ πνεύματι (two short syllables being equivalent to one long one, and the last syllable of καρδίᾳ being treated as short) or as its mirror image (see n. 4 above), with καρδίᾳ treated as a dissyllable.

    7.   See Goulder, *Midrash*, p. 252. Puech, '4Q525', p. 94, draws attention to the Hebrew of Sir. 14.20-24, which has beatitudes in two four-line strophes each of 23 words.

    8.   J. Schniewind, *Das Evangelium nach Matthäus* (NTD; Göttingen: Vandenhoeck & Ruprecht, 1936), p. 40, with acknowledgement to W. Weber (no

ago, contains exactly the same number of words (36).[9]

What do the formal characteristics of the composition that we have so far identified have in common?

(a) Parallelism is of course the defining characteristic of Hebrew poetry,[10] and its use within a complex formal structure is typical of the

reference given), and reading αὐτοὶ with the majority of MSS at 5.9; cf. apparatus to the text of the Beatitudes.

9.   Di Lella, 'Structure', has carried the analysis further, finding in each half one beatitude of six words, one of eight, one of ten, and one of twelve. He is probably right to find in the word count an explanation for the addition of τὴν (diffPs. 36.11 LXX [but = Isa 61.7]; cf. n. 41 below) in III and the omission of τῆς (diffIV) in VIII. But his attribution of the suffix τῷ πνεύματι in I to the same motivation is unconvincing. His insistence on transposing II and III produces, in Puech's hands (see '4Q525', p. 97), the following analysis of the total word count:

$$
\begin{array}{lll}
\text{I} & 5 + 7 = 12 \\
\text{III} & 3 + 5 = 8
\end{array} \Big\} \; 20 \\[4pt]
\begin{array}{lll}
\text{II} & 3 + 3 = 6 \\
\text{IV} & 7 + 3 = 10
\end{array} \Big\} \; 16
\quad \Bigg\} \; 36
$$

$$
\begin{array}{lll}
\text{V} & 3 + 3 = 6 \\
\text{VI} & 5 + 5 = 10
\end{array} \Big\} \; 16 \\[4pt]
\begin{array}{lll}
\text{VII} & 3 + 5 = 8 \\
\text{VIII} & 5 + 7 = 12
\end{array} \Big\} \; 20
\quad \Bigg\} \; 36
$$

Neat as this is, it represents a chiasmus of word counts rather than of the words themselves, and an imperfect one at that, unless II and IV, and V and VI, are, respectively, counted together. It ignores (and thus obscures) the alternating pattern in the apodoses noted above (and its part in effecting the *inclusio* between VIII and I), and it imposes itself on the meanings of the words instead of arising out of them. The justification for this last assertion must await the treatment of the individual beatitudes in Part II.

10.   On the whole subject see W.G.E. Watson, *Classical Hebrew Poetry* (JSOTSup, 26; Sheffield: JSOT Press, 1984) (on parallelism pp. 114-59); B. Hrushovski, 'Prosody, Hebrew', in *Encyclopedia Judaica* (New York: Macmillan, 1973), XIII, pp. 1195-1203; R. Alter, *The Art of Biblical Poetry* (New York: Basic Books; London: George Allen & Unwin, 1985) (on parallelism pp. 1-24). For further work subsequent to 1984 see Berlin, *Dynamics*; Follis (ed.), *Directions*; L.A. Schökel, *A Manual of Hebrew Poetics* (Rome: Pontifical Biblical Institute, 1987); W. van der Meer and J.C. de Moor (eds.), *The Structural Analysis of Biblical and Canaanite Poetry* (JSOTSup, 74; Sheffield: JSOT Press, 1988); W.G.E. Watson, *Traditional Techniques in Hebrew Poetry* (JSOTSup, 170;, Sheffield: Sheffield Academic Press, 1994); for a simpler introduction, A. Fitzgerald, 'Hebrew Poetry', in R.E. Brown,

later and more self-conscious phase of the poetic tradition associated with the 'wisdom' school.[11] (b) Chiasmus, (c) *inclusio*, (d) rhyme, both terminal and internal, and assonance, and (e) alliteration, while fully at home in that tradition,[12] are not of course confined to it, but shared by it with many literatures including the Greek. Of these (b) and (c), like (a), can in principle survive translation, while (d) and (e), failing a translator's *tour de force* (of which there is no evidence in extant translations) cannot. This, and the occurrence of (f) quantitative scansion (which of course played no part in the Hebrew verse tradition) is evidence that the composition has been done in Greek; but the fact that the incidence of (f) is internal to words or short phrases rather than coextensive with the lines establishes that Greek poetry, as Matthew's contemporaries and co-linguals would have written it, is not the name of the game here, while the line arrangement of the piece, and the evidence of rhythmic stress structure within it (see below), indicate that it is more than a stretch of Hellenistic rhetorical prose (in which internal rhyme and alliteration and some use of quantitative scansion would all have been at home[13]). The conclusion to which this points is that the composer of the Beatitudes was working within the conventions of Hebrew verse, but by writing in Greek transplanted them to a linguistic soil to which they were not native[14] (absorbing at the same time from that soil such features as its practice of quantitative scansion, which, like rhyme and alliteration, could be used to complement or reinforce parallelism).

J.A. Fitzmyer and R.E. Murphy (eds.), *The New Jerome Bible Commentary* (London: Geoffrey Chapman, 1989), pp. 201-208.

11. See Watson, *Hebrew Poetry*, pp. 160-200; on acrostics, pp. 192-99.

12. Watson, *Hebrew Poetry*, pp. 201-207 (b); (see further *Traditional Techniques*, pp. 313-91); pp. 282-85 (c); pp. 222-23, 229-33 (d); pp. 225-28 (e).

13. See G.A. Kennedy, *New Testament Interpretation through Rhetorical Criticism* (Chapel Hill: University of North Carolina Press, 1984), p. 59. In Greek literature, however, they are less characteristic of poetry.

14. F.V. Filson, 'How Much of the New Testament is Poetry?', *JBL* 67 (1948), pp. 125-34 (132), allowed the possibility of this, suggesting as a parallel the Wisdom of Solomon, which, in whole or part, was composed directly in Greek. In addition to extensive use of alliteration, this book contains no fewer than 80 instances of pairs of lines (or triplets) with endings in matching (quantitative) scansion; couplets with 7 or 8 syllables of equal scansion are common, and at 8.3 the count is 11. For the evidence see H.St J. Thackeray, 'Rhythm in the Book of Wisdom', *JTS* 6 (1905), pp. 232-37.

2. *Metre in Hebrew Verse*

What we have found not only argues a high level of technical sophistication in the composition, but raises questions in connection with the ongoing debate about the nature of metre in Hebrew verse. The classical understanding of this as based on patterns of stressed words (more strictly, of stressed syllables in certain words[15]) has come under fire in recent years.[16] Among the alternatives proposed have been a count of the total number of syllables,[17] or (more recently) of words,[18] a structure based on syntactical line forms,[19] and the reduction of all metrical regularity to parallelism.[20] With the situation as fluid as this it might be supposed that there are few, if any, firm guidelines to be expected from current study of Hebrew metrics. However, the present dissonance would seem on the face of it to be the consequence of expecting a single exclusive answer to the question at issue. If on the other hand it is answered inclusively, as by Hrushovski[21] (whose account of Hebrew prosody is brilliantly summarized by Alter[22] as 'a "free rhythm" in which, within fixed quantitative limits, there are shifting parallelisms of meaning, accentual stress, and syntax, with a coincidence of all three elements always possible but by no means obligatory'), there is then the possibility of admitting new discoveries about the way Hebrew verse works in certain cases without either treating these as universal or

15. Watson, *Hebrew Poetry*, pp. 97-102; cf. W.H. Cobb, *A Criticism of Systems of Hebrew Metre* (Oxford: Clarendon Press, 1905). For a lively restatement of this position see M.C.N. Kospel and J.C. de Moor, 'Fundamentals of Ugaritic and Hebrew Poetry', in van der Meer and de Moor (eds.), *Structural Analysis*, pp. 1-62.

16. See Watson, *Hebrew Poetry*, pp. 103-10.

17. E.g. D.N. Freedman, *Poetry, Prophecy and Pottery* (Winona Lake, IN: Eisenbrauns, 1980); R.C. Culley, 'Metrical Analysis of Early Hebrew Poetry', in J.W. Wevers and D.B. Redford (eds.), *Essays on the Ancient Semitic World* (Toronto: Toronto University Press, 1970), pp. 12-28.

18. Suggested by D.N. Freedman, 'Another Look at Biblical Hebrew Poetry', in Follis (ed.), *Directions*, pp. 11-27 (18), as an alternative to syllable counting.

19. T. Collins, *Line-Forms in Hebrew Poetry* (Rome: Pontifical Biblical Institute, 1978); cf. Watson, *Hebrew Poetry*, pp. 106-108.

20. J.L. Kugel, *The Idea of Biblical Poetry: Parallelism and its History* (New Haven: Yale University Press, 1981); cf. Watson, *Hebrew Poetry*, p. 109; *Traditional Techniques*, pp. 44-53.

21. Hrushovski, 'Prosody', pp. 1200-202.

22. Alter, *Poetry*, pp. 26-27.

jettisoning a well-tried account which may nevertheless admit of exceptions. The subject as a whole, moreover, is one to be studied diachronically, and our concern here is not with the full history of its development, but only with a limited segment of it: namely, the way it would have been understood and practised towards the end of the first century of our era.[23]

There had actually been phonological developments in the Greek language, not very long before the period of the New Testament writings, which would have made it hospitable, in a way in which it had not been before, to reproduction of the stress system of Hebrew verse as that has been traditionally understood. The earlier distinctions of tone codified in the Alexandrian system of accentuation which for orthographical purposes we still use gave way to a simple stress accent, still in the position indicated in the older system, but applied only to the more significant words.[24] The older system had excluded certain words, defined as enclitic if they followed an accented word and under certain conditions could throw back their accent upon it, or proclitic if they were allowed to precede it. Enclitics were largely unaffected by the new system, but proclitics become part of the larger category of 'prepositives', including articles, conjunctions, prepositions and some pronouns; these would not be stressed separately, but would form a cluster around a single stressed word.[25] This is sufficiently close to the general metrical rules for Hebrew poetry (as the majority tradition has received them[26]) to make composition in accordance with them possible in Greek.

23. See Hrushovski, 'Prosody', pp. 1199, 1207-12, for the development of early post-biblical Hebrew poetry, including Ben Sira and other wisdom poetry, which employed 'a variety of rhythmic formulae, occasional rhymes, and parallelism', but without a discernibly regular formal system. For the poetry of Qumran see M.P. Horgan and P.J. Kobielski, 'The Hodayot (1QH) and New Testament Poetry', in *idem* (eds.), *To Touch the Text*, pp. 179-93; Puech, '4Q525'.

24. See P. Maas, *Greek Metre* (Oxford: Clarendon Press, 1962), p. 21, with acknowledgment to earlier German philologists (including, interestingly, Friedrich Nietzsche).

25. Thus, following Maas, J. Irigoin, 'La composition rythmique des cantiques de Luc', *RB* 98 (1991), pp. 5-50 (7-8).

26. Kospel and de Moor, 'Fundamentals', pp. 1-2, speak of the 'foot' (defined as 'a word containing at least one stressed syllable') as 'the smallest building block' in the composition of Hebrew verse. Cf. Schökel, *Manual*, pp. 34-36.

A recent and intensive examination by J. Irigoin[27] of the canticles of Luke 1–2 in the light of the Greek accentual changes argues that their rhythmical structure has a syllabic basis, exhibited both in the subtle and varied patterns of accented and unaccented syllables and in close correspondence of the total syllable count of the major sections of these canticles, which compensates for the irregular length of the individual lines. Its author further claims to have found a comparable pattern in certain of the LXX Psalms, and also suggests a continuity in the opposite direction with the liturgical texts of later Greek-speaking Christianity.[28]

This hypothesis still awaits a full scholarly appraisal. If sustained, it could become a landmark in the literary study of the Lukan poetry in its wider context. We should however be cautious about including Matthew in that context.[29] Whereas the two strophes of the Beatitudes poem contain, as we have seen, an equal number of words (and we shall find that this is not an isolated instance[30]), neither there nor in the other texts that we shall be examining have I discovered (with one insignificant exception[31]) any evidence of an interest in the counting of syllables within lines or stanzas.[32] Irigoin's more ambitious conclusions are therefore not applicable to them. His starting point, however, is a different matter. The criteria for distinguishing words containing stressed syllables from the prepositives listed above offer a valid basis for identifying metrical stress in texts written in Greek without assuming translation. Since however the Hebrew metrical tradition which is the start-

27. Irigoin, 'Composition'.

28. 'Composition', pp. 49-50. If the suggested 'trajectory' has any foundation, the most likely link is the Hellenistic synagogue. This would account for the relative independence of Matthew's prosody (see next note).

29. While Matthew's community was evidently Greek-speaking, and he himself steeped in the LXX, the same cannot be assumed for the synagogues with which he found himself in conflict; even if they had gone over to the *lingua franca*, they could not be said to have had a long tradition in it. His exercises in Hebraic Greek verse are thus likely to have been his own independent work, which is what the internal evidence suggests.

30. See below, Chapter 4 §6 on 11.20-24.

31. The first part of the formula quotation at 4.15-16; see Chapter 3 §3 below.

32. J. Smit Sibinga, 'Eine literarische Technik im Matthäusevangelium', in Didier (ed.), *L'Evangile*, pp. 99-105, claims to find evidence of it in a number of passages in Matthew; but since virtually none of them can be construed as verse his findings are not strictly relevant here.

ing point is nothing if not flexible,[33] we should not expect a rigid uniformity among those attempting to reproduce it in Greek. I have found the following liberties occurring regularly enough in the poetic material in Matthew to be treated as characteristic of it:

(1) while prepositions and relative pronouns are normally unstressed, some flexibility with these as required by the meaning can be allowed for;[34]

(2) a negative may receive a stress if an emphatic form (e.g. οὐδαμῶς) is used, or if the simple form governs a whole clause rather than a single word within it;[35]

(3) personal pronouns (which Koine Greek tended to use wherever possible, in marked contrast to their suppression in classical Greek) can be stressed if the sense requires it, and this can extend to the enclitic forms;[36]

(4) a pair of words that would otherwise be stressed individually may receive a single metrical stress if it conveys a hendiadys or stands for a single referent.[37] Suggested examples are υἱοὶ θεοῦ (5.9 above), υἱὸς Δαυείδ (1.20), σοφοὶ καὶ συνέτοι (cf. 11.25), σὰρξ καὶ αἷμα (16.17).

Only (4) applies to the Beatitudes. Within that composition the count of stresses in the individual lines yields a result, on my reckoning, of 3-3, 2-2, 2-3, 4-2; 2-2, 3-3, 2-3,[38] 3-3—a total of 21 in each strophe.

What this suggests is in line with the position of Hrushovski cited above:[39] that word counting is not alternative to regularity of metrical

---

33. See Watson, *Hebrew Poetry*, pp. 98, 160-62.

34. For flexibility with these cf. C.F. Burney, *The Poetry of Our Lord* (Oxford: Clarendon Press, 1925) (a book which argued for the synoptic sayings of Jesus as translations from Aramaic verse originals), p. 58.

35. Cf. Kospel and de Moor, 'Fundamentals', p. 12.

36. This is especially the case in 11.28-30 and 28.18-20. See Chapter 4 Sections 7 and 10 below, and cf. H.B. Green, 'Matthew 28.19, Eusebius, and the *Lex Orandi*', in R. Williams (ed.), *The Making of Orthodoxy* (Festschrift H. Chadwick; Cambridge: Cambridge University Press, 1989), pp. 124-40 (132-33).

37. Cf. Kospel and de Moor, 'Fundamentals', pp. 2-3, on the flexibility of Semitic verse in the expansion and contraction of stressed feet (originally for musical reasons); though the norm is 1-5 accented syllables, Ps. 59.15 has 8 and Ps. 20.6 has 7.

38. Assuming a single stress on υἱοὶ θεοῦ (see [4] above).

39. See n. 21 above.

stress but complementary to it, and prepares for the possibility that the latter will not be universally present. Its presence in the Beatitudes may not unreasonably be connected with unevenness in the length of the individual lines of the poem.[40]

What remains to be observed, while of central importance, is hardly disputable: the pervasive influence of the Old Testament on both the content and wording of the composition. The full extent of this is part of what my investigation sets out to discover; but we may begin by acknowledging the unquestionable influence of Isa. 61.1-2 on I and II, of Ps 36.11[41] on III, and of Ps 23.4 on VI. These, as we shall find, are only the tip of the iceberg.

3. *The Poet and the Evangelist*

Can this writer of Hebraic verse in Greek be identified with the Evangelist? Source, form and redaction critics have all tended to think in terms of stages in the formation of a Gospel, and of a 'final redactor' responsible for its present form.[42] Stages there may well have been, but it should not be assumed that the person responsible for its final form was involved only in the last of them, or had no personal part in the creation of the materials which he assembled. In a striking and valuable chapter of *Midrash and Lection in Matthew*[43] (and independently of his final conclusions in favour of a lectionary origin for the Gospel) Goulder has shown how widespread and varied, and how unregarding of conventional source attributions, is the evidence of Hebrew poetic rhythms in the sayings material of this Gospel. He challenges the usual explanation of this as the result of translation from Aramaic or Hebrew, preferring to see the pronounced individual characteristics of the sayings as the impress of a single mind steeped in the scriptures of the Old Testament. He allows in principle that the presence of rhythmic quality does not by itself establish originality: that Matthew regularly improves

40. We shall find that the same applies to 11.20-24 (see n. 30).

41. All Old Testament citations from this point, including the numeration of the Psalms, are from the LXX unless otherwise stated.

42. This is especially true of those who, like G. Strecker, *Der Weg der Gerechtigkeit* (Göttingen: Vandenhoeck & Ruprecht, 1962), argue for a Gentile setting and author for the final form of the Gospel, and have thus to treat material with a clearly Jewish-Christian background as 'pre-Matthaean'.

43. 'Matthew's Poetry', in *Midrash*, pp. 70-94.

on Mark, and Luke, very occasionally, on Matthew.[44] But this does not dispose of his case for Matthew's creative imprint, even if in places he seems to overstate it. I am unable to dismiss as confidently as he does the evidence of redaction (and sometimes of subtle juxtaposition of sayings that seem to reflect a conservative Jewish-Christian outlook with others that serve to neutralize their original force) in such contexts as 5.17-20, 10.5 with v. 23b,[45] 18.15-20 and 23.2-7, and thus to rule out the presence of at any rate some (oral?) source material.[46] Nor do I feel any pressure to assume that all the logia contributed by the Evangelist must have been originally composed for the contexts in which we find them now. But despite these reservations I find the argument convincing in a sufficiently large number of cases to make it the starting point for my own, and it is by way of supplement to it that two groups of texts are submitted to further examination here: first, the bulk of Matthew's direct quotations from the Old Testament, in the form of which his own hand can be detected;[47] and, secondly, a series of logia, all found at structurally or dramatically significant, not to say climactic, points in the Gospel, which appear collectively to exhibit the same verse characteristics as we have noted in the Beatitudes (not all of which Goulder allows for—in fact he denies the presence of rhyme, alliteration, or metric stress in the material[48]), and at the same time, like them, to reflect, in a special degree, the influence of the Old Testament. They will be examined in the light of the evidences of verse composition, but within the wider context of current commentary and not apart from it.

44. *Midrash*, pp. 74, 88-89.

45. A suggestion of A. Loisy, *Les Evangiles synoptiques*, I (Ceffonds: published privately, 1907), p. 887, taken up by B.H. Streeter, *The Primitive Church* (London: Macmillan, 1929), pp. 34-35; J. Dupont, 'Vous n'aurez pas achevé les villes d'Israel avant que le Fils d'homme ne vienne', *NovT* 2 (1959), pp. 228-44: 231, 238; modified by the exclusion of 10.6 in H.B. Green, *The Gospel According to Matthew* (New Clarendon Bible; Oxford: Oxford University Press), p. 111.

46. It does not of course follow that such material necessarily contains authentic *verba Christi*; and the line between it and previous composition by the Evangelist is not easy to draw.

47. See authorities cited in n. 1 to Chapter 3.

48. *Midrash*, p. 70.

Chapter 3

MATTHEW AS VERSIFIER (1): THE REMODELLING
OF OLD TESTAMENT QUOTATIONS

The 'formula' quotations, a special characteristic of this Gospel, were long regarded as deriving from a special source independent of the Evangelist to which he had at best secondhand access. In recent study[1] (with the exceptions of Ulrich Luz's commentary[2] and of the work of scholars for whom the 'final redactor' of the book was a Gentile[3]) they have increasingly come to be seen as closely related to their present contexts in the Gospel, and their formulation as a process in which the Evangelist had a considerable if not decisive hand, and to which he brought a familiarity not only with the LXX, but with the Hebrew text and probably also with the Aramaic targums current in his day. It cannot however be claimed that there is a comparable consensus about

1. In particular: R.H. Gundry, *The Use of the Old Testament in St Matthew's Gospel* (NovTSup, 18; Leiden: E.J. Brill, 1967); *idem, Matthew*; K. Stendahl, *The School of St Matthew* (Philadelphia: Fortress Press, 2nd edn, 1968; see preface to this edition only); W. Rothfuchs, *Die Erfüllungszitäte des Matthäus-Evangelium* (BWANT, 88; Stuttgart: Kohlhammer, 1969); F. Van Segbroeck, 'Les citations d'accomplissement dans l'Evangile selon saint Matthieu d'après trois ouvrages récents', in Didier (ed.) *L'Evangile*, pp. 105-30; L. Hartman, 'Scriptural Exegesis and the Problem of Communication', in Didier (ed.), *L'Evangile*, pp. 131-52; G.M. Soares Prabhu, *The Formula Quotations in the Infancy Narrative of Matthew* (AnBib, 67; Rome: Pontifical Biblical Institute, 1976); B.M. Nolan, *The Royal Son of God* (OBO, 23; Fribourg: Presses Universitaires; Göttingen: Vandenhoeck & Ruprecht, 1979). See survey by Stanton, *Gospel*, pp. 346-63 (= D.A. Carr and H.G.M. Williamson [eds.], *It is Written* [Festschrift B. Lindars; Cambridge: Cambridge University Press, 1988], pp. 205-19).
2. Luz, *Matthew*, I, pp. 156-64 seems to make unnecessarily heavy weather of the discrepancies from both the LXX and the MT in these quotations (e.g. at 2.23), especially since he assumes, as I do, an author who, though his starting point is the LXX, is familiar with the Hebrew.
3. Of whom Strecker, *Weg*, has been the most influential.

the part played by the LXX in the creation of 'mixed' text forms, nor over the question how justly it can be called the Bible not only of Matthew's readership but of himself.[4] It seems to be too readily assumed that direct quotation was the sole object of the exercise, and therefore that when Matthew departs from the LXX text he does so in order to quote an alternative version which he has reason to prefer. The possibility of this in individual cases of course remains open.[5] But contemporary Jewish exegesis embraced not only comparison of different versions but cross-referencing of different texts on the basis of words they have in common,[6] and this could be done, and in my submission has been predominantly done here, by working from the LXX. A number of the texts are generally recognized as composite, but the degree to which this factor has affected those still thought of as unitary needs further exploration.

Another aspect was pointed out many years ago by C.C. Torrey.[7] The texts, it will be remembered, are all taken from the prophetic books (the Psalter being reckoned as prophetic for this purpose).[8] The books of the

4. Cf. J.M. van Cangh, 'La Bible de Matthieu: les citations d'accomplisse-ment', *RTL* 6 (1975), pp. 205-11; Stanton, *Gospel*, pp. 353-58 (= *It is Written*, pp. 210-13).

5. It is considered below in connection with 12.18-21; see §4.

6. For a summary of the *middôt* attributed to Hillel (of which this is the second) see C.K. Barrett, 'The Interpretation of the Old Testament in the New', *CHB*, I, pp. 383-84; cf. B. Gerhardsson, *The Shema in the New Testament* (Lund: Novapress, 1996), pp. 209-12.

7. C.C. Torrey, *Documents of the Primitive Church* (New York: Harper, 1941), pp. 41-90.

8. David was reckoned a prophet on the basis of 1 Kgdms 16.13 and 2 Kgdms 23.2; cf. J.A. Fitzmyer, 'David, "Being Therefore a Prophet" (Acts 2.30)', *CBQ* 34 (1972), pp. 332-39; M. de Jonge, 'The Earliest Christian Use of *Christos*', *NTS* 32 (1986), pp. 321-43 (334-35) and notes. It is implied at Mk 12.36//Mt. 22.43. In addition, the quotation of Ps. 77.2 (an Asaph psalm) at 13.35 (see §5 below) is ascribed to 'the prophet', and the name of Asaph, like that of Amos, finds its way, according to the best supported text, into the genealogy of Christ in Matthew's prologue (1.8, 10), contra M.D. Johnson, *The Purpose of the Biblical Genealogies* (SNTSMS, 8; Cambridge: Cambridge University Press, 2nd edn, 1988), p. 182, who does not however consider the possibility that an intentional choice of these variants by the Evangelist could reflect not confusion but haggadic conflation, as could also the famous crux at 23.35, or the ascription of 27.9-10 to Jeremiah (see now M. Knowles, *Jeremiah in Matthew's Gospel* [JSNTSup, 68; Sheffield: JSOT Press, 1993], pp. 52-81).

prophetic canon proper are a mixture of verse and prose, with the former predominating especially in the pre-exilic prophets; but the LXX translators of them (though not of the Psalter) made no distinction, although the verse structure often, if unevenly, shows through. Now a striking feature of Matthew's formula quotations is that although they are sometimes composite, and on occasion combine a verse quotation with one in prose, yet he almost always, if the text is of sufficient length, gives the result a clear rhythmic structure,[9] even if it is in this respect some way removed from the original. The validity of Torrey's observation does not stand or fall by the mistaken conclusion that he drew from it, that the Gospel had been translated; it is really evidence of the author's ability not only to render but to create Hebraic verse forms in Greek.

Since these texts are presented as explicit quotations, the first stage in the examination of them is necessarily the identification of their source(s) in the Old Testament. This will involve both comparison of the basic text with the LXX (and other versions where relevant) and concordance work on words not found in the LXX version of it but used elsewhere in the LXX in texts that could have influenced the writer. The context in the Gospel will often suggest such influences. Finally the text as it stands in Matthew must be examined for evidence of verse characteristics, and these compared with the forms found in the Hebrew original.[10]

1. *Matthew 2.6*

1a   καὶ σὺ Βηθλέεμ, γῆ Ἰούδα,
 b   οὐδαμῶς ἐλαχίστη εἶ ἐν τοῖς ἡγεμόσιν Ἰούδα·

---

9. *Documents*, p. 46.

10. Of the recognized formula quotations, this survey omits 2.15 and 8.17 as too brief to allow of significant metrical analysis, 2.23 both for that reason and as not corresponding to any known text and probably a summary in indirect speech (cf. AV, RV; Green, *Matthew*, p. 61; Gundry, *Matthew*, pp. 39-40; Davies and Allison, *Matthew*, I, p. 275; contra Luz, *Matthew*, I, pp. 148-50), and 27.9-10, though it is not too difficult to set out in five lines of more or less rhythmical verse, because the complexities and obscurities of the underlying exegesis (cf. Knowles, *Jeremiah*) would take us too far from our primary objective. 1.23, for reasons which will become clear when we reach it, is deferred to the following chapter. (13.14-15, even if not an interpolation, reproduces LXX *verbatim* and thus offers no evidence of Matthaean intervention.)

2a ἐκ σοῦ γὰρ ἐξελεύσεται ἡγούμενος,
b   ὅστις ποιμανεῖ τὸν λαόν μου τὸν Ἰσραήλ.

Mic. 5.1: **καὶ σὺ Βηθλέεμ**, οἶκος τοῦ Εφραθά, ὀλιγοστὸς **εἶ** τοῦ εἶναι ἐν χιλιάσιν **Ἰούδα**. ἐκ σοῦ μοι **ἐξελεύσεται** τοῦ εἶναι εἰς ἄρχοντα ἐν τῷ Ἰσραήλ... (3) καὶ **ποιμανεῖ** τὸ ποίμνιον αὐτοῦ ἐν ἰσχύϊ κυρίου.

Ruth 1.1: ἀπὸ **Βηθλέεμ** τῆς Ἰούδα... (7) ἐπιστρέψαι εἰς τὴν **γῆν Ἰούδα**.

Jer. 38(31).23: ... Ἔτι ἐροῦσιν τὸν λόγον τοῦτον ἐν **γῇ Ἰούδα** καὶ ἐν πόλεσιν αὐτοῦ.

Ps. 67.28: ἐκεῖ Βενιαμὶν νεώτερος ἐν ἐκστάσει, |ἄρχοντες **Ἰούδα ἡγεμόνες** αὐτῶν, |ἄρχοντες Ζαβουλών, ἄρχοντες Νεφθαλί.

1 Kgdms 9.21: καὶ ἀπεκρίθη Σαοὺλ καὶ εἶπεν Οὐχὶ ἀνδρὸς υἱὸς Ἰεμιναίου ἐγώ εἰμι τοῦ μικροῦ σκήπτρου φυλῆς Ἰσραὴλ καὶ τῆς φυλῆς τῆς **ἐλαχίστης** ἐξ ὅλου σκήπτρου Βενιαμίν;

Isa. 60.22: ὁ ὀλιγοστὸς ἔσται εἰς χιλιάδας καὶ ὁ **ἐλάχιστος** εἰς ἔθνος μέγα.

2 Kgdms 5.2 (= 1 Chron. 11.2): καὶ εἶπεν κύριος πρός με Σὺ **ποιμανεῖς τὸν λαόν μου τὸν Ἰσραήλ**, καὶ σὺ ἔσει εἰς **ἡγούμενον** ἐπὶ τοῦ Ἰσραήλ.

This composite text, now generally reckoned among the formula quotations although lacking the characteristic introduction,[11] clearly has as its starting point the quatrain in Mic. 5.1, and its rhythm corresponds approximately to that of the Hebrew text (which is very difficult to discern in the LXX). But the wording can be derived entirely from the combination of the latter with other LXX texts linked to it by catchword connections. The combination γῆ Ἰούδα is rare in the LXX; its occurrence in Ruth makes the connection with Bethlehem (and with the genealogy of the previous chapter; see 1.5), while the Jeremiah text is from a context which has also supplied the quotation which will be examined next. The words also echo γῆ Ζαβουλών, γῆ Νεφθαλίμ in 4.15, a text which gathers up themes from this chapter. All three names are found in Ps. 67.28, together with Βενιαμίν which is a further clue to the interpretation.[12] The strong negative οὐδαμῶς, which at first sight contra-

11. See, e.g., Soares Prabhu, *Formula Quotations*, p. 40; Stanton, *Gospel*, p. 348 (= *It is Written*, p. 206).

12. B. Lindars, *New Testament Apologetic* (London: SCM Press, 1961), p. 193 n. 2, brings up this text, but only as the contributor of ἡγεμών which Matthew's version has substituted for χιλιάς (see following note). He notes that the alteration

dicts the meaning of the Micah text, conveys a double paradox: the son of David (cf. Mt. 1.1), like his prototype, will rise from humble origins (hence preference of Bethlehem over Jerusalem) to greatness (thus Isa. 60.22).[13] Yet, again like his prototype, his original littleness does not preclude superiority to what he is to displace, here typified by Saul on the basis of the latter's own admission (1 Kgdms 9.21). Saul was a Benjamite; if his tribe is the least, the Davidic tribe of Judah, even as represented by little Bethlehem, is above it.[14] And as the historical David displaced Saul, so the Son of David will displace the present leaders of his people, represented in this chapter by Herod, and in subsequent ones by scribes and Pharisees. The theme of displacement is near the surface at 11.28-30; 16.17-19; 21.33–22.14; 28.18-20.

The fourth verset of Mic. 5.1 (in spite of its reference to ancestors which would have made a link with the genealogy of the previous chapter) is suppressed in favour of a partial quotation of 2 Kgdms 5.2 (or 1 Chron. 11.2, here identical), made possible by catchword connection from ποιμανεῖ in Mic. 5.3.[15] ἡγούμενος in line 2a is overflow from the same source.

'calls attention to the possibility of rival dynasties', but without recognizing the relevance of Benjamin to this theme. Lindars started from the assumption of an independent history for 2.6 as a Christian proof-text, and thus missed its associations with the larger context in Matthew, such as the tribal patronymics shared with Ps. 67.28.

13.   ὀλιγοστός and ἐλαχίστος are found in parallelism at Isa. 60.22, which gives warrant for Matthew's substitution, but they are not strictly synonymous in Greek, though the LXX used them indiscriminately to render synonyms. The numerical sense of ὀλιγοστός ('fewest') is not quite contradicted by a qualitative understanding of οὐδαμῶς ἐλαχίστος (compare the expression 'last but not least'). The substitution of 'leaders' for 'thousands' has altered the terms of the argument. The population of Bethlehem will remain small, but one born from her is the true Son of David, with whom the future of God's people lies.

14.   That a reference to Saul—the prototype of Herod as *de facto* ruler of Israel —is intended is confirmed by (and is probably one reason for) the incorporation of wording from 2 Kgdms 5.2 in 2b. That text relates the recognition of David as king by all Israel after the years of conflict with Saul (who is mentioned by name at the beginning of the verse). For this theme elsewhere in the New Testament cf. Acts 13.21-22 (on this Green, 'Clement', pp. 18-21).

15.   ποιμαίναιν and its cognates are used repeatedly in the Old Testament of the office of a king, including Jer. 3.15; for the part played by the passage containing this text in Matthew's thinking see Chapter 4 §1 below.

The cento (for that is what it must really be called) has been constructed to be read as a single tetrastich. The two distichs which comprise it each consist of 12 words (5-7: 5-7); the stress-system on the other hand is uneven (4-4, 3-3), though in the context of biblical poetry this hardly calls for comment.

2. *Matthew 2.18*

In order to be in a position to compare Matthew with the LXX here it is necessary first to get some idea of the LXX text form that would have been known to him. Our present MSS of Jer. 38(31).15 (all of course of Christian provenance) represent at this point two main forms: B (followed in the main by ℵ Q V) and A.

B: φωνὴ ἐν Ῥαμὰ ἠκούσθη,
       θρήνου καὶ κλαυθμοῦ καὶ ὀδυρμοῦ,
       Ῥαχὴλ ἀποκλαιομένη[ς]
       [καὶ] οὐκ ἤθελεν παύσασθαι ἐπὶ τοῖς υἱοῖς αὐτῆς,
       ὅτι οὐκ εἰσίν.

       [ ] ℵ Q V

A: φωνὴ ἐν τῇ ὑψήλῃ ἠκούσθη,
       θρήνου καὶ κλαυθμοῦ καὶ ὀδυρμοῦ,
       Ῥαχὴλ ἀποκλαιομένης ἐπὶ τῶν υἱῶν αὐτῆς,
       καὶ οὐκ ἤθελεν παρακληθῆναι,
       ὅτι οὐκ εἰσίν.

Mt.:
1a   φωνὴ ἐν Ῥαμὰ ἠκούσθη,
 b   κλαυθμὸς καὶ ὀδυρμὸς πολύς·
2a   Ῥαχὴλ κλαίουσα τὰ τέκνα αὐτῆς,
 b   καὶ οὐκ ἤθελεν παρακληθῆναι,
3   ὅτι οὐκ εἰσίν.

Lines 1b and 3 are identical in B and A (their agreement against MT in 3 represents a sounder text than the latter[16]); and A's substitution of τῇ ὑψήλῃ for Ῥαμὰ in 1a is unsupported by any other witness to the LXX text (but found in Aquila). These three lines, then, can be confidently assigned to LXX. There remains the problem of 2a and 2b.

Here Ῥαχὴλ and οὐκ ἤθελεν are common to all. A's παρακληθῆναι is found in Aquila as well as in Matthew, and although these two are

16. The singular in the MT is surely corrupt; see Gundry, *Use*, p. 104.

presumably independent of one another, it is difficult to believe that A which was exposed to influence from both[17] was indebted to neither. The likelihood of such assimilation makes B's παύσασθαι the more probable verb in the LXX. But the words ἐπὶ τοῖς υἱοῖς which follow it imply a repetition of ἀποκλαιομένη or of an equivalent dependent participle. παρακληθῆναι cannot carry this, and the substitution of it in A has thus dictated the shifting of these words to follow ἀποκλαιομένη in the previous line. This means that their original position was as in B.

Whether the same factor was also responsible for the extension of the dependent genitives (diffMT) of 1b into 2a is more doubtful. It certainly reads more naturally in A than in א Q V which agree with A at this point while leaving 2b otherwise untouched; for there can be no smooth transition from a genitive participle in 2a to a nominative one, dependent on παύσασθαι understood, in line 2b. This can mean either that the reading of א Q V is primary (*difficilior lectio potior*) and the B reading an attempt to improve on its infelicities, or, as I should prefer to say, that the former have been affected by the text of A.

With this reservation, the B version is probably as near to the text of the LXX current in Matthew's time as we can expect to get.[18] Matthew agrees with it *verbatim* in 1a and 3. In 1b he has retained two of the LXX's three nouns;[19] his replacement of the third by an adjective is in line with the Hebrew construction at this point, and the colourlessness of the word chosen (πολύς, where the Hebrew would lead the reader to expect πικρός[20]) helps to concentrate attention on the two that he has retained. By keeping these in their LXX order (which reverses that of

17. From Matthew, as with all Christian texts of the LXX, as part of their total canon of scripture; from Aquila through the influence of the Hexapla, of which A shows special evidence (see M.J. Lagrange, *Evangile selon saint Matthieu* [Paris: Gabalda, 1923], p. 35; Stendahl, *School*, p. 102; Torrey, *Documents*, pp. 51-53; Gundry, *Use*, p. 89). Matthew will hardly have known Aquila's version as such, but it could have incorporated earlier readings that were already current in his day (cf. nn. 29, 63 below).

18. This accords with the judgment of J. Ziegler, *Jeremias* (Septuaginta auctoritate Societatis Litterarum Gottingensis, 15; Göttingen: Vandenhoeck & Rupecht, 1957), p. 358.

19. Rothfuchs, *Erfüllungszitäte*, p. 64, concludes that Matthew's choice of words is dependent on the LXX.

20. Lagrange (*Matthieu*, p. 36) wondered if πολύς had crept in as a corruption of πικρός. But the word is classed by Goulder (*Midrash*, p. 483) as 'semi-Matthaean', and is used with emphasis at 5.12 and 9.37.

their Hebrew equivalents) he sets up his own parallelism with the following lines, κλαίουσα in 2a corresponding to κλαυθμὸς and οὐκ ἤθελεν παρακληθῆναι in 2b to ὀδυρμός.[21] He also reverts to the MT's paratactic construction of the verse, in preference to the LXX's dependent genitives. Taken as a whole, his version looks more like a revision of the LXX made by a writer familiar with the Hebrew than a fresh translation. The result, a stanza of two bicola in 3-3 rhythm with a short extra-metrical tailpiece, is rhythmically an improvement on LXX[B] (and vastly better than ℵ Q V which can scarcely be construed as verse at all).

The remaining changes are likely to have been made for reasons of applied exegesis[22] rather than of style or exact correspondence to the original. τέκνον is elsewhere in the LXX a perfectly acceptable equivalent for *bēn*, but the choice of it here in preference to υἱός must be studied in the light of (1) the reverse substitution in the previous formula quotation at 2.15;[23] (2) the associations of τέκνα elsewhere in this Gospel, in particular at 23.37; 27.25.[24] παρακληθῆναι, though in any case a better rendering of the Hebrew than that of the LXX, has further associations with Jeremiah 38. The implications of both words will be examined below in connection with the beatitude on the mourners.[25]

3. *Matthew 4.15-16*

1a	γῆ Ζαβουλών,
b	καὶ γῆ Νεφθαλίμ,
2a	ὁδὸν θαλάσσης,
b	πέραν τοῦ Ἰορδάνου,
3	Γαλιλαία τῶν ἐθνῶν·
4a	ὁ λαὸς ὁ καθήμενος ἐν σκότει
b	φῶς εἶδεν μέγα·
5a	καὶ τοῖς καθημένοις ἐν χώρᾳ καὶ σκιᾷ θανάτου,
b	φῶς ἀνέτειλεν αὐτοῖς.

21. See Gundry, *Matthew*, p. 36.

22. For the meaning and scope of this expression see G. Vermes, 'Bible and Midrash: Early Old Testament Exegesis', *CHB*, I, pp. 199-231 (221-28).

23. Hos. 11.1: ἐξ Αἰγύπτου μετεκάλεσα τὰ τέκνα αὐτοῦ. Mt. 2.15: ἐκάλεσα τὸν υἱόν μου.

24. Cf. Nolan, *Royal Son*, p. 138; Gundry, *Matthew*, p. 36; Knowles, *Jeremiah*, p. 37.

25. See Chapter 4 §9b, and Chapter 7 §3a.1, below.

Isa. 8.23–9.1: τοῦτο πρῶτον ποίει, ταχὺ ποίει, χώρα **Ζαβουλών**, ἡ **γῆ Νεφθαλίμ ὁδὸν θαλάσσης** καὶ οἱ λοιποὶ οἱ τὴν παραλίαν κατοικοῦντες καὶ **πέραν τοῦ Ιορδάνου, Γαλιλαία τῶν ἐθνῶν**, τὰ μέρη τῆς Ιουδαίας. **ὁ λαὸς ὁ πορευόμενος ἐν σκότει**, ἴδετε **φῶς μέγα**· οἱ κατοικοῦντες **ἐν χώρᾳ καὶ σκιᾷ θανάτου, φῶς** λάμψει ἐφ᾽ ὑμᾶς.

Isa. 42.7: ἐξαγαγεῖν...ἐξ οἴκου φυλακῆς **καθημένους ἐν σκότει**.

Ps. 106.10: **καθημένους ἐν σκότει καὶ σκιᾷ θανάτου**...

Zech. 6.12: Ἰδοὺ ἀνήρ, Ἀνατολὴ ὄνομα αὐτῷ καὶ ὑποκάτωθεν αὐτοῦ **ἀνατελεῖ**...

Mal. 3.20: καὶ **ἀνατελεῖ** ὑμῖν...ἥλιος δικαιοσύνης.

If Matthew seems to assume the unity of the oracle that he quotes from Isaiah (now vigorously defended by A. Alt[26]) his treatment nevertheless reflects the metrical diversity between the two verses: a series of five short versets (which some do not recognize as verse[27]) in the first, and a straightforward tetrastich in the second.

His handling of the first is bold: instead of reproducing the complete text, he has excerpted from it phrases which serve to make his geographical point, and formed them into a five-colon strophe with two stresses to each colon.[28] The wording of these corresponds with the *textus receptus* of the LXX throughout,[29] except for the substitution of

26. A. Alt, *Kleine Schriften*, II (Munich: Beck, 1953), pp. 206-25.

27. E.g. G. Fohrer, *Das Buch Jesaja* (Zürich: Zwingli, 1960), p. 123; J. Lindblom, *A Study on the Immanuel Section in Isaiah* (Scripta Minora 1757–58: 4; Lund: C.W.K. Gleerup, 1958), p. 53.

28. Cf. Torrey, *Documents*, pp. 57-59. The metrical analysis involves stress on the prepositions in lines 2a and 2b; a reasonable assumption, especially as the first is a noun doing duty as a preposition (see next note).

29. ὁδὸν θαλάσσης (a literal rendering of the Hebrew), found in LXX אᶜ A Q, is missing in B and א*, and seems to duplicate the following words: οἱ τὴν παραλίαν κατοικοῦντες. Rahlfs included it in his edition, as did Ziegler, *Isaias* (Septuaginta, XIV; Göttingen: Vandenhoeck & Ruprecht, 1939), p. 67, with some hesitation. Gundry, *Use*, p. 106, attributes it to influence from the text of Matthew. As regards the textual history of LXX this may well be right; but it does not explain the preference of both Aquila and Theodotion for this version of the text (see H-R s.vv., and cf. Torrey, *Documents*, pp. 57-59). This would not be the only instance of a reading adopted by the later Greek versions which appears to have been already current in the first century (cf. n. 63 below), and it seems the most plausible explanation here. It hardly amounts to an argument for Matthew's general independence of the LXX.

γῆ for χώρα, which enhances his parallelism as well as conforming more closely to the MT (which has the same word in both places), and also to γῆ Ἰούδα in 2.6. The verse structure is more complex than appears at first sight. In terms of parallelism the scheme is AABB: in terms of scansion it is ABA'B' (those marked ' having an extra initial short syllable); in terms of word count it is 2.3.2.3. None of these allows adequately for the inclusion of the final line Γαλιλαία τῶν ἐθνῶν as the climax. If syllables are counted, however (to which I have found no parallel in Matthew), and the first four lines are taken as pairs (as form and sense both indicate), the count is: 4-5, 5-6, 7.

Matthew's version of the lines which follow is closer both in rhythm and in general sense to the MT than is the LXX, but apart from his rearrangement of the words within the lines to make the parallelism stand out more sharply,[30] he has effected this exclusively by the selection of words available to him from cross-referencing of the LXX, two of which (καθήμενος for πορευόμενος[31] and ἀνέτειλεν for λάμψει) actually diverge from the MT where the LXX agrees with it. The rhyming correspondence of ἀνέτειλεν with εἶδεν recalls the association of ἀνατολή with ἰδεῖν in 2.2, 9, and the connection of the former word not only with the star but with the 'young shoot' as an image of the Messiah.[32] 4.15-16 is the final item in the Gospel's initial presentation of Jesus before the beginning of his ministry,[33] and it naturally reflects its larger context.

30. φῶς, though object in the second line and subject in the fourth, occupies the same position in both, and there is assonance between εἶδεν and ἀνέτειλεν.

31. καθήμενος, which replaces both πορευόμενος and κατοικῶν, is a recognized LXX alternative for the Hebrew word behind the latter (*yāsab*). Its substitution for both is sufficiently explained by the LXX parallels in Isa. 42 and Ps. 106 cited above.

32. ἀνατολή, used of Joshua (= Jesus) the high priest at Zech. 3.8; 6.12 (see above), and found also at Jer. 23.1, translates the Hebrew *semāḥ*; the latter may be a contributor to the enigmatic Ναζωραῖος at 2.23, either by association with its synonym *nēser*, or by a more complicated route involving ναζίρ at Judg. 13.5, 'holy' there and at Isa. 4.3 (and perhaps also *semāḥ* [no LXX equivalent] at Isa. 4.2); see Davies and Allison, *Matthew*, I, pp. 276-77; Gundry, *Matthew*, pp. 39-40 (for ναζίρ cf. n. 3 to Chapter 4 §1 below).

33. 4.14, which introduces this quotation, repeats 2.22 (which introduces that at 2.23) almost verbatim; and at 4.17 the words ἀπὸ τότε introduce, as a fresh phase in the Gospel narrative, the proclamation and ministry of Jesus. (I agree so far with E. Krentz, 'The Extent of Matthew's Prologue: Toward the Structure of the First

Matthew has thus displayed great freedom in his handling of the text, and some of the features noted, such as quantitative scansion and internal rhyming, though found regularly, as we shall see, where he is composing, are rare in cases where (with dependence on predecessors) he is translating. This is possibly an indicator of the thinness of the line, in his literary practice, between free quotation and composition on biblical models.

4. *Matthew 12.18-21*

1a Ἰδού, ὁ παῖς μου, ὃν ᾑρέτισα,
 b   ὁ ἀγαπητός μου, εἰς ὃν εὐδόκησεν ἡ ψυχή μου·
2a θήσω τὸ πνεῦμά μου ἐπ᾽ αὐτόν,
 b   καί κρίσιν τοῖς ἔθνεσιν ἀπαγγελεῖ.
3a οὐκ ἐρίσει οὐδὲ κραυγάσει,
 b   οὐδὲ ἀκούσει τις ἐν ταῖς πλατείαις τὴν φωνὴν αὐτοῦ.
4a κάλαμον συντετριμμένον οὐ κατεάξει,
 b   καὶ λίνον τυφόμενον οὐ σβέσει·
5a ἕως ἂν ἐκβαλῇ εἰς νῖκος τὴν κρίσιν,
 b   καὶ τῷ ὀνόματι αὐτοῦ ἔθνη ἐλπιοῦσιν.

Isa. 42.1-4: Ἰακὼβ **ὁ παῖς μου**, ἀντιλήμψομαι αὐτοῦ, |Ἰσραὴλ **ὁ ἐκλεκτός μου**, προσεδέξατο αὐτὸν **ἡ ψυχή μου** |ἔδωκα **τὸ πνεῦμά μου ἐπ᾽ αὐτόν**· |**κρίσιν τοῖς ἔθνεσιν** ἐξοίσει.|**οὐ** κεκράξεται **οὐδὲ** ἀνήσει, |**οὐδὲ ἀκουσθήσεται** ἔξω ἡ **φωνὴ αὐτοῦ**. |**κάλαμον** τεθλασμένον οὐ συντρίψει |**καὶ λίνον** καπνιζόμενον **οὐ σβέσει**, |ἀλλὰ **εἰς** ἀλήθειαν ἐξοίσει **κρίσιν**. |ἀναλάμψει καὶ οὐ θραυσθήσεται, |ἕως ἂν θῇ ἐπὶ τῆς γῆς **κρίσιν·|καὶ** ἐπὶ **τῷ ὀνόματι αὐτοῦ ἔθνη ἐλπιοῦσιν**.

Mt. 3.16: ...καὶ εἶδεν πνεῦμα θεοῦ...ἐρχόμενον **ἐπ᾽ αὐτόν**· (17) καὶ ἰδοὺ φωνὴ ἐκ τῶν οὐρανῶν λέγουσα· οὗτός ἐστιν ὁ υἱός **μου**, **ὁ ἀγαπητός**, ἐν ᾧ **εὐδόκησα**.

1 Chron. 28.6: καὶ εἶπέν μοι ὁ θεὸς Σαλωμὼν ὁ υἱός σου οἰκοδομήσει τὸν οἶκόν μου...ὅτι **ᾑρέτικα** ἐν αὐτῷ εἶναί μου υἱόν, κἀγὼ ἔσομαι αὐτῷ εἰς πατέρα...

Gospel', *JBL* 83 [1964] pp. 409-15; J.D. Kingsbury, *Matthew: Structure, Christology, Kingdom* [London: SPCK, 1975], pp. 1-39; Bauer, *Structure*, pp. 42-45, 73-84, though without commitment to their overall structural hypothesis.) Cf. λαός here and at 1.21; γῆ followed by tribal patronymic here and at 2.6; Ναζαρά at 4.13 and apparently read by p^{70} (our earliest witness) at 2.23 (ignored by Tuckett, *Q*, p. 228, as by J.M. Robinson, 'The Sayings Gospel Q', in Van Segbroeck *et al.* [eds.], *Four Gospels 1992*, pp. 360-88 [373-75]).

Isa. 61.1: **Πνεῦμα** Κυρίου ἐπ᾽ ἐμέ, οὗ εἵνεκεν ἔχρισέν με· εὐαγ-γελίσασθαι πτωχοῖς ἀπέσταλκέν με, ἰάσασθαι τοὺς **συντετριμμένους** τῇ καρδίᾳ...

Isa. 44.2: μὴ φοβοῦ, **παῖς** μου Ἰακὼβ καὶ ὁ **ἠγαπημένος** Ἰσραήλ, ὃν ἐξελεξάμην· (3) ὅτι ἐγὼ δώσω ὕδωρ...ἐπιθήσω τὸ **πνεῦμά μου ἐπὶ** τὸ σπέρμα σου...

Hab. 1.4: ...καὶ οὐ διεξάγεται **εἰς** τέλος κρίμα,...

Job 23.7: ἀλήθεια γὰρ καὶ ἔλεγχος παρ᾽ αὐτοῦ, |ἐξαγάγοι δὲ **εἰς** τέλος τὸ κρίμα μου.

Ps. 71.1: Ὁ θεός, τὸ κρίμα τῷ βασιλεῖ δὸς |καὶ τὴν δικαιοσύνην τῷ υἱῷ τοῦ βασιλέως |κρίνειν τὸν λαόν σου ἐν δικαιοσύνῃ |καὶ τοὺς πτωχούς σου ἐν κρίσει...(17) ἔστω **τὸ ὄνομα αὐτοῦ** εὐλογημένον εἰς τοὺς αἰῶνας...πάντα **τὰ ἔθνη** μακαριοῦσιν αὐτόν.

Isa. 11.10: Καὶ ἔσται ἐν τῇ ἡμέρᾳ ἐκείνῃ ἡ ῥίζα τοῦ Ἰεσσαὶ καὶ ὁ ἀνιστάμενος ἄρχειν ἐθνῶν, ἐπ᾽ **αὐτῷ ἔθνη ἐλπιοῦσιν**...

The Hebrew of Isa. 42.1-4 is a poem of 12 versets in an unusually regular 3-stress metre, arranged as three bicola followed by two tricola. The LXX is basically faithful to this pattern, as is Matthew until he comes to the first tricolon; the third verset of this is detached, and its content, together with that of the final tricolon, compressed into a single distich. It is nevertheless at this point that his vocabulary is closest to that of the LXX: 11 of his 14 words are found there, as against only 28 (and those not the most significant) of the 49 in the first part of his version of the quotation. This led a majority of earlier scholars[34] to the conclusion that for the latter he is following an independent Greek version of the text that had circulated in the tradition—possibly as a christological proof text. Recent studies,[35] however, have challenged this account, notably those of O.L. Cope,[36] who points out the influence of the baptism narrative on Matthew's version of the opening lines, and

---

34. E.g. C.H. Dodd, *According to the Scriptures* (London: Nisbet, 1952), p. 89; J. Jeremias, 'παῖς θεοῦ', *TDNT*, V, pp. 677-717 (701); Lindars, *Apologetic*, pp. 144-52; Rothfuchs, *Erfüllungszitäte*, p. 77.
35. See, in addition to the two scholars named in the text, Torrey, *Documents*, pp. 64-66; J. Grindel, 'Matthew 12.15-21', *CBQ* 29 (1967), pp. 110-15; Kingsbury, *Structure*, pp. 94-95; J. Gnilka, *Das Matthäusevangelium* (HTKNT, 1.1, 1.2; Munich: Kösel, I 1986, II 1988), I, p. 453; Davies and Allison, *Matthew*, II, pp. 323-24.
36. Cope, *A Scribe*, pp. 35-45.

J.H. Neyrey,[37] who relates the quotation to its proximate context in the Gospel. Both arguments can be carried further.

The opening distich, while actually nearer as it stands to the MT than is the LXX, seems to be dictated by a Christian hermeneutic familiar not only with the synoptic baptism narrative but with Matthew's modifications of the version he found in Mark. Matthew has assimilated the form of the utterance of the heavenly voice at the baptism to that already found in Mark at the transfiguration,[38] putting it in the third person; his motive for this must be sought in the overall plan of his Gospel, in which Jesus has already been introduced as the Son of God in the infancy narrative and cannot be presumed ignorant of the fact, so that the heavenly voice at the baptism is addressed to the witnesses, and carries revelation to them,[39] not (as in Mark) to him (and to the implied reader).[40] The combination of ἀγαπητός and εὐδόκησεν (the latter is not in the transfiguration narrative of either Gospel) indicates that the writer has the baptism text in mind,[41] and ἐπ᾽ αὐτόν in the following distich corresponds to (and helps to explain; see below) Matthew's redaction of Mark at 3.16.[42] αἱρετίζειν is the word used at 1 Chron. 28.6 of God's adoption of Solomon.[43] The Messianic overtones which

37. J.H. Neyrey, 'The Thematic Use of Isaiah 42.1-4 in Matthew 12', *Bib* 63 (1982), pp. 457-73.

38. Mk 9.7: οὗτός ἐστιν ὁ υἱός μου ὁ ἀγαπητός. Cope, through declining all source-critical assumptions, misses this point.

39. Cf. J.P. Meier, *The Vision of Matthew* (New York: Crossroad, 1979), p. 58. For the significance of this for Matthew's understanding of revelation see on 11.27; below, Chapter 4 §7c.

40. Mk 1.12 conveys to the implied reader the true identity of Jesus: a knowledge that from that point the reader shares with the Evangelist and with the demonic forces, but not with the other characters in the narrative.

41. The partial parallels to ἀγαπητός at Isa. 41.8 (ἠγάπησα) and 44.2 (ἠγαπημένος) do not invalidate this point, though they may have helped with Matthew's alteration of 42.1.

42. Luke's agreement with Matthew at this point (in a context where he is basically following Mark) is not coincidental.

43. The context of this passage is God's election of Solomon to build the temple, another function in which he is the prototype of Jesus (see on 16.18, Chapter 4 §8c below). Cf. H.B. Green, 'Solomon the Son of David in Matthaean Typology', *SE* 7 (TU, 126; Berlin: Akademie Verlag, 1982), pp. 227-30 (229). (For the date of its appearance this short paper was seriously under-documented. I would therefore beg to put on record that the conference to which it was communicated

this introduces into the prophecy (and which will be continued in its conclusion) support Cope's argument[44] for an implied double meaning for παῖς here: he is Son as well as Servant.[45] The use of the future θήσω with reference to the Spirit turns a prophetic statement originally made, it would seem, about contemporary Israel or an individual person in relation to it (the LXX has clearly opted for the former) into a promise about a future figure, which Jesus fulfils. The significance of the choice of verb[46] is not immediately apparent, but ἐπ' αὐτόν is an allusion to the opening words of Isaiah 61, another Messianic text which Matthew has drawn upon not only at 11.5 but, as I shall be showing, at 5.3.[47] εὐαγγελίσασθαι in the same verse explains the substitution of ἀπαγ-

---

took place in 1973, and that the delay in the publication of its proceedings was due to circumstances over which the contributors had no control.)

44. *A Scribe*, p. 45; cf. Jeremias, 'παῖς θεοῦ', p. 701.

45. Matthew could hardly have substituted υἱός in the actual quotation, but his other modifications (ἀγαπητός especially) give sufficient clues to his real intention here. There is also the evidence of 8.5-13. If this is read without reference to Lk. 7.1-10 (which on my assumptions is dependent on it; see Green, 'Credibility', p. 138), and if Matthew's version of the healing of the Canaanite woman's daughter (15.21-28) is recognized as its counterpart (cf. R. Bultmann, *The History of the Synoptic Tradition* [trans. J. Marsh; Oxford: Basil Blackwell, 1963], p. 38; F.W. Beare, *The Earliest Records of Jesus* [Oxford: Basil Blackwell, 1964], p. 132; Green, *Matthew*, p. 146), the most natural construction makes the boy the centurion's son, not (as Luke seems to have thought) the slave mentioned in v. 9. Jn 4.46-54, which is related in some way to the synoptic pericope (a relationship of dependence is not ruled out; contra Davies and Allison, *Matthew*, II, p. 20), supports this interpretation. Cf. Bultmann, *Tradition*; J. Jeremias, *Jesus' Promise to the Nations* (trans. S.H. Hooke; SBT, 24; London: SCM Press, 1958), p. 35; Beare, *Records*, p. 74; Goulder, *Midrash*, p. 320; *Luke*, p. 376; Green, *Matthew*, p. 99; J.S. Kloppenborg, *Q Parallels* (Sonoma, CA: Polebridge Press, 1988), pp. 48-51; contra Gundry, *Matthew*, p. 142; Davies and Allison, *Matthew*, II, p. 21; and the majority of Q supporters. If the argument is accepted, a double meaning for παῖς is in order here, despite the absence of parallels elsewhere in the New Testament to its use in the sense of 'son'. See also the arguments of Kingsbury, *Structure*, pp. 94-95, against the view that Matthew develops a 'Servant' Christology here. The 'slave' connotation will appear in the passion narrative, notably in the named price for the betrayal (26.15; 27.3).

46. The nearest LXX parallel is in Isa. 44.3, a text linked to 42.1 by a number of catchword connections: notably the address to Jacob/Israel. ἐπιθήσω, though it represents a different Hebrew word from δώσω, is found there in parallelism with it, with πνεῦμα as its object.

47. See on Beatitude I; below, Chapter 7 §1a, d.

γελεῖ for ἐξοίσει. The mission of Jesus to the poor is finally to embrace the evangelization of the Gentiles (cf. 24.14, 28.19); their inclusion in the scope of God's κρίσις (already understood in a positive sense by Deutero-Isaiah[48]) will be effected by direct proclamation. The activity of the Spirit is much in evidence in this chapter; cf. 12.22-28, 31-32.

The two following distichs make a series of four negative statements about the Servant-Son:[49] collectively they depict him as πραΰς (non-assertively gentle; cf. 11.29, and behind it 5.5[50]), but it need not follow that each of the several items corresponds to something said about him in the surrounding text.[51] That they are denied of him implies that they are asserted of someone else: in this context the Pharisaic scribes. The word chosen to translate the Hebrew *yiṣ^ʿaq*, ἐρίζειν (literally to 'wrangle', 'be contentious')[52] has controversial and indeed forensic associations: to 'assert one's rights', which is just what the Pharisees have been doing, on behalf of their interpretation of the law, in the foregoing pericopes. They will shortly repeat the performance with the Beelzebul slander. It can hardly be said that the Jesus of this Gospel formally eschews controversy at any point before the conclusion of ch. 23 (contrast much of 12.22-45).[53] ἐν ταῖς πλατείαις echoes 6.5, where atten-

---

48. κρίσις renders *mišpāṭ*, a word which changed its meaning in the later Old Testament period; see V. Herntrich, 'κρίνω κτλ.', *TDNT*, III, pp. 923-30. The earlier insistence on strict judgment gives way to a new emphasis on salvation and deliverance, and this can be extended to Gentile nations. Isa. 42.1-4 is a primary text for the latter development.

49. Cf. Neyrey, 'Thematic Use', pp. 459-60.

50. See on Beatitude III; below, Chapter 7 §1b.

51. This is not to say that Neyrey is wrong to look for indications of the fulfilment of the prophecy quoted at 12.18-21 in the section that follows, but only in supposing that they must all be positive points about Jesus, rather than negative ones about the Pharisees.

52. B. Gärtner, 'The Habakkuk Commentary and the Gospel of Matthew', *ST* 8 (1954), pp. 1-24 (21), cites Sir. 8.2 for the word and Isa. 53.7 for the meaning. The difficulty about the latter is that its fulfilment at 26.63; 27.14 is a long way ahead and does not seem to be anticipated in the immediate context of the quotation.

53. Davies and Allison, *Matthew*, II, p. 324 explain the implied silence by reference to 12.15. While this, and the injunction to secrecy at 12.16 (which Matthew took over from Mark with less than total comprehension) provide the starting point for the quotation, its significance for the Evangelist goes far beyond the elucidation of such small details. Neyrey, 'Thematic Use', pp. 461-62, struggles to explain it in terms of the immediate context, but does not really convince.

tion is drawn to the ostentatious piety of the 'hypocrites' (= Pharisees); here, though the starting point is Jesus' refusal of publicity for his miracles,[54] the point is made against his opponents rather than expressly for him. Next, συντρίβειν is now used not of the Servant's (non-)action but of the situation of the objects of it. In this form it recalls the συντετριμμένους τῇ καρδίᾳ of Isa. 61.1, who are there identified with the 'poor'; for Matthew these are the marginalized, tax collectors and others crushed and cowed by the weight of the Pharisees' demands (11.28) and their judgment of failures (12.7).[55] The substitution of τυφόμενον for καπνιζόμενον is harder to explain; but what lexical evidence there is[56] suggests that the former word lends itself more readily to metaphorical use, e.g. of prophetic inspiration by the Spirit.[57]

These two distichs thus convey four aspects of Matthew's gravamen against the Pharisees (who are presented in high relief in these chapters [cf. 12.1-14, 24, 34, 38]): their insistence on finding legal fault,[58] their love of publicity, their judgmental attitude towards those who have difficulty in fulfilling the demands of the law ('lost sheep of the house of Israel' and Gentiles), and their resistance to prophecy.[59] It is with the whole picture that Jesus is contrasted.

The examination so far shows that virtually all Matthew's departures from the LXX version can be attributed to his own theological purpose in writing, while the framework in which they are set remains essentially that of the LXX. Once again, his version is best seen as a modifi-

54. Cf. ἐν ταῖς ῥύμαις in 6.2 (both words being paired with ἐν ταῖς συναγωγαῖς); Davies and Allison, *Matthew*, II, p. 326. Neyrey, 'Thematic Use', pp. 460-61, construes the line to mean 'no one will listen to his voice in the streets'. While it is true that ch. 13 distinguishes sharply between disciples, who can understand plain language (and are addressed in private; cf. 13.36), and the rest, who have to be spoken to in parables, it would be difficult to maintain that the 'crowds' who were 'astonished' at the authority of his teaching (7.28-29), and who are found in the present context (12.23), paid no attention to it.

55. See on Beatitude I; below, Chapter 7 §1d.

56. Cf. LSJ, s.v., II.2 fin.

57. Cf. 1 Thess. 5.19-20: τὸ πνεῦμα μὴ σβέννυτε, προφητείας μὴ ἐξουθενεῖτε. See n. 59 below.

58. Cf. 12.1-14.

59. Cf. 23.29-33. The insertion of τοῦ προφήτου at 12.39 (diff16.4) may be connected with this. On the hostility of neo-Pharisaic Judaism to prophecy see A.A.T. Ehrhardt, *The Framework of the New Testament Stories* (Manchester: Manchester University Press, 1964), pp. 103-31.

cation of the LXX carried out by a writer familiar with the Hebrew. The same is more obviously true of his final distich which compresses the last four versets of the original. The second of these, almost unintelligible in the LXX, is simply suppressed; the fourth reproduces the LXX unaltered apart from the omission of ἐπί. The first and third, both of which end with κρίσιν, are conflated, and the LXX's εἰς ἀλήθειαν is replaced by εἰς νῖκος.[60] This expression is sometimes used in the LXX to translate the Hebrew *lāneṣaḥ*;[61] the commoner rendering there is εἰς τέλος.[62] But Aquila is said to have used it uniformly, and it appears that versions of individual texts containing it were already in circulation in the first century.[63] However, *lāneṣaḥ* is not found in the MT of Isa. 42.3-4, and Matthew's introduction of an equivalent to it must therefore be put down to the influence of other texts. An author familiar with the underlying Hebrew word need not have confined his attention to passages where the LXX has εἰς νῖκος (none of which is particularly helpful). Habakkuk 1.4[64] and Job 23.7, where it has εἰς τέλος, both have a forensic ring, catchword connection with Isa. 42.3-4, and a verb compounded with ἐκ of which κρίμα is the object.[65] The comprehensive meaning recently proposed for the expression[66] (with only the

60. See Grindel, 'Matthew 12.15-21', p. 115; R.A. Kraft, 'Eis Nikos = Permanently/Successfully: 1 Cor. 15.54, Matt. 12.21', *Septuagintal Lexicography 1* (SBLSCS, 1; Missoula, MT: Scholars Press, 1972), pp. 153-56 (contra G.B. Caird, 'Towards a Lexicon of the Septuagint', p. 77 of the same volume).

61. 2 Kgdms 2.26; Job 36.7; Amos 8.7. It appears to have been originally a LXX translators' coinage.

62. Job 14.20; 20.7; 23.7; Hab. 1.4, plus some 20 instances in the Psalter (exclusive of those conveying a direction to the choirmaster).

63. On Aquila see A. Rahlfs, 'Über Theodotion-Lesarten im Neuen Testament und Aquila-Lesarten bei Justin', *ZNW* 20 (1921), pp. 182-89 (186). Paul read the word at Isa. 25.8, making it the basis of a word play with Hos. 13.14 at 1 Cor. 15.54.

64. Cf. Stendahl, *School*, p. 113; Lindars, *Apologetic*, p. 149 (both perhaps over-influenced by the recently discovered Qumran *Habakkuk Commentary* [1QpHab]).

65. κρίσις in Hab. 1.3 (κρίμα in 1.4); ἀλήθεια and κρίμα in Job 23.7 (both κρίσις and its cognate render *mišpāṭ*). For the conjunction of Isa. 42.3 and Hab. 1.4 at 1QH 4.25 see Grindel, 'Matthew 12.15-21', p. 115.

66. See Kraft, 'Eis Nikos'. Underlying the Hebrew expression is the etymology of the verb *nēṣāḥ*, meaning originally to 'shine', 'be brilliant'; hence (1) to 'be preeminent', and (in late Hebrew) 'conquer'; (2) to 'be enduring'. Cf. BDB, s.v.

faintest connection with the dictionary meaning of νῖκος[67]) is 'perma-
nently/successfully':[68] Job looks for final vindication in his case with
God, and Jesus' achievement is presented in terms of a case brought to
a successful, even triumphant, conclusion.[69]

There is moreover a further text which could have influenced Matthew's form of the quotation: Psalm 71, headed Εἰς Σαλωμών in the
LXX, and already a background text for the second chapter of the
infancy narrative,[70] has the same catchword connection with Isa. 42.1-4
(both κρίμα and κρίσις) in its first two verses; *mišpāṭ* is understood in
terms of the vindication of the poor; the kingdom is to be extended to
the Gentiles, and is to last for ever (here εἰς τοὺς αἰῶνας).[71] The
significance of this is, first, that there are tacit allusions to Solomon all
over these chapters:[72] the reaction of the crowds to the exorcism in
12.23 is 'can this be the son of David?' (referring to the traditional role
of Solomon as exorcist[73]); 12.41 speaks of Jesus as 'something greater

67. Except for texts containing forensic language or imagery, the expression
usually means no more than 'for ever', without reference to the literal meaning of
the noun (compare 'for good' in English; and see Kraft, 'Eis Nikos', p. 156).

68. Gundry, *Matthew*, p. 230, and Davies and Allison, *Matthew*, II, p. 326, by
omitting the first of these two renderings, fail to do justice to the element of finality
in the meaning.

69. Gundry, *Matthew*, p. 230, argues from the use of the verb at 12.35 that
ἐκβάλλειν τὴν κρίσιν is here a matter of teaching rather than action. In that case
Matthew's exegesis here would only add a more decisive thrust to what has already
been said in line 2b above; cf. 24.14, which makes the coming of the end depend on
the completion of the proclamation of the gospel to all nations. While the interpretation accords with a number of Matthaean emphases, it is unnecessary to
restrict the significance of εἰς νῖκος to this alone. 28.18-20 clearly implies as the
basis for the disciples' mission something already decisively achieved through the
death and exaltation of Jesus (cf. 26.28). In view of his practice elsewhere it is
probable that Matthew here, like Paul at 1 Cor. 15.54 (n. 63 above), intends a double meaning. The same goes for κρίσις; for the judgment theme in these chapters
see 11.20-24; 12.36-37; 13.36-51; cf. Neyrey, 'Thematic Use', pp. 462, 466-67.

70. Note the influence of Ps. 71.10-11 on 2.1, 11.

71. Ps. 71.17. The Hebrew word here is *'ôlām*.

72. See Green, 'Solomon', p. 228; *Matthew*, p. 17, for a suggested literary and
typological explanation.

73. The principal evidence for this is Josephus, *Ant.* 8.45-49; see D.C. Duling,
'Solomon, Exorcism and the Son of David', *HTR* 68 (1975), pp. 235-53; *idem*, 'The
Therapeutic Son of David', *NTS* 24 (1977–78), pp. 392-419, and literature cited
by him.

than Solomon', and Jesus' parables in ch. 13 recall Solomon's *mᵉšālîm* (LXX παραβολάς) at 3 Kgdms 5.12. Secondly, it is in accordance with the Messianic interpretation of the quotation,[74] which is further borne out by the coincidence of the final wording with that of Isa. 11.10.

In his recasting of the text Matthew has respected the rhythmic pattern of the original in his first four distichs, but by his compression of the final lines he has created a foreshortened climax to the prophecy which concentrates attention on his own pro-Gentile hermeneutic.[75]

5. *Matthew 13.35*

ἀνοίξω ἐν παραβολαῖς τὸ στόμα μου·
ἐρεύξομαι κεκρυμμένα ἀπὸ καταβολῆς.*

*κόσμου C D L W Θ f13 etc.

Ps. 77.2: ἀνοίξω ἐν παραβολαῖς τὸ στόμα μου· |φθέγξομαι προβλήματα ἀπ᾽ ἀρχῆς.

Sir. 20.30 (= 41.15): σοφία **κεκρυμμένη** καὶ θησαυρὸς ἀφανής· τίς ὠφέλεια ἐν ἀμφοτέροις;

The first half of 13.35 reproduces the LXX *verbatim*; the second has no word in common with it except ἀπό. Nor is there anything to suggest familiarity with the alternatives later favoured by the versions of Aquila and Symmachus.[76] Matthew's version is compatible with the Hebrew, but not so decisively better than the others that accuracy could have been the motive behind its changes. We have therefore to fall back on the internal evidence of Matthew's Greek wording in relation to its context in the Gospel.

In the light of what has already been discovered about the way Matthew writes verse, what should strike the reader of this text is that καταβολῆς is not only alliterated with κεκρυμμένα but rhymes with

74. For the presence of this theme in 11.25-30, see below, Chapter 4 §7a,b, and n. 151 to Chapter 4.

75. Possibly even more striking if the LXX originally read ἐπὶ τῷ νόμῳ and its present reading was the result of assimilation to Matthew; cf. Ziegler, *Isaias*, p. 277 (citing as parallels the LXX of Exod. 16.4; Ps. 118.165). Note that 18.20 speaks of disciples gathered together, εἰς τὸ ἐμὸν ὄνομα, where *m. Ab.* 3.2 (often seen as a Jewish counterpart; see Chapter 4 §§7a, 8e and 10c below) has them gathered to hear 'words of Torah'.

76. For these see Stendahl, *School*, p. 116.

παραβολαῖς.[77] This is unexpected in that it is in tension with the parallelism of the couplet, in which κεκρυμμένα would seem to be the natural counterpart of ἐν παραβολαῖς. But the more unexpected, even paradoxical, the rhyming, the more it demands serious attention. If the lines are now rearranged so that the rhyming words correspond structurally, we get the following:

ἀνοίξω ἐν παραβολαῖς
τὸ στόμα μου· ἐρεύξομαι
κεκρυμμένα ἀπὸ καταβολῆς.

This involves a double enjambment in the second line, which would be exceptional and daring for Hebrew verse as we know it. But it is difficult to ignore the exact parallelism of lines 1 and 3, or their correspondence (given the classical equivalence of two short syllables to one long) in scansion, as well as in word count, or the possibility of reading the two outer lines consecutively as a single sentence. As a clue to further meaning below the surface it is therefore worth exploring. ἀπὸ καταβολῆς is at one level equivalent to the LXX's ἀπ' ἀρχῆς and their common Hebrew exemplar. At that level it has to be understood as equivalent to ἀπὸ καταβολῆς κόσμου (cf. 25.34), and the larger part of the MS tradition has supplied the missing word. But Matthew may have his reasons for not being explicit here. καταβολή can mean, in addition to the laying of a foundation, the sowing of seed,[78] and this has been, in one way or another, the theme of three of the four parables so far narrated in this chapter. In these sowing is clearly seen as essentially an act of concealment, which will finally have visible and public consequences, both desired and undesired. The fourth of these parables (13.33) actually says that the woman 'hid' (ἐνέκρυψεν) the leaven in the meal. But the purpose of hiding anything is 'that it may be revealed' (cf. 10.26, Matthew's version of a Markan logion that in Mark belongs

---

77. If the 'itacist' pronunciation later characteristic of Byzantine Greek was already current in the Koine, it is an exact rhyme. For further evidence of this in Matthew see on 16.17 (Chapter 4 §8a below). L.R. Palmer, *The Greek Language* (London: Faber & Faber, 1980), p. 216, gives a mid-second century date for it in Attic Greek; F.T. Gignac, 'Phonological Phenomena in the Greek Papyri Significant for the Text and Language of the New Testament', in Horgan and Kobielski (eds.), *To Touch the Text*, pp. 33-46 (38-39, 42-44), finds evidence for it in first-century Koine.

78. LSJ, s.v., I.a (i.e., the basic meaning); BAGD, s.v., 2. F. Hauck, 'καταβολή' *TDNT*, III, p. 620, ignores this sense.

to the parables chapter [Mk 4.22]), and the formula quotation stands between the two halves of Matthew's chapter. The second half contains the interpretation of the parable of the tares, the parable of the dragnet with its interpretation, and the paired parables of the hidden treasure (θησαυρὸς κεκρυμμένος) and the pearl, which are matched chiastically with the leaven and the mustard seed in the first half. Everything here is concentrated on the disclosure of what had been hidden (note, e.g., that whereas the leaven was simply hidden in the meal, the hidden treasure is discovered and acquired).

If the importance, and the relevance, of these details is accepted, the clue to the significance of the quotation in its context is a play on the two meanings of καταβολή; in short, a pun. The surface meaning of the word as it stands in the psalm ('from the foundation of the world') is not excluded (it is needed to make the connection with the original text); but the meaning that links it with its immediate context is 'sowing', and this can itself be taken in two ways according to the two audiences addressed in the two halves of this chapter. With reference to the crowds, to whom everything is said in parables,[79] it will mean:

> 'I will teach hidden truths from (comparison with[80]) sowing' [synonymous parallelism];

and with reference to the disciples, who can receive plain language,[81] it will mean:

> 'I will disclose [lit. 'blurt out'[82]] matters hidden from (the time of) sowing' [antithetical parallelism].

There is a clear reminiscence of Sir. 20.30 and its parallel in the wording of the parable of the treasure trove at 13.44 (θησαυρῷ κεκρυμμένῳ), as there is also in the parable of the talents, when the servant is condemned for *hiding* his master's money in the ground. The latter parable, like the interpretation of those in ch. 13, is set in an eschatological context, and the comments of the master at the end of it pick up and repeat (25.29) the threat to take away from 'the one who has not even what he has'—that is, the kingdom (cf. 13.12//Mk 4.25).[83]

---

79. See 13.11.

80. For this use of ἀπό cf. Mk 13.26 (//Mt. 24.32).

81. See 13.16-18, 51-52.

82. For the double meaning of the Hebrew *'abbî'āh* see Stendahl, *School*, p. 117; Gundry, *Matthew*, p. 270.

83. The general sense seems to be that while the growth of the kingdom from its

6. Matthew 21.5

1a   εἴπατε τῇ θυγατρὶ Σιών,
 b   ἰδοὺ ὁ βασιλεύς σου ἔρχεταί σοι,
2a   πραῢς καὶ ἐπιβεβηκὼς ἐπὶ ὄνον,
 b   καὶ ἐπὶ πῶλον υἱὸν ὑποζυγίου.

Isa. 62.11: **Εἴπατε τῇ θυγατρὶ Σιών**...

Zech. 9.9: Χαῖρε σφόδρα, **θύγατερ Σιών**· κήρυσσε, θύγατερ Ἰερου-
σαλήμ· **ἰδοὺ ὁ βασιλεύς σου ἔρχεταί σοι**, δίκαιος καὶ σώζων αὐτός,
πραῢς καὶ ἐπιβεβηκὼς ἐπὶ ὑποζύγιον καὶ **πῶλον** νέον. (10) καὶ
ἐξολεθρεύσει ἅρματα ἐξ Ἐφραίμ καὶ ἵππον ἐξ Ἰερουσαλήμ...

Zechariah 9.9-10 in Hebrew consists, like Isa. 42.1-4, of 12 versets in a
more or less strict 3-3 rhythm. The section used by Matthew is just half
that, but scaled down still further. The probable explanation of his
elimination of the first line of the Zechariah prophecy and substitution
of a half-line from another prophetic context which makes the daughter
of Zion the recipient rather than the proclaimer of the message is that in
the narrative that follows the acclamations come from the crowds accompanying Jesus rather than the inhabitants, let alone the religious
authorities, of the city itself.[84] The displacement of δίκαιος and σώζων
brings the remaining predicates into higher relief; one is the subject of a
beatitude (III), and the other a major clue to the interpretation of a second (VII).[85] This, and the shuffling of the words denoting the animal(s),
will be discussed when we come to consider those beatitudes.[86]

small beginnings is a hidden matter which no one can assess before the final day,
the response of individual disciples to its claims is not. They are to witness to it by
their life, proclamation and example, according to the gifts they have received; cf.
5.13-16 (8.3, below). The day that reveals the progress of the gospel will reveal also
the secrets of the hearts of those who out of sloth or fearfulness have failed in this
witness.

    84. Mt. 21.9, 11; contrast vv. 10, 15.
    85. See (1) 5.5, (2) 5.9. The connection with the latter is indicated by the way
the Zechariah prophecy continues at v. 10. To the Hebrews, as to contemporary
Egyptians and Greeks (and in contrast with their Asiatic neighbours to the north and
east), horses were not for riding but for drawing chariots; to enter a city behind one
was the ancient equivalent of arriving in a tank, whereas any kind of ass, even the
swift Asian onager, signified that its rider came in peace.
    86. See Chapter 7 §§1a and 2d, below.

The result is a stanza of two distichs in 3-3 rhythm, constructed from composite materials, which can all be found in the LXX but owe their verse structure to the Evangelist. Each of the distichs contains 10 words. In all these respects it is a close counterpart of 2.6 (see §1 above).

Thus far the formula quotations. But Torrey also pointed out[87] that the same phenomenon, of Old Testament quotations moulded into a verse form which they had previously lacked, extends to other, non-prophetic texts quoted from a prose context. Two of the three texts quoted from Deuteronomy in the temptation narrative fall into this category.

7. *Matthew 4.4 and 4.10*

Mt. 4.4 (Deut. 8.3):
οὐκ ἐπ᾽ ἄρτῳ μόνῳ
    ζήσεται ὁ ἄνθρωπος,
ἀλλ᾽ ἐπὶ παντὶ ῥήματι * ἐκπορευομένῳ
    διὰ στόματος θεοῦ.

*τῷ LXX

Mt. 4.10 (Deut. 6.13):
κύριον τὸν θεόν σου προσκυνήσεις*,
    καὶ αὐτῷ μόνῳ** λατρεύσεις.

*φοβηθήῃ LXX **μόνῳ om. LXX

The form of 4.10 is evidently the work of the creator of the temptation narrative, who has substituted προσκυνήσεις for the LXX φοβηθήῃ. προσκυνεῖν in the LXX of Deuteronomy is always used of false worship, that of rival divinities; the one apparent exception at 26.10 denotes only a single specific cultic act, not a habitual devotion of the heart, which is always conveyed by φοβεῖσθαι (Heb. *yāre*).[88] The framer of the temptation narrative was clearly working from the LXX, and there is therefore little likelihood that he was familiar with a text-form that read προσκυνήσεις;[89] the alteration is due to the context, in which Satan has invited Jesus to worship him.[90] Both it and the addition of μόνῳ, which

---

87. *Documents*, p. 46.
88. A point missed by Catchpole, *Quest*, p. 14 n. 35.
89. Contra Stendahl, *School*, p. 89.
90. So, rightly, Catchpole, *Quest*, p. 14.

transforms the (originally prose) text into a 3-3 stress distich,[91] are found in Luke (4.8) as well as Matthew, and the two alterations are therefore to be ascribed to the same agency.

4.4 similarly turns a prose passage into a 3-2 stress tetrastich. Here Luke has only the first half, which makes the rhythm less obvious; but since, as we have seen, he was familiar with the example at 4.10 which he reproduces, it seems more probable that he has here reduced what was before him in his source than that Matthew has added to the material that they have in common.[92] The versifier was thus either the unknown author of a passage afterwards incorporated in Q,[93] or, given Lukan dependence on him, Matthew. The evidence that Matthew treats his formula quotations (and others; see next section) redactionally in the same way favours the second alternative.

8. Matthew 21.13

γέγραπται,
ὁ οἶκός μου οἶκος προσευχῆς κληθήσεται,
    ὑμεῖς δὲ αὐτὸν ποιεῖτε σπήλαιον λῃστῶν.

cf. Mk 11.17 (LXX quotations in bold):

οὐ γέγραπται ὅτι
Ὁ οἶκός μου οἶκος προσευχῆς κληθήσεται
    πᾶσιν τοῖς ἔθνεσιν;
ὑμεῖς δὲ πεποιήκατε αὐτὸν **σπήλαιον λῃστῶν**.

The Markan version of Isa. 56.7 is based on the LXX and retains the prose character of that translation; it betrays no awareness of a verse original. Mark works it into a controversial argument which contrasts it with a single phrase quoted from Jer. 7.10. Matthew by dropping πᾶσιν

91. Cf. Torrey, *Documents*, p. 57.

92. Luke's literary practice is dominated by 'the habit of variation' (H.J. Cadbury, 'Four Features of Lucan Style', in L.E. Keck and J.L. Martyn [eds.], *Studies in Luke–Acts* [London: SPCK, 1968], pp. 89-101 [91-92]), and the extent of quotations found in his sources was a convenient field for its exercise. His reduction of the one here is balanced by his enlargement (and pedantic correction) of that from Ps. 90 at Mt. 4.6 (Lk. 4.10-11), which is clearly secondary. Contra Torrey, *Documents*, p. 57; Catchpole, *Quest*, p. 13.

93. A number of Q proponents regard the temptation narrative as a late arrival in the Q tradition, partly on account of its use of scripture: e.g. Schulz, *Q*, pp. 177-90; Jacobson, *First Gospel*, pp. 94, 126-27; Kloppenborg, *Formation*, pp. 246-62.

τοῖς ἔθνεσιν[94] moves even further away from the Hebrew, but by doing so is able to form what remains of the two texts into a composite one, framed as a distich in 4-4 rhythm, with 6 words to each line. Whereas in Mark the adversative force of δὲ in the final line answers to the introduction οὐ γέγραπται ὅτι, in Matthew ὑμεῖς δὲ answers to ὁ οἶκός μου, and γέγραπται introduces the whole couplet as scripture. For Matthew's hermeneutic, as the formula quotations repeatedly show, the interpretation tends to be assimilated into the sacred text.[95]

9. *Summary of Findings*

The examination has so far revealed the following characteristics in Matthew's handling of Old Testament material:

(a) composite texts based on the LXX: §§ 1, 6, 8;

(b) single texts, the wording of which has been influenced by that of other (LXX) texts: §§3, 4;

(c) compression of texts drawn from the LXX: §§3, 4 (final couplet), 6, 8;

(d) prose quotations turned into verse or worked into a composite verse form: §§1, 7 (*bis*), 8;

(e) evidence of familiarity with the Hebrew: §§2, 4, ?3, ?6;

(f) influence from context in the Gospel or features peculiar to it: §§1, 2, 3, 4, 5, 6, 7 (*bis*);

(g) a recognizable preference for lines arranged in a multiple of four: §§1, 2, 3 (second part), 4, 6, 7(a);

(h) in one case, an arrangement of five short lines followed by distichs: §3;

(j) quantitative scansion: §§3, 5;

(k) rhyme or assonance: §§3, 5;

(l) alliteration: §5;

(m) word play based on the Greek: §§3, 4, 5;

---

94. His objection is not to the invitation of the Gentiles but the part in it predicted for the temple. See on 23.38, Chapter 4 §9b below. It is striking that Lk. 19.46 agrees with Matthew both in the omission and, with characteristic minor variations of wording, in the form of the conflated text (including the introductory γέγραπται). F. Neirynck, *The Minor Agreements of Matthew and Luke against Mark* (BETL, 37; Leuven: Peeters, 1974), p. 147, includes it in his Cumulative List, but without comment.

95. Cf. §3 above.

(n)   equivalent word count between two distichs: §§1, 6; or be-
        tween two versets: §3 (alternating), 5, 8;
(o)   possible evidence of syllable counting: §3;
(p)   parallelism of alternate lines: §§3 (second part), 5 (as rear-
        ranged).

It will be seen that the most constant features are the influence on a text
from its context in the Gospel, the priority given to the LXX, and the
preference for quatrains. The first of these establishes, and the second
supports, the decisive part played in the construction of these texts by
the Evangelist himself; the third is an important indicator in the recognition of his hand elsewhere. The other poetic features listed at (j)-(p)
above are largely confined, as can be seen, to two texts that are very
freely treated. They are not easily worked into translations, as opposed
to free compositions. If Matthew can exercise such freedom as he already does when (officially) he is just translating, what is to be expected when he is working without that constraint? The question makes an
appropriate transition to the examination of his own efforts in this genre.

Chapter 4

MATTHEW AS VERSIFIER (2): NEW COMPOSITIONS INFLUENCED BY THE OLD TESTAMENT

The texts which follow, although almost all of them reflect intense study of the Old Testament, are not quotations but free compositions from the hand, as I shall argue, of the Evangelist. The method of their examination is thus necessarily different from that of the quotations in the previous chapter, and more directly in line with what has aleady been said of the priorities in the study of a poetic text.[1] The verse characteristics and their significance for the understanding of the poem will be examined first, and then the 'vertical' relationships to Old Testament texts and the 'horizontal' relationships to other parts of the Gospel, in whichever order seems most appropriate.

1. *Matthew 1.20b-21 (with 1.23)*

Matthew 1.20b-21 is something of a halfway house between the formula quotations and the verse sayings found in the mouth of Jesus at specially significant points in the Gospel, both because the speaker is not Jesus himself but an angel in a dream, and because the passage is followed by and linked to a further formula quotation which has not been examined so far, but held back until this point so that the two texts can be examined together.

1a Ἰωσὴφ υἱὸς-Δαυίδ, μὴ φοβηθῇς
 b   παραλαβεῖν Μαρίαν τὴν γυναῖκά σου·
2a τὸ γὰρ ἐν αὐτῇ γεννηθὲν
 b   ἐκ πνεύματός ἐστιν ἁγίου.
3a τέξεται δὲ υἱόν, καὶ καλέσεις
 b   τὸ ὄνομα αὐτοῦ Ἰησοῦν·
4a αὐτὸς γὰρ σώσει τὸν λαὸν αὐτοῦ
 b   ἀπὸ τῶν ἁμαρτιῶν αὐτῶν.

---

1.   Chapter 1 §1 above.

Gen. 15.1: **Μὴ φοβοῦ**, Ἀβράμ...

Gen. 17.19: ἰδοὺ Σαρρὰ ἡ γυνή σου **τέξεταί** σοι **υἱόν, καὶ καλέσεις τὸ ὄνομα αὐτοῦ** Ἰσαάκ.

Ps. 129.8: καὶ **αὐτὸς** λυτρώσεται τὸν Ἰσραὴλ |ἐκ πασῶν τῶν ἀνομιῶν αὐτοῦ.

Judg. 13.5 (LXX^B): ὅτι ἰδοὺ σὺ ἐν γαστρὶ ἕξεις καὶ **τέξῃ υἱόν, καὶ**... ναζὶρ θεοῦ ἔσται τὸ παιδάριον ἀπὸ τῆς κοιλίας, καὶ αὐτὸς ἄρξεται τοῦ **σῶσαι** τὸν Ἰσραὴλ ἐκ χειρὸς Φυλιστιίμ.

Ps. 27.9: **σῶσον τὸν λαόν** σου...καὶ ποίμανον αὐτοὺς...

Isa. 53.8: ἀπὸ τῶν ἀνομιῶν τοῦ **λαοῦ** μου ἤχθη εἰς θάνατον...(11)...καὶ **τὰς ἁμαρτίας αὐτῶν αὐτὸς** ἀνοίσει.

Sir. 46.1: Κραταιὸς ἐν πολέμῳ **Ἰησοῦς** Ναυή |καὶ διάοχος Μωυσῆ ἐν προφητείαις, |ὃς ἐγένετο κατὰ **τὸ ὄνομα αὐτοῦ** |μέγας ἐπὶ σωτηρίᾳ ἐκλεκτῶν αὐτοῦ...

1.23 (Isa. 7.14 + 8.8b):

5a   ἰδοὺ ἡ παρθένος ἐν-γαστρὶ-ἕξει,
  b   καὶ τέξεται υἱόν,
6a   καὶ καλέσουσιν* τὸ ὄνομα αὐτοῦ Ἐμμανουήλ,
      (ὅ ἐστιν μεθερμενευόμενον)
  b   μεθ᾽ ἡμῶν ὁ θεός.

*LXX καλέσεις

Jer. 3.17: ἐν ταῖς ἡμέραις ἐκείναις καὶ ἐν τῷ καιρῷ ἐκείνῳ **καλέσουσιν** τὴν Ἰερουσαλὴμ Θρόνος κυρίου, καὶ συναχθήσονται εἰς αὐτὴν πάντα τὰ ἔθνη...

The angel's message is in the form of a stanza of four enjambed couplets, in a basically 3-2 metre.[2] It is rhythmically loose, and lacks some of the features that we have noted in the Beatitudes and shall be noting again in other Matthaean poetry. But the web of scriptural allusion is clear. The poem takes up the heading of the Gospel at 1.1, where Jesus is called 'son of David, son of Abraham'; the former is reflected in the form of address to Joseph (and possibly in the quotation from the [officially Davidic] Psalter), the latter in the Genesis passages quoted in 3a-b

---

2.   First noted by G.H. Box, *St Matthew* (Century Bible; Edinburgh: T.C. & E.C. Jack, 1926), p. 75.

(which are prose in the original). The wording of Ps. 129.8 (best understood as a conflation of the LXX with other texts)[3] will be taken up in the Last Supper narrative at 26.28, where the cup is called 'my blood of the covenant shed for many *for the forgiveness of sins*'. The meaning of the name Jesus is thus associated with the temporal mission of the Messiah, while 'Emmanuel' in the Isaiah prophecy which follows is taken up in the final commission at 28.18-20, where the reference is to the post-resurrection presence of the Son of God (see below).

The wording which the message takes from Genesis recurs unaltered (apart from the changed person of καλέσουσιν) in the text of the prophecy, and confirms that they are to be taken closely together. As the former is a composition in verse, the latter, though taken from a prose passage in Isaiah, is surely to be read as verse also. It would be possible to construe it, without the interpretation, as consisting of three cola of three stresses each, the middle line corresponding to 3a of the angelic message. But the four-line arrangement and 3-2 stress of the latter, as well as Matthew's clear preference for multiples of four,[4] incline the verdict in favour of the corresponding arrangement (with the rubric about translation treated as anacrusis[5]) that is offered here. This is supported by the observation that the prophecy, exclusive of the anacrusis, consists of 19 words, as does each of the two quatrains that make up the angel's message.

---

3.   The significant words for Matthew's purposes are σώσει, as conveying the meaning of the name Jesus/Joshua, and λαόν, as a more comprehensive designation of a community that will eventually include Gentiles (prefigured by the magi of the next chapter, and in the use of the Isaiah prophecy at 4.15-16; so, with the majority, Davies and Allison, *Matthew*, I, p. 210, contra Luz, *Matthew*, I, p. 121). Ps. 129.8 has neither word; Ps. 27.9 (cf. Lindars, *Apologetic*, p. 114 n. 2) has both. Judg. 13.5 which has σώζειν but retains Ἰσραήλ, makes a bridge between the two, and also contains the word ναζίρ (LXX[A] ναζιραῖον) which has probably contributed to Ναζωραῖος at 2.23 (so Stanton, *Gospel*, p. 361 [= *It is Written*, p. 216]; Goulder, *Midrash*, pp. 240-41; Davies and Allison, *Matthew*, I, pp. 276-80).

4.   See Chapter 3 §9 above.

5.   See Watson, *Hebrew Poetry*, pp. 110-11. Compared with his examples the expression may seem a little unwieldy to describe what we have here; alternatively it could be treated as a parenthesis containing an author's gloss. What matters is that the words stand outside the metrical pattern.

The different inflection of καλεῖν is not due solely to the context, in which Joseph has already been instructed to call the child by another name. καλέσουσιν occurs only 3 times in the LXX (Deut. 25.8; Jer. 3.17; and Ezek. 8.18 [LXX^A]), and only the second of these has anything to do with naming. But its context, Jer. 3.11-18, is one of the key passages in the development of a 'Zion-eschatology' during and after the exile, in which T.L. Donaldson finds the clue to Matthew's use of mountain symbolism, with the place of Zion taken by the presence of the risen Christ in the midst of his people.[6] These associations of the meaning of the name Emmanuel (especially at 28.20) support a reference to the Jeremiah text here.

2. *Matthew 6.9b-13: The Lord's Prayer*

1	Πάτερ ἡμῶν ὁ ἐν τοῖς οὐρανοῖς,
2a	ἁγιασθήτω τὸ ὄνομά σου·
b	ἐλθέτω ἡ βασιλεία σου·
c	γενηθήτω τὸ θέλημά σου,
3	ὡς ἐν οὐρανῷ καὶ ἐπὶ γῆς·
4a	τὸν ἄρτον ἡμῶν τὸν ἐπιούσιον
b	δὸς ἡμῖν σήμερον·
5a	καὶ ἄφες ἡμῖν τὰ ὀφειλήματα ἡμῶν,
b	ὡς καὶ ἡμεῖς ἀφήκαμεν τοῖς ὀφειλέταις ἡμῶν·
6a	καὶ μὴ εἰσενέγκῃς ἡμᾶς εἰς πειρασμόν,
b	ἀλλά ῥῦσαι ἡμᾶς ἀπὸ τοῦ πονηροῦ.

As the Beatitudes form the exordium of the Sermon on the Mount, the Lord's Prayer is its centrepiece. The main body of the Sermon runs from 5.21–7.11 and falls into three sections: the antitheses on the Greater Righteousness, the threefold instruction on true and false piety, and the remaining items in 6.19–7.11, of which a structured account will be offered in due course.[7] The middle item in the threefold instruction is prayer, and it is to this that the Lord's Prayer is appended. It is therefore in the kind of context where, if my working hypothesis is

6.   T.L. Donaldson, *Jesus on the Mountain* (JSNTSup, 8; Sheffield: JSOT Press, 1985): see pp. 228 n. 64, 230 n. 86 for Jer. 3.11-18 (cf. Knowles, *Jeremiah*, p. 268); pp. 174-90 on 28.16-20 (cf. p. 183 for Jer. 3.17 in that context). Cf. n. 336 below.

7.   See Chapter 6, Chapter 7 §§1e.3, 2b, below.

right, we should expect to find verse of an elevated kind (though it does not follow from this that the Prayer was composed originally for its present position[8]). But how far is it legitimate to cite even this version of the Prayer as evidence for *Matthew's* poetic style and practice? The justification for this rests on two observations about the Prayer which can be offered with some confidence:

(1) Those lines of the composition which are found only in Matthew's version show obvious marks of his vocabulary and style: 'Father in heaven',[9] 'heaven...and earth',[10] and ὁ πονηρός as a designation of the devil[11] are all characteristic of his usage, while to do God's will is virtually a synonym for 'righteousness' in his vocabulary.[12]

(2) The whole composition, inclusive of those lines, has a recognizable verse structure[13] to which there is no clear counterpart in the Lukan version.[14] Let us examine this.

8.   Goulder's argument (*Midrash*, pp. 262-63) that the triple injunction on almsgiving, prayer and fasting is too repetitious to have stood on its own is hardly convincing; the theme that its parts have in common, the incompatibility of ostentation with true piety, clearly marks them off from the inserted matter at 6.6-15. (Cf. Gerhardsson, *Shema*, pp. 75-83; K. Syreeni, 'Separation and Identity: Aspects of the Symbolic World of Matthew 6.1-18', *NTS* 40 [1994], pp. 522-47; Betz, *Sermon on the Mount*, pp. 348-49.) Nor is it possible to regard the Lord's Prayer as having been composed originally for the context of warnings against Jewish insincerity and Gentile loquacity which now introduce it. Whatever the answer to the question of its origins, it must have taken shape as a prayer to be *used*, and its appearance in the text of a Gospel written for a Christian community is an indication that it was already being so used.

9.   Matthew 20 (inclusive of 5 instances of ὁ πατήρ...ὁ οὐράνιος); Mark 1 (11.25; see below); rest of New Testament 0.

10.   Matthew 5; Mark 0; Luke 2 (both Q = Matthew); Paul (undisputed letters) 4; Colossians 2, Ephesians 2 (in parallel texts); Catholic Epistles 3; Revelation 4. But see n. 325 below.

11.   Matthew 5; Mark 0; Luke–Acts 0; John 1; 1 John 5; Ephesians 1.

12.   Cf. 7.21; 12.50 (//Mk 3.35); 21.31; 26.42 (diffMk 14.39); and see discussion in Chapter 7 §3b, with n. 209 to Chapter 7.

13.   An original analysis of the poetic form of Matthew's Greek version appeared anonymously in *Modern Liturgical Texts* (Church of England Liturgical Commission; London: SPCK, 1968), pp. 1-3. R.C.D. Jasper in his last published work *The Development of the Anglican Liturgy: 1662–1980* (London: SPCK, 1989), pp. 292-93, gave a summary quotation and revealed that it was the work of Austin Farrer. In words which anticipate the thesis of this book (see Chapter 1 §1a above), Farrer wrote: 'The force and meaning of the prayer in this form is inseparable from the shape; if the shape is not in essentials preserved, the prayer goes to

a. *The Structure of the Prayer*
The composition falls into two halves:
(1) The line ὡς ἐν οὐρανῷ καὶ ἐπὶ γῆς forms an *inclusio* with the opening address Πάτερ ἡμῶν ὁ ἐν τοῖς οὐρανοῖς. Of the three cola enclosed by it, the two outer ones

ἁγιασθήτω τὸ ὄνομά σου

γενηθήτω τὸ θέλημά σου

pieces... In the second half of the prayer, as in the first, the phrases in balance against one another are pointed with assonance or rhyme' (*Texts*, p. 1). The details of his analysis also, repeatedly, match my own.

Farrer does not directly concern himself with the Lukan form, except to say that it 'can be consulted to throw light on the Matthaean'. Earlier ('Dispensing', pp. 64-65), he excepted it from his general account of the relationship between Matthew and Luke, treating the two forms as deriving from separate liturgical traditions. But the view of the Matthaean form implicit in his later analysis is one of a literary creation in Greek. So also, explicitly, Betz, *Sermon on the Mount*, pp. 375-76, despite having concluded for dominical authorship (*Sermon on the Mount*, p. 349).

14. Attempts at a retroversion of the Matthaean form into Aramaic have been made by Burney, *Poetry*, pp. 113, 165; modified by E. Lohmeyer, *The Lord's Prayer* (trans. J. Bowden; London: Collins, 1965), pp. 27-28, and by K.G. Kuhn, *Achtzehngebet und Vaterunser und der Reim* (WUNT, 1; Göttingen: Vandenhoeck & Ruprecht, 1961) (commented on by Davies, *Setting*, pp. 310-20), and into Hebrew by J. Carmignac, *Recherches sur le Nôtre Père* (Paris: Letousey & Ané, 1969), p. 395, cf. pp. 29-52. Lohmeyer also offers (p. 29) a retroversion (based on earlier work by Torrey and E. Littman) of the Lukan form; this is too divergent to admit of any literary relationship between the two. He is clearly influenced, here as elsewhere, by his own theory of the early relationship between Jerusalem and Galilean Christianity. But he, Kuhn and Davies all admit the uncertainty of such reconstructions in view of our ignorance of the precise nature of the language spoken by Jesus (so, even more emphatically, Betz, *Sermon on the Mount*, p. 375 n. 344). This has not inhibited yet more recent efforts: G. Schwarz, 'Matthäus vi.9-13/Lukas xi.2-4: Emendation und Rückübersetzung', *NTS* 15 (1968–69), pp. 233-47, attempts to establish an *Ur-Text* in Aramaic with a Greek counterpart, which, interestingly, includes a form of the 'your will be done' clause; and J.C. de Moor, 'The Reconstruction of the Aramaic Original of the Lord's Prayer', in van der Meer and de Moor (eds.), *Structural Analysis*, pp. 397-422, starting from a critically conservative position, concentrates on the Matthaean version as a valid witness to the original form of the Prayer. Betz's hypothesis of the origins of the Sermon on the Mount allows him to treat the Matthaean Lord's Prayer as textually independent of the Lukan version; he assumes a dominical original behind both, but is reticent about its content. See *Sermon on the Mount*, pp. 370-83.

have an obvious rhyming correspondence (even more impressive if the accent on θέλημα was already an indication of stress[15]) from which the middle line stands apart.[16] It establishes that this first stanza is concentric[17] in form, and thus that the line 'your kingdom come' is pivotal[18] to the structure of the opening section of the Prayer, as it has long been recognized as fundamental to its content.

(2) The remainder of the Prayer falls into three distichs, each containing a single petition. While this is generally accepted for the second, the first has commonly been read as one line, and the third as two petitions.[19] But in fact the petition for daily bread, as Burney,[20] Lohmeyer,[21] Gaechter,[22] Farrer[23] and others[24] have rightly seen, should be read as an enjambed couplet:

> The bread we need for the day ahead
> (or 'the bread that is ours in the time to come'[25])
> Give———us——— today.

15. See above in Chapter 2.

16. This is my one real difference with Farrer, who treated the three aspirations as straightforward coordinates. Obviously the three have a common syntactical structure, but the closer correspondence of the outer pair distinguishes them from the one enclosed by them.

17. For concentric patterns see Watson, *Hebrew Poetry*, pp. 187-88, where the expression denotes a five-line chiastic stanza ABCBA (or, more rarely, AACBB).

18. Watson however (*Hebrew Poetry*, pp. 214-21) reserves the term 'pivot' for a particular form of the device known as 'gapping' (*Hebrew Poetry*, p. 48; cf. Berlin, *Dynamics*, p. 40; Goulder, *Midrash*, p. 71, who calls it 'pardic' in view of its occurrence at Jer. 13.23).

19. Cf., e.g., Kuhn, *Achtzehngebet*, p. 39; T.W. Manson, 'The Lord's Prayer', *BJRL* 38 (1955–56), pp. 99-113, 436-48: 439-41; H. Schürmann, *Das Gebet des Herrn* (Freiburg: Herder, 1981), pp. 45-47.

20. *Poetry*, pp. 112-13.

21. *Lord's Prayer*, pp. 26-27.

22. P. Gaechter, *Das Matthäus-Evangelium* (Innsbruck: Tyrolia, 1962), p. 211. This very conservative commentator had a sharp ear for Hebraic poetic rhythms when not deflected by critical assumptions that were unacceptable to him.

23. *Texts*, p. 1.

24. Goulder, *Midrash*, p. 300; Luz, *Matthew*, I, p. 369; de Moor, 'Reconstruction', pp. 409, 423; also Davies and Allison, *Matthew*, I, p. 591 in their reconstruction of the 'original' Prayer; contra Gerhardsson, *Shema*, p. 87: 'five stichoi'.

25. Cf. Farrer, *Texts*, p. 1: 'the terms of the antitheses are patient of more than one meaning'. See below, on the third petition.

(which has obvious implications for the meaning of ἐπιούσιον);[26] and it is only the absence of the second line of the petition against temptation from the Lukan version, and the assumption of the latter's priority, that has concealed from scholars that

> And do not expose [and then abandon] us to temptation,
> (or 'to the testing time')
> But deliver us from the one that is evil.

is equivalent to a single petition expressed in antithetical parallelism.[27] Moreover the final words of the two lines are alliterated, and have, in inverse form, the same quantitative scansion: πειρασμόν...πονηροῦ (the trochaic ending of the former inviting some sort of rejoinder, while the spondaic conclusion of the latter conveys a sense of finality, as in the Greek hexameter line).[28]

The three petitions are respectively for sustenance, for forgiveness, and for supernatural assistance, and it is not fanciful to see them as corresponding in detail to the three aspirations of the first stanza in which the praying disciples are to identify themselves with the purposes of God. The counterpart of 'your kingdom come', the master clause of the first stanza, is the petition for forgiveness, as Matthew makes clear by singling it out for special comment at 6.14-15; the heart of the gospel is that it promises forgiveness of sins (and requires repentance of those

26. The parallelism between ἐπιούσιον and σήμερον gives strong support to the derivation of the former from ἡ ἐπιοῦσα ἡμέρα. The objections of Strecker, *Sermon on the Mount*, p. 118, and Betz, *Sermon on the Mount*, p. 398 to this on grounds of a supposed clash with 6.34 are misplaced: regular prayer for a particular need expresses confidence that God can and will supply it, not anxiety that he will not, and the 'tomorrow' of 6.34 stands for worry about the indefinite future, as opposed to living in the present, of which the supply of bread for the day ahead is a part.

27. So Kuhn, *Achtzehngebet*, p. 39; cf. Schürmann, *Gebet*, pp. 20, 120-21; de Moor, 'Reconstruction', pp. 411-12; Betz, *Sermon on the Mount*, p. 412. Farrer (*Texts*, p. 1) sees antithesis in all three petitions: '(today/tomorrow, our debts/our debtors, *not* temptation *but* deliverance). These antitheses develop in strength, until in the third petition the line is almost broken in two'.

The petition does not ask for immunity from temptation, but for proportionate spiritual resources for resistance to it. It thus expresses both an admission of the petitioner's weakness and confidence in the power of God's assistance to overcome it. Cf. 1 Cor. 10.13 (the relevance of this is too readily dismissed by Betz, *Sermon on the Mount*, p. 408. See further n. 58 below).

28. Cf. Kennedy, *Rhetorical Criticism*, p. 59.

who would enter the kingdom).[29] The prayer that God's will may be done, followed by the petition for daily bread, at once recalls the conclusion of the long poem at 6.25-33: 'seek first his kingdom and his righteousness, and all these things shall be yours as well'.[30] The petition for divine assistance will then be a reflection of the ascription of holiness to God, to which any surrender to or compromise with evil is an affront (cf. 4.10, where the final and comprehensive temptation is answered with 'you shall worship the Lord'[31].)

If this is the case, then the overall arrangement of the Lord's Prayer, like that of the Beatitudes,[32] is chiastic (and would be even more emphatically so if we could assume some form of doxology as its conclusion[33]). It also contains instances, once again, of internal rhyming in lines not immediately contiguous with each other, and of single words in parallel positions matched by both alliteration and quantitative scansion. With the first of these we may compare 6.26, 28:

29. On forgiveness and the kingdom cf. 9.2-9 (//Mk 2.1-12).

30. See on Beatitude IV, Chapter 7 §3b.1, below.

31. A similar position is reached, according to G. Schneider, 'Das Vaterunser des Matthäus', in *A cause de l'Evangile* (Festschrift J. Dupont; Paris: Gabalda, 1985), pp. 57-90 (83), by S. Sabugal, 'La redaccion mateana del Padrenuestro (Mt 6,9-13)', *EstE* 68 (1983), pp. 307-29: 313-14 (not directly available to me). Goulder, however, sees the three aspirations and the three petitions as linked in the order in which they stand (*Midrash*, pp. 299-300). The Gethsemane associations of 'your will be done' are undeniable, but an Exodus link between the hallowing of God's name (Decalogue) and the petition for daily bread seems forced.

32. See Chapter 2, above.

33. On this see the balanced discussion in Davies, *Setting*, Appendix VIII, pp. 451-52; for a more recent view (highly favourable), de Moor, 'Reconstruction', p. 414; also M. Black, 'The Doxology to the *Pater Noster*, with a Note on Matthew 6.13b', in P.R. Davies and R.T. White (eds.), *A Tribute to Geza Vermes* (JSOTSup, 100; Sheffield: JSOT Press, 1990), pp. 327-38. It may be added that if Matthew is reproducing a prayer composed by himself that was already in regular use in his community, he may have literary reasons for omitting its conclusion here. Davies and Allison, *Matthew*, I, p. 615 n. 54, note that 'while 6.14-15 is striking enough following 6.13, it would be even stranger coming after a doxology'. Thus while the older textual tradition is right about the Gospel text as Matthew wrote it, the use of a doxology with the Lord's Prayer could have been already established in liturgical practice. *Did.* 8.2 offers indirect confirmation of this. Betz, *Sermon on the Mount*, pp. 414-15, confines himself to excluding the authenticity of the forms found in the later MS tradition.

ἐμβλέψατε εἰς τὰ **πετεινὰ** τοῦ οὐρανοῦ
καταμάθετε τὰ **κρίνα** τοῦ ἀγροῦ·

(where the interval is rather longer); and with the second the distich at
11.19b.[34]

b. *The Content of the Prayer*
The influence of other texts on the content of the Prayer is a question
which must not be tackled pedantically, as if it had been entirely shaped
by literary study, rather than by the praxis of a Christian community in
living contact both with the tradition that came originally from Jesus
and with the practice of contemporary (i.e. neo-Pharisaic) Judaism.[35] It
is always possible that Old Testament texts influenced the wording of
the Prayer indirectly through these channels rather than from direct
study. The converse, however, is also true. Not all the suggested exam-

---

34. §5 below.
35. I. Abrahams, *Studies in Pharisaism and the Gospels* (Cambridge: Cambridge University Press, 1924), II, pp. 94-108, 'The Lord's Prayer', quotes (pp. 98-
99) a cento (ascribed by him to I. Elbogen or someone writing under his editorship,
by Davies and Allison, *Matthew*, I, p. 595 to Abrahams himself) of phrases culled
from early rabbinic writings as parallels to each line of the Prayer. But he goes on
to say that it 'is clearly not altogether of this type. Composed under the influence of
Hebraic ideas, modelled to a large extent on Jewish forms, it was not in its primitive
form a mosaic but a whole and fresh design' (p. 100). By 'primitive form' he meant
Harnack's three-petition original (beginning at 'Give us today...'; cf. *Sayings of
Jesus* [trans. J.R. Wilkinson; London: Williams & Norgate, 1908], p. 136). One
wonders if without that assumption he would still have seen the 'additions' in
Matthew's Prayer as mosaic; 'a whole and fresh design' is exactly what I am
claiming for his version. It is interesting in this connection to find Abrahams
suggesting a little further on that 'Such mosaic appearance, as the Lord's Prayer
really presents, is explicable on the theory that it is the work not of Jesus himself
but of disciples who knew his career and interpreted his mind. It is possible to find
for each of the clauses a basis in either the experiences or the doctrines attributed to
Jesus. This theory would account for both the close parallel to Jewish prayer and for
a certain difference' (p. 101). Cf. M.D. Goulder, 'The Composition of the Lord's
Prayer', *JTS* NS 14 (1963), pp. 32-45; B. Standaert, 'Crying "Abba" and Saying
"Our Father"', in Draisma (ed.), *Intertextuality*, pp. 141-58 (151): 'we see the
Lord's Prayer detach itself more and more clearly as a formula redacted by a Christian community rather than one pronounced as such by the historical Jesus. By its
thematic it recapitulates the whole preaching of Jesus; by its form it appears destined to be pronounced by those who enter the community and receiving [*sic*]
pardon.'

ples of Christian borrowing from contemporary Jewish practice are equally convincing;[36] and Goulder's argument that the content of the Jesus tradition was largely mediated to Matthew's church through its reading of the Gospel of Mark[37] has to be taken seriously by those who have found reason to dispense with Q. A Greek-speaking church, moreover, or someone writing for it, would have needed to find words to convey both what was new and what was old in its understanding of prayer and worship, and would have sought them in the version of the scriptures that it habitually used.[38]

Goulder rightly draws attention to the influence of the Markan Gethsemane narrative;[39] this is hardly to be thought of as being in the other direction (that is, reflecting Mark's own familiarity with the Prayer), since it is not only in Mark's text but also, and more particularly, in Matthew's redaction of it that the parallels emerge. Thus Mark's Jesus addresses God as ἀββὰ ὁ πατηρ (cf. Rom. 8.15; Gal. 4.6); Matthew, who gives Jesus' words in two versions, has πάτερ μου in both. The

---

36. The closest parallels are those between the first half of the Prayer and the Kaddish (see n. 41 below). The case for the Amidah or *Shemoneh Esreh* (Prayer of XVIII Benedictions) is much less clear. The substance of this text was in use in the synagogue in the time of Matthew (if less certainly, in the case of some sections, in that of Jesus; for a convenient comparative table see C.W. Dugmore, *The Influence of the Synagogue on the Divine Office* [London: Faith Press, 2nd edn, 1964], pp. 114-25). But only three of its sections (3, 7, 9) are comparable to the Lord's Prayer in subject matter, and only in the first of these is there any verbal correspondence, even there by no means as striking as with the Kaddish. The 'Abbreviated' form quoted by Davies, *Setting*, p. 312, from the Gemara on *m. Ber.* 4.3 and regarded by him as a more likely counterpart to the Lord's Prayer than the full XVIII, contains parallels to the content of all three of the Lord's Prayer petitions but none to the actual wording. Kuhn's arguments from internal rhyming in *Shemoneh Esreh* and the Lord's Prayer (*Achtzehngebet*, p. 33 and *passim*) presuppose his own retroversion of the latter.

37. See *Midrash*, pp. 137-52; *Luke*, pp. 22-26.

38. This can only have been the LXX, whatever variants from it for particular texts may have been available to the Evangelist, whether from current alternative versions or from his own knowledge of the Hebrew text.

39. *Midrash*, pp. 289-90. S. van Tilborg, 'Form-Criticism of the Lord's Prayer', *NovT* 14 (1972), pp. 94-105 (95), argues that Matthew's redaction of Mk 14.34-40 was influenced by the wording of the (previously existing) Lord's Prayer. On my view the same thinking that created the Lord's Prayer will have been concurrently at work in the redaction of Mark. Compare the account of 11.5 in relation to the Markan material in chs. 8–9, in Appendix B.

opening address of the Prayer merely pluralizes this, very possibly with the assistance of Isa. 63.16 LXX: ...ἀλλὰ σὺ, κύριε, πάτηρ ἡμῶν· ῥῦσαι ἡμᾶς... (The two last words will be taken up at the conclusion of the Prayer).[40] Mark 11.25, a text which, as will be seen shortly, underlies the second of the three petitions in the second half of the Prayer, speaks of God (uniquely for that Gospel) as ὁ πάτηρ ὑμῶν ὁ ἐν τοῖς οὐρανοῖς.

(1) 'Your name be hallowed' can be taken in two ways: (a) an expression of praise, for the great things already done by God. Cf. Lk. 1.47, 49: 'My soul magnifies the Lord...for the Mighty One has done great things for me; and holy is his name'; (b) a petition: not only that all may thus acknowledge his greatness, but that he may himself bring about those things which redound to the glory of his name; cf. Ezek. 36.23: 'and I will hallow my great name which has been profaned among those nations' (NEB). The coordination of the clause with the two following petitions clearly requires (b). The Kaddish,[41] which contains parallels to all three and evidently reflects the influence of Ezek. 36.23, points in the same direction.

'Your kingdom come', the heart of the Prayer, is without direct Old Testament parallel. Contemporary Jewish prayers regularly contained a petition relating to God's kingdom; but to pray specifically for its 'coming', as emphasized in the word order of this one, gives it an urgency not ordinarily found in the others and links it with the heart of Jesus' message, whatever view is taken of the actual origin of the Prayer.[42]

---

40. De Moor, however ('Reconstruction', p. 404), cites 1 Chron. 29.10 (from a context on which we have already found Matthew drawing; cf. Chapter 3 §4 above [αἱρετίζειν]).

41. 'Magnified and hallowed be his great name in the world which he has created according to his will' (note the passive form here and in the Lord's Prayer, without parallel in the background texts from the Old Testament; cf. de Moor, 'Reconstruction', p. 405). This 'ancient Aramaic doxology' (Dugmore, *Influence*, p. 109) is the nearest evidence for direct influence of Jewish liturgical forms on the Prayer, especially if the fifth line of the latter is to be taken as governing all three aspirations (see below, and n. 44). The words which follow are 'May he establish his kingdom during your life and during your days' (cf. Lohmeyer, *Lord's Prayer*, p. 100). De Moor argues from this for an Aramaic original for the Prayer; but an author familiar with Aramaic (even if writing in Greek) is all that is required. Standaert however ('Abba', p. 147) suggests a Greek-language counterpart for a 'Hellenist' community.

42. See Betz, *Sermon on the Mount*, pp. 390-92, for an unemphatic statement of

'Your will be done': Mark's version of Jesus' prayer in Gethsemane (14.36) ends with the words ἀλλ᾽ οὐ τί ἐγὼ θέλω ἀλλὰ τί σύ. Matthew's first version (26.39) remains close to this; but his second (26.42, unparalleled in his source) reads: '...if this cup cannot pass unless I drink it, γενηθήτω τὸ θέλημά σου'. Where the Markan wording conveys resignation to God's will, the Matthaean suggests positive action in cooperation with it; this is supported by such texts as Ps. 39.9: τοῦ ποιῆσαι τὸ θέλημά σου...ἐβουλήθην, and Ps. 142.10: διδαξόν με τοῦ ποιεῖν τὸ θέλημά σου, as well as by Matthew's own emphasis in such passages as 7.21.[43]

'As in heaven so on earth' evidently applies to all three foregoing clauses.[44] In the first it hardly calls for scriptural justification, but if required, the threefold 'Holy' of Isaiah's vision (Isa. 6.3) surely suffices. The other two are linked in Ps. 102.19, 21; for the third cf. Ps. 134.6: πάντα, ὅσα ἠθέλησεν ὁ κύριος, ἐποίησεν |ἐν τῷ οὐρανῷ καὶ ἐν τῇ γῇ.

(2) The background to the petition for daily bread is clearly Exodus 16 (cf. v. 15: Οὗτος ὁ ἄρτος ὃν ἔδωκεν κύριος ὑμῖν φαγεῖν). If 6.25-33 can be taken as extended comment on this petition, the story of the manna of which only a day's provision could be gathered at a time was for Matthew a potent image of God's care for his people and their need to depend wholly on him. In view of the fact that in later Hebraic and Jewish tradition the manna was interpreted in an eschatological sense, as the food (and all thereby implied) of the final kingdom,[45] this understanding of the petition probably cannot be excluded, but it would seem nevertheless not to be the immediate or primary one.[46]

this, which points forwards to the development of early Christian eschatology rather than backwards to the distinctive message of Jesus (despite his cautious acceptance of a dominical origin for the Lord's Prayer). For the virtual absence of rabbinic parallels to this petition cf. R. Freudenberger, 'Zum Text der zweiten Vaterunserbitte', *NTS* 15 (1968–69), pp. 419-32 (426-27).

43. See n. 12.

44. So, rightly, Sabugal, 'Padrenuesto', p. 312 (contra Schneider, 'Vaterunser', p. 87); Betz, *Sermon on the Mount*, p. 377. Abrahams (*Studies*, II, p. 100 n. 4) notes the closeness of this clause to the Prayer of R. Eleazar b. Hyrcanus (*b. Ber.* 29b, possibly as early as 65 CE), but goes on to say that the ultimate source is Ps. 134.6 (quoted below).

45. See Carmignac, *Recherches*, pp. 198-200; Lohmeyer, *Lord's Prayer*, pp. 153-59.

46. Cf. Luz, *Matthew*, I, pp. 380-82; contra Standaert, 'Abba', p. 148, whose

(3) The starting point of the petition for forgiveness is Mk 11.25, of which, as already noted, Matthew gives a modified and extended version as his final comment on the whole Prayer.[47] The wording of the petition itself, however, seems to owe something to Deut. 15.1-6, the direction for the remission of debt after seven years (cf. 15.2: ἀφήσεις πᾶν χρέος ἴδιον, ὃ ὀφείλει σοι ὁ πλήσιον...). By New Testament times 'debt' was widely understood as a metaphor for sin,[48] as Matthew himself clearly understands it in his parable of the unmerciful servant (18.23-35; esp. v. 35); but the literal meaning need not be totally excluded for the second half, in view of the Evangelist's stringent teaching on the disposal of wealth.[49] The other text behind the petition (and probably behind Mk 11.25 as well) is Sir. 28.2: ἄφες ἀδίκημα τῷ πλησίόν σου, |καὶ τότε δεηθέντος σου αἱ ἁμαρτίαι σου λυθήσονται. The absence of any close verbal echo (after the first word) in either Prayer or comment in Matthew is in favour of the original influence having come through Mark, although Matthew, who knew Sirach well,[50] would presumably have recognized the allusion.

(4) For the prayer against temptation the starting point is, once again, Gethsemane. In Mk 14.38 (here followed closely by Mt. 26.41) the remonstration of Jesus to the sleeping disciples may be rendered thus: Keep awake, and pray that you may be spared the testing (πειρασμός); the spirit is eager enough, but the flesh is weak. πειρασμός here means 'a time of testing', in the sense of severe affliction and danger, par-

revival of the attempt to derive ἐπιούσιος from οὐσία is still etymologically implausible (it would require ἐπούσιος), and Betz, *Sermon on the Mount*, pp. 398-99.

47. See J. Schlosser, 'Marc 11,25, tradition et redaction', in *A cause de l'Evangile* (Festschrift J. Dupont), pp. 277-300; Standaert, 'Abba', pp. 150-51.

48. See Lohmeyer, *Lord's Prayer*, pp. 162-76. De Moor, 'Reconstruction', p. 410, points out that the combination of ὀφείλημα and ἀφιέναι is not found before 1 Macc. 15.8, and that no Hebrew word can both denote financial debt and offer a basis for word play between debt/sin and debtor/sinner in the way that Aramaic *hôb* does. Once again the evidence calls for an author capable of thinking in Aramaic, but not necessarily for an Aramaic original text.

49. See on 13.44-45, Chapter 7 §1e.3 below; and cf. S. van Tilborg, *The Sermon on the Mount as an Ideological Intervention* (Assen: Van Gorcum, 1986), p. 114.

50. Cf. Orton, *Scribe*, p. 104 n. 2: 'In a whole range of matters Sirach bears comparison with the First Gospel'. It is to be hoped that the fuller investigation for which he calls will be followed up. See also n. 19 to Chapter 6, and a further suggestion in Chapter 10.

ticularly from persecution.[51] Its cognate πειράζειν however, in the usage of this Gospel, means 'try to get the better of', either of human controversialists with baited questions or of the devil.[52] In the latter case the meaning is not far from that conveyed by the noun: exposure to trials can be the occasion for temptation, as in the first of the three temptations of Jesus at 4.3 (a 'testing hunger' leads to the temptation to relieve it),[53] and both situations call for endurance and for prayer for assistance. What from the devil's point of view is the temptation of Jesus to unfaithfulness is for God who exposed him to it the testing of the obedience of his newly acknowledged Son; while the implication of the devil in the testing time of the passion, though not made explicit as in Luke[54] and John,[55] is hardly to be questioned.[56]

The ambiguity of πειρασμός is mirrored by a corresponding ambiguity in τοῦ πονηροῦ in the second half of the petition. At 5.39, where non-resistance τῷ πονηρῷ is recommended, the expression must denote the human aggressor, not the devil; at 5.37 ἐκ τοῦ πονηροῦ (unless the word is neuter and means moral evil, which is very rare in the New Testament;[57] even if that were the source of oaths sworn to reinforce

51. Luke uses it repetitively in his parallels to these contexts and introduces it redactionally into two others, 8.13 and 22.28. In all of them it denotes a time of trial or persecution, except for 4.13, the only place in the Synoptic Gospels where it means temptation by the devil.

52. 4.1; 16.1; 19.3; 22.18 (all //Mk); 22.35 (MtR), where its insertion turns a friendly encounter into a confrontation); 4.3 (where ὁ πειράζων to mean the devil is paralleled in the New Testament only at 1 Thess. 3.5). Cf. 4QpPs[a] 2.10-11: 'delivered from all the traps of Beliar' (on this G.J. Brooke, 'The Wisdom of Matthew's Beatitudes', *ScrB* 19 [1989], pp. 35-41 [38]).

53. 4.2-3; see B. Gerhardsson, *The Testing of God's Son* (ConBNT, 2.1; Lund: C.W.K. Gleerup, 1966), pp. 41-53 (and note choice of title).

54. Lk. 22.3, 31.

55. Jn 13.27; cf. 14.30.

56. Note especially the echoes of the temptation story at 27.42-43; cf. B. Gerhardsson, 'Jésus livré et abandonné d'après la passion selon saint Matthieu', *RB* 76 (1969), pp. 206-27 (221) (= *Shema*, p. 127 [there in German]).

57. Only at Rom. 12.9 and (probably) 1 Thess. 5.22; both in parenetic passages. Cf. Sabugal, 'Padrenuesto', pp. 327-28. G. Harder, 'πονηρός', *TDNT*, VI, pp. 546-62 (550-55), offers parallels from *Test. XII Patr.*, but notes the growth of references to demonic influences there in comparison with the Old Testament. Abrahams, *Studies*, II, p. 105, considered the possibility that the word in the Lord's Prayer carried a reference to the evil *yēṣer*, but questioned whether πειρασμός could mean 'temptation' in the later sense as early as this. That assumed a rather earlier dating

truthful speech, it could hardly be called the agent of πειρασμός[58]) must mean the devil, as it does at 13.19, 38. Matthew's usage thus allows only two possible meanings for τοῦ πονηροῦ in the Prayer, the human enemy and the diabolical one, and they are not alternatives, as is borne out by the rest of the line.

ῥῦσαι is used, in addition to Isa. 63.16 (see above), no less than 23 times in the LXX Psalter to introduce a prayer for deliverance. Several of the passages are relevant to this petition:

Ps. 78.9: ἕνεκα τῆς δόξης τοῦ **ὀνόματός σου**, κύριε, **ῥῦσαι ἡμᾶς**.[59]

Ps. 139.1: ἐξελοῦ με, κύριε, ἐξ ἀνθρώπου πονηροῦ· |ἀπὸ ἀνδρὸς ἀδίκου **ῥῦσαί** με.

Ps. 17.30: ὅτι ἐν σοὶ **ῥυσθήσομαι** ἀπὸ **πειρατηρίου**.

and cf. also Ps. 21.21;[60] 30.16; 33.20.

All these (and others not cited), where they specify the enemy, do so in terms of a human persecutor, not a supernatural one. This is only what we should expect for the Psalter, which was composed well before later Jewish (and Christian) thought had expanded the role of Satan to that of universal tempter.[61] Matthew, as his temptation narrative shows, stands fully within this later development, yet not so much so as to deny human responsibility, and therefore the possibility of autonomous human wickedness.[62] A reference to the earlier understanding of πειρ-

---

for the Prayer than is proposed here. Both concepts are clearly present at Jas 1.13. But the *yēṣer* will hardly help with 5.37.

58. Contra Harder, 'πονηρός', pp. 560-61. For Betz, *Sermon on the Mount*, pp. 406-13, the agent of temptation in the sermon (diffMt.) is God himself. This involves taking τοῦ πονηροῦ in the Prayer as a neuter (*Sermon on the Mount*, p. 413). He offers no Greek evidence for τὸ πονηρόν as abstract or collective evil (there is none in LSJ, s.v.); and the fact that the later Christian tradition of taking the expression as neuter derives mainly from Western Fathers working from the Latin *a malo* which (as he says, n. 571), tended to be 'felt as a neuter' favours the masculine understanding of the original. It is difficult to acquit Betz of rationalizing here, and his interpretation misses the poetic tension in the total petition.

59. See above on the Kaddish.

60. This psalm has strong associations with the passion for both Mark and Matthew; cf. n. 56 above.

61. On this development see W. Foerster, 'διάβολος', *TDNT*, II, pp. 78-79; *idem*, 'Σατανᾶς', *TDNT*, VII, pp. 152-56 (with further evidence from Qumran).

62. Cf. 26.24 with 18.7; on this Green, *Matthew*, p. 161; 'Clement', p. 17 n. 69.

ασμός is therefore not excluded, and is in line with the double meanings that we have detected elsewhere in the Prayer.

The Matthaean Lord's Prayer turns out not only to contain examples
of the characteristics of verse composition that have been noted in the
Beatitudes, but to be itself what I am attempting to show that the
Beatitudes are, a poem whose structure throws light on its meaning: a
meaning which must not be assumed, so far as the individual words are
concerned, to be confined to a single univocal sense. For a view of the
Lukan version from this perspective see Appendix A.

The next group of examples is to be found in ch. 11, a section of
central significance both in position and content.[63] It stands as a kind of
watershed of the developing action of the Gospel after the formal and
largely static presentation of Jesus as authoritative Messianic teacher
and healer and the involvement of the disciples in his mission (chs. 5–
10); and its content can be read as an epitome of the argument of the
whole book.[64] The essentially Matthaean character of the composition,
with its skilful building up of smaller units into larger wholes, so familiar from the great discourses of this Gospel, has been obscured for
much of the world of scholarship by the Q hypothesis, as has the structure of the chapter;[65] those who maintain that the Lukan version is

---

63. Noted by Luz, *Matthew*, I, p. 37, who speaks of the 'transitional' character
of the whole chapter. Cf. T. de Kruijf, *Der Sohn des Lebendiges Gottes* (AnBib, 14;
Rome: Pontifical Biblical Istitute, 1962), pp. 41-43, who sees a major break
between chs. 10 and 11; Green, *Matthew*, pp. 16-17, 113-14; V. Schönle, *Johannes,
Jesus und die Juden* (Frankfurt: Peter Lang, 1982), pp. 26 n. 18, 146 n. 43. But see
now R. Scroggs, 'Eschatological Existence in Matthew and Paul', in J. Marcus and
M.L. Soards (eds.), *Apocalyptic and the New Testament* (Festschrift J.L. Martyn;
JSNTSup, 24; Sheffield: JSOT Press, 1989), pp. 125-46: 136 n. 4, who maintains
that 11.25-30 serves as the conclusion of the first part of the Gospel and a summary
of its whole message. The close formal correspondence between 11.28-30 and
28.18-20 (noted in Chapter 4 §10 below) supports this account of the overall
structure.

64. (1) Jesus' affirmation of his own Messianic and John's prophetic role (11.2-
15); (2) 'this generation's' rejection of both (11.16-24); (3) the open invitation to
discipleship (so that the divine purpose is not frustrated) (11.25-30). So Green,
Matthew, p. 114. But see now Appendix B, 'The Making of Matthew 11'.

65. Luke has been obliged to concentrate all the material concerning John the
Baptist at a point before 9.2-9 (//Mk 6.14-16), where John is spoken of as already
dead (Matthew does not reach the corresponding point in his narrative until 14.1-2).
But by doing so he has spoiled the coherence of the material he has transferred, as

closer to the original have tended to group the simile of the children's game (11.16-19), even in Matthew, with the foregoing material about John the Baptist, instead of with the part about rejection which it clearly introduces.

The units from which the chapter is built up are, I shall argue, predominantly verse compositions, and it is the identification of these that is of primary importance for the argument of this book. In a number of cases, however, the process will be found to call for a measure of redaction criticism, and the implication of this is that the chapter reached its present form by stages. An account of what these may have been is reserved for Appendix B.

3. *Matthew 11.5*

1a	τυφλοὶ ἀναβλέπουσιν
b	καὶ χωλοὶ περιπατοῦσιν
2a	λεπροὶ καθαρίζονται
b	καὶ κωφοὶ ἀκούουσιν
3a	καὶ νεκροὶ ἐγείρονται
b	καὶ πτωχοὶ εὐαγγελίζονται

The suggestion that this logion is poetry is not new, but there has so far been little in the way of detailed analysis.[66] As we have already begun to detect in the Beatitudes,[67] there are separate vertical relationships for the two halves of each verse, the indicators being alliteration, internal rhyming and quantitative scansion for the left-hand column, and terminal rhyming and quantitative scansion for the right-hand one. Matthew's basic scheme would appear to be ABABAB for the former and AABCCB for the latter. In practice he does not quite achieve this. On

---

well as that of the fragments he has left to be used later. See Green, 'Credibility', pp. 136, 139.

66. M. Dibelius, *Die urchristliche Überlieferung von Johannes der Täufer untersucht* (Göttingen: Vandenhoeck & Ruprecht, 1911), p. 35; Burney, *Poetry*, 117; Gaechter, *Matthäus-Evangelium*, pp. 361-62; J. Jeremias, *New Testament Theology*, I (trans. J. Marsh; London: SCM Press, 1971), p. 21; Schulz, *Q*, p. 196; Goulder, *Midrash*, p. 85. R. Morgenthaler, *Lukas und Quintilian* (Zürich: Gotthelf, 1993), pp. 197-98, has recognized some of the complex pattern of assonance, alliteration and rhyme noted here on the basis of the asyndetic but otherwise identical version at Lk. 7.22; but it is easier to believe that Luke 'streamlined' his version than that Matthew added his καὶ's to one that had originally lacked them. N-A[26, 27], curiously, print Luke's form as verse, but not Matthew's.

67. See Chapter 2 above.

the left-hand side λεπροὶ and νεκροὶ have rhyming vowels and near-rhyming consonants; τυφλοὶ shares neither, though its scansion is the same, but its consonants occur in inverse order in the three remaining adjectives χωλοι–κωφοὶ–πτωχοὶ, which themselves have rhyming vowels and a guttural κ or χ in each. On the right ἀναβλέπουσιν and περιπατοῦσιν are matched in rhyme for their two final syllables, and in scansion for all five; so are καθαρίζονται and εὐαγγελίζονται for their final three and final four respectively. ἀκούουσιν and ἐγείρονται correspond in scansion, but the latter rhymes not with the former but, a little weakly, with εὐαγγελίζονται. If scansion controls the pattern, then it is AABCCB as above; if rhyme controls it, it is AABABB. Perhaps the ambivalence was intentional. The thrust of the final couplet is towards the climax of the whole stanza in the proclamation to the poor; it was appropriate that both verbs should have the rhyming passive form expressing the action of God.

> Isa. 42.18: οἱ **κωφοί, ἀκούσατε, καὶ** οἱ **τυφλοί, ἀναβλέψατε** ἰδεῖν.

> Isa. 29.18: καὶ **ἀκούσονται** ἐν τῇ ἡμέρᾳ ἐκείνῃ **κωφοὶ** λόγους βιβλίου, καὶ οἱ...ὀφθαλμοὶ **τυφλῶν βλέψονται·**

> Isa. 35.5: τότε ἀνοιχθήσονται ὀφθαλμοὶ **τυφλῶν**, καὶ ὦτα **κωφῶν ἀκούσονται**. τότε ἁλεῖται ὡς ἔλαφος ὁ **χωλός**... (8) ἐκεῖ ἔσται ὁδὸς **καθαρά**...καὶ οὐ μὴ παρέλθῃ ἐκεῖ **ἀκάθαρτος**...

> Ezek. 36.25: καὶ **καθαρισθήσεσθε** ἀπὸ πασῶν τῶν ἀκαθαρσιῶν ὑμῶν...

> 4 Kgdms 5.10: Πορευθεὶς λοῦσαι...καὶ **καθαρισθήσῃ**.

> Isa. 26.19: ἀναστήσονται οἱ **νεκροί**, καὶ **ἐγερθήσονται** οἱ ἐν τοῖς μνημείοις...

> Isa. 61.1: **εὐαγγελίσασθαι πτωχοῖς** ἀπέσταλκέν με, κηρῦξαι...**τυφλοῖς ἀνάβλεψιν**...

As the above apparatus shows, every line of the text is paralleled in the LXX version of Isaiah except the third; as regards that, although λεπρός and its cognates occur nowhere in the prophetic books, the text cited from Ezekiel speaks of cleansing from uncleanness, and Isa. 35.8 of its consequences. There may also be a reference to the healing of Naaman the leper by the prophet Elisha (4 Kgdms 5); and less probably (since the theme is sufficiently covered by the prophetic text quoted) to the raising of the dead in 4 Kingdoms 4 or 3 Kingdoms 17.

Each of these prophetic signs corresponds to a specific event narrated in the miracles section of chs. 8–9.[68] This need not imply that 11.5 was composed ad hoc with the miracles already, so to speak, in position. All of them have been taken over from Mark, and 11.5 could quite well be the product of direct reflection on Mark and thus anterior or parallel to the selection of miracles which Matthew made to form his chapters 8–9. Its subtle and complex formal arrangement supports this, and is in contrast with certain passages that we shall be examining further on, whose less polished form does suggest that they took shape as part of the actual writing process of the Gospel.

The chreia which contains this verse, though commmonly assigned to Q, has caused difficulty to scholars who assume Q (some of whom would regard it as a late arrival in that stratum of the tradition, chiefly on account of its Septuagintal formulation).[69] On the other hand it fits admirably into its present context in Matthew (as it does not in Luke[70]); were it not for the existence of the latter there would have been no reason to question its Matthaean provenance.

a. With the 'left-hand column' of 11.5 we may compare the list of the afflicted in 15.30. Although this passage is not verse, the words are arranged in a way that is reminiscent of what we have already observed of Matthew's habits in verse composition; the fact that no less than six permutations of the word order have good MS support[71] suggests that the copyists saw the need to take the order seriously, though the variety of their solutions implies that they had lost the key to it.[72] Since we know of Matthew's fondness for chiasmus, one of the two solutions based on this is likely to be right. The order in B (followed by N-A[25]), χωλοὺς, κυλλοὺς, τυφλοὺς, κωφοὺς, is strictly chiastic both for vowels

68. Blind: 9.27-31; lame: 9.2-8; leper: 8.1-4; deaf: 9.32-34; dead: 9.18-26; poor (in Matthew's sense; see below, Chapter 7 §1d, on Beatitude I): 9.9-13 (and/or, possibly, 10.6).

69. Cf. Schulz, *Q*, p. 190. Kloppenborg, *Formation*, p. 108, also recognizes the Septuagintal character of τυφλοὶ ἀναβλέπουσιν, but does not draw the same conclusion. Jacobson, *First Gospel*, p. 112, stresses rather the logion's implied familiarity with the narrative miracles tradition.

70. Contrast what Luke has had to do in 7.1-17 and particularly at 7.21; see Green, 'Credibility', p. 139.

71. See apparatus to N-A[26, 27] *ad loc.*

72. B.M. Metzger, *A Textual Commentary on the Greek New Testament* (London: United Bible Societies, 2nd edn, 1994), p. 32, has evidently not rediscovered it.

(ω-υ-υ-ω) and inner consonants (λ-λλ-φλ-φ). The reading now adopted by N-A²⁶, ²⁷, χωλοὺς, τυφλοὺς, κυλλοὺς, κωφοὺς, is chiastic for the vowels, but less logically (or more subtly) so for the consonants. A possible justification for preferring it is the rearrangement of the words in the following verse, presumably to remove τυφλοὺς βλέποντας as far as possible from ὥστε τὸν ὄχλον θαυμάσαι βλέποντας... If the B reading (where τυφλοὺς is already in third place) were original, this would have been superfluous.

It is not necessary for our present purpose to resolve this question. Whatever the answer to it, the words reveal Matthew the author (for this paragraph, replacing rather than redacting Mark, is clearly his own composition[73]) as capable of dropping into semi-verse reminiscent of the passage (assigned to Q by the majority) in which we have found the same verse characteristics.

b. There are also obvious affinities between 11.5 and another six-line stanza, that at 10.8.[74]

ἀσθενοῦντας	θεραπεύετε,
νεκροὺς	ἐγείρετε,
λεπροὺς	καθαρίζετε,
δαιμόνια	ἐκβάλλετε,
δωρεάν	ἐλάβετε,
δωρεάν	δότε.

11.5 in its Matthaean context, as we have seen, takes up the healing miracles of chs. 8–9 as witness to the authenticity of Jesus' Messiahship; 10.8 does so to convey the extension of his mission to his disciples. Old Testament references are minimal, and the structure is looser, but a scheme of some sort can be recognized. In the first four lines there is an ABBC pattern (rhyming and scansion of νεκροὺς–

73. See discussion in Donaldson, *Mountain*, pp. 122-35, and authorities cited by him at p. 260 nn. 31, 32. He shows (p. 127) that Mark, despite the suppression of 7.31-37, is not totally absent from Matthew's version, nor the background influence of Isa. 35.5-6, which has contributed μογιλάλος to the Markan pericope and three of its four adjectives to Matthew's substitute. He does not however observe that this text is a link between 15.29-31 and 11.5, of which the former has sometimes been seen as a Gentile-orientated paraphrase (for the Gentile associations of these vv. cf. A.H. McNeile, *The Gospel according to St Matthew* [London: Macmillan, 1915], p. 107; Jeremias, *Promise*, pp. 29 n. 1, 35; Davies, *Setting*, pp. 325-32).

74. Noted by Jeremias, *Theology*, I, p. 21.

λεπροὺς) on the left, and on the right an ABAB one (as indicated by the scansion). The final couplet stands somewhat on its own, but δωρέαν is linked to δαιμόνια by alliteration, and ἐλάβετε to ἐκβάλλετε by alliteration of consonants and assonance of vowels. The less highly wrought quality of this verse suggests that, unlike 11.5, it was composed ad hoc for its present context.

4. *Matthew 11.7-9 (11a, 13)*

There is clearly a short poem at the heart of this section, but it has to be disinterred from an overlay of later redaction.[75] The removal of intrusive material discloses a strophe of three 3-3 bicola,[76] with a concluding coda. ἰδοὺ οἱ τὰ μαλακὰ...βασιλέων εἰσίν is evidently a gloss on the previous line,[77] and therefore not part of the original poem.

ναὶ λέγω ὑμῖν, which interrupts the basic rhythm, has been inserted to prepare the way for the addition of v. 10, which Matthew found (misattributed to Isaiah) at Mk 1.2 and uses here to modify the sense in which John is accounted more than a prophet. Nowhere else does he use ναὶ to introduce the solemn λέγω ὑμῖν in preference to the more Hebraic ἀμήν,[78] and this indicates that words introduced by ἀμήν in v. 11 already stood in the text he was modifying. Not so however all the words that follow in the present text: if the original sense of the poem has been modified, the paradoxical and virtually contradictory ὁ δὲ μικρότερος...μείζων αὐτοῦ ἐστιν must belong to the modification.[79] It has been suggested that οὐκ ἐγήγερται...βαπτιστοῦ originally stood on its own,[80] but the abrupt and unrhythmical conclusion that this leaves

75. See fuller treatment in Green, 'Matthew 11.7-15'.
76. This requires a stress on ἀλλὰ in the second and third distichs. According to Gundry, *Matthew*, p. 207, the word has the force of the Aramaic *'ella'*, 'if not'. Being thus an adverbial expression and not merely a conjunction, it can carry a metrical stress.
77. Compare what Matthew has done at 12.27b.
78. Matthew uses ἀμήν to introduce λέγω ὑμῖν/σοι 30 times (9 of them from Mark); ναὶ with the same combination only here.
79. Cf. J.P. Meier, 'John the Baptist in Matthew's Gospel', *JBL* 99 (1980), pp. 383-405 (394-95).
80. By, e.g., Dibelius, *Täufer*, pp. 12-14; Lührmann, *Redaktion*, p. 27; A.P. Polag, *Die Christologie der Logienquelle* (Neukirchen: Neukirchener Verlag, 1977), p. 47; R.A. Edwards, 'Matthew's Use of Q in Chapter 11', in J. Delobel (ed.), *LOGIA: Les Paroles de Jesus* (BETL, 59; Leuven: Peeters, 1982), pp. 257-75 (265).

would be uncharacteristic of Matthew. There is however a further state-ment of John's greatness a little further on, at 11.13: πάντες γὰρ οἱ προφῆται καὶ ὁ νόμος ἕως Ἰωάννου ἐπροφήτευσαν. The words καὶ ὁ νόμος are seemingly superfluous in this context; Matthew has intro-duced the law into a statement about the prophets as he has inserted the prophets into statements about the law at 5.17 and 22.40.[81] The particle γὰρ does nothing, in its present context, to clarify the relation of this verse to the preceding one; the prophetic activities of the (former) proph-ets do not obviously explain the violence currently offered to the king-dom.[82] But if detached from their present immediate context the words make an appropriate conclusion to v. 11a, indicating in what sense the poem in its original form understood John's greatness: he is the prophet who is the climax and conclusion of the (Old Testament) prophetic line.

The original form will then read as follows:

1a	τί ἐξήλθατε εἰς τὴν ἔρημον θεάσασθαι;
b	κάλαμον ὑπὸ ἀνέμου σαλευόμενον;
2a	ἀλλὰ τί ἐξήλθατε ἰδεῖν;
b	ἄνθρωπον ἐν μαλακοῖς ἠμφιεσμένον;
3a	ἀλλὰ τί ἐξήλθατε ἰδεῖν;[83]
b	προφήτην καὶ περισσότερον προφήτου.
	(ἀμήν λέγω ὑμῖν)

81. This is clear from the verb ἐπροφήτευσαν, which is what prophets do, but is not a natural choice of word for the combined subject if that was there from the beginning. Luke's ὁ νόμος καὶ οἱ προφῆται (16.16) is thus not the original form (contra virtually all Q adherents, with the exception of Hoffmann, *Studien*, p. 57, and Kloppenborg, *Formation*, pp. 114-15), but a redaction arrived at by cross-reference with Mt. 5.17, as is confirmed by (1) the paraphrase of Mt. 5.18 at Lk. 16.17; (2) the conflation of 5.32 with Mk 10.11 at Lk. 16.18; (3) the pinpointing of the division between the old dispensation and the new with ἀπὸ τότε, a *hapax* for him and for the rest of the New Testament, but characteristic of Matthew and used by him at 4.17 to mark the inauguration of the *kerygma* of Jesus. Cf. on 23.39, Chapter 4 §9b below; and see further Green, 'Matthew 11.7-15', pp. 461-62.

82. Both provenance and interpretation of 11.12 are unresolved problems. For the history of its interpretation see P.S. Cameron, *Violence and the Kingdom* (ANTJ, 5; Frankfurt: Lang, 1982). It is introduced by the temporal expression 'From the days of...', paralleled elsewhere in Matthew (23.30; 24.37) and indicative of *past* time; in 11.12 it must distinguish the time of John's proclamation of the coming kingdom (3.1–4.16) from that of Jesus (4.17 onwards). Whether a previous *Sitz im Leben* without this time scheme is possible for the logion is an open question.

83. Assuming present text as given in N-A[26, 27]; contra that of F.L. Huck and

4a   οὐκ ἐγήγερται
b   ἐν γεννητοῖς γυναικῶν
c   μείζων Ἰωάννου·
d   πάντες γὰρ οἱ προφῆται
e   ἕως Ἰωάννου ἐπροφήτευσαν.

These lines have evidently been composed in Greek, not translated into it, as is shown by the internal rhyming and word play: the succession of short syllables in 1b conveys in an almost onomatopoeic way the swaying of a reed in the wind. κάλαμον, σαλευόμενον and μαλακοῖς repeat the insistent αλ-sound, and the consonants of μαλακοῖς (inflections apart) are those of κάλαμον in inverse order. ἄνθρωπον echoes the initial syllable of ἀνέμου. Both these lines give rejected answers to the initial question; 3b with its three alliterated initial π's[84] gives emphatic expression to the true one.

I have hesitated about construing what follows ἀμὴν λέγω ὑμῖν as verse, and other arrangements are possible. But the alliterative pattern is the most likely clue to the structure. The inner lines 4b and 4d have alliteration of the initial letters γ and π, and there is internal repetition of the same letter in the corresponding outer lines 4a and 4e; between them is 4c, naming John who is the subject of the whole strophe. The latter is thus concentric,[85] with the pattern AA'CB'B. The insertion of καὶ ὁ νόμος, as well the the qualification of John as τοῦ βαπτιστοῦ, can then be seen as belonging to the final redaction.

γεννητοῖς γυναικῶν reproduces in plural form an expression found several times in the LXX of Job;[86] otherwise there are no clear Old Testament allusions. But the poem displays other characteristic features of Matthaean poetry, and there are therefore no good grounds for questioning his authorship. Why then should he have wished to alter it?

The most likely reason is a christological one, prompted by further reflection on the Christology of Mark. I have argued elsewhere[87] that

H. Greeven, *Synopsis der drei ersten Evangelien* (Tübingen: J.C.B. Mohr, 1981), p. 61 *ad loc.* See Metzger, *Textual Commentary*, pp. 23-24.

84. Alliterated π may justifiably be called a mark of Matthew's personal style; cf. 5.3-6 (Chapter 2, above, with n. 5); 11.27, 28-30; 16.18; 28.18-20 (see §10 below).

85. See Watson, *Hebrew Poetry*, pp. 187-88; and note that it is in the middle line that John is named; cf. §2 with n. 17 above, on the Lord's Prayer.

86. Job 11.2, 12; 14.1; 15.14; 25.4 (γεννητὸς γυναῖκος); cf. Sir. 10.18 (γεννήματα γυναικῶν).

87. 'Matthew 11.7-15', pp. 464-66.

whereas for the original form of the poem (and for 11.16-19 and 12.41-42) Jesus and John are peers, but only John is a prophet, for Mark, and for the final form of Matthew, John, as the forerunner, is clearly subordinate,[88] but both are prophets (and thus share the fate of prophets in suffering and death).[89] (For further discussion see Appendix B.)

5. *Matthew 11.16-19b*

Form-critical treatments of this pericope have fallen into two main categories: those that separate the application from the parable proper, regarding the latter as early and probably authentic, the former as secondary;[90] and those which maintain the unity, and usually the authenticity, of the whole passage.[91] Two further possibilities demand consideration: (1) that the pericope is a unity but not authentic; (2) that such redaction as has taken place may not be coterminous with the interpretation but internal to it.

While the 'interpretation' could conceivably have stood on its own in a way that the 'parable', uninterpreted, clearly could not, the essential literary unity of the pericope is indicated by the correspondence of the two couplets between which it is, as it were, stretched. Both are in 3-3 rhythm, and each contains 9 words. The first of these:

ηὐλήσαμεν ὑμῖν καὶ οὐκ ὠρχήσασθε,
ἐθρηνήσαμεν καὶ οὐκ ἐκόψασθε,

carries a clear reference to Eccl. 3.4b: καιρὸς τοῦ κόψασθαι καὶ καιρὸς τοῦ ὀρχήσασθαι;[92] it is thus to be seen as a literary creation.

---

88. See Mk 1.2-3//Mt. 11.10; Mk 9.11-13//Mt. 17.10-12. Mt. 11.14, which has no counterpart in Luke, is clearly 'throwback' from the latter (for the force of this expression see n. 177 below).

89. Mt. 5.12; 14.1-12; 17.12; 21.23-43; 23.29-36 (all but the first and last MtR of Mk).

90. E.g. Dibelius, *Täufer*, p. 16; Bultmann, *Tradition*, p. 172; Hoffmann, *Studien*, pp. 224-28; E. Arens, *The 'ΗΛΘΟΝ Sayings in the Synoptic Tradition* (OBO, 10; Fribourg: Presses Universitaires; Göttingen: Vandenhoeck & Ruprecht, 1976), p. 223.

91. J. Jeremias, *The Parables of Jesus* (trans. S.H. Hooke; London: SCM Press, 1963), pp. 160-62; N. Perrin, *Rediscovering the Teaching of Jesus* (London: SCM Press, 1967), pp. 119-21 (who maintains the improbability of a formulation of the later Church having referred to Jesus in such terms after the situation of his own ministry had been removed. Would it therefore have been simply forgotten?)

92. Cf. Gnilka, *Matthäusevangelium*, I, p. 423. Luke's alteration of ἐκόψασθε

Eccl. 3.4b is part of a larger poem on the theme 'a time for everything', and this is the essential significance of the children's game.[93] The complaint of the group demanding activity from the others (ἑτέροις; the parallelism of the couplet implies a single group [even if divided into boys and girls] making both demands) could have been matched by one from the 'others': 'you piped to us when we needed to mourn, and you wailed to us when we wanted to celebrate'. The charge against 'this generation' is that it would take neither John nor Jesus seriously, and so found fault, perversely and inconsistently, with each. John comes to them with a call to repentance because the kingdom is near (which for him, and by implication for them, involves fasting), and they say he is mad (that is, too ascetic);[94] Jesus follows him with an invitation to celebrate because it is, proleptically, present, and they complain that he is a glutton (that is, not ascetic enough). We in fact have evidence (shared with the Evangelist) of complaints about Jesus' failure to fast (see Mk 2.18-19//Mt. 9.14-15).[95] We have none of protests against John's penitential stance or attempts to get him to relax it (though Matthew, who at

to ἐκλαύσατε (7.32) is probably due to Eccl. 3.4a (which he has already drawn on at 6.21; cf. Goulder, *Luke*, p. 350). Variation of the wording of a LXX quotation found by him in a source with words also taken from the LXX is characteristic of him. The terminal rhyming of the two pairs of verbs (3 syllables for the first pair and 2 for the second) and near-matching scansion for the first pair are equally characteristic of Matthew's Greek-language parallelism.

93. Jeremias, *Parables*, pp. 160-62, and Perrin, *Rediscovering*, pp. 85-86 (both with acknowledgment to E.F.F. Bishop, *Jesus of Palestine* [London: Lutterworth, 1955], p. 104) interpret the game correctly. The exegesis requires Matthew's ἑτέροις; Luke's ἀλλήλοις is clearly secondary (contra Hoffmann, *Studien*, p. 197), and O. Linton's suggestion of ἄλλοις as *Vorlage* ('The Parable of the Children's Game', *NTS* 22 [1975–76], pp. 159-79 [162 n. 1]) is not preferable to ἑτέροις, which accurately describes a situation where there are a number of individual participants but only two groups. Cf. W.J. Cotter, 'The Parable of the Children in the Market Place', *NovT* 29 (1987), pp. 289-304 (291), followed by Tuckett, *Q*, p. 176.

94. The piping thus stands for an inappropriate response (or proposition) to John. It is therefore not the case, as some have claimed, that the order of the interpretation does not correspond to that of the parable.

95. It is interesting to find that whereas Mk 2.18 speaks of a joint approach to Jesus by John's disciples and the Pharisees, Matthew's redaction eliminates the latter and has John's disciples speaking for both groups. This may simply reflect the greater polarization of the Pharisees in Matthew and an unwillingness to suggest any sort of identification with them. See next note.

certain points in this chapter seems to be in closer contact with the Baptist tradition than any other synoptic source, may conceivably have known of one[96]). But the saying at 21.32 (also beginning ἦλθεν γὰρ Ἰωάννης) speaks of John coming 'in the way of righteousness' and the leaders of the people (cf. 21.22) refusing to believe him.

The 'interpretation' reads as if it had originally been composed as a quatrain, with the first and third lines in antithetical parallelism, but the counterpart to the single phrase δαιμόνιον ἔχει in the second is the self-contained distich:

ἄνθρωπος φάγος καὶ οἰνοπότης,
τελωνῶν φίλος καὶ ἁμαρτωλῶν.

The matching of the two lines[97] depends on features only possible in Greek, and already instanced in Matthaean usage.[98] φάγος and φίλος are alliterated, parallel in scansion, and terminally rhymed. ἄνθρωπος and τελωνῶν are paired by inverse, and οἰνοπότης and ἁμαρτωλῶν by (imperfect) converse, quantitative scansion. οἰνοπότης may have been suggested by Prov. 23.20, and the combined expression may also owe something to Deut. 21.20 which in the LXX is nearer to it than it is to its Hebrew original (as are also the Targums).[99] But more significant than these partial parallels is the closeness of the second line to μετὰ τῶν τελωνῶν καὶ ἁμαρτωλῶν ἐσθίει in Mk 2.16b.[100] On the assumption that Matthew works from Mark it is difficult to reject influence from the latter here.

While it could be argued that in an earlier form of the 'interpretation' the comment on Jesus was more nearly parallel to that on John (e.g.,

96. See §4 above (with notes); also Appendix B. The evidence that the first Evangelist has moved from a strongly pro-Baptist stance to a more nuanced one associated with a higher Christology (so Green, 'Matthew 11.7-15', pp. 464-66) suggests the possibility of close contact, perhaps even identification, with a 'Baptist' group in his earlier background.

97. Obscured in Luke's version by the inversion of the order of the first two words (a characteristic Lukan alteration for alteration's sake). Gundry's explanation (*Matthew*, p. 213) is inadequate; Goulder's (*Luke*, p. 397) more to the point.

98. See the final petition of the Lord's Prayer, §2b.4, above.

99. For the connection with these texts see Jeremias, *Parables*, p. 61; Gundry, *Use*, pp. 80-81; *Matthew*, p. 213; Hoffmann, *Studien*, p. 228; Goulder, *Midrash*, p. 358.

100. Schulz, *Q*, p. 361, notes the closeness of 11.19ab to Mk 2.15-17 both in terminology and content.

'Look, a glutton') and the expansion of this into the present couplet a piece of later redaction, it would not be easy to maintain that the Markan impress on the logion came about in two separate stages. If the complaint at Mk 2.18 lies behind the entire passage,[101] the contribution of Mk 2.16b to its concluding distich can hardly have come much later. This accords with the structural prominence of the two couplets in the whole composition.

A suggestive parallel to the comparison-cum-contrast of John and Jesus in this pericope is provided by the double logion at 12.41-42. In its present context both the components of this must refer to Jesus (cf. 12.40: 'the Son of man').[102] But it is evident that this is not their original context, since together they clearly constitute a formal unity, yet only one of them is concerned with Jonah. If they are detached from it, it becomes possible to see in Jonah the type of John's prophetic preaching of repentance,[103] and in Solomon that of Jesus' healings,[104] and of his teaching and embodiment of wisdom, especially in the understanding of the divine law. The former topic belongs to the logion at 11.7-9; the latter is developed further in 11.28-30 (see below). Some implications for history of the composition of the chapter are considered in Appendix B.

6. *Matthew 11.21-24*

a   Οὐαί σοι, Χοραζίν,
      οὐαί σοι, Βηθσαϊδά,
      ὅτι εἰ ἐν Τύρῳ καὶ Σιδῶνι ἐγένοντο
      αἱ δυνάμεις αἱ γενόμεναι ἐν ὑμῖν,
      πάλαι ἂν ἐν σάκκῳ καὶ σποδῷ μετενόησαν.

101. The chreia containing this text is followed immediately by the question about fasting (see above). The association of the two in 11.16-19 is hardly coincidental, and from what we have already discovered about the allusive quality of Matthew's verse, a reference to a written text he certainly had before him is a more economical, and a safer, explanation than one to a conjectural oral source behind that text.

102. On the overall significance of the 'sign of Jonah' see Green, 'Matthew 12.22-50', pp. 166-70.

103. For previous attempts to argue this, see n. 13 to Appendix B.

104. For Solomon as healer (and exorcist) see Duling, 'Exorcism' and 'Therapeutic Son', cited in n. 73 to Chapter 3.

(πλὴν λέγω ὑμῖν)
Τύρῳ καὶ Σιδῶνι ἀνεκτότερον ἔσται
ἐν ἡμέρᾳ κρίσεως ἢ ὑμῖν

b   καὶ σύ, Καφαρναούμ,
μὴ ἕως οὐρανοῦ ὑψωθήσῃ;
ἕως ᾅδου καταβήσῃ.
ὅτι εἰ ἐν Σοδόμοις ἐγενήθησαν
αἱ δυνάμεις αἱ γενόμεναι ἐν σοί,
ἔμεινεν ἂν μέχρι τῆς σήμερον.
(πλὴν λέγω ὑμῖν ὅτι)
γῇ Σοδόμων ἀνεκτότερον ἔσται.
ἐν ἡμέρᾳ κρίσεως ἤ σοί.

There are two particular reasons for including this little poem in the survey. First, it is the clearest example that I have been able to discover, apart from the Beatitudes,[105] of a two-strophe poem with the same number of words (39) in each strophe. The number of stresses is also, on my reckoning, the same (23) in each, if emphasis on ἕως in the second and third versets of b is allowed; that this preposition can more easily be used emphatically[106] may be a reason for its displacement of εἰς in the Old Testament model. The exact correspondence of the word count compensates for freedom in the line arrangement, b having one more verset than a. The word count depends on the presence of ὅτι after πλὴν λέγω ὑμῖν in b but not a,[107] which indicates that though the phrase is, strictly speaking, extra-metrical it is still reckoned part of the composition.

Secondly, the introduction of the poem by an abrupt reference to unrepentant towns (of which nothing has so far been narrated in the Gospel), and the need for a further formula after it to introduce 11.25 before ταῦτα in that verse can recall τὰ ἔργα (v. 2) and τῶν ἔργων (v. 19c), constitutes an aporia for its present context. This suggests that the composition was originally independent of that. It appears to belong with such pieces as 12.41-42[108] (see above) and the lament over Jerusalem at 23.37-38.[109]

105. See Chapter 2.
106. Cf. 28.20; see n. 305 below.
107. Cf. the suggestion of Di Lella ('Structure') on the Beatitudes: see n. 9 to Chapter 2.
108. Parallel suggested by Bultmann, *Tradition*, p. 113.
109. See §9a below.

Jer. 13.27: **οὐαί σοι**, Ἰερουσαλήμ, ὅτι οὐκ ἐκαθαρίσθης ὀπισώ μου,...

Zech. 9.2: **Τύρος καὶ Σιδών**, διότι ἐφρόνησαν σφόδρα.

Jon. 3.6: καὶ ἤγγισεν ὁ λόγος πρὸς τὸν βασιλέα τῆς Νινευή,...καὶ περιεβάλετο **σάκκον** καὶ ἐκάθισεν ἐπὶ **σποδοῦ**.

Dan. 9.3: ἐν νηστείαις καὶ **σάκκῳ καὶ σποδῷ**.

Isa. 34.8: **ἡμέρα** γὰρ κρίσεως **κύριου**...

Isa. 14.13-15: σὺ δὲ εἶπας ἐν τῇ διανοίᾳ σου Εἰς τὸν **οὐρανὸν** ἀναβήσομαι,...καθιῷ ἐν ὄρει **ὑψηλῷ**...ἔσομαι ὅμοιος τῷ **ὑψίστῳ**...νῦν δὲ εἰς **ᾅδου καταβήσῃ**...

Isa. 2.2: Ὅτι ἔσται ἐν ταῖς ἐσχάταις ἡμέραις ἐμφανὲς τὸ ὄρος κύριου καὶ ὁ οἶκος τοῦ θεοῦ ἐπ' ἄκρων τῶν ὀρέων καὶ **ὑψωθήσεται** ὑπεράνω τῶν βουνῶν.

Josh. 4.9: καί εἰσιν ἐκεῖ ἕως **τῆς σήμερον** ἡμέρας.

1 Esd. 8.74: **μέχρι τῆς σήμερον** ἡμέρας...

Lam. 4.6: καὶ ἐμεγαλύνθη ἀνομία θυγατρὸς λαοῦ μου ὑπὲρ ἀνομίας **Σοδόμων**...

The address of the first strophe to the two cities is taken up in the traditional pairing of Tyre and Sidon, and that in its turn by the conventional (and in Greek alliterated) pairing of σάκκος and σποδός. (The cities are denounced in Isa. 23 and Ezek. 26–28 for their pride and luxury; though there are no verbal reminiscences of those chapters here, the irony of seeing Tyre, a byword for its costly fabrics and dyes, in the garb of penitents and mourners should not be missed.)

That Matthew has ὑψωθήσῃ in b where the LXX of Isaiah has ἀναβήσῃ may have been partly suggested by catchword connection with ὑψηλὰ/ὑψίστῳ in the latter context, but its closest LXX parallel is the use of the verb in Isa. 2.2. In its Isaiah context this oracle is a promise of peace and a message of hope to Jerusalem. Matthew's attitude to Jerusalem is ambivalent; it is the 'holy city' (4.5; 27.53), and an abiding image of God's people, but at the same time it is, in the literal sense, the city that has suffered destruction for the faithlessness of its inhabitants. The exaltation of Mount Zion promised in the oracle will not be fulfilled in the literal sense. And it is in this sense that Capernaum is being compared to Jerusalem; although no one could plausibly call the lakeside town a 'city set on a hill', a comparison may be intended between the house of God on Zion and the house (οἰκία; 9.10; 13.1, 36) of Jesus at Capernaum. The general point being made is that repentance was the proper response to Jesus' miracles as well as to John's preaching, and the people of Capernaum failed to make it. The thought fits only loosely into the overall argument of ch. 11. But it may serve as a corrective to a distinction of their roles which concentrated the preaching of repentance on the figure of John.[110]

The usual LXX expression for a place (cult, etc.) surviving to the present day is that cited from Josh. 4.9. Matthew however has already used ἕως in a spatial sense in the first two versets of b (see above). Hence his variation from it and use of wording found in the LXX only at 1 Esd. 8.74.

7. *Matthew 11.25-30*

A full account of past treatment of this long-standing *crux criticorum*[111] is not practicable within the compass of the present study. But it is possible, in summary, to indicate two principal, and, on conventional critical assumptions, probably irreconcilable, lines of approach. The first of these[112] recognizes the extensive parallels between the text in its en-

110. See Appendix B.

111. The best account of earlier treatment of this text (going back ultimately to D.F. Strauss) is that of H.D. Betz, 'The Logion of the Easy Yoke and of Rest', *JBL* 86 (1967), pp. 10-24 (though his position with regard to some more recent theories is controversial; see nn. 115, 124 below). For summaries of past positions down to their date of publication see also Schulz, *Q*, pp. 213-28; Hoffmann, *Studien*, pp. 104-28; for more recent work, C. Deutsch, *Hidden Wisdom and the Easy Yoke* (JSNTSup, 18; Sheffield: JSOT Press, 1987), pp. 21-53; A. Denaux, 'The Q-Logion Mt 11,27/Lk 10,22 and the Gospel of John' in *idem* (ed.), *John and the Synoptics* (BETL, 101; Leuven: Peeters, 1992), pp. 163-99 (bibliography pp. 188-93).

112. See E. Norden, *Agnostos Theos* (Leipzig: Teubner, 1913), pp. 276-308, 394-95; T. Arvedson, *Das Mysterium Christi* (Uppsala: Lundqvist, 1937); M. Rist, 'Is Matt. 11.25-30 a Primitive Baptismal Hymn', *JR* 15 (1935), pp. 63-77; K. Stendahl, 'Matthew', in M. Black and H.H. Rowley (eds.), *Peake's Commentary on the Bible* (London: Nelson, 1962), pp. 769-98 (784). M. Dibelius, *From Tradition to Gospel* (trans. B.L. Woolf; London: Ivor Nicholson & Watson, 1934), p. 279, agreed with Norden about the unity of the passage, but not about its literary antecedents. U. Wilckens, 'σοφία κτλ.', *TDNT*, VII, pp. 496-526 (517), also favours unity on grounds of continuity of theme. There has been a strange reluctance on the part of representatives of this position (Rist excepted) to allow that the Evangelist could have known and worked from the Greek text of Sirach as we have it. The admission of this makes arguments from the pre-history of Sir. 51 (e.g. M.J. Suggs, *Wisdom,*

tirety and Sirach 51, and in seeking to make sense of the connection treats the former as a unity. The other,[113] relying (as we have found with the Beatitudes) on the genetic method, notes the absence of vv. 28-30 from the parallel passage in Luke 10.21-22, assumes (as a rule, rather than argues) that this could only have been due to Lukan ignorance of them,[114] and so assigns the two parts to separate sources, vv. 25-27 to Q, and vv. 28-30 to M[115] (or, less usually, to the Evangelist himself[116]).

Christology and Law in Matthew's Gospel [Cambridge, MA: Harvard University Press, 1970], pp. 42, 80) irrelevant here.

113. So Harnack, *Sayings*, pp. 272-95; J. Weiss, 'Das Logion Mt 11,25-30', in *idem* (ed.), *Neutestamentliche Studien* (Festschrift G. Henrici; Leipzig: J.C. Hinrichs, 1914), pp. 120-30; W. Bousset, *Kyrios Christos* (Göttingen: Vandenhoeck & Ruprecht, 2nd edn, 1921), pp. 45-50; Bultmann, *Tradition*, p. 159; W. Bussmann, *Synoptische Studien*. II. *Zur Redenquelle* (Halle: Waisenhause, 1929), p. 65; and more recent Q adherents generally.

114. The underlying reasons for this conclusion seem to be (1) a residual 'scissors-and-paste' conception of Luke's editorial work; (2) an over-simplistic assumption of his humanity and compassion (contrast Lk. 19.27; Acts 12.19); (3) failure to grasp what Mt. 11.28-30 is really about (see §7a below; cf. Franklin, *Luke*, p. 325; Ravens, *Restoration*, p. 221). For answers to it cf. Dibelius, *From Tradition*, p. 279 n. 2; J.M. Creed, *The Gospel according to St Luke* (London: Macmillan, 1930), p. 148; B.T. Viviano, *Study as Worship: Aboth and the New Testament* (SJLA, 26; Leiden: E.J. Brill, 1978), p. 185; Goulder, 'Order of a Crank', p. 117; *Luke*, p. 480; Green, 'Credibility', p. 136; Franklin (as above); Ravens (as above). The number and variety of these rejoinders is no argument against the proposition they seek to establish; if anything, they enhance its probability. None of us has direct access to the mind of Luke; it is by a convergence of separate viewpoints that we can best hope to approach it.

115. The symbol M covers all material in Matthew not shared with either Mark or Luke, and no stricter classification of such various matter is feasible. Strauss, Bultmann (see *Tradition*, p. 159) and E. Dinkler, 'Jesu Wort von Kreuztragen', in W. Eltester (ed.), *Neutestamentliche Studien* (Festschrift R. Bultmann; BZNW, 21; Berlin: Alfred Töpelmann, 1954), pp. 110-29 (117), thought in terms of quotation of a 'floating' saying from Jewish wisdom tradition; since the parallels adduced were literary, the evidence for oral tradition of this sort was defective, though the affinities of the text were correctly identified. More recent work (see Betz, 'Logion', pp. 19-23) has seen the shorter forms of this logion at *Gos. Thom.* 90 and *Pistis Sophia* 95 (ed. G.R.S. Mead; London: J.M. Watkins, 1921, p. 182) not as quotations or derivatives but as collaterals, with Matthew's the product of enlargement of the original form. On this see n. 124 below.

116. As by Bacon, *Studies*, pp. 322-23; E. Hirsch, *Die Frühgeschichte des Evangeliums* (Tübingen: J.C.B. Mohr, 1941), II, p. 285; G. Barth, 'Matthew's Understanding of the Law', in G. Bornkamm, G. Barth and H.J. Held, *Tradition*

The origin of vv. 25-27 thus gets pushed back to an earlier stage of the tradition, and discussed in terms of the theology of the 'Q community',[117] or in some cases identified, in whole or part, as an authentic *verbum Christi*.[118]

The strength of the second approach (though not of all the inferences that have been drawn from it) has lain in the fact that the passage is not a continuous unity but actually comprises three formally distinct and disparate items: (1) (vv. 25-26): a thanksgiving (addressed by Jesus to the Father); (2) (v. 27): a soliloquy by the Son about the Father; (3) (vv. 28-30): an invitation addressed by the Son to those weary of their burden. Of these the last is at once the most self-contained and the most poetically elaborated.[119] It will therefore be examined first.

---

and Interpretation in Matthew (trans. P. Scott; London: SCM Press, 1963), pp. 58-164 (103) n. 1; W.P. Weaver, 'A History of the Tradition of Matt. 11.25-30 (Luke 10.21-22)' (PhD dissertation; Drew University, 1968) [not available to me]; Goulder, *Midrash*, p. 385; Green, *Matthew*, p. 122; Gundry, *Matthew*, pp. 218-20; A. Sand, *Das Matthäusevangelium* (Regensburg: Regensburger, 1986), p. 251; S.H. Brooks, *Matthew's Community* (JSNTSup, 16; Sheffield: JSOT Press, 1987), pp. 95-97. Strecker's objection (*Weg*, p. 172) from the presence of six *hapax legomena* ignored the fact that all six are found in the LXX.

117. E.g. Lührmann, *Redaktion*, pp. 64-68; P. Hoffmann, 'Die Offenbarung des Sohnes', *Kairos* NS 12 (1970), pp. 270-88; *Studien*, pp. 104-42.

118. Bultmann's uncharacteristic espousal (*Tradition*, pp. 160, 410; following Bousset, *Kyrios*, pp. 46-47) of the dominical origin of vv. 25-26 (although, as he admitted, they fall right outside his usual criteria for the identification of genuine sayings of Jesus) has been widely followed, though it does not amount to more than an acknowledgment that the saying is possible in Aramaic and has an undeniably Semitic ring about it. This consensus does not extend to v. 27, though that too is held to be authentic by Schniewind, *Matthäus*, pp. 151-53; O. Cullmann, *The Christology of the New Testament* (trans. S.C. Guthrie and C.A.M. Hall; London: SCM Press, 1959), p. 288; J. Jeremias, *The Prayers of Jesus* (SBT, 2.6; London: SCM Press, 1967), pp. 45-47 (who reads the verse as a generalizing statement about fathers and sons); B.M.F. van Iersel, *'Der Sohn' in den synoptischen Jesusworten* (NovTSup, 3; Leiden: E.J. Brill, 1961)—as well as by those who maintain this for 11.25-30 as a whole: e.g. L. Cerfaux, 'Les sources scripturaires de Mt 11,25-30', in *Recueil Lucien Cerfaux*, III (Gembloux: Ducoulot, 1962), pp. 139-59; E. Percy, *Die Botschaft Jesu* (Lund: C.W.K. Gleerup, 1953), pp. 108-10; A.M. Hunter, 'Crux Criticorum—Matt 11.25-30: A Re-Appraisal', *NTS* 8 (1961–62), pp. 241-49.

119. Cf. Gundry, *Matthew*, p. 218: 'a distinctive composition that exhibits his characteristic attention to parallelism, diction typical of him, and his habit of conforming phraseology to the Old Testament'.

a. *Matthew 11.28-30*

1a δεῦτε πρός με, πάντες οἱ κοπιῶντες
b καὶ πεφορτισμένοι, κἀγὼ ἀναπαύσω ὑμᾶς.
2a ἄρατε τὸν ζυγόν μου
b ἐφ᾽ ὑμᾶς, καὶ μάθετε ἀπ᾽ ἐμοῦ·
3a ὅτι πραΰς εἰμι καὶ ταπεινὸς τῇ καρδίᾳ,
b καὶ εὑρήσετε ἀνάπαυσιν ταῖς ψυχαῖς ὑμῶν·
4a ὁ γὰρ ζυγός μου χρηστός,
b καὶ τὸ φορτίον μου ἐλαφρόν ἐστιν.

The stanza consists of four distichs, and is comparable in that respect to the two strophes that make up the Beatitudes. It points to Jesus as the alternative to the heavy burden under which those invited at present labour. There is therefore (since Jesus is the speaker) an emphasis on the first person pronoun which extends to the enclitic forms με and μου. The basic rhythm is thus a 3-3 stress, though the first couplet looks more like a 4-4,[120] with enjambment of the second participle καὶ πε-φορτισμένοι. Its structure is clearly chiastic, and this is a characteristic of the whole poem.[121] Enjambment is found also in the second couplet; this, as I have arranged it, is comparable to the petition for daily bread in the Lord's Prayer.[122] ἐφ᾽ ὑμᾶς is parallel with ἄρατε (for it is upon

120. In a previous analysis of the poem (see 'Matthew 28.19', pp. 132-33) I proposed a 3-3 stress throughout. This involved, in the first distich, treating δεῦτε πρός με as a single 'thought unit'. This is at variance with what we find at Sir. 51.23 (clearly a 3-stress line).

121. The first distich, as arranged here, is chiastic (and near-concentric) in its parallelism:

δεῦτε
    πρός με
        πάντες οἱ κοπιῶντες
        καὶ πεφορτισμένοι
    κἀγὼ
ἀναπαύσω ὑμᾶς:

and, spanning the poem as a whole, we find (1b) πεφορτισμένοι–(2a) ζυγὸν–(4a) ζυγός–(4b) φορτίον, which is *inclusio* as well as chiasmus. (Noted also by Viviano, *Study*, p. 190, who however offers a different [concentric] analysis of the composition; cf. Deutsch, *Wisdom*, p. 40. Watson, as previously noted [n. 17 above] speaks of concentric structure in connection with 5-line strophes; it is far from obvious that 11.28-30 can be called that.)

122. 6.11 (§2a.2 above) has the verb δὸς in structural parallelism with its object, the other words being in (broadly) synonymous parallelism. For noun-verb parallelism in the Old Testament see Watson, *Hebrew Poetry*, pp. 157-58.

themselves that the persons addressed are to take the new yoke), and to learn from Jesus as a disciple (μάθετε ἀπ᾽ ἐμοῦ) is equivalent to taking his yoke upon oneself (though there may also be a distinction here—which would not invalidate the parallelism—between his precept and his example).

It should also be observed that, as in the Beatitudes, there is alternating correspondence of couplets: 1 and 3 are linked[123] by the cognates ἀναπαύειν/ἀνάπαυσις and by repeated alliteration, both initial and internal, of the letters π and κ, 2 and 4 by ζυγός and the repetition of the enclitic pronouns. The parallelism in 4 between ζυγός and φορτίον makes an *inclusio* with πεφορτισμένοι in 1.

Mk 6.31: **δεῦτε** ὑμεῖς αὐτοὶ κατ᾽ ἰδίαν εἰς ἔρημον τόπον καὶ **ἀναπαύ-** ΄**σασθε** ὀλίγον.

Ps. 45.9: **δεῦτε** ἴδετε **τὰ ἔργα** κυρίου,|ἃ ἔθετο τέρατα ἐπὶ τῆς γῆς (cf. Ps. 65.5).

Ps. 65.16: **δεῦτε** ἀκούσατε καὶ διηγήσομαι,|πάντες οἱ φοβούμενοι τὸν θεόν,|ὅσα ἐποίησεν τῇ **ψυχῇ** μου.

Ps. 33.12: **δεῦτε**, τέκνα, ἀκούσατέ μου·| φόβον κυρίου διδάξω ὑμᾶς.

Sir. 51.23: ἐγγίσατε **πρός με**, ἀπαιδευτοί,| καὶ αὐλίσθητε ἐν οἴκῳ παιδείας.|...(26) τὸν τράχηλον ὑμῶν ὑπόθετε ὑπὸ **ζυγόν**,| καὶ ἐπιδεξάσθω ἡ **ψυχὴ** ὑμῶν παιδείαν.|...(27) ἴδετε ἐν ὀφθαλμοῖς ὑμῶν ὅτι ὀλίγον **ἐκοπίασα**| καὶ **εὗρον** ἐμαυτῷ πολλὴν **ἀνάπαυσιν**.

Zeph. 3.9: ὅτι τότε μεταστρέψω ἐπὶ λαοὺς γλῶσσαν εἰς γενεὰν αὐτῆς τοῦ ἐπικαλεῖσθαι πάντας τὸ ὄνομα κυρίου τοῦ δουλεύειν αὐτῷ ὑπὸ **ζυγὸν** ἕνα...(12) καὶ ὑπολείψομαι ἐν σοὶ λαὸν **πραῢν καὶ ταπεινὸν**...

Lam. 3.27: ἀγαθὸν ἀνδρὶ ὅταν ἄρῃ **ζυγὸν** ἐν νεότητι αὐτοῦ.

Sir. 6.28: ἐπ᾽ ἐσχάτων γὰρ **εὑρήσεις** τὴν **ἀνάπαυσιν** αὐτῆς.

123. Contra Stanton, *Gospel*, pp. 369-70, who treats 3a as Matthew's redactional insertion into a traditional wisdom saying. πραῢς is a preferred Matthaean word; cf. 5.5, 21.5 (both of them free quotations from LXX: see Chapter 3 §6 above and Chapter 7 §1b.1 below). Stanton rightly sees its presence (and that of μάθετε in 2b) as evidence of the Evangelist's own hand, but his distinction between these lines and the rest of the logion is unnecessary, and his argument that the alleged redactional insertion breaks up the argument of the original misconstrues the character of the composition, which must be read as a poem and not as a syllogism. (Professor Stanton, in a private communication, has informed me that he now accepts a unitary account of the composition of this passage.)

Isa. 28.12: λέγοντες αὐτῷ Τοῦτο τὸ **ἀνάπαυμα** τῷ πεινῶντι καὶ τοῦτο τὸ σύντριμμα, καὶ οὐκ ἠθέλησαν ἀκούειν.

Jer. 6.16: καὶ ἴδετε, ποία ἐστιν ἡ ὁδὸς ἡ ἀγαθή, καὶ βαδίζετε ἐν αὐτῇ, καὶ **εὑρήσετε** [ἁγνισμὸν] **ταῖς ψυχαῖς ὑμῶν**·...(17)...καὶ εἶπαν Οὐκ ἀκουσόμεθα.

2 Chron. 10.4: Ὁ πατήρ σου ἐσκλήρυνεν τὸν **ζυγὸν** ἡμῶν, καὶ νῦν ἄφες ἀπὸ τῆς δουλείας τοῦ πατρός σου τῆς σκληρᾶς καὶ ἀπὸ τοῦ **ζυγοῦ** αὐτοῦ τοῦ βαρέος...

The germ of the invitation can be found in Mk 6.31,[124] which must be read in context. The disciples have returned from their mission of 6.7-13, and are now invited to come away and rest. But the crowds follow them, and Jesus perceives these as 'sheep without a shepherd'. The most apposite of the several Old Testament contexts in which these words occur is Num. 27.17, where they preface the appointment of Joshua to succeed Moses.[125] Now between the commissioning of the disciples for their mission and their return Mark has inserted his account of the end of John the Baptist. The typology of his Gospel certainly sees John as Elijah (meaning primarily the forerunner of the Messiah, but without excluding the thought of Jesus as Elisha, as seems to be implied in this same context by his feeding of the multitudes

124. This suggestion of de Kruijf, *Der Sohn*, p. 71, was repeated by Goulder in his review of my *Matthew* (*JTS* NS 27 [1976], p. 456) and is hinted at in his *Luke*, p. 481. The presence of the latter word makes the text a more likely parallel than the more commonly cited Mk 1.17, which Matthew has already used in his parallel at 4.19. If it is right, the theory of a simpler *Vorlage* witnessed to by *Gos. Thom.* 90 and *Pistis Sophia* 95 (see n. 115 above) can hardly be right as well. Nor does the complexity of the verse structure of 11.28-30 encourage the view that it has been built up piecemeal from earlier materials. One does not make a silk purse out of a sow's ear. On *Gos. Thom.* 90 see W. Schrage, *Das Verhältnis des Thomas-Evangelium zur synoptischen Tradition* (BZNW, 29; Berlin: Alfred Töpelmann, 1964), pp. 172-74; on the whole subject of *Gos. Thom.* in relation to the synoptic tradition, C.M. Tuckett, ' "Thomas" and the Synoptics', *NovT* 30 (1988), pp. 132-57; J.P. Meier, *A Marginal Jew* (New York: Doubleday, 1991), I, pp. 124-39; C.A. Evans in Chilton and Evans (eds.), *Historical Jesus*, pp. 496-507; for the opposite view cf. n. 10 to Chapter 9.

125. I owe my account of Markan typology at this point originally to recollection of lectures delivered by Austin Farrer at Oxford in 1949, though it did not find its way into *A Study of St Mark* (Westminster: Dacre, 1951), or *St Matthew and St Mark* (London: A. & C. Black, 1954), and no trace of it is to be found in his unpublished remains.

[6.35-44; cf. 4 Kgdms 4.42-44]). The implication of the allusion to Num. 27.17 at this point is that John is also the antitype of Moses (presumably as summing up the Old Testament dispensation), while Jesus, as his name conveys, is that of Joshua, the successor to Moses and thus both compared and contrasted with him.

Matthew has separated these themes from the narrative context in which he found them in Mark. 'Sheep without a shepherd' is anticipated at 9.35, where it forms part of the run-up to the disciples' mission in ch. 10.[126] The relation of Jesus to John and of both to the old dispensation has been considered in the earlier part of the present chapter;[127] now he concentrates on Jesus, and on the contrast between the old dispensation and the new: that is, between the Mosaic law as currently interpreted in (Pharisaic) Judaism and as newly interpreted by Jesus. In effect, he has transformed an invitation to disciples into an invitation to discipleship.[128]

The short saying in Mark has been developed into a poem by cross-referencing of the two words δεῦτε and ἀναπαύειν/ἀνάπαυσις.

The words ἔργα κυρίου in Ps. 45.9 recall the ἔργα τοῦ Χριστοῦ at 11.2; this text and Ps. 65.5 speak of seeing them, and Ps. 65.15 of hearing of them. The saying in 11.4 'Go and tell John what you hear and see' is probably connected, despite the use of a different word for seeing. This echo of the opening of the chapter supports the position that 11.28-30 has been composed with the themes of the whole chapter in

126. For the disciples as themselves fulfilling Joshua-typology see on 28.19-20, §10c below.

127. 11.2-15; see §4 above.

128. Stanton, *Gospel*, p. 374, rightly concludes (though the logical connection with his preceding argument is far from clear) that 'a hard and fast line should not be drawn between crowds and disciples in Matt'. This would appear to exclude the primary reference to disciples facing opposition and rejection for which he argues in this context. Unlike the Markan parallel, Matthew does not bring his disciples back for rest and refreshment after their mission. They are apparently referred to in 11.25 as the νήπιοι who have received the revelation denied to the 'wise and understanding' (see nn. 161, 162 below), and 11.28 is the invitation to join their number. Cf. Deutsch, *Wisdom*, p. 32; Luz, *Matthew*, II, p. 219 and n. 235; W.L. Kynes, *A Christology of Solidarity: Jesus as the Representative of his People in Matthew* (Lanham, MD: University Press of America, 1991), p. 94; contra Dupont, *Béatitudes*, III, p. 530.

mind and not simply appended to it, and that in the chapter as originally drafted it could have stood on its own, independently of 11.25-27.[129]

Psalm 33, after an extended thanksgiving to God, turns at v. 12 to address its audience on the fear of the Lord, i.e. *wisdom*,[130] a word later associated with the scribal function of expounding the Torah, as found first in Sirach[131] and afterwards in the rabbinic tradition. δεῦτε, τέκνα makes a bridge with ἐγγίσατε πρός με, ἀπαιδευτοί in Sir. 51.23; Matthew's wording combines elements from both.

Sir. 51.23-27 is thus the pivot between the two catchwords; it also supplies the word ζυγός which, as we have seen, plays its part with ἀνάπαυσις in the structuring of the Matthaean poem. The implied author—i.e., Jesus ben-Sira (*not* the personified Wisdom as in ch. 24[132])—invites his hearers to put their necks under the yoke and receive instruction from Wisdom as he has done, and in doing so to find rest (ἀνάπαυσιν) from labour. The yoke is thus not the burden from which they are to be relieved; it is to be the means of their relief from it. In the same way Matthew's Jesus uses the word only in a positive sense, reserving it for what he himself offers: '*my* yoke'. When he wants to contrast this with a burden seen by him as oppressive, his middle term is φορτίον: hence πεφορτισμένοι in 1b, but φορτίον also in parallelism with ζυγός in 4b. The contrast implied is between an imposition and a demand which claims a willing response.

In the light of this usage of the Evangelist, as well as of the known signification of the word for his near-contemporaries,[133] it is a mistake to look for Old Testament antecedents in texts that use 'yoke' of the oppression of Israel by its enemies, whether in Egypt before the Exodus or in prophetic allusions to the captivity.[134] The positive sense is a surer

---

129. See further Appendix B.

130. Cf. Ps. 110.10; Prov. 1.7; 9.10; Sir. 1.14, 27; 23.27.

131. Cf. Sir. 6.37; 15.1; 24.23; 39.1-11; 51.19. See Orton, *Scribe*, pp. 47-58 (and notes), 68; Deutsch, *Wisdom*, pp. 114-15 (cf. pp. 125-26 for later rabbinic usage).

132. This is the natural reading of the text. The implied speaker of the soliloquy at Sir. 51.13-22 is clearly a human being who claims to have sought and found Wisdom, and there is no change of subject when the invitation is reached at v. 23; at v. 27 he still speaks of himself as one who has toiled (if not very much; but cf. 24.34 where the sage is again the speaker [diff24.3-22]).

133. For the contemporary sense and associations of 'yoke' see Deutsch, *Wisdom*, pp. 126-28; Allison, *New Moses*, p. 226.

134. Contra B. Charette, 'To Proclaim Liberty to the Captives', *NTS* 38 (1992),

guide here. At Zeph. 3.9 ζυγὸν conveys the promise of a single discipline for Jews and Gentiles (cf. 28.18-20), which will make them a single people, πραΰν καὶ ταπεινὸν (3.12).[135] Jesus is seen both as himself the fulfilment of this prophecy and, by example and precept, the source of its fulfilment in those who respond to his invitation to discipleship.[136]

The associations of ἀνάπαυσις are extended by the texts from Isa. 28.12 and Jer. 6.16; 3b quotes the latter directly from the LXX apart from the restoration of ἀνάπαυσιν (which corresponds to the Hebrew) in place of the LXX's ἁγνισμόν. The fulfilment of these two texts in Jesus rests partly on the recollection that in their original setting the appeal was disregarded. 12.1-13 correspondingly depicts in two scenes the Pharisees' rejection of more lenient interpretations of the Torah; and this is only the beginning of the story of rejection.[137]

The poem thus, like much else in the Gospel, operates at two, if not three levels: that of the story of Jesus (but foreshadowing also that of his future disciples), and that of the scriptures of the old Israel which are to find their fulfilment in him. Central to all these is the contrast between the 'easy yoke' of Jesus and the heavy burden imposed on the subjects of the invitation. Both the immediate context and the recurrence of φορτίον in that of the denunciation of the Pharisaic scribes in 23.4 (and there alone in this Gospel) make a reference to the latter context unavoidable.[138] But for its deeper meaning the reader must look to

pp. 290-97, and the suggestion of W.D. Davies reported but not endorsed by Allison, *New Moses*, p. 230.

135. The only text in the LXX to combine the two adjectives (apart from Isa. 26.6, which is not helpful here). Cf. Charette, 'To Proclaim', p. 296; *idem, The Theme of Recompense in Matthew's Gospel* (JSNTSup, 79; Sheffield: JSOT Press, 1992), p. 86 (to which I owe the reference). πραΰς may also carry an allusion to the meekness of Moses at Num. 12.3, though the argument of Allison, *New Moses*, pp. 217-33, exaggerates the prominence of Moses in the typology of this text of Matthew.

136. The line arrangement makes it implausible to construe the ὅτι-clause as epexegetic (as does Strecker, *Weg*, p. 174); it would involve enjambment of two distichs.

137. Knowles, *Jeremiah*, p. 216, rejects Jer. 6.16 as a contributor to Mt. 11.29 on the grounds that the latter's context in the Gospel gives no hint of a rejection of the invitation. Actually Mt. 12–28 as a whole is the story of that rejection and its consequences, which opens with the two disputes with Pharisees at the beginning of Mt. 12.

138. So, rightly, Deutsch, *Wisdom*, pp. 40-41 and notes; contra Stanton, *Gospel*, p. 375 (see n. 150 below).

evidences of Old Testament prefiguration; an 'applied exegesis'[139] is clearly called for. Who made Israel's yoke heavy—turned a positive obligation, which he was empowered to require,[140] into a negative imposition? The figure in Israel's history of whom, above all, this may be said is Solomon, who was both its traditional exponent of wisdom and the king who imposed forced labour on his subjects (cf. 2 Chron. 10.4 above).

The link between the Old Testament type and the situation to which it is applied is the equation, fully established by Matthew's time,[141] of wisdom and Torah. The professional exponents of Torah had come to be known as *ḥᵃkāmîm*, 'wise men' (cf. 11.25), and of this tradition of exposition, seen in its dominant Pharisaic form as oppressive, Solomon is made the representative figure. Who then is available to represent the contrasted approach of Jesus? There was a latecomer to the literature of the Hebrew wisdom tradition, who wrote, untypically, in his own name and not in that of Solomon, Jesus ben-Sira, whose words are here made the model for those placed on the lips of his namesake. 'Not Solomon but one called Jesus is the bearer of the divine wisdom'.[142] The relationship of Matthew's poem to the book of Sirach is thus typological as well as literary.

The words 'bearer of the divine wisdom' were carefully chosen. A number of commentators in recent years have represented the Matthaean Christ as the 'incarnation' of the personified Wisdom.[143] The

139. See n. 22 to Chapter 3.
140. The Matthaean counterpart to this is surely 23.2, where the scribes' authority to teach is acknowledged, but the way they exercise it is under judgment.
141. See n. 131 above.
142. Green, 'Solomon', p. 229; cf. Deutsch, *Wisdom*, n. 20 (to ch. 4) on p. 175.
143. E.g. F. Christ, *Jesus-Sophia* (Zürich: Zwingli, 1970); Suggs, *Wisdom*; and, following him, R.G. Hamerton-Kelly, *Pre-Existence, Wisdom and the Son of Man* (SNTSMS, 21; Cambridge: Cambridge University Press, 1973), pp. 30-36; J.M. Robinson, 'Jesus as Son of Man and Sophia: Wisdom Tradition and the Gospels', in R.L. Wilken (ed.), *Aspects of Wisdom in Judaism and Early Christianity* (CSJCA, 1; Notre Dame: University of Notre Dame Press, 1975), pp. 9-11; F.W. Burnett, *The Testament of Jesus–Sophia* (Washington, DC: Catholic University of America Press, 1981), esp. pp. 69-71; J.D.G. Dunn, *Christology in the Making* (London: SCM Press, 1980), pp. 197-206; Deutsch, *Wisdom*, pp. 130-39. The position rests ultimately on the validity of Q and consensus among its advocates that Lk. 11.49 represents its original wording as against Mt. 23.34 (against the arguments urged in favour of this see Green, 'Clement', pp. 21-23; M.D. Goulder, 'Is Q a Juggernaut?',

expression carries overtones of the Christology of the Johannine prologue which not all of them may have intended (despite the fact that it was long fashionable to see Mt. 11.25-27 as 'a Johannine thunderbolt in a synoptic sky'). But it is generally admitted that Matthew's infancy narrative knows nothing of a pre-existent Christ; and if indeed he had conceived of this, it is highly unlikely, as a number of scholars have insisted,[144] that he could have identified him with a feminine figure. On the other hand 18.20 speaks of the future presence of the risen Christ with his assembled disciples in terms closely parallel to those used by contemporary Jews about the Torah;[145] he is thus the 'embodiment' (which is by no means the same as 'incarnation') or the 'impersonation' of Torah, as Moses was for Matthew's Jewish contemporaries.[146] If the Matthaean Jesus can be in any sense assimilated to the personified Wisdom, it will be by way of his identification with Torah and not the other way round.[147]

Solomon, as Israel's archetypal wise man, could be called the 'embodiment' of wisdom; but for the personified Wisdom he is no more than a mouthpiece,[148] and when wisdom comes to be understood as

JBL 115 [1996], pp. 667-81 [673-74]). But it is no longer unchallenged even on its own assumptions; see M.D. Johnson, 'Reflections on a Wisdom Approach to Matthew's Christology', *CBQ* 36 (1974), pp. 44-64; Stanton, *Gospel*, pp. 369-71 (who however rejects any contact between 11.28-30 and Sirach); and the careful and balanced study of F.T. Gench, 'Wisdom Christology in the Gospel of Matthew' (PhD dissertation; Union Theological Seminary, Virginia, 1988).

144. So Johnson, 'Reflections', pp. 61-62; Stanton, *Gospel*, p. 370; Kynes, *Solidarity*, pp. 88-89. Deutsch's rejoinder to Stanton (*Wisdom*, p. 178) begs the question.

145. The best known example (slightly later than Matthew) is the saying ascribed to R. Hananiah b. Teradion in *m. Ab.* 3.2: 'If two sit together and words of Torah (are spoken) between them, the divine presence rests between them.' By analogy with this Matthew's (risen; cf. 28.20) Jesus embodies both Torah and Shekinah.

146. For 'impersonation' cf. Philo, *Vit. Mos.* 162; for this, and for Moses as 'living Torah' see Allison, *New Moses*, p. 230. Luz, *Matthew*, II, p. 218 speaks of a 'functional' identification.

147. The final position of Deutsch is close to this, though she has previously made steady and unnuanced use of 'Wisdom incarnate' language; cf. *Wisdom*, p. 143.

148. Cf. Prov. 1.22-33; 8.4-36; 9.4-6, for direct utterances of Wisdom within the collection of which Solomon is the official author: a possible model for Lk. 11.49, especially if its author was familiar with *1 Clem.* 57.3, as suggested in Green, 'Clement', p. 23.

Torah he does not have Moses' association with its origins. He is thus a convenient type-figure for that aspect of developed Jewish practice which Matthew wants to repudiate: not Torah as such, nor Moses as representative of it (although both are transcended in Jesus),[149] but the interpretations of the Pharisaic scribes and the heavy burdens they bind on people's backs.[150]

If, as suggested, 11.28-30 could originally have stood on its own, then the thought of Jesus as 'one greater than Solomon' (12.42) need have conveyed no more for it than his miracles of healing and his fresh approach to the requirements of the divine law. But Solomon, as son of David, has Messianic as well as sapiential significance;[151] and a special concern of this Gospel, developed from Mark, is to emphasize that the Messiah is Son of God.[152] This offers a motive for the expansion of the section, and indeed of the whole chapter, to make room for that dimension.

b. *Matthew 11.25-26*

1a   ἐξομολογοῦμαί σοι, πάτερ,
 b   κύριε τοῦ οὐρανοῦ καὶ τῆς γῆς,
2a   ὅτι ἔκρυψας ταῦτα ἀπὸ σοφῶν καὶ συνετῶν
 b   καὶ ἀπεκάλυψας αὐτὰ νηπίοις·
3a   ναὶ ὁ πατήρ, ὅτι οὕτως
 b   εὐδοκία ἐγένετο ἔμπροσθέν σου.

Sir. 51.1: ἐξομολογήσομαί σοι, κύριε βασιλεῦ, |καὶ αἰνέσω σε θεὸν τὸν σωτῆρά μου, |ἐξομολογοῦμαι τῷ ὀνόματί σου, |ὅτι...

Tob. 7.17: ὁ κύριος τοῦ οὐρανοῦ καὶ τῆς γῆς δῴη σοι χάριν...

Jdt. 9.12: δέσποτα τῶν οὐρανῶν καὶ τῆς γῆς,...

149. Cf. Allison, *New Moses*, pp. 232-33.

150. Stanton, *Gospel*, pp. 372-76, resists such a construction on the passage on the grounds of the tension involved between this verse and 5.20. But the pericopes which immediately follow the present context are an indication of the burdens that disciples of Jesus are to be spared (see further Chapter 7 §1a below), and Stanton only escapes the tension in this form to meet it in another, between the lightness of Jesus' burden here and the cost of discipleship (pp. 375-76). For further discussion of the question see Kynes, *Solidarity*, pp. 96-99.

151. See especially 2 Kgdms 7.12-16, and the parallel at 1 Chron. 17.11-14; also Ps. 71 (addressed to Solomon in the LXX title). Cf. on 12.18-21 (Chapter 3 §4 above).

152. See Kingsbury, *Structure*, pp. 40-127.

Dan. 4.17 LXX: ἕως ἂν γνῷ τὸν **κύριον τοῦ οὐρανοῦ** ἐξουσίαν ἔχειν πάντων τῶν ἐν τῷ **οὐρανῷ** καὶ τῶν ἐπὶ **τῆς γῆς**...

Hos. 14.10: τίς σοφὸς καὶ συνήσει **ταῦτα**; ἢ συνετὸς καὶ **ἐπιγνώσεται αὐτά**; διότι εὐθεῖαι αἱ ὁδοὶ τοῦ κυρίου, καὶ δίκαιοι πορεύσονται ἐν αὐταῖς, οἱ δὲ ἀσεβεῖς ἀσθενήσουσιν ἐν αὐταῖς.

Isa. 29.14: καὶ ἀπολῶ τὴν σοφίαν τῶν **σοφῶν** καὶ τὴν σύνεσιν τῶν **συνετῶν κρύψω**.

Dan. 2.21 LXX: καὶ αὐτὸς ἀλλοιοῖ καιροὺς καὶ χρόνους,...δίδους **σοφοῖς** σοφίαν καὶ **σύνεσιν** τοῖς ἐν ἐπιστήμῃ οὖσιν· (22) **ἀνακαλύπτων** [Thdt. **ἀποκαλύπτει**] τὰ βαθέα καὶ σκοτεινὰ [Thdt. ἀπόκρυφα]...(23) σοί, **κύριε** τῶν πατέρων μου, **ἐξομολογοῦμαι** καὶ αἰνῶ, ὅτι **σοφίαν** καὶ φρόνησιν ἔδωκάς μοι...

Sir. 3.19 (added in a later hand to LXXᴬ,[153] but corr. to Hebrew): πολλοὶ εἰσὶν ὑψηλοὶ καὶ ἐπίδοξοι, ἀλλὰ **πραέσιν ἀποκαλύπτει** τὰ μυστήρια αὐτοῦ.

Ps. 8.3: ἐκ στόματος **νηπίων** καὶ θηλαζόντων κατηρτίσω αἶνον. (cf. Mt. 21.16)

Ps. 18.8: ἡ μαρτυρία κυρίου πιστή, **σοφίζουσα νήπια**.

Ps. 118.130: ἡ δήλωσις τῶν λόγων σου φωτιεῖ |καὶ **συνετιεῖ νηπίους**

Wis. 10.21: ὅτι ἡ **σοφία** ἤνοιξεν στόμα κωφῶν |καὶ γλώσσας **νηπίων** ἔθηκεν τρανάς.

Sir. 1.27: **σοφία** γὰρ καὶ παιδεία φόβος κυρίου, |καὶ ἡ **εὐδοκία** αὐτοῦ πίστις καὶ **πραότης**.

The introduction of the Baptist's question at the beginning of this chapter (11.2) speaks of τὰ ἔργα τοῦ Χριστοῦ, a general designation for the miracles of chs. 8–9; these are the deeds by which wisdom is justified (11.19c), and it is to these that ταῦτα in 11.25 refers: it is their Messianic significance which has been hidden from the 'wise and prudent', that is, the *ḥᵃkāmîm*, the professional interpreters of the Torah. The latter's rejection of the fulfilment of prophetic testimony in Jesus (contrast 11.14-15) has disqualified them as exponents of the law, a matter not explicitly raised so far in the chapter, but possibly hinted at in the addition to 11.13, certainly alluded to in vv. 28-30, and immediately illustrated in 12.1-13.

---

153. See apparatus to A. Rahlfs, *Septuaginta* (Stuttgart: Württemburgische Bibelanstalt, 6th edn, 1952), II, p. 382.

Verses 25-26 are thus integral to their context in the present form of the chapter, and their own form and content do not encourage the conclusion that a previous composition from another source has been incorporated here. The verse composition is relatively loose, and the single rhyme, that of ἔκρυψας ταῦτα/ ἀπεκάλυψας αὐτὰ in 2ab (cf. Hos. 14.10), somewhat lame; it confirms however that the lines were composed in Greek and not translated,[154] and the enjambment of 3ab is characteristic of Matthew. The whole piece has been built up from borrowings from and allusions to Old Testament texts, clearly in their LXX form;[155] if it gives the impression of a pastiche rather than a carefully wrought composition, that is to be seen as evidence that it was created ad hoc in the course of writing, probably at the stage of the enlargement of the chapter. (See Appendix B.)

ἐξομολογεῖσθαι is too common an expression for praise in LXX[156] for a single text containing it to account conclusively for its presence here; but the fact that it occurs four times in Sir. 51.1-12, together with the model that the later verses of Sirach 51 have provided for vv. 28-30, means that the influence of that chapter on this passage is not to be excluded. If, as I have proposed, vv. 28-30 were composed first, a project for their expansion would naturally have begun by looking to the wider context of their model. The word, however, has influenced form rather than content; whereas Ben Sira (like Psalm 33) gives thanks for deliverance from death or danger, Jesus' thanksgiving here is concerned with the bestowal of wisdom on the simple (and childlike), contrasted with and at the expense of those traditionally or conventionally accounted wise. The content of this is drawn, in its negative aspect, from

---

154. Contra Bultmann, *Tradition*, p. 159; F. Hahn, *The Titles of Jesus in Christology* (trans. H. Knight and G. Ogg; London: Lutterworth, 1969), p. 309.

155. Of those cited above, Tob. 7.17 is noted also by Hoffmann, *Studien*, p. 110 n. 37, Gnilka, *Matthäusevangelium*, I, p. 434, and Luz, *Matthew*, II, p. 204; Dan. 2.21-23; Sir. 3.27; Ps. 18.8; 118.30 and Wis. 10.21 by H. Frankemölle, *Biblische Handlungserweisungen* (Mainz: Grünewald, 1983), p. 89, cf. pp. 91-93; the three latter and Isa. 29.14 also by E. Schweizer, *The Good News according to Matthew* (trans. D.E. Green; London: SPCK, 1976), p. 269.

156. On this word see R.J. Ledogar, *Acknowledgement: Praise-Verbs in the Early Greek Anaphoras* (Rome: Herder, 1968); O. Michel, 'ὁμολογέω, ἐξομολογέω κτλ.', *TDNT*, V, pp. 199-220; J.M. Robinson, 'Die Hodajot-Formel in Gebet und Hymnus des Frühchristentums', in W. Eltester and F.H. Kettler (eds.), *APOPHORETA* (Festschrift E. Haenchen; Berlin: Alfred Töpelmann, 1964), pp. 194-235 (226-28).

Isa. 29.14, and in its positive from Dan. 2.21-23, a thanksgiving for the
wisdom given to Daniel and enabling him to perceive God's revelation,
but withheld from the professional wise men.

The words cited from Tobit are the closest that LXX comes to the
parallel expression in 1b; those from Judith indicate how naturally they
could be used as a form of address.[157]

Of the remaining texts alluded to, the two from Sirach speak of the
aptness of the humble (πραεῖς) to receive revelation from God, and his
good pleasure (εὐδοκία) in bestowing it. Why then does Matthew not
use the former word here? The most likely answer is that he has already
used it of Jesus at 11.29,[158] and although disciples are indeed expected
to reproduce this attribute of their Master,[159] that is a consequence and
not a condition of the revelation that is spoken of here. He might perhaps have called them μικροί (cf. 10.42; 18.6-14), though the controversial overtones that this word seems to have had in his community[160]
could have been a dissuasive. νήπιοι recurs only once in the Gospel, in
the quotation of Ps. 8.3 at 21.16 (where the children seem to be symbolic of those who have accompanied Jesus' entry into Jerusalem[161]).
But the two remaining quotations from the Psalter in which it occurs
speak explicitly of God's power to impart σοφία and σύνεσις to whom
he will (cf. also Ps. 118.98-100[162]), and this is sufficient explanation of
his choice of word.

157. Contra Robinson, 'Hodajot', p. 227.

158. Assuming my theory of the order of composition. Even if this is not
accepted, Matthew as author (or indeed as mere redactor) would have been aware of
his intentions for vv. 28-30.

159. See 5.5. The Beatitudes (to anticipate my conclusions in Chapter 10) are
meant for a portrait of the Master as well as a pattern for the disciple; and at 11.29
he teaches by example as well as by precept.

160. On the evidence of 18.1-14 see the discussion at the conclusion of Chapter 7
§1d below.

161. The children's acclamation (21.15) takes up that of the crowds who accompanied Jesus' entry into Jerusalem (v. 9); cf. Duling, 'Therapeutic Son', pp. 404-
405. They are thus distinguished from those who speak for the city. The suggestion
of Howell, *Story*, p. 150, that the children stand for 'characters on the margin of
society' seems over-specific. The number of the disciples in Matthew certainly
includes such (note his identification of the tax-collector Levi [Mk 2.14] with 'Matthew', one of the twelve [9.9; 10.3]), but is not restricted to them, and the contrast is
more probably, as at 11.25-26, between the acquired learning of the (Pharisaic)
scribes and the unlettered but graced disciples. See next note.

162. In this text, though it does not contain the word νήπιος, the state of the

The revelation with which the whole chapter in its final form is concerned is the identification of Jesus as 'the one who should come',[163] the Messiah and Son of God. It is confirmed by his public acts and their conformity to the testimony of the prophetic scriptures. But the true revealer, without respect to the qualifications of those to whom he discloses the mystery, is God himself.

c. *Matthew 11.27*
We have recognized a formal and thematic continuity between vv. 25-26 and vv. 28-30, conveyed by their common model in Sirach 51 and by the hostility of both to the dominant Pharisaic tradition. But there remains also a discontinuity between the two passages as they stand: the former speaks of revelation by the Father to the νήπιοι, the latter of receiving instruction from Jesus as the true interpreter of Torah, that is of the Father's will. Between these two thoughts a transition is called for, and the purpose of v. 27 is to supply it.[164] It can therefore only be understood in context; it is the method of abstracting it from the latter on form-critical grounds and then interpreting it against a presumed

recipients of the revelation of 11.25-26 is strikingly prefigured. The speaker claims more wisdom than his adversaries, more understanding than his teachers and his elders. (Compare the use to which the same text is put, *pace* almost all commentators, in Lk. 2.40-51. Luke, characteristically, conveys his insight in a narrative, Matthew in a poem.)

163. On this expression see Hahn, *Titles*, pp. 352-406.

164. Schulz, *Q*, p. 215, and Hoffmann, *Studien*, p. 109 (cf. pp. 122-23), have already shown that the content of v. 27 is by no means unrelated to that of vv. 25-26: πάντα...πατρός μου corresponds to the address πάτερ, κύριε...γῆς; οὐδεὶς ἐπιγινώσκει to ἔκρυψας (cf. also Hos. 14.10, cited above); ᾧ ἐὰν βούληται to εὐδοκία; and ἀποκαλύπτειν is common to both. Kloppenborg, *Formation*, p. 198, concludes from this that 11.27 is 'an interpretive addition' to 11.25-26. Luz, *Matthew*, II, p. 200, notes that πάντα presupposes something to be understood on the basis of vv. 25-26; these verses express the matter from the Father's standpoint (hence they are framed as a thanksgiving); v. 27 from the Son's. All that is missing in this analysis is that the content of the revelation is spelled out in vv. 28-30. Davies and Allison, *Matthew*, II, pp. 283-87, argue for influence of Exod. 33.12-13 on v. 27, with καταπαύσω in 33.12 as catchword connection with ἀναπαύσω in vv. 28-30. While this is quite possible, the difficulty about it as a clue to the meaning of v. 27 is the lack of clear verbal reminiscence in the latter.

previous *Sitz im Leben*, whether 'gnostic'[165] or 'Jewish',[166] that has produced an exegetical impasse.

1 πάντα μοι παρεδόθη ὑπὸ τοῦ πατρός μου,
2 καὶ οὐδεὶς ἐπιγινώσκει τὸν υἱὸν εἰ μὴ ὁ πατὴρ,
3 οὐδέ τὸν πατέρα τις ἐπιγινώσκει εἰ μὴ ὁ υἱός,
4 καὶ ᾧ ἐὰν βούληται ὁ υἱὸς ἀποκαλύψαι.

Ruth 2.10: Τί ὅτι εὗρον χάριν ἐν ὀφθαλμοῖς σου τοῦ **ἐπιγνῶναι** με;

Sir. 44.23: εὐλογίαν πάντων ἀνθρώπων καὶ διαθήκην |κατεπαυσεν ἐπὶ κεφαλὴν Ιακώβ· |**ἐπέγνω** αὐτὸν ἐν εὐλογίαις αὐτοῦ |καὶ ἔδωκεν αὐτῷ ἐν κληρονομία·

Mt. 7.16, 20: ἀπὸ τῶν καρπῶν αὐτῶν **ἐπιγνώσεσθε** αὐτούς.

Mt. 17.12: Ἡλιάς ἤδη ἦλθεν, καὶ οὐκ **ἐπέγνωσαν** αὐτὸν...

Hos. 2.21: μνηστεύσομαί σε ἐμαυτῷ ἐν δικαιοσύνῃ...καὶ ἐν ἐλέει... (22) ...καὶ **ἐπιγνώσῃ** τὸν κύριον.

Hos. 4.1: διότι οὐκ ἐστιν ἀλήθεια οὐδὲ ἔλεος οὐδὲ **ἐπίγνωσις** θεοῦ ἐπὶ τῆς γῆς;

Hos. 6.6: διότι ἔλεος θέλω καὶ οὐ θυσίαν, καὶ **ἐπίγνωσιν** θεοῦ ἢ ὁλοκαυτώματα.

Mk 13.32: περὶ δὲ τῆς ἡμέρας ἐκείνης ἢ τῆς ὥρας οὐδεὶς οἶδεν, οὐδὲ οἱ ἄγγελοι ἐν οὐρανῷ, **οὐδὲ ὁ υἱός, εἰ μὴ ὁ πατήρ**.

Mt. 3.17: καὶ ἰδοὺ φωνὴ ἐκ τῶν οὐρανῶν λέγουσα· οὗτός ἐστιν **ὁ υἱός** μου ὁ ἀγαπητός, ἐν ᾧ εὐδόκησα.

The four lines are in 4-stress rhythm, and there is chiastic correspondence of the word count of the lines (7-9-9-7), as well as π-alliteration of the three significant words in line 1. But despite these formal characteristics they do not, at a first reading, have much of a poetic ring about them. They look more like an argument put in verse form for the sake of its context, but not in itself poetic. Old Testament allusion appears to be limited to the single word ἐπιγινώσκει. Yet, ironically, it is to the possibilities of double meaning in this word that we have finally to look for elucidation of the text.

---

165. Norden and Dibelius, Bousset, Weiss and Bultmann were in agreement on this point, across the divide of their divergent views on the source criticism.
166. Schniewind, *Matthäus*, pp. 150-53, Hahn, *Titles*, pp. 309-17, W.D. Davies, *Christian Origins and Judaism* (London: Darton, Longman & Todd, 1962), pp. 119-44, Hoffmann, 'Offenbarung', and *Studien*, pp. 122-42, all fall in various ways under this heading.

The prevailing consensus is that there is no semantic distinction in the Greek Bible between this word and the uncompounded γινώσ-κειν;[167] and this is broadly true in passages where they translate the Hebrew *yāda'*,[168] as is mostly the case with the latter throughout the LXX, and with the former in the prophetic books (only five exceptions). Elsewhere in the LXX, however, ἐπιγινώσκειν represents a number of other words, and in particular *nākar*,[169] which often means to 'recognize', in the sense of being able to identify (cf., e.g., Gen. 42.7). It is used thus in Ruth 2.10, but with the further nuance of something gratuitously bestowed on the object of recognition. Its importance for our present purpose is that Matthew's entire usage outside the present context (which includes 14.25 in addition to the two texts quoted above) falls under this head.[170] 17.12 (which is MtR of Mk 9.13) is particularly apposite here, since it speaks of failure to recognize a person with a significant part in the divine purpose for what he is.

yāda' is used by the classical prophets, especially Hosea, for the mutual knowledge of God and his people; this, as Eichrodt has written, 'does not denote the contemplative knowledge of the wise, but a perceiving which at the same time always includes an interior relation to the one known. In the case of Man's knowledge of God this is a relation of surrender and obedience, in that of God's knowledge of Man one of care and election.'[171] It is thus less a matter of notional understanding than of love. The ethical implications are plain enough. These are conveyed also by the cognate ἐπίγνωσις, as in the two texts cited from Hosea above.[172] There is no question that this emphasis was carried over into early Christianity.[173]

---

167. See R. Bultmann, 'γινώσκω, ἐπιγινώσκω κτλ.', *TDNT*, I, pp. 689-719 (703-704).

168. *TDNT*, I, pp. 696-701.

169. It is strange not to find this word even mentioned in Bultmann's survey.

170. By contrast, it is found in Mark (of personal recognition) only in the parallel to Mt. 14.25 at 6.54; in Luke only in the Emmaus story at 24.16, 32, and four times in the early chapters of Acts. The distinctiveness of Matthew's usage is noted also by Deutsch, *Wisdom*, pp. 35-36, and found theologically significant.

171. W. Eichrodt, *Theology of the Old Testament* (trans. J.A. Baker; London: SCM Press, 1957), II, p. 292.

172. Note that the first part of Hos. 6.6 is quoted in the sequel to this discourse at 12.7.

173. Cf., e.g., Col. 1.9-10, and see Bultmann, 'γινώσκω', I, pp. 707-708.

The use of 'Father' and 'Son' absolutely was known to Matthew from Mk 13.32,[174] a context to which the thought of revelation is central, but expressed negatively: the day and the hour of the parousia are not known to the Son because the Father has not revealed them to him; that is, they are not revealed at all. Matthew would seem to concur on that point, since he leaves it unaltered in his own version at 24.30. But he evidently finds no inconsistency between this and the words attributed to Jesus here: πάντα μοι παρεδόθη ὑπὸ τοῦ πατρός μου. The parallel between this and 28.18 has been noted often enough;[175] but my approach to the history of the composition of 11.25-30 may suggest a new angle on it. The true formal correspondence is between 11.28-30 and 28.18-20; these, as will be shown,[176] are companion pieces, verse compositions of four distichs apiece in the same metre. This by itself will not suffice to explain the correspondence in content between 28.18 and 11.27a if the latter text is studied in isolation. Either 28.18 draws on the content of the complete composition 11.25-30, or 11.28-30 and 28.18-20 were composed first and 11.27a is 'throwback'[177] from the latter. The suggestion of an earlier draft of ch. 11 enhances the plausibility of the second alternative. Not total throwback, however: the full authority (πᾶσα ἐξουσία) in *heaven and* earth which Jesus claims at 28.18 and in virtue of which he will judge the world at the eschaton is the consequence of his death and exaltation;[178] hitherto he has had

174. If Mk 13.32 rests on earlier tradition, the specification of Father and Son is probably MkR of it; cf. R. Pesch, *Naherwartung* (Dusseldorf: Patmos, 1968), pp. 190-98.

175. E.g. Bultmann, *Tradition*, p. 160; Schniewind, *Matthäus*, p. 150; Hahn, *Titles*, pp. 310, 312; Betz, 'Logion', p. 24; J. Lange, *Das Erscheinen der Auferstandenen* (FB, 12; Würzburg: Echter, 1973), pp. 488-506; J.D. Kingsbury, 'The Composition and Christology of Matt 28.16-20', *JBL* 93 (1974), pp. 573-84 (581-82); E. Schweizer, 'υἱός', D, *TDNT*, VIII, pp. 363-92 (374 n. 277); Hoffmann, *Studien*, pp. 140-41. For the debate over the significance of πάντα in 11.27 see further Hoffmann, 'Offenbarung', pp. 272-74.

176. See below, §10b.

177. An expression coined by this author in 'Matthew 12.22-50', p. 160, to refer to passages in which Matthew anticipates a (usually) fuller version later on in the Gospel: e.g. 9.27-31 (cf. 20.29-34); 9.32-34 (cf. 12.22-24). See H.J. Held, 'Matthew as Interpreter of the Miracle Stories', in Bornkamm, Barth and Held, *Tradition*, pp. 165-299 (223-26); and for another angle on it, Howell, *Story*, pp. 100-106.

178. Cf. the future tense at 12.21 (see Chapter 3 §4 above). Commentators who seek to establish links between 11.27 and 28.18 in the tradition behind the Gospel

authority only on earth,[179] to exorcize and heal (12.22-30, anticipated throughout chs. 8–9), to forgive sins (9.6),[180] and to deliver the definitive Messianic exposition of Torah (7.29).[181] These functions are to be continued on earth after his exaltation by his disciples in dependence on him (10.8; 16.19; 18.18; 28.20). On this view the revelation with which the present passage is concerned is not, except in a very general sense, eschatological revelation;[182] for the earthly Jesus, as for his disciples, to know the Father is not to be privy to the details (or the timing; cf. 24.30) of the last things, but to understand his will.

The relationship spoken of at Mk 13.32 is clearly a quite asymmetrical one, with heavy emphasis on the subordination of the Son. Matthew has moved towards a more mutual relationship; the question is how far. It is not necessary that all thought of subordination should be eliminated before it can be called fully reciprocal (this is clearly not the case even in John; cf. Jn 14.28), nor that such a relationship should be defined in terms of mutual knowledge (Jn 10.15 is unparalleled even in John, and the analogy offered there does not call for a very high intensiveness in the knowledge).[183] For it to be defined thus requires that the force of 'know' shall be the same in both directions, as in John 10.15 and 1 Cor. 13.12. Since this is hardly possible on the basis of Hebrew usage,[184] we are left with two clear options: either to insist that the par-

---

before examining their relationship within it are commonly in danger of ignoring the development of its plot.

179. Both the Sermon on the Mount and the miracles section have been developed (not to say 'exploded') out of the two references to ἐξουσία in Mk 1.22, 27. Mt. 12.22-30 is Matthew's version of the final Jewish challenge to that authority.

180. On 9.6 see Strecker, *Weg*, pp. 220-21.

181. See Davies, *Setting*, especially pp. 173-80, 446-50.

182. *Contra* Davies, *Origins*, pp. 142-43.

183. Bultmann, 'γινώσκω', I, pp. 711-13, emphasizes that while the mutual relationship of Father and Son in John has its cognitive aspect, fundamentally it rests on love rather than knowledge. Cf. Eichrodt's account of *yāda'* in the Old Testament (*Theology*, II, p. 292).

184. See previous note. In general it may be said that the more reciprocal the relationship, the less its cognitive aspect is stressed; and, conversely, that the more explicitly it is defined in cognitive terms, the less fully reciprocal it is found to be. It is not possible for humankind within the confines of earthly life (to which the traditional Hebrew perspective was restricted) to have the kind of knowledge of God that God himself has of the individual person (Ps. 138), of a 'chosen vessel' (Exod. 33.12, 17; Jer. 1.5) or of the chosen people (Amos 3.2). The reply to Moses'

allelism of the two inner lines must convey a fully reciprocal relationship, and so, abandoning all Hebraic connections, to conclude that its conceptual roots are Hellenistic and probably, in some sense, 'gnostic';[185] or to let go of full reciprocity and to construe ἐπιγινώσκει with reference to two related but not identical kinds of knowledge; i.e., to treat it as intentionally equivocal. This has been previously attempted on the assumption that the Hebrew *yāda'* underlies both uses of the word:[186] a necessary move so long as an early origin and thus a non-Greek original had to be postulated for the logion. If however we think in terms of Matthaean formulation (and the Evangelist's liking for double meanings encourages this, as well as unsatisfactory details in the 'Hebraic' analysis[187]), the starting point becomes the Greek word which offers a larger range of alternative connotations. I therefore propose to

request at Exod. 33.18 says it all. The mutual knowledge looked for in 1 Cor. 13.12 implies eschatological fulfilment (its counterpart in Matthew is 5.8; see Chapter 7 §4b below); that in Jn 10.15 presupposes pre-existence of the Son (to which Matthew, for all the attempts to foist a Wisdom Christology on him, has not yet found his way). Hoffmann's attempted way out of the dilemma by concentrating on the present (post-Easter) Son of man and investing him with a combination of attributes of the Old Testament Wisdom and apocalyptic revelation figures (*Studien*, pp. 131-42; 'Offenbarung', pp. 277-88) is too conjectural to carry much conviction, especially with those for whom the Q community, like Q itself, never existed.

185. That the wording is exposed to this line of interpretation is not to be disputed; but the very fact that the variant versions witnessed to by some Fathers and favoured by, e.g., Harnack, *Sayings*, pp. 282-95; Weiss, 'Das Logion', p. 126; Bultmann, *Tradition*, p. 159; T.W. Manson, *The Sayings of Jesus* (London: SCM Press, 1949), p. 80; and P. Winter, 'Matthew 11.27 and Luke 10.22 from the First to the Fifth Century: Reflections on the Development of the Text', *NovT* 1 (1956), pp. 112-48, by omitting or displacing the line about the Father's knowledge of the Son, bring it closer to a Gnostic position (so Hoffmann, 'Offenbarung', p. 276) suggests that it was otherwise with the original.

186. Originally by J. Schniewind, 'Zur Synoptischer-Exegeser', *TRu* NS 2 (1930) pp. 169-71; cf. his *Matthäus*, pp. 151-53; Hahn, *Titles*, p. 309; Schweizer, 'υἱός', p. 373. It understands ἐπιγινώσκει in line 2 of the Father's *choosing* of the Son, and in line 3 of the Son's *acknowledgment* of the Father. On this interpretation line 2 is a truism (who else would choose him?), and line 3 an insufficient ground for the revelation spoken of in line 4, which clearly has a cognitive aspect. See the criticisms of Hoffmann, 'Offenbarung', p. 277; Luz, *Matthew*, II, p. 212.

187. In addition to the above, the Father's choice of the Son would strictly require a past tense (for which there is no good textual evidence in either Gospel) while the ongoing relationship between them demands the present.

take ἐπιγινώσκειν as equivalent to *yāda'* where the object is the Father, and to *nākar* where it is the Son:

> Line 2: Only the Father knows to whom he has committed this relationship to himself, and only he can disclose this knowledge to humankind. This he has done, first, at the baptism of Jesus (3.17, where, in distinction from Mark, the words identifying Jesus as the Son are addressed not to him but to the bystanders;[188] the Sonship itself has been his from birth[189]), and then in the acts for which Messianic significance has been claimed at 11.2, 5-6, 19c, 25.[190] (It is the chief recipient of the revelation at 3.17, John the Baptist, whose appeal for reassurance has been the starting point of the whole chapter.)

> Lines 3-4: If only the Father can know and reveal the identity of the Son (*who* he is),[191] only the Son in his turn can know the true character of the Father (*what* he is),[192] and only he can reveal this understanding of him to others—which in this Gospel he has been doing in the Lord's Prayer and throughout the Sermon on the Mount (see 5.16, 45, 48; 6.1-18 *passim*, 26, 32-33; 7.9-11, 21). To know the Father is preeminently to know what he requires of men and women;[193] hence the emphasis on fulfilling his will (see 7.21; 12.46-50;[194] also 5.16, 48; 6.33). The yoke of Christ that is offered in vv. 28-30 is Jesus' instruction on how this is to be done.

In the light of this exegesis it is now possible to recognize in these lines the poetic device known as anaphora: 'the rhetorically emphatic reiteration of a single word or brief phrase, in itself not a syntactically complete unit'. Robert Alter, from whom that definition is taken,[195] goes on to say that it

> shifts the attention from the repeated element to the material that is introduced by the repetition, at once inviting us to see all the new utterances as locked into the same structure of assertion and to look for strong differences or elements of development in the new material. There is, in other words, a productive tension between sameness and difference, reiteration and development, in the use of anaphora.

---

188. See Chapter 3 §4 above on 12.18-21.

189. 1.18-23; 2.15.

190. See §§ 3, 5 and 7b above.

191. Cf. 16.17.

192. This distinction (ironed out in the Lukan version) is a further argument against the claims of the 'shorter' text-form (n. 185 above).

193. See the texts from Hosea, above and nn. 171, 172; cf. Mic. 6.8 (echoed in 23.23).

194. For the relevance of this passage see Deutsch, *Wisdom*, pp. 37, 132, 138.

195. *Poetry*, p. 62.

On this account, the new element in line 2 is the Father's knowledge of the Son, in line 3 the Son's knowledge of the Father (which is thus not simply the counterpart of what is said in line 2; this would tend to confirm that ἐπιγινώσκει is not used univocally), and in line 4 the Son's revelation of what he knows to others. We are in the presence of poetry after all.[196]

My tentative conclusion, therefore, is that of the three unequal pieces that make up 11.25-30, the third (vv. 28-30), which is a more studied construction than the others, was composed first, but originally for a less developed version of the discourse which it concludes; its handling of the theme of wisdom did not explicitly include the Father's revelation of Jesus' Sonship, nor the withholding of this from the teachers of the old Israel and its delivery to the disciples. These are the emphases added by vv. 25-26, which belongs to and arises out of its context in the present form of ch. 11 (though later separated from it by Luke[197]), and there is a certain improvised quality about its verse form. This is also true of v. 27, which has been composed as a bridge between vv. 25-26 (revelation by the Father) and vv. 28-30 (instruction by the Son).

The implications of this for the composition history of ch. 11 as a whole are examined in Appendix B.

The theme of Sonship is continued and developed in the passage to be considered next, which shares also something of the improvised quality of the verse of 11.25-27.

8. *Matthew 16.17-19*[198]

This is the promise to Peter which Matthew has inserted into the Markan context of the latter's confession of Jesus' Messiahship. The

196. A different analysis based on an *inclusio* is proposed by van Iersel, *'Der Sohn'*, pp. 150-51.

197. See Goulder, *Luke*, pp. 479-80.

198. The literature is vast. For general documentation see R. Pesch, 'The Position and Significance of Peter in the New Testament', *Concilium* 4.7 (1971), pp. 21-35 (23 n. 5); Davies and Allison, *Matthew*, II, pp. 642-47; Luz, *Matthew*, II, pp. 450-52. For important critical overviews: P. Hoffmann, 'Der Petrus-Primat im Matthäusevangelium', in J. Gnilka (ed.), *Neues Testament und Kirche* (Festschrift R. Schnackenburg; Freiburg: Herder & Herder, 1974), pp. 94-114; C. Kähler, 'Zur Form- und Traditionsgeschichte von Matth. XVI.17-19', *NTS* 23 (1977), pp. 36-58; J.D. Kingsbury, 'The Figure of Peter in Matthew's Gospel as a Theological Problem', *JBL* 98 (1979), pp. 67-83; U. Luz, 'Das Primatwort Matthäus 16.17-19

material added has often been thought to have been derived from independent floating tradition,[199] but in fact it carries marks both of his own
poetic style and of his exegetical methods. It is also closely related to
its context in the narrative, and particularly to redactional alterations
and additions which Matthew has made to Mark: notably the prefigurations of a Gentile mission in ch. 15,[200] the repetition of the sign of
Jonah saying (16.4) without the interpretation that follows its earlier
appearance at 12.40,[201] and the severe warning against the teaching of
the Pharisees and Sadducees which follows in 16.5-12. All this suggests
that it was composed *currente calamo* for its present context, like
11.25-27, not fitted into one of which it had originally been independent.[202] The unpolished quality of the verse (in marked contrast with the
complexity and intensity of the poetic imagery) bears this out. It falls
into three tristichs, (a) in 3-stress rhythm,[203] (b) and (c) in 4-stress, 'so

als wirkungsgeschichtlicher Sicht', *NTS* 37 (1991), pp. 415-33. For Old Testament
and linguistic background: J. Jeremias, 'ᾅδης', *TDNT*, I, pp. 146-49; 'Ἰωνᾶς',
TDNT, III, pp. 406-10; 'κλείς', *TDNT*, III, pp. 744-53; 'λίθος', *TDNT*, IV, pp. 265-
80; 'πύλη', *TDNT*, VI, pp. 921-28; O. Cullmann, 'πέτρα, Πέτρος, Κηφᾶς', *TDNT*,
VI, pp. 95-112; O. Michel, 'οἶκος κτλ.', *TDNT*, V, pp. 119-59; K.L. Schmidt,
'ἐκκλησία', *TDNT*, III, pp. 501-36 (518-20); F. Büchsel, 'δέω', TDNT, II, pp. 60-
61; H. Traub, 'οὐρανός', *TDNT*, V, pp. 509-36 (518-20); J.A. Emerton, 'Binding
and Loosing: Forgiving and Retaining', *JTS* NS 13 (1963), pp. 325-31; J. Kahmann,
'Die Verheissung an Petrus', in Didier (ed.), *L'Evangile*, pp. 261-80; G. Vermes,
'The Targumic Versions of Genesis IV 3-16', in *Post-Biblical Jewish Studies*
(Leiden: E.J. Brill, 1975), pp. 92-128; M. Wilcox, 'Peter and the Rock: A Fresh
Look at Matt 16.17-19', *NTS* 22 (1975–76), pp. 75-88; P. Lampe, 'Das Spiel mit
dem Petrus-Namen—Matt 16.18', *NTS* 25 (1979), pp. 227-45; J.A. Fitzmyer, 'Ara-
maic *Kepha* and Peter's Name in the New Testament', in *To Advance the Gospel*
(New York: Crossroad, 1981), pp. 114-24; C. Caragounis, *Peter and the Rock*
(BZNW, 58; Berlin: de Gruyter, 1990); Kynes, *Solidarity*, pp. 101-17.

199. This is more or less assumed by R.E. Brown, K.P. Donfried and J. Reumann, *Peter in the New Testament* (Minneapolis: Augsburg; New York: Paulist
Press, 1963), pp. 96-101.

200. A motif already present in Mark. For the Gentile orientation of Mt. 15.29-31
see n. 73 above. On the preparation of the context in general cf. Meier, *Vision*, pp.
100-106.

201. See §4a, below.

202. Hoffmann, 'Petrus-Primat', p. 105, allows the possibility of composition by
the Evangelist from Old Testament and early Christian materials; so also Gundry,
Matthew, p. 330.

203. 1a and c are clearly 3-stress; b can be read thus if σὰρξ καὶ αἷμα is taken as
a single unit (see Chapter 2 above), and the pronoun σοι (or the negative οὐ) as

constructed that in each a theme is elucidated by antithetical parallelism'.[204]

1a μακάριος εἶ, Σίμων Βαριωνᾶ,
 b ὅτι σὰρξ καὶ αἷμα οὐκ ἀπεκάλυψέν σοι,
 c ἀλλ᾽ ὁ πατήρ μου ὁ ἐν τοῖς οὐρανοῖς.
2a κἀγὼ δέ σοι λέγω ὅτι σὺ εἶ Πέτρος,
 b καὶ ἐπὶ ταύτῃ τῇ πέτρᾳ οἰκοδομήσω μου τὴν ἐκκλησίαν
 c καὶ πύλαι ᾅδου οὐ κατισχύσουσιν αὐτῆς.
3a δώσω σοι τὰς κλεῖδας τῆς βασιλείας τῶν οὐρανῶν.
 b καὶ ὃ ἐὰν δήσῃς ἐπι τῆς γῆς ἔσται δεδεμένον ἐν τοῖς οὐρανοῖς,
 c καὶ ὃ ἐὰν λύσῃς ἐπὶ τῆς γῆς ἔσται λελυμένον ἐν τοῖς οὐρανοῖς.

Isa. 28.15: Ὅτι εἴπατε Ἐποιήσαμεν διαθήκην μετὰ τοῦ **ᾅδου** καὶ μετὰ τοῦ θανάτου συνθήκας... (16) διὰ τοῦτο οὕτως λέγει κύριος Ἰδοὺ ἐγὼ ἐμβαλῶ εἰς τὰ θεμέλια Σιὼν **λίθον** πολυτελῆ ἐκλεκτὸν ἀκρογωνιαῖον ἔντιμον...καὶ ὁ πιστεύων ἐπ᾽ αὐτῷ οὐ μὴ καταισχυνθῇ.

Zech. 6.12: Ἰδοὺ ἀνήρ, Ἀνατολὴ ὄνομα αὐτῷ, καὶ ὑποκάτωθεν αὐτοῦ ἀνατελεῖ, καὶ **οἰκοδομήσει** τὸν οἶκον κυρίου.

Gen. 28.17: οὐκ ἔστιν τοῦτο ἀλλ᾽ ἢ οἶκος θεοῦ, καὶ αὕτη ἡ **πύλη** τοῦ **οὐρανοῦ**...(22) καὶ ὁ **λίθος** οὗτος, ὃν ἔστησα στήλην, ἔσται μοι οἶκος θεοῦ...

Ps. 117.19: ἀνοίξατέ μοι **πύλας** δικαιοσύνης...|(20) αὕτη ἡ **πύλη** τοῦ κυρίου, |δίκαιοι εἰσελεύσονται ἐν αὐτῇ.

Isa. 22.22 (Hebrew): And on his shoulder I will place the *key* of the house of David; he shall open and none shall shut, and he shall shut and none shall open.[205]

Targ. Neofiti on Gen. 4.7: If you perform your deeds well in this world |it shall be *loosed* and forgiven you in the world to come. |But if you do not perform your deeds well in this world |your sin shall be retained for the day of the great Judgment.[206]

The debate continues over the question whether the primary emphasis

unemphatic. But there is no need to presume a rigid uniformity here.

204. Jeremias, 'κλείς', p. 751 (cf. p. 749); 'πύλη', p. 927.

205. The LXX, according to the best attested text, omits these words. The MS tradition is in great confusion here (cf. Ziegler, *Isaias*, pp. 199-200) and the fact that later translators like Theodotion restored an equivalent to the Hebrew suggests that the pressure to do so was not confined to Christian circles.

206. See Vermes, *Studies*, p. 95. Targum Yerushalmi (Geniza Fragment) and the Second Jerusalem Targum have a text virtually identical with Neofiti; Onkelos and Ps.-Jonathan lack the word 'loose' and the reference to judgment.

of this text is christological or ecclesiological.[207] They are not, of course, mutually exclusive; but whereas a definitive christological statement is already in place at 11.25-30, the new ground broken in the present passage concerns the relationship between Jesus revealed as Son of God and those who receive the revelation.

The starting point of the whole poem is Peter's answer to the question of Jesus in 16.16. The expression ὁ υἱὸς τοῦ θεοῦτοῦ ζῶντος carries a clear reference to Hos. 2.1 LXX: 'And in the place in which it was said to them, You are not my people, ἐκεῖ κληθήσονται υἱοὶ θεοῦ ζῶντος',[208] and may be said positively to invite a reply which takes account of the plural υἱοὶ by associating others with that sonship. The three stanzas progressively build this up, and in the course of doing so avail themselves of no less than three plays on words.

a. *'Sign of Jonah' and 'Simon Barjonah'*
Strophe 1, which refers back to 11.25 (revelation of the Son's identity by the Father), cites no Old Testament text directly, but the address Σίμων Βαριωνᾶ shows signs of a play on σημεῖον Ἰωνᾶ at 16.4.[209] I have argued elsewhere[210] that while the sign of Jonah in both 12.40 and 16.4 is essentially a sign of contradiction, a negative sign both directed at and incomprehensible (because unacceptable) to unbelievers, its content varies according to the stages of the unfolding of the gospel story. At 12.40, where the context is concerned with the rejection of Jesus' own mission (the Beelzebul slander), it speaks of the *absence* of Jesus from the sight of those who thought they had seen the last of him when they rejected him; in 16.4 (where the reference to the whale is omitted) it speaks rather of his continued *presence* in the Church of his disciples, located now, like Jonah's preaching at Nineveh, in the lands of the Gentiles, and thus still unrecognizable for what it is to those who

207. For the former position cf. Kingsbury, *Structure*, p. 36; Bauer, *Structure*, pp. 143-45; Caragounis, *Peter*, especially pp. 110-13. Meier, *Vision*, p. 106, rightly declines to regard them as alternatives.

208. For the influence of this text on Beatitude VII (5.9) and its reflection at 5.45, see Chapter 7 §2d below. See also on 17.24-27, §8b and n. 214 below.

209. Orignally proposed by H.M. Gale, 'A Suggestion Concerning Matthew 16', *JBL* 60 (1941–42), pp. 255-60; cf. S. van Tilborg, *The Jewish Leaders in Matthew* (Leiden: E.J. Brill, 1972), p. 35. See also Gundry, *Matthew*, p. 332, though I cannot follow him in detail.

210. 'Matthew 12.22-50', pp. 168-70.

demand the sign. The paranomasia on Peter's patronymic indicates that he is the representative figure for this Church, not in himself as an individual, nor as typifying the individual disciple, but as standing for the whole body of those who have followed him in confessing the Sonship of Jesus.[211]

b. *Son and Stone*

Peter at 16.16 has acknowledged Jesus not only as Christ but as Son; Jesus' reply turns on the meaning of the name previously bestowed on him,[212] 'stone'. It is not fanciful to see in this an instance of the familiar Jewish pun between *bēn* (son) and *'eben* (stone).[213] The image serves to convey that extension of sonship to God which Paul expresses by the metaphor of adoption (Rom. 8.15; Gal. 4.6), and the Johannine tradition by that of rebirth (Jn 1.12; 3.3-5; 1 Jn 2.28; 5.1). But whereas those figures can accommodate a plurality of adopted or regenerate sons, the one-to-one matching of 'son' and 'stone' calls rather for the notion of an extended sonship to be conveyed by an inclusive singular. The meaning is reflected in the little chreia of the temple tax at 17.24-27,[214]

211. Hoffmann, 'Petrus-Primat', pp. 107-108, comes to a similar conclusion, if not by this route. Kingsbury, 'Peter', p. 72, and Luz, *Matthew*, II, p. 406 (cf. 'Primatwort', p. 422) also recognize that the text sees Peter as representative of the rest of the disciples, but understand this in too individualistic a way. What Peter represents is what all the disciples are corporately rather than what each is individually; see below, §8e.

212. Though Matthew omits the calling-with-naming of the Twelve at Mk 3.14-16, he has transferred the list to 10.2-4; the narrative of the call of the first disciples at 4.18 speaks of Σίμωνα τὸν λεγόμενον Πέτρον, and thereafter the implied narrator uses his sobriquet throughout (Σίμων without it is used only by Jesus to address Peter, and then only at 16.17, with patronymic, and 17.25). It is thus unlikely that Matthew intended the present passage to represent the actual bestowal of the name (contra Schweizer, *Matthew*, p. 341), though it clearly is the fruit of long reflection on its meaning.

213. So, rightly, Wilcox, 'Rock', pp. 84-85. For the history of the pun see M. Black, 'The Christological Use of the Old Testament in the New Testament', *NTS* 18 (1971–72), pp. 1-14; P. Carrington, *According to Mark* (Cambridge: Cambridge University Press, 1960), pp. 256-59.

214. Bacon, *Studies*, pp. 222-30, bracketed 17.24-27 with 14.28-33 and 16.16b-19 as the three 'Petrine supplements' inserted by Matthew into material received from Mark. All three speak of sonship to God, with progressive involvement of the disciple. Cf. Kahmann, 'Verheissung', pp. 270-72; P.F. Ellis, *Matthew: His Mind and his Message* (Collegeville, MN: Liturgical Press, 1974), pp. 64-66; P. Rolland,

where the basic question concerns Jesus' own exemption as a 'son', but Peter (presumably in his representative capacity) is finally associated with him in the *ex gratia* payment which follows, 'for me and you'.

The fact that *'eben* is almost invariably rendered by λίθος in the LXX is no objection to the part here suggested for it in the thinking behind this text; poetry, and Hebrew poetry in particular, depends on the ready availability of synonyms. Both Hebrew word and Greek equivalent are used respectively in the MT and LXX of Isa. 28.16, the principal background text, as we shall see,[215] for the present passage. While however the pun suggested here, like that on Peter's patronymic, is only implicit, the third, between 'rock' and 'stone', is explicit and generally recognized, if not universally understood.

c. *Rock and Stone*

The basic meaning of πέτρα is 'rock'; that of πέτρος 'stone'.[216] While πέτρα is found in parallelism with λίθος at Isa. 8.16,[217] the context here requires its basic meaning; and while Πέτρος entered the tradition as the translation of the Aramaic *kēpha*[218] (which can be used in both senses, though 'rock' is relatively rare and apparently not the original one[219]) the Greek equivalent chosen for it cannot carry the same range of meaning. It does not follow from this that no word-play is possible between the two, or that the 'imperfect' play in the Greek points to an unambiguous Aramaic original.[220] Punning requires no more than ap-

---

'From the Genesis to the End of the World: The Plan of Matthew's Gospel', *BTB* 2 (1972), pp. 135-76 (too lightly brushed aside by Bauer, *Structure*, p. 43); Green, *Matthew*, p. 158; Meier, *Vision*, p. 126 n. 131.

215. See §8d, below.

216. See LSJ, s. vv.

217. The reference of both words in that text is to a boulder that one can trip over, not to a quarried stone. It is thus relevant to the σκάνδαλον of 16.23, but not at this point.

218. Caragounis, *Peter*, pp. 20-25, maintains, against previous consensus (cf. Lampe, 'Spiel', p. 228; Fitzmyer, 'Aramaic Kepha', p. 119) that it was already in use as a proper name in pre-Christian times. If so, it would have been ready to hand for use in the second generation of Greek-speaking Christianity (already in Mark; contrast Pauline usage). It is nevertheless as the equivalent of the Aramaic *Kepha* that it enters the tradition (cf. Jn 1.42). But this does not justify treating it as, in effect, the adjectival form of πέτρα ('The Rock-man').

219. See Lampe, 'Spiel', pp. 231-39.

220. Caragounis, *Peter*, pp. 45-57; contra O. Cullmann, *Peter: Disciple, Apostle,*

proximation in sound, and by definition rules out semantic identity.

The image of building is developed differently here from what we find in the Pauline tradition.[221] The latter nowhere speaks of the bedrock foundation, only of a foundation stone or stones laid upon it, whether Christ himself (1 Cor. 3.11; 1 Pet. 2.4) or of apostles and prophets with him (Eph. 2.20).[222] Paul speaks of himself as 'a wise master builder' on a foundation already laid (1 Cor. 3.10); later contributors to the tradition see the building as growing by the addition of fresh individual stones representing new Christians (Eph. 2.22; 1 Pet. 2.5). Behind all these texts lies Isa. 28.16 which, though differently treated here, is central to Matthew's exegesis also.[223] For this Jesus is himself the builder[224] (like Joshua [= Jesus] the high priest in Zech. 6.12, who rebuilds the temple originally built by Solomon;[225] once again the latter's original role is superseded by that of one named Jesus[226]); and what is built is founded upon a rock.[227] For light on the nature and identity of that rock we turn first to the Gospel's only parallel to this kind of language: the parable that concludes the Sermon on the Mount (7.24-27).[228] There the man who hears and does what Jesus has taught is compared to one who has built his house upon a rock which the

Martyr (trans. F.V. Filson; London: SCM Press, 1962), p. 193.

221. Cf. Hoffmann, 'Petrus-Primat', p. 103.

222. Luz, 'Primatwort', p. 425, sees Eph. 2.20 (with Rev. 21.14) as a development of the sub-apostolic age when the Church was beginning to look back on the time of the original apostles as foundational (a possible point of contact with the Matthaean text). All the same, the image of Christ as the cornerstone remains distinct from that of Christ the builder which we have in Matthew; contra Goulder, *Midrash*, pp. 388-90.

223. See Cullmann, 'πέτρα', pp. 95-99; Jeremias, 'κλείς', pp. 748-51; 'πύλη', p. 927; Kahmann, 'Verheissung', pp. 264-68.

224. At Mk 14.58 Jesus is (falsely) alleged to have claimed that he would destroy the temple and rebuild it in three days. Matthew's redaction alters the prediction to a affirmation of his ability to do so, and the testimony is no longer qualified as false. It would seem that he wants to emphasize building as an aspect of Jesus' work.

225. See Lindars, *Apologetic*, p. 197.

226. Green, 'Solomon', p. 229; §7a, above.

227. For Jewish traditions of the temple as built on the 'foundation rock' (*'eben setiyyāh*) now covered by the Dome of the Rock, see J. Jeremias, 'Golgotha und die heilige Felse', in *Angelos* 2 (Leipzig: Pfeiffer, 1926), pp. 74-128 (93); R.J. McKelvey, *The New Temple* (Oxford: Clarendon Press, 1969), pp. 188-92.

228. Cf. Hoffmann, 'Petrus-Primat', pp. 109 n. 54; Gundry, *Matthew*, p. 334; Caragounis, *Peter*, pp. 65, 107.

autumn floods cannot sweep away. While this is only simile, it is nevertheless a pointer to the meaning of the metaphor at 16.18: as what Jesus *says* is a firm foundation for the life of one who obeys it, so what he *is* (that is, Son of the living God) is the foundation for the community of those who confess their faith in it.[229] The bedrock on which the Church is built *is* Peter's faith, but in the sense of 'that which is believed' (*fides quae creditur*), not of what enables him to believe it (*fides qua...*); and he himself represents the Church in distinction from the personal Christ. That is not to deny it, or him, all qualitative affinity with the rock. Stone, although, once quarried, it ceases to be rock, is still in the nature of things derived from it (hence the very possibility of a word-play on Peter's name); and the Church for which Peter stands takes on, like the precious corner-stone of Isa. 28.16, something of the enduring and bedrock character of its foundation.[230]

We can now return to the examination of the oracle from Isaiah 28, of which Matthew's whole text can be seen as an extended midrash.[231] In its original context this accuses the ruling group in Jerusalem of having come to an accommodation with the powers of death and the underworld, of living, in effect, on borrowed time, whereas they can neither avert the coming cataclysm nor survive it. The text is tailor-made for transposition to the situation of Matthew's church; what we have here is a piece of what Vermes calls 'applied' exegesis.[232] If Matthew, as many hold, saw the events of 70 CE as a definitive judgment, within history, on the old Israel for its rejection of its Messiah, the escape of R. Johanan b. Zakkai from death in the besieged city to make terms with its conquerors would indeed have struck him as 'a covenant with death, and with Hades an agreement' (Isa. 28.15), and the reorganized and aggressive neo-Pharisaic Judaism that resulted as an anomalous and uncovenanted survival.[233] Against this, his own interpretation insists

229. The whole argument of Caragounis, *Peter*, pp. 103-10, on this point is weighty and, to my mind, compelling.

230. Contra Caragounis, who makes too sharp a disjunction here: 'Πέτρος has given utterance to a πέτρα, but the πέτρα is not Πέτρος' (*Peter*, p. 108).

231. Kahmann, 'Verheissung', pp. 265-69; developed in Green, *Matthew*, pp. 246-48.

232. See n. 22 to Chapter 3.

233. Suggested in Green, *Matthew*, p. 247. For the tradition about R. Johanan see J. Neusner, *A Life of Rabban Yohanan ben Zakkai* (Leiden: E.J. Brill, 1962), pp. 104-28; *idem*, *The Development of a Legend* (Leiden: E.J. Brill, 1970), pp. 114-19, 162-66, 228-32; E. Schürer, *The History of the Jewish People* (trans. and rev.

that only the community founded on the rock (of the faith concerning the Son of God) will survive the final (and not too distant) eschatological cataclysm.

d. *Gates and Gate*

Matthew, unlike his basic Old Testament text, speaks of πύλαι ᾅδου (thus giving an additional stress in the line, and continuing the π-alliteration of the two previous ones). The expression is not only rare in the LXX[234] but, where found, speaks of Hades (Sheol) as the abode of the departed and thus conveys the irrevocability of death rather than positive assault from the forces of the underworld, which seems clearly to be implied here.[235] If πύλαι adds anything to the sense that ᾅδης has at Isa. 28.15, it will be that instead of closing on the dead, the gates are thought of as opening to allow the enemy within to sally forth.[236] But they are contrasted with the gate of heaven which the keys of the following strophe are intended to open, and the transition to this is provided by Gen. 28.16-17, the exclamation of Jacob after his dream at Bethel, which he calls both (as its name implies) 'house of God' (cf. οἰκοδομήσω in 16.18) and 'gate of heaven'.[237] This text links the meta-

---

G. Vermes, F. Millar and M. Goodman; Edinburgh: T. & T. Clark, 1979), II, pp. 369-70. The hypothesis does not stand or fall by the veracity of the details of the tradition; it is not in question that R. Johanan was a survivor of the Jerusalem Sanhedrin and that his project at Jamnia was established with official Roman sanction. The latter fact may go some way towards explaining the strange bracketing of 'Pharisees and Sadducees' at 16.6, 12, since to make common cause with the Romans was a distinguishing stance of the latter.

234. Isa. 38.10; Wis. 16.13; *Pss. Sol.* 16.2; cf. πύλαι θανάτου at Job 38.17; Ps. 9.14; 106.18. The two words are used interchangeably to render both *še'ôl* and *māwet*.

235. Thus Jeremias, 'πύλη', p. 927 (preferred to no fewer than 11 alternatives by Davies and Allison, *Matthew*, II, pp. 632-34).

236. For 'gates' as the source of aggression cf. 1QH 6.24-27. 'Gates are a metaphor for might, especially military might, on the attack' (Meier, *Vision*, p. 112 n. 111); contra Kynes, *Solidarity*, pp. 116-17.

237. Cf. on 23.38 (§9b below); and see Luz, *Matthew*, II, pp. 461-62 for Qumran parallels to the *house* as image of the elect community. Further catchword connection (with Isa. 28 in particular) is provided by the stone (λίθος) used by Jacob for a pillow and afterwards set up by him as a pillar (στήλη), which he identifies with the οἶκος θεοῦ (Gen. 28.19); cf. 1 Tim. 3.15, which expounds the latter as 'the church of the living God [?an echo of Mt. 16.16; there could be dependence on Matthew here], the pillar (στῦλος) and ground of the truth'. The

phor of the Church as a building both with its function in the Matthaean *Heilsgeschichte*, where it is to supersede the οἶκος (i.e. the temple) of the old Israel,[238] and with its future responsibility for the salvation of the individual believer: thus the gate of heaven is identical with the gate of righteousness, the 'gate of the Lord' which the righteous will enter (Ps. 117.19-20).[239]

e. *Gate and Keys*

The added word thus assists the transition to the third strophe, which is controlled by the image of the keys. Here a reference to Isa. 22.22, despite the apparent absence of the words from the LXX,[240] is inescapable. Some form of that text is clearly quoted at Rev. 3.7 (though there probably with reference to the gates of death and Hades; cf. Rev. 1.18), and was therefore current in late first-century Christian use. The Old Testament type for Peter here is Eliakim the principal officer in the court of the Davidic king— not merely the comptroller of the royal household,[241] but vicegerent in the kingdom (cf. 22.21), and thus the *šālîyaḥ* whose actions bind his principal.[242] What Eliakim is to be to the kingdom of Judah (as distinct from the palace),[243] Peter is to be to the king-

setting at Bethel, in the northern territory, and visited by Jacob on his way to what was to be Gentile territory for his descendants, is significant for Matthew's own location of the dialogue, along with other prefigurations of a Gentile future for the Church (cf. §8a above, and §10c below).

238. See 23.38: ὁ οἶκος ὑμῶν; for the pronoun cf. 23.34 (of synagogues), also 4.23; 9.35; 13.53, where the narrator's αὐτῶν has the same force.

239. The correlation of kingdom and righteousness is a Matthaean commonplace; see n. 256 below. Note the theme of deliverance from death in vv. 17a, 18b of the same Psalm, and the expression ἔργα κυρίου (cf. 11.2, 19) in v. 17b. For a further combination of Jacob/Israel typology with a text from the Psalter see on Beatitude VI, Chapter 7 §4b, below.

240. See n. 205 above.

241. Contra Jeremias, 'κλείς', p. 752. In Isa. 22.21 Eliakim's responsibilities are not confined to the palace; he is to be 'a father to the inhabitants of Jerusalem and to the house of Judah'.

242. See K.H. Rengstorf, 'ἀπόστολος', *TDNT*, I, pp. 407-47 (413-20).

243. B.D. Chilton, *A Feast of Meanings* (Leiden: E.J. Brill, 1994), p. 53 (cf. 'Shebna, Eliakim and the Promise to Peter', in *idem, Targumic Approaches to the Gospels* [Lanham, MD: University Press of America, 1986], pp. 63-80) argues for a pre-Matthaean exegesis of this text in the light of the Targum which saw it as giving Eliakim right of access to the temple, and so in effect investing him with priestly attributes. Chilton admits that Matthew's own interest in the text is dif-

dom of heaven (as distinct from the Church); his role is concerned with admission to the final eschatological reign.

In the larger context of Isa. 22.15-25 Eliakim's appointment is in place of Shebna, the unfaithful steward who has been disgraced. In view of Matthew's redaction of the context into which he has inserted the Petrine text,[244] this aspect of the typology must not be overlooked; the displacement of the old Israel by the new 'nation' (21.43) is already implicit in these chapters. But the symbolism is hardly applicable to individuals on either side. There is no Shebna on that of Jesus and the apostles, unless it be Judas Iscariot; the synoptic tradition knows of no special responsibility exercised by him, and only Acts 1 (probably post-Matthaean) has any suggestion of replacing him. Nor was there any representative figure on the Jewish side, be it high priest or Pharisaic leader, whom Peter could be seen as displacing, whether historically or typically. (He was, it must be presumed, dead before the establishment of Jamnia; and while certain high priests, notably Caiaphas,[245] had achieved notoriety in his time, he could hardly be said to take over from them their function with regard to the existing temple.) The contrast is not between individuals but between communities, rival claimants to be the real continuator of the Israel of God and the true interpreter of his will to the present age. We catch a whiff of the competition at ground level at 23.13, where Pharisaic scribes are accused of locking people out of the kingdom of heaven (that is, claiming possession of keys which they have not got, since they cannot enter themselves). If this does not actually reflect the operation of the *birkāt ha' minîm*,[246] it is

ferent; and a theology that saw Peter's role in priestly terms is hardly thinkable before the destruction of the Second Temple (especially if, as he argues, the Petrine circle was temple-friendly), and this is at once too far in time from the disgrace of Caiaphas and too near to Matthew.

244. See §8 *ad init.*, and cf. n. 237.

245. Caiaphas was deposed from the high priesthood by Vitellius in 36 CE; cf. Chilton, *Feast*, pp. 60-63, 80, for possible connections between this and Jesus' cleansing (Chilton glosses 'occupation') of the temple.

246. The force and application of this is disputed by L.H. Schiffman, 'At the Crossroads: Tannaitic Perspectives on the Jewish-Christian Schism', and R. Kimelman, 'Birkat Ha-Minim and the Lack of Evidence for an Anti-Christian Prayer in Late Antiquity': both in E.P. Sanders *et al.* (eds.), *Essays in Jewish and Christian Self-Definition*, II (London: SCM Press, 1981), pp. 115-56 and 226-44 respectively. See also Stanton, *Gospel*, pp. 142-45.

certainly evidence for the polarization that gave rise to it.[247] Matthew's response in the text that we are examining is that the authority to pronounce on a person's final destiny belongs now to the Church and not to the synagogue; the latter cannot claim to exclude from God's future (as the wording[248] of that anathema implied).

What the keys are for is conveyed by the promise about binding and loosing, which is repeated in virtually identical wording[249] at 18.18 (there addressed to all the disciples). How, in terms of source and redaction, are the two related? 18.18, while apparently self-contained and not integral to the disciplinary procedure outlined in 18.15-17, is clearly introduced as comment on it; the authority to deal with grave sin in that way has been given in the promise about binding and loosing. But λύειν is not a normal Greek expression for 'forgive'; it conveys the remission of debt, and 'debt' as an Aramaic metaphor for sin is a usage which we have already met in the Lord's Prayer. There is an important partial parallel to the bind/loose language in the Neofiti version of the Targum on Gen. 4.7.[250] Matthew clearly still has Genesis 4 in mind at 18.22,[251] when he has moved on from formal church discipline to the duty of personal forgiveness, and the language of 'loosing' from debt dominates the concluding (and strongly Matthaean) parable of the unmerciful servant.[252] Apart from 18.15-17, which presumably reflects current practice in Matthew's church, there is no item in the second half

---

247. Nothing in Matthew actually compels the conclusion that it reflects the working of the 'Test' Benediction, but the process that led up to its promulgation has surely left its mark on the Gospel, and 23.13 in particular reads like a riposte to it; so Green, *Matthew*, pp. 191-92; cf. Meier, *Vision*, p. 163; contra M. Pamment, 'The Kingdom of God according to the First Gospel', *NTS* 27 (1981), pp. 211-32 (223).

248. '...let them be blotted out of the book of the living and not be written among the righteous' (quoted in Davies, *Setting*, p. 275).

249. That the object of binding/loosing is expressed in the singular in 16.19 and in the plural in 18.18 is sufficiently explained by the respectively singular and plural subjects in the two texts.

250. See n. 206 above, and Vermes, *Studies*, p. 95, for the textual variants. No extant witness retains the word 'bind', but the wording of Mt. 18.18 implies that it was originally there, while the paraphrasing in the Targum is an important clue to the first-century interpretation of 'bind'/'loose'.

251. 18.22 clearly recalls and reverses Gen. 4.24.

252. See §2b.3, above, on the debt image in the Lord's Prayer, and Chapter 7 §2b, below, for the parable.

of that chapter that demands to be treated as 'traditional'.[253] Reflection by the Evangelist on Genesis 4 in the light of the Targum offers sufficient explanation of the rest.

The implication of this is that, for a diachronic account of the development of the Evangelist's thinking, 18.18, which can be sufficiently interpreted in terms of its own context, is prior to 16.19, which cannot, and is the starting point for the wording of the latter.[254] Has he then, in incorporating the wording here, modified the meaning? In particular, is there any room for the regular rabbinic understanding of bind/loose to convey an authoritative ruling on what is forbidden/allowed in the Torah?[255]

The function of the keys is to admit to the final kingdom, and what qualifies a person for admission is of course 'righteousness', doing the will of the Father (5.20; 7.21; 12.50; 21.31).[256] The responsibility of the Church, corporately or through authorized representatives,[257] is to make known by preaching, teaching and exemplary behaviour what that will is. It has discretion to receive or to challenge those seeking the forgiveness of their past sins in baptism (cf. 3.7),[258] and, against that

253. I include in the scope of this judgment 18.19-20, which contains a Christian answer (Matthew's own?) to the Jewish problem of the location of the Shekinah after the destruction of the temple (cf. §7a, above, and §10c, below). Since this was a question contemporary with the Evangelist himself it is hardly to be classed as 'tradition'. For its relation to the context see n. 260 below.

254. Cf. Hoffmann, 'Petrus-Primat', pp. 99-102; Luz, 'Primatwort', p. 423; contra G. Bornkamm, 'The Authority to Bind and Loose in Matthew's Gospel', in G.N. Stanton (ed.), *The Interpretation of Matthew* (London: SPCK, 2nd edn, 1995), pp. 101-14 (110).

255. Bornkamm, 'Authority', p. 104, speaks for a long line of exegetes who (following later rabbinic usage; see Jeremias, 'κλείς', p. 751) have insisted on interpreting Mt. 16.19 in this way. See further n. 262 below.

256. In Matthew, as is generally recognized, kingdom and righteousness are correlatives; it is the latter that admits to the former (cf. 5.6, 20; 6.33; on these see further, in connection with Beatitude IV, Chapter 7 §3b.1, below).

257. These two ways of proceeding are complementary rather than alternative. Even if, as many believe, the Matthaean community acknowledged no other ministries than those of 'prophets, wise men and scribes' (23.34), it was clearly ready to be taught 'the way of righteousness' by those whose authority it recognized (the Evangelist presumably included); yet substantive judgments are the responsibility of the whole body. Compare the procedure envisaged in 1 Cor. 5 (n. 260 below).

258. Some scholars (for whom see R.E. Brown, *The Gospel according to John* [AB; New York: Doubleday; London: Chapman, 1971], pp. 1041-44) have seen the

background, to bring its knowledge of God's will, both by committed pastoral care (18.6-7, 10-14) and, where necessary, by the exercise of church discipline (18.15-17), to bear on those among its membership who persistently ignore or transgress it, even to the point of anticipating in the earthly community that exclusion which such behaviour will have as its consequence in the final judgment (18.18). These things are the responsibility of the whole community (note the plural at 18.18),[259] but they are not undertaken arbitrarily; they are done in the name of Christ, who has promised his presence in their midst (18.19-20).[260]

Can there then be any distinction between the meaning there and that at 16.18-19? If, as is commonly maintained, ἐκκλησία in 16.18 denotes the universal Church and in 18.17 the local, it must be remembered that for primitive ecclesiology the local church is not a part of the whole so much as the whole in the part.[261] If the universal Church comes to have

reception of new disciples by baptism as the primary application of the related saying at Jn 20.23. That text 'unpacks' the language of binding and loosing as do the later versions of the Targum on Gen. 4.7. Most scholars take it for independent tradition; but if Matthew is himself responsible for 18.18, there is a case for direct dependence of John on Matthew here. For Johannine knowledge of Matthew in general see F. Neirynck, *Evangelica*, I (BETL, 60; Leuven: Peeters, 1982), pp. 143-78, 365-488; II (BETL, 99; Leuven: Peeters, 1991), pp. 407-712; cf. Denaux (ed.), *John and the Synoptics*, esp. pp. 3-62 (Neirynck, 'John and the Synoptics 1975–90'), pp. 63-75 (C.K. Barrett, 'The Place of John and the Synoptics within the Early History of Christian Thought').

259. 18.18 is addressed to all the disciples, and to them, in the opinion of most scholars, as comprising the nucleus of the future Church rather than as authority figures within it. Cf. R. Hummel, *Die Auseinanderzetzung zwischen Kirche und Judentum im Matthäusevangelium* (Munich: Chr. Kaiser Verlag, 1967), p. 61; H. von Campenhausen, *Ecclesiastical Authority and Spiritual Power in the Church of the First Three Centuries* (trans. J.A. Baker; London: A. & C. Black, 1969), p. 128; Strecker, *Weg*, p. 223; Bornkamm, 'Authority', p. 104; Hoffmann, 'Petrus-Primat', 107; contra Jeremias, 'κλείς', p. 752; Goulder, *Midrash*, pp. 389-90, *Luke*, p. 640. This is in line with the interpretation of 16.17-19 which sees it as addressed to Peter as representing the whole Church.

260. Cf. 1 Cor. 5.3-5, where the excommunication is to be carried out 'in the name of' and 'with the power of' the Lord Jesus. For Matthew the process rests on (1) agreement, (2) prayer, (3) the support of the indwelling Christ.

261. This account of the matter does not stand or fall with the view that every local ἐκκλησία was seen from the beginning as embodying the new counterpart of the qᵉhal yhwh of Deut. 23.1-8, the idea coming first and influencing the choice of name for the local worshipping community. See the critical comments of M.E. Thrall, *II Corinthians* (ICC; 2 vols.; Edinburgh: T. & T. Clark, 1994, 2000), I,

notional priority, the local still has experiential priority. It is where the action is; what is done in it must express what is true of the whole. If then the functions associated with the keys are in the local church the responsibility of the whole body, that holds good for the universal Church as well, and confirms our conclusion that Peter in 16.17-19 stands for the Church corporately, not for a specific office or function in it distinct from the whole. By the same token it is a mistake to polarize the possible meanings of binding/loosing into *halakah* and the ban, and to assign one to the universal Church and the other to the local,[262] because it is in the local church that the universal is to be found. For the Matthaean ecclesiology the one true teaching authority is in any case Jesus Christ (23.8-10; cf. 28.19),[263] and he is a living presence with the local community (18.20). Even if the Jamnia academy could claim to speak with authority to and for the contemporary synagogue, there was no counterpart to this for the Christian churches at this time.[264] If the Church of Jerusalem under James had claimed such a role (which may be the case), the question of who or what succeeded to its authority after its destruction or flight does not get even a provisional answer for a

pp. 89-93. But if, as seems more likely, the word was first used, possibly in a quite secular sense, of the local church, that would not have inhibited reflection on its biblical associations; and when the concept of the universal Church emerges it is seen as something more dynamic than an association of local churches, a perspective which informs a local church's understanding of itself. Thrall connects this, in the Pauline context, with the idea of the Church as the Body of Christ; the Matthaean counterpart may be the spiritualized οἶκος that has superseded the Jerusalem Temple (see above, and §9b, below). The pre-70 CE synagogue was seen as a place of spiritual communion with the worship of the Temple; both the destruction of that and the divergence from the new Judaism will have contributed to this development. Note the convergence of the two images in Eph. 4.16; Jn 2.21.

262. As do, e.g., Hummel, *Auseinandersetzung*, p. 61; Campenhausen, *Ecclesiastical Authority*, p. 126; Bornkamm, 'Authority', pp. 104, 109-10. Davies and Allison, *Matthew*, II, pp. 638-39, consistently but questionably understand both texts in terms of *halakah* only. Hummel (p. 63) and Bornkamm (p. 111) repeat Streeter's designation of Peter as 'chief rabbi' (*Four Gospels*, p. 515), which cannot be sustained in the face of 23.8; cf. Hoffmann, 'Petrus-Primat', pp. 111-12. For the more inclusive interpretation suggested here cf. also Kynes, *Solidarity*, p. 124.

263. Cf. Hoffmann, 'Petrus-Primat', pp. 110-12.

264. For Hoffmann, 'Petrus-Primat', pp. 109-10, the primacy of Peter (so far as Matthew is concerned) is a matter of unrepeatable past history; cf. also Luz, 'Primatwort', p. 424.

further century. Matthew is an early product of that phase of post-apostolic Christianity.

9. *Matthew 23.37-39*

The part played by ch. 23 in the structure of the Gospel can be understood in two alternative ways: as a preliminary to the eschatological discourse in the following two chapters,[265] or as an integral part of it.[266] If it is the former, its function can be compared to that of 12.22-50 in relation to ch. 13;[267] if the latter, it conveys a judgment on Israel as a nation (the execution of which Matthew clearly identifies with the events of 70 CE[268]), within history, to be followed by his forecast of the final judgment of all people and nations at the parousia. Each of the four previous discourses, as I have argued elsewhere,[269] divides into two parts, the second of which (beginning at 7.13; 10.24; 13.36; and 18.15 respectively) is specifically directed at contemporary Christians facing the prospect of final judgment still probably seen as imminent. If chs. 24–25 are treated as the entire discourse, the function of the second

265. This remains the majority view; most of the current New Testament introductions do not even consider an alternative (W. Marxsen, *Introduction to the New Testament* [trans. G. Buswell; Oxford: Basil Blackwell, 1968], p. 146, excepted). It is also assumed by the classic study of E. Haenchen, 'Matthäus 23', *ZTK* 48 (1951), pp. 38-63.

266. So Bacon, *Studies*, pp. xvii, 427; Taylor, 'Order of Q', p. 29; 'Original Order', pp. 260-62; Marxsen, *Mark*, pp. 198-99; Ellis, *Mind and Message*, pp. 77-82; Frankemölle, *Jahwebund*, pp. 270, 335; W. Pesch, 'Theologische Aussagen der Redaktion von Matthäus', in P. Hoffmann (ed.), *Orientierung an Jesus: Theologie der Synoptiker* (Festschrift J. Schmid; Freiburg: Herder, 1973), pp. 286-99 (295-96); Green, *Matthew*, p. 186; D.E. Garland, *The Intention of Matthew 23* (NovTSup, 52; Leiden: E.J. Brill, 1979), pp. 26-30; Gundry, *Matthew*, p. 453; (cautiously) Stanton, *Gospel*, p. 327, cf. p. 320. The most effective argument is still that of Hummel, *Auseinandersetzung*, pp. 85-90.

267. Mt. 12.22-50 (virtually all discourse from 12.25) is generally recognized as marking the final challenge of the Jewish religious authorities to Jesus' mission, leading to a clear parting of the ways, which is then reflected on from the point of view of the disciple in the parables discourse. If the second option is adopted, its function can be compared with that of 21.23–22.14, which like it is concerned with authority.

268. See especially 22.7; 27.25; Hummel, *Auseinandersetzung*, pp. 87-90.

269. *Matthew*, pp. 19-20.

part will have to be assigned to the seven parables of warning that begin at 24.32, where there is no obvious structural break, or to the more extended final three in ch. 25, where there is still no thematic one. There is in addition good reason to see the conditions predicted at 24.4-14 as those of Matthew's contemporary church.[270] It makes better sense to treat the pointed departure of Jesus from the temple[271] to the Mount of Olives as the counterpart of his withdrawal from the crowds to the house at 13.36.[272]

The reproach to Jerusalem at 23.37-39 is thus the climax of the first part, the judgment upon Israel within history. It is needed in order to establish that the judgment is on the nation as a whole and not only on its religious leaders, the object of the preceding denunciation (23.13-36), though theirs is the 'greater sin', and to give advance interpretation of 24.1-2 in which the temple is symbolically abandoned[273] and its destruction predicted. But its introduction after the woes against the scribes and Pharisees, which have their own climax in vv. 34-36, is more than a little abrupt, and there is not only a change of address but a marked change of tone as vituperative denunciation of the perceived guilty party gives way to reproaches for the people they have carried

270. See Marxsen, *Mark*, pp. 198-204; for parallels between this section and the final sections of the Sermon on the Mount (7.13-23) and the parables discourse (13.36-51), Barth in Bornkamm, Barth and Held, *Tradition*, p. 75; Green, *Matthew*, pp. 197-99; and for the cruciality of the Gentile mission, D.R.A. Hare, *The Theme of Jewish Persecution of Christians in the Gospel According to St Matthew* (SNTSMS, 6; Cambridge: Cambridge University Press, 1967), pp. 156-62, 164-66, 170-71. Meier, *Vision*, p. 169, is surely in error in taking the following section, 24.15-22, to refer to the events of 70 CE.

271. As Hummel points out (*Auseinandersetzung*, pp. 85-86), Matthew's omission of the pericope of the widow's mite (Mk 12.41-44), which in another context he might well have found congenial (see Chapter 7 §1e below), leaves his redaction of Mk 12.37-40 (= Mt. 23) continuous with that of Mk 13 (= Mt. 24–25). His alteration of Mk 13.2 at 24.2 (βλέπετε ταῦτα πάντα;) deflects attention from the buildings themselves to what has just (23.38) been predicted for them.

272. J.C. Fenton, *The Gospel of St Matthew* (Pelican Gospel Commentaries; Harmondsworth: Penguin Books, 1963), pp. 15-16, and Ellis, *Mind and Message*, p. 13, treat 13.36 as a break not just in the discourse but in the entire Gospel, and Bauer, *Structure*, p. 38, though he professes to reject this interpretation, still exaggerates the significance of the break for the total narrative pattern.

273. See n. 301 below.

with them. There is a real aporia at this point, and it suggests that here, as at 11.20-24, the Evangelist has inserted a piece not originally composed for its present position: an earlier response, perhaps, to the destruction of Jerusalem, or even a counter-charge to comments on that from controversial opponents. There is an interesting formal parallel in a saying from the Talmud ascribed to R. Johanan b. Zakkai, to which O.H. Steck has drawn attention: 'Oh Galilee, Galilee! You have despised the Torah! You will soon have to deal with extortioners.'[274] If this alludes, as Hengel has argued,[275] to the Roman expropriations of land in the years following the suppression of the Jewish revolt of 66–70 CE, R. Johanan is putting the blame for that disastrous venture on Galilee where it began, and sees the confiscations that have followed as punishment for its notoriously casual attitude to observance of the Torah.[276] A Christian rejoinder to this could turn the charge back on Jerusalem and its record of violence to prophets and rejection of their warnings.[277] This is the right message, as well as the right time and place,[278] for the author of this Gospel; we have still to determine, from examination of the text, whether it is also the right language.

274. *y. Šab* 15d 50 (Bar.); see O.H. Steck, *Israel und das gewaltsame Geschick der Propheten* (WMANT, 23; Neukirchen: Neukirchener Verlag, 1967), p. 58 n. 1.

275. M. Hengel, *The Zealots* (trans. D. Smith; Edinburgh: T. & T. Clark, 1989), p. 53.

276. Hengel here follows S. Klein, 'Neue Beitrage zur Geschichte und Geographie Galiläas', *PS* 1 (1923), p. 15; contra J. Klausner, *Jesus of Nazareth* (London: George Allen & Unwin, 1925), p. 173 n. 103.

277. See Chapter 3 §4 above, with nn. 57, 59 to Chapter 3, for Matthew's emphasis on the prophetic, and §4 above for his habit of adding 'and the prophets' to his assertions about the law.

278. There are scattered indications elsewhere in the Gospel that the Evangelist's personal roots were in Galilee, and that he viewed Jerusalem and Judaea from a Galilaean perspective. See on 11.20-24, §6, above, and on 2.18, Chapter 7 §3a.1, below. It is even possible that the 'very high mountain' of Mt. 4.8, from which all the kingdoms of the world can be seen (cf. 17.2; 28.16; for the connection between the three texts see Donaldson, *Mountain*, pp. 100-103, 153-56, 178; for reservations about his conclusions see n. 336 below) was inspired by familiarity with Mt Hermon; cf. G.W.E. Nickelsburg, 'Enoch, Levi and Peter: Recipients of Revelation in Upper Galilee', *JBL* 100 (1981), pp. 575-600 (582), for explicit references to that in *1 En.* 12–14. See however the comments of S. Freyne, *Galilee, Jesus and the Gospels* (Dublin: Gill & Macmillan, 1988), pp. 188-89.

a. *The Shape of the Poem*

1 Ἰερουσαλήμ Ἰερουσαλήμ,
2a ἡ ἀποκτείνουσα τοὺς προφήτας
b καὶ λιθοβολοῦσα τοὺς ἀπεσταλμένους πρὸς αὐτήν,
3a ποσάκις ἠθέλησα ἐπισυναγαγεῖν
b τὰ τέκνα σου,
4a ὃν τρόπον ὄρνις ἐπισυνάγει
b τὰ νοσσία αὐτῆς ὑπὸ τὰς πτέρυγας,
5 καὶ οὐκ ἠθελήσατε.

6 <ἰδοὺ>
a ἀφίεται
b ὑμῖν
c ὁ οἶκος
b' ὑμῶν
a' ἔρημος.[279]

7 (λέγω γὰρ ὑμῖν)
a οὐ μή με ἴδητε
b ἀπ' ἄρτι ἕως ἂν εἴπητε,
c Εὐλογημένος ὁ ἐρχόμενος
d ἐν ὀνόματι κυρίου.

If the lament in fact antedates the Gospel, does its present form show evidence of redaction? I find indications of this at three points.

(1) If vv. 37-38 are taken by themselves, the implied speaker is clearly God, not the earthly Jesus as the total context in ch. 23 now requires. The alternative ascription to the personified Wisdom of the Old Testament presupposes (a) Q; (b) Wisdom as the original speaker of vv. 34-36 (as at Lk 11.49);[280] (c) the implied contiguity of the two passages

279. A majority of commentators now accept this word as belonging to the authentic text of Matthew (but reject it for the Lukan parallel); see Knowles, *Jeremiah*, pp. 185-88, for details. Most of these (for whom Knowles speaks) treat it as Matthew's addition to Q, and seek to identify a specific LXX text that could have suggested the addition. The hypothesis of Matthaean creation allows more room for the cumulative influence of prophetic texts with this theme; see §9b below. Tob. 14.4 (quoted by Knowles, p. 187) is an earlier example of the same process. Luke's omission of the word from his source (which this account requires) can be attributed to its dramatic inappropriateness to the context to which he has moved the lament. Lk. 13.35b (//Mt. 23.39) now looks forward only as far as Jesus' entry into Jerusalem; that will be soon enough to speak of the coming devastation of the city (cf. 19.41-44).

280. See n. 143 above.

in Q,[281] despite the aporia noted above in Matthew and the separate contexts in Luke. It is not required by the wording of the text,[282] while the image of the nesting bird, however appropriate in theory to a female figure, is used in the Old Testament only of God himself.[283]

(2) This however changes with v. 39, where the emphasis on *seeing* (οὐ μή με ἴδητε) addressed to non-believers (only the pure in heart will see *God*: 5.8), and on the inception of a changed situation with regard to the speaker (ἀπ᾽ ἄρτι) only makes sense on the lips of the earthly (not to be confused with the historical) Jesus. The verse has close parallels with two redactional passages in the passion narrative: 26.29, 64. All three are introduced by λέγω ὑμῖν, indicating both emphasis and a slight break between the words and the material that precedes them; and all three use the characteristic Matthaean expression ἀπ᾽ ἄρτι[284] to con-

---

281. So Bultmann, *Tradition*, pp. 114-15 (who ascribes both to his lost Wisdom apocalypse; cf. n. 115 above); Suggs, *Wisdom*, pp. 64-66. Steck, *Israel*, p. 47 (following Strauss and Haenchen), rejects this, arguing that the two utterances attributed to Wisdom speak from entirely different temporal situations (future and past respectively). See also T.F. Glasson, *The Second Advent* (London: Epworth Press, 1947), pp. 99-103.

282. As Suggs admitted, *Wisdom*, p. 67 n. 14.

283. So Garland, *Intention*, p. 190 n. 6; cf., in addition to the texts printed above, Ps. 16.8; 35.8; 60.5; 62.8; Isa. 31.5; Ruth 2.12; and see the well argued case of Gench, 'Wisdom', pp. 113-17.

284. Matthew 3 Mark 0 Luke 0 John 2 Revelation 1. If the figures for its 'past tense' ἀπὸ τότε (Matthew 3 Mark 0 Luke 1 [see n. 81 above]) are counted in, the evidence of characteristic Matthaean usage is overwhelming (cf. Frankemölle, *Jahwebund*, pp. 355-56). Note also that the Lukan parallels to the two latter texts (Lk. 22.18, 69) both have ἀπὸ τοῦ νῦν (Luke avoids ἄρτι as a vulgarism). These are to be reckoned among the minor agreements of Matthew with Luke against Mark in Markan contexts (see Neirynck, *Minor Agreements*, pp. 172, 178); the absence of exact verbal agreement (the reason why they have not received more attention) means that they cannot be dismissed as scribal assimilations, while the repetition of the correspondence in two parallel contexts is difficult to regard as coincidence. In Lk. 13.35 ἥξει ὅτε is the *lectio difficilior* and therefore presumably the true reading, but stylistically untypical of Luke and so probably due to the constraints of a source that he needed to alter (cf. Lk. 11.49-51 [see Green, 'Clement', p. 23 n. 98], 11.13 [see n. 12 to Appendix A, below]). Luke knows very well what ἀπ᾽ ἄρτι means for Matthew, and its inappropriateness for the new position of the logion, which being an indeterminate point on Jesus' journey to Jerusalem, has no particular temporal significance. He has therefore to divert its reference to the journey's end (the entry into Jerusalem), and thus to foreshorten its perspective as compared with Matthew's version (see n. 279 above). ἥξει ὅτε is thus his substitute for ἀπ᾽ ἄρτι. The verb

vey the opening of a fresh temporal situation. The two latter have a rhythmic quality distinct from the Markan material in their contexts,[285] but it does not distinguish them sharply from the surrounding narrative to which they remain integral. 23.37-38 has no immediately surrounding narrative, but it has surrounding discourse, and v. 39 has the function of keying in the lament to the predictions that follow, and thus of indicating the distinct, and prior, judgment on Israel.[286] The weak

was probably suggested by Matthew's use of it at 23.36, which Luke has altered; compare his use of οἶκος (which he has retained in the present context from Mt. 23.38) in place of ναός (Mt. 23.36) at 11.51. For a Lukan parallel to the strange syntax that results cf. Lk. 17.22 (so Metzger, *Textual Commentary*, p. 138; Goulder, *Luke*, p. 581; contra Steck, *Israel*, p. 50).

285. Cf. 26.64b:

πλὴν λέγω ὑμῖν,
ἀπ᾿ ἄρτι ὄψεσθε τὸν υἱὸν τοῦ ἀνθρώπου
καθήμενον ἐκ δεξιῶν τῆς δυνάμεως
καὶ ἐρχόμενον ἐπὶ τῶν νεφελῶν τοῦ οὐρανοῦ

See further discussion in §10c, below.

286. A number of defenders of Q note the change of subject in 23.39//Lk. 13.35b, and see the verse as a secondary addition to the original text: Hoffmann, *Studien*, pp. 176-77; Neirynck, *Evangelica*, II, p. 51; Kloppenborg, *Formation*, p. 228; Catchpole, *Quest*, pp. 273-74; Tuckett, *Q*, p. 175. Does 23.39 convey for Matthew (whether as redactor or original author of the verse) a definitive rejection or the possibility of eleventh hour repentance? Opinion is sharply divided. A distinction must be drawn between judgment on Israel as God's chosen people and the prospects of individual Jews. Of the former the first alternative must surely be true, and Matthew sees the events of 70 CE as the execution of it (cf. n. 268 above). The kingdom of God is to be taken away from the old Israel and given to 'another people' (ἄλλο ἔθνος; see 21.43). Membership of the former people will no longer be a path to salvation, but again not an automatic impediment to it. It is rather that, being now dispersed and having no organized national structure of their own, Jewish survivors of the destruction of their nation will meet the judgment, as individuals, alongside the nations among whom they live; if converts to Christianity (which can hardly be ruled out, given the probable composition of Matthew's church, to say nothing of his personal background), they will presumably do so as members of the ἄλλο ἔθνος. The question debated between D.R.A. Hare and D.J. Harrington, ' "Make Disciples of All Nations" ', *CBQ* 37 (1975), pp. 350-69, and J.P. Meier, 'Nations or Gentiles in Matthew 28.19?', *CBQ* 39 (1977), pp. 94-102, was thus insufficiently nuanced. See further Stanton, *Gospel*, pp. 249-50. Matthew may once again be working with double meanings: the acclamation in 23.39 is suggestively close to the confession 'Jesus (Christ) is Lord'. That suggested by T.B.

attempt at rhyming (ἴδητε...εἴπητε; cf. 11.25) suggests that it was constructed ad hoc for this purpose.

(3) If this is the case, ἰδοὺ in 6a can be taken as introducing the climax of the original lament. The words that follow, like 6.9b-10[287] and 11.11a, 13,[288] may be read (as printed) as a concentric construction, in this case pivoted on the word οἶκος.

Burney's observation[289] that the whole lament has been composed, appropriately, in the qinah metre (basically 3-2, though used here with a certain freedom) certainly holds good for 1-5 (the stresses, as I see them, are 2-2-2-3-2[290]-3-2-2), and this can be extended to 6 also if the concentric analysis does not find favour.

b. *The Poem Interpreted against its Old Testament Background*

Isa. 52.9: ῥηξάτω εὐφροσύνην ἅμα τὰ **ἔρημα Ἰερουσαλήμ**, ὅτι ἠλέησεν κύριος αὐτὴν καὶ ἐρρύσατο Ἰερουσαλήμ... (12) ...πορεύσεται γὰρ πρότερος ὑμῶν κύριος καὶ ὁ **ἐπισυνάγων** ὑμᾶς κύριος ὁ θεὸς Ἰσραήλ.

2 Chron. 24.19: καὶ **ἀπέστειλεν** πρὸς αὐτοὺς **προφήτας** ἐπιστρέψαι πρὸς κύριον καὶ οὐκ ἤκουσαν· καὶ διεμαρτύραντο αὐτοῖς, καὶ οὐκ ἤκουσαν. (20) καὶ πνεῦμα θεοῦ ἐνέδυσεν τὸν Ἀζαρίαν... (21) καὶ ἐπέθεντο αὐτῷ καὶ **ἐλιθοβόλησαν** αὐτόν...ἐν αὐλῇ **οἴκου** κυρίου.

Isa. 55.11: οὕτως ἔσται τὸ ῥῆμά μου...ἕως ἂν συντελεσθῇ ὅσα **ἠθέλησα**.

Jer. 38(31).15 *ap.* Mt. 2.18: Ῥαχὴλ κλαίουσα τὰ **τέκνα** αὐτῆς...

Ps. 90.4: ἐν τοῖς μεταφρένοις αὐτοῦ ἐπισκιάσει σαι, |καὶ **ὑπὸ τὰς πτέρυγας** αὐτοῦ ἐλπιεῖς...

Ps. 83.4: καὶ γὰρ στρουθίον εὗρεν ἑαυτῷ οἰκίαν |καὶ τρυγὼν νοσσιὰν ἑαυτῇ, οὗ θήσει **τὰ νοσσία αὐτῆς**...

Isa. 28.12: **καὶ οὐκ ἠθέλησαν** ἀκούειν.

Deut. 1.26: **καὶ οὐκ ἠθελήσατε** ἀναβῆναι...

Cargal, ' "His blood be on us and on our children": A Matthean Double Entendre?', *NTS* 37 (1991), pp. 101-12, is however questionable in the light of Matthew's use of τέκνα; see conclusion to this section, and the discussion of Beatitude II, Chapter 7 §3a.1, below.

287. See on the structure of the Lord's Prayer, §2a above.

288. See §4, above.

289. *Poetry*, p. 146.

290. I take σου in this verset, though enclitic, to be emphatic; cf. μου in 11.30; 16.17; 28.19.

Jer. 8.5: διὰ τί ἀπέστρεψεν ὁ λαός μου οὕτως ἀ ποστροφὴν ἀναιδῆ...**καὶ οὐκ ἠθέλησαν** τοῦ ἐπιστρέψαι;

Hos. 11.5: κατῴκησεν Ἐφραὶμ ἐν Αἰγύπτῳ... ὅτι **οὐκ ἠθέλησαν** ἐπιστρέψαι.

Isa. 64.9: πόλις τοῦ ἁγίου σου ἐγενήθη **ἔρημος**, Σιὼν ὡς **ἔρημος** ἐγενήθη **Ἰερουσαλὴμ** εἰς κατάραν. (10) ὁ **οἶκος**, τὸ ἅγιον ἡμῶν, ...ἐγενήθη πυρίκαυστος...

Jer. 12.7: ἐγκαταλέλοιπα τὸν **οἶκόν** μου, **ἀφῆκα** τὴν κληρονομίαν μου...

Jer. 22.5: ὅτι εἰς **ἐρήμωσιν** ἔσται ὁ **οἶκος** οὗτος.

Hag. 1.9: Ἀνθ᾽ ὧν ὁ **οἶκός** μου ἐστιν **ἔρημος**...

The Old Testament echoes and allusions are considerably more extensive than most commentators seem to have recognized, and once again the primary reference is to the LXX. This will explain Matthew's adoption of the form Ἰερουσαλήμ here, as against his preference elsewhere for Ἱεροσόλυμα (a comparable phenomenon is observable in Galatians, where Paul uses the latter, like Matthew, in narrative contexts, but the former where the name has theological significance).[291]

Isa. 52.9-12 and 55.11 are originally positive prophecies which, for Matthew, Jerusalem and the people for whom it stands have frustrated by their refusal to listen.

The episode recounted in 2 Chron. 24.17-22 is the only Old Testament stoning of a prophet, and its language has influenced Matthew both here and in his redaction of the parable of the wicked vinedressers at 21.33-41 (//Mk 12.1-9); the victim of it is at least one of the referents of the Zechariah of 23.35. But if, as suggested above, 23.37-38 were originally independent of 23.29-36, they are not necessarily concerned, as the latter are, with a post-biblical continuation of the killing of prophets. The plural noun is sufficiently accounted for by the two missions of 2 Chron. 24.19. However, in view of the echoes of Jeremiah in this passage (see below), a reminiscence of the prophet Uriah, whom

291. J.K. Elliott, 'Jerusalem in Acts and in the Gospels', *NTS* 23 (1976–77), pp. 462-69, notes the Pauline parallel, but explains the Hebraic form in Gal. 4.25-26 as due to the Semitic character of the story of Hagar which is its starting point. Its use here he attributes to Q. The LXX, which, with very few exceptions, transliterates the Hebrew, seems a more likely as well as a more verifiable source.

Jehoiakim brought back to Jerusalem to be killed, and whose fate, recorded in the book of Jeremiah (33[26].20-33), Jeremiah himself so nearly shared,[292] is not unlikely.

ἐπισυνάγειν in Isa. 52.11 represents the Hebrew ʾāsap, used here and at 58.8 of Yahweh as the rearguard of his people, but in other contexts of other forms of protection, including gathering into a place of safety (cf. Deut. 22.2, of a neighbour's ox or ass; Ps. 26.10 of God's protection of the orphan).[293] Matthew has combined it with the metaphor of the protecting wings at Ps. 90.4 and elsewhere[294] to produce a simile which probably owes something also to his close observation of animal life.[295] The reminiscence of Ps. 83.3 in the words τὰ νοσσία αὐτῆς associates it directly with the temple.[296] Cf. Deut. 32.11 where the image is not quite the same, but the vocabulary has clear affinities. τέκνα anticipates 27.25 and recalls its foreshadowing at 2.18,[297] and as in both those texts is evidence of the Evangelist's redaction.

οὐκ ἠθελήσατε reproduces the exact wording of Deut. 1.26, which reminds Israel of its refusal to take the daunting direct route into the promised land and its hankering after a return to the fleshpots of Egypt. Isa. 28.12 is a link with the exegesis which has produced 11.28-30 and 16.18, and the texts from Jeremiah and Hosea, where θέλειν represents a different Hebrew word from that used in Deuteronomy and Isaiah,[298] speak of the refusal to repent which is the burden of the complaint against Jerusalem.[299]

---

292. According to some post-biblical traditions (datable to the first century CE) he actually had shared it, and by stoning. See Knowles, *Jeremiah*, pp. 183-84.

293. Cf. BAGD, s.v.

294. See n. 283 above.

295. See Goulder, *Midrash*, pp. 101-103.

296. Ps. 83 is a song for pilgrims going up to the temple; the shelter the latter affords for birds is an image of the spiritual home that it represented for Israelites. Luke's substitution of τὴν ἑαυτῆς νοσσίαν for τὰ νοσσία αὐτῆς (which puzzles Goulder [*Luke*, p. 580]) indicates that he has recognized the allusion; cf. Lk. 7.32 (n. 92 above), and 13.22, where he retains from Ps. 6.9 what Mt. 7.23 omits, and vice versa.

297. See Chapter 3 §2, above, and Chapter 7 §3a.1, below; and cf. Goulder, *Luke*, p. 579.

298. Here mā'on, not ʾābāh as in Deut. and Isa.

299. See below, Chapter 7 §3a.1, on 2.18 in connection with Beatitude II.

οἶκος has multiple associations in the Old Testament:[300] (a) the temple (as in Isa. 64.10; Jer. 12.7; Hag. 1.9 above); (b) the royal palace (as in Jer 22.5 above); (c) the nation ('house of Israel'). (b) was no longer significant by Matthew's time; Jer. 22.5 is interpreted both literally of (a) and symbolically of (c) for which (a) stands. The final comment in v. 38 speaks of the 'house' as both abandoned and in ruins:[301] in ruins because of the foreseen destruction by the Romans (itself foreshadowed by the earlier destruction in 587 BCE of which the Old Testament prophecies speak), and abandoned because of the departure of the indwelling presence of God (the Shekinah; see also Ezek. 10.22-23). It is significant that the text speaks of ὁ οἶκος ὑμῶν, as 23.34 has of 'your synagogues'.[302] For the successors of the old Israel the indwelling presence will be mediated not by a building but by the assembling of disciples in the name of Jesus (18.20), and by the mission to the nations which will bring it about (28.18-20; see below).

10. *Matthew 28.18-20*

I have argued elsewhere,[303] against majority opinion, that the Eusebian version of this text is the original; it offers a regular rhythmic pattern

300. Cf. Knowles, *Jeremiah*, pp. 142-46.

301. To 'abandoned' corresponds the very pointed departure from the temple area of Jesus (who is to be 'God with us' for his disciples; cf. 1.23; 18.20; 28.20, and see §10c below) at 24.1; and to 'in ruins' (Hag. 1.9 confirms that this is the meaning intended) the prediction of 'no stone upon another' at 24.2; cf. Hummel, *Auseinandersetzung*, pp. 85-89; Garland, *Intention*, p. 200 n. 3.

302. Cf. 4.23; 9.35; 13.54.

303. 'Matthew 28.19'. (This entirely supersedes my earlier contribution 'The Command to Baptize and Other Matthaean Interpolations', *SE* 4 [TU 102; Berlin: Akademie Verlag, 1968], pp. 60-63). The heart of the argument is that the retreat during the second half of this century from the implications of the Eusebian form of the text pressed by F.C. Conybeare ('The Eusebian Form of the Text Matth. 28.19', *ZNW* 2 [1901], pp. 275-88) has not been accompanied by any systematic re-examination of the Eusebian evidence for it (with the partial and late exception of B.J. Hubbard [*The Matthean Redaction of a Primitive Apostolic Commissioning* (SBLDS, 19; Missoula, MT: Scholars Press, 1974)]), and that the alternative explanations so far offered for the latter do not bear close scrutiny. It is therefore probable that Eusebius had textual authority for his shorter (S) reading—which makes him a senior contemporary of the earliest extant MS witnesses for this passage.

The suspicion of Donaldson, *Mountain*, p. 280 n. 48, that 'Conybeare and his

very close to that of 11.28-30, which the insertion of the Trinitarian baptism formula completely breaks up.[304]

followers have allowed dogmatic predispositions to overrule the usual canons of textual criticism' allows greater dogmatic weight to the latter than they can properly carry (cf. my 'Matthew 28.19', pp. 128-29); and while Conybeare's anti-dogmatic prejudice is well enough known (and was shared to some extent by most of the early enthusiasts for the S text), it can hardly be attributed to Ernst Lohmeyer (cf. his 'Mir ist gegeben alle Gewalt!', in W. Schmauch [ed.], *In Memoriam Ernst Lohmeyer* [Stuttgart: Evangelisches Verlagswerk, 1951], pp. 22-49), and is no truer of this writer.

304. What I have proposed for Mt. 11.7-13 (see §4 above) may encourage the suggestion that the interpolation of the command to baptize into the commission was the work of Matthew himself (thus D.A. Hagner, *Matthew*, II [WBC; (Dallas: Word Books, 1995], p. 889). Against this is the problem of explaining Eusebius' access to a discarded draft of the Evangelist's own work.

Attempts to find thematic continuity between the earlier chapters and the baptismal triad have been forced and artificial. Frankemölle's parallel with ch. 1 (*Jahwebund*, p. 323) assumes a reference to the Father whom that chapter never names as such, and to the Holy Spirit, whom it only introduces, 'anarthrously and prior to the Son, as the agent of the latter's conception' ('Matthew 28.19', p. 134). While it is probable that some form of the synoptic baptism narrative lies behind the triad (p. 135), Kingsbury's assertion (*Structure*, pp. 77-78) that the Evangelist intended a connection between them does not ring quite true. The basic difficulty is the reluctance to refer to the Spirit in terms or in contexts that would allow of the latter being 'named' alongside Father and Son. 11.27 (see above, §7c, for the link between this and the baptism narrative) says nothing of the Spirit; nor does 28.20 when it speaks of the abiding presence of the risen Christ with his disciples. (For the context of Kingsbury's argument see n. 319 below.)

J. Schaberg, *The Father, the Son, and the Holy Spirit: The Triadic Phrase in Matthew 28.19b* (SBLDS, 61; Chico, CA: Scholars Press, 1982), argues that the triad was part of the pre-Matthaean core of the commission, and (following Lohmeyer and R.H. Fuller) that its antecedents are to be found in a Jewish apocalyptic triad consisting of God, the Son of man, and the angels which has left traces in several places in the New Testament (e.g. Mk 8.38; 13.32; Rev. 3.5; 14.10; 1 Tim. 5.21; 2 Thess. 1.7-8) On this it may be said (1) that the impression of multiple attestation can be misleading: the non-Markan texts cited are relatively late and could well be dependent on Mark (or even Matthew); (2) while imagery of that sort could have played a part in the early development of Christian thought in this area, an association with baptism, by way either of liturgical formula or of elementary theology, is hardly thinkable before an explicitly Christian language has been evolved; the Jewish triad offers no *name* in(to) which baptism can be effected (contrast 1 Cor. 6.11); (3) to insist on the pre-Matthaean status of the triad is effectively to treat it as contemporary with, if not prior to Mark, our earliest witness to the

In its Eusebian form it runs thus:

1a ἐδόθη μοι **πᾶσα**
 b   ἐξουσία ἐν οὐρανῷ καὶ ἐπὶ [τῆς]* γῆς.
2a πορευθέντες οὖν μαθητεύσατε **πάντα**
 b   τὰ ἔθνη ἐν τῷ ὀνόματί μου,
3a διδάσκοντες αὐτοὺς τηρεῖν **πάντα**
 b   ὅσα ἐνετειλάμην ὑμῖν·
4a καὶ ἰδοὺ ἐγὼ μεθ' ὑμῶν εἰμι **πάσας**
 b   τὰς ἡμέρας ἕως τῆς συντελείας τοῦ αἰῶνος.

*For authorities favouring and rejecting τῆς see apparatus to N-A[26, 27] *ad loc.*

a. *The Shape of the Poem*

This final example of Matthew's poetic art corresponds closely in form to 11.28-30: a strophe of four distichs in basically 3-3 rhythm—though the final one, like the first in the earlier composition, is easier to construe as 4-4;[305] if so, the second piece is rhythmically a mirror image of the first. It is however more tightly constructed: each distich has integral enjambment,[306] and the repeated forms of πᾶς at the end of the first verset of each serve to bind the composition together formally as well as thematically. Their rhyming inflections are arranged chiastically: πᾶσα–πάντα–πάντα–πάσας; and the chiastic structure is reinforced by the placing of the participles πορευθέντες...διδάσκοντες, which occupy corresponding positions in the inner couplets, and are matched by quantitative scansion. As in 11.28-30, but even more insistently, stress falls on the personal pronouns, irrespective of the enclitic forms: μοι–μου–ὑμῖν–ὑμῶν, with ἐγὼ μεθ' ὑμῶν (cf. 1.23) forming a final *inclusio*.

synoptic baptism narrative; this both makes influence from the latter less assured, and puts the triad on an evolutionary fast track for which other evidence is missing.

305. See n. 120, above. In 'Matthew 28.19', p. 132, I argued for a 3-3 rhythm throughout, making ἐγὼ μεθ' ὑμῶν a 'single thought pattern' (on the basis of the Hebrew *Immanuel* [cf. 1.23]), and ἕως unstressed as a preposition. I now see that if my analysis of 1.23 (§1, above) is right, Matthew did not treat the *Greek* rendering of *Immanuel* there as carrying a single stress; while ἕως seems to be stressed at 11.23 (see §6, above).

306. That is, where the sense of a line (properly, distich) is carried over from the first verset to the second; see Watson, *Hebrew Poetry*, p. 334.

b. *Sources of the Poem*

The contribution of Old Testament texts and models to Matthew's final commission is a complex question, which has been bedevilled by the insistence of so many scholars on identifying a single comprehensive principle, whether formal or theological, or a single dominant text, which can serve as a key to the whole passage.[307] Ironically, it is the failure of the latest, and in the opinion of many the most promising, of recent attempts[308] to classify the genre to which it belongs that throws most light on how scripture is being used in this context. B.J. Hubbard's monograph,[309] starting from the assumption that behind the different post-resurrection commissionings (assumed to be independent of one another) there lies a single proto-commission preserved in the tradition behind our written Gospels,[310] systematically combed the Old Testament for texts which could have contributed to it, and came up with a wealth of material which, if it did not establish his case,[311] nevertheless, by its sheer repetitiveness (so characteristic of the Deuteronomic tradition from which the bulk of it derived) as much as anything, indicated where an answer might be looked for. Matthew, as we have discovered, is a systematic searcher of the scriptures, which he handles by the methods of contemporary Jewish exegesis. We have already found

307. For a useful account of these see Donaldson, *Mountain*, pp. 174-79 and notes.

308. Surveyed by Meier, 'Two Disputed Questions'.

309. Hubbard, *Matthean Redaction*.

310. It was unfortunate that Hubbard's work had to be done in the first flush of redaction-critical enthusiasm in the United States and only shortly before the appearance of a number of monograph studies which allowed and concluded for the position that Matthew was capable of producing this pericope without requiring an exemplar to work on: e.g. Frankemölle, *Jahwebund*; Lange, *Erscheinen*; Kingsbury, 'Matt 28.16-20'; cf. G. Friedrich, 'Die formale Struktur von Mt 28,18-20', *ZTK* 80 (1983) pp. 137-83 (174); while the appearance of Goulder, *Midrash*, was to herald potential alternative ways of accounting for his material. The view of 28.16-20 as redaction of previously existing tradition is still by no means dead, however; cf. Strecker, *Weg*, pp. 209-11; Meier, 'Two Disputed Questions', pp. 408-16; Schaberg, *The Father*, pp. 43-44; Donaldson, *Mountain*, p. 171; Allison, *New Moses*, pp. 263-66. But see next note.

311. Meier, 'Two Disputed Questions', p. 424, while in principle a supporter of the redactionist view, had reluctantly to concede that Hubbard had not made out his case and that Matthew's commission, so far as form-critical genre is concerned, is *sui generis*. (The argument of this study, that it is not *sui generis* within the components of the Matthaean *oeuvre*, is another story.)

abundant evidence of his use of the second of Hillel's *middôt*, the method of cross-referencing texts on the basis of the words they have in common;[312] an exegete who practised this on Old Testament commissioning texts might be expected to anticipate Hubbard's findings, without dependence on previous Christian tradition for either form or content. Most of the texts quoted below appear in his material, to which this study acknowledges its indebtedness.[313]

2 Chron. 36.23: τάδε λέγει Κῦρος βασιλεὺς Περσῶν **Πάσας** τὰς βασιλείας τῆς **γῆς ἔδωκέν μοι** κύριος ὁ θεὸς τοῦ **οὐρανοῦ**, καὶ αὐτὸς **ἐνετείλατό** μοι οἰκοδομῆσαι αὐτῷ οἶκον ἐν Ἰερουσαλὴμ ἐν τῇ Ἰουδαίᾳ. τίς ἐξ ὑμῶν ἐκ παντὸς τοῦ λαοῦ αὐτοῦ; ἔσται ὁ θεὸς αὐτοῦ **μετ' αὐτοῦ**, καὶ ἀναβήτω.

Dan. 4.17 LXX: ἕως ἄν γνῷ τὸν κύριον τοῦ οὐρανοῦ **ἐξουσίαν** ἔχειν **πάντων τῶν ἐν τῷ οὐρανῷ** καὶ τῶν **ἐπὶ τῆς γῆς**.

Dan. 7.14 LXX: καὶ **ἐδόθη** αὐτῷ **ἐξουσία**, καὶ **πάντα τὰ ἔθνη τῆς γῆς** κατὰ γένη...

Gen. 18.18 (cf. 26.4): ...καὶ ἐνευλογηθήσονται ἐν αὐτῷ **πάντα τὰ ἔθνη τῆς γῆς**.

Exod. 29.35: καὶ ποιήσεις...κατὰ **πάντα, ὅσα ἐνετειλάμην** σοι...

Jer. 1.7: πρὸς **πάντας**, οὓς ἐὰν ἐξαποστείλω σε, **πορεύσῃ**, καὶ κατὰ **πάντα, ὅσα ἐὰν ἐντείλωμαί** σοι, λαλήσεις·

Deut. 4.14: καὶ ἐμοὶ **ἐνετείλατο** κύριος ἐν τῷ καιρῷ ἐκείνῳ **διδάξαι** ὑμᾶς δικαιώματα καὶ κρίσεις ποιεῖν αὐτὰ ὑμᾶς **ἐπὶ τῆς γῆς** εἰς ἣν ὑμεῖς εἰσπορεύεσθε ἐκεῖ κληρονομεῖν αὐτήν.

Josh. 1.5: οὐκ ἀντιστήσεται ἄνθρωπος κατενώπιον ὑμῶν **πάσας τὰς ἡμέρας** τῆς ζωῆς σου, καὶ ὥσπερ ἤμην μετὰ Μωϋσῆ οὕτως **ἔσομαι μετὰ σου**...(7) ἴσχυε οὖν καὶ ἀνδρίζου φυλάσσεσθαι καὶ ποιεῖν καθότι **ἐνετείλατό** σοι Μωϋσῆς ὁ παῖς μου...(8)...ἵνα συνῇς ποιεῖν **πάντα** τὰ γεγραμμένα...(9) ἰδοὺ **ἐντέταλμαί** σοι. ἴσχυε καὶ ἀνδρίζου, μὴ δειλιάσῃς μηδὲ φοβηθῇς, ὅτι **μετὰ σου** κύριος ὁ θεὸς σου εἰς **πάντα** οὗ ἐὰν **πορεύῃ**...(16) καὶ ἀποκριθέντες τῷ Ἰησοῖ εἶπαν **Πάντα, ὅσα** ἄν ἐ ν-

312. See Chapter 3 *passim*, with n. 6 to it.

313. The selection is mostly my own, though I have accepted from Allison, *New Moses*, p. 263, Exod. 29.35 (as he says there [n. 308], not a commissioning text) for its verbal closeness, and Jer. 1.7 for its inclusiveness (though I question whether Matthew, for whom Jeremiah is a type-figure in his own right [see Knowles, *Jeremiah*, esp. pp. 223-46] thought of him here only as a Moses-surrogate). On Josh. 1 (pressed by Allison) see n. 329 below.

τείλῃ ἡμῖν, ποιήσομεν καὶ εἰς πάντα τόπον, οὗ ἐὰν ἀποστείλῃς ἡμᾶς, **πορευσόμεθα**.

Dan. 12.13 LXX: ἔτι γάρ εἰσιν **ἡμέραι** καὶ ὧραι εἰς ἀναπλήρωσιν **συντελείας**, καὶ ἀναπαύσῃ καὶ ἀναστήσῃ ἐπὶ τὴν δόξαν σου εἰς **συντέλειαν ἡμερῶν**.

c. *The Sources and the Meaning*
I have put 2 Chron. 36.23[314] in first place, although its wording is not so close to Matthew as that of some of the other texts cited, because, though written in prose, it comes nearest to providing a comprehensive formal model for the whole composition: it begins with a statement of the commissioner's authority, then gives the commission, and ends with assurance of the accompanying divine presence. Since the genealogy with which the Gospel begins draws heavily on those at the beginning of 1 Chronicles,[315] it is not inappropriate that its conclusion should be modelled on that of 2 Chronicles; and since Isa. 45.1 calls Cyrus 'my anointed' (LXX ὁ χριστός μου), the thought of him as a type of Christ would not have had for the Evangelist the strangeness with which it strikes modern ears. Cyrus claims in his commission to have been given the nations of the world by the 'God of heaven' (i.e., the God of the Old Testament), and the object of the commission is to build a house for the latter in Jerusalem as he has commanded. The counterpart of this in Matthew's salvation history is, as we have already seen in connection with 16.18,[316] the building of the Church, its place no longer (whatever some conservative Jewish Christians may have thought[317]) in Jerusalem, but in the lands of the Gentiles wherever the gospel is taken. The 'house' in Jerusalem, on the other hand, is 'abandoned and in ruins' (see 23.38); the Old Testament type is fulfilled, as so often in Matthew, by contrast.[318]

314. Included (as the identical Ezra 1.2-3) in the 'commissioning' texts collected by Hubbard, *Matthean Redaction*, p. 65, and suggested independently by Frankemölle, *Jahwebund*, pp. 51-61, and by B.J. Malina, 'The Literary Structure and Form of Matt xxviii.16-20', *NTS* 17 (1970–71), pp. 87-103; rejected by Meier, 'Two Disputed Questions', pp. 418-20, as by many others, usually on the assumption of an obligatory choice between alternatives.
315. 1 Chron. 1.34; 2.4-5, 9-12; 3.5, 10-17, 19.
316. §8c, above.
317. Contra Goulder, *Midrash*, pp. 258, 287, who included the Evangelist in their number.
318. See Green, 'Solomon', p. 227.

The first two texts cited from Daniel complement one another: 4.17 states that the Lord (God) has authority over all things in heaven and earth, 7.14 that authority was given to the Son of man, but limited to the nations of the earth. But the authority conferred on Matthew's Jesus, by virtue of his death and exaltation, extends to all that the Father has. Some scholars,[319] mostly for reasons connected with their overall view of Matthaean Christology, have resisted a reference to Dan. 7.14 here; they have been right to reject the idea of an 'enthronement' text[320] (the scene is clearly set on earth), but it does not follow from this that no enthronement has yet taken place. Already, by the insertion of his own expression ἀπ' ἄρτι at 26.64,[321] Matthew has emphasized that the reversal of the relative situations of Jesus and his interlocutors of which his *Vorlage* speaks is to take effect as from his death;[322] now the sub-

319. E.g. A. Vögtle, *Das Evangelium und die Evangelien* (Dusseldorf: Patmos, 1971), pp. 255, 257-58, 259; W. Trilling, *Das Wahre Israel* (Munich: Kösel, 1964), pp. 22-23; Strecker, *Weg*, p. 209; Donaldson, *Mountain*, pp. 179-88 (see n. 336 below); Kingsbury, 'Matt 28.16-20', pp. 579-84; *Structure*, p. 121; Bauer, *Structure*, pp. 111-12. The two latter are persuaded that they cannot argue for a Son of God Christology in the commission unless all reference to the Son of man is excluded. This either/or methodology is inappropriate to Matthew's inclusive use of the Old Testament. More subtly, Meier, 'Two Disputed Questions', pp. 410, 413-14 (followed by Schaberg, *The Father, passim*; Allison, *New Moses*, pp. 265-66), accepts the allusion to Dan. 7.14 in 28.18, but assigns it to the pre-Matthaean tradition of the commission which Matthew enhanced to produce his final version. But (1) the objections to breaking up a poetic composition into 'tradition' and 'redaction' which I have noted in connection with 11.28-30 (n. 123) apply here too; (2) even if that method were appropriate here, it would be wrong to infer the Evangelist's meaning only from what he has added; (3) the poem in any case reverts to Daniel in the final verset (see n. 329 below).

320. Proposed by O. Michel, 'The Conclusion of Matthew's Gospel' (= *EvT* 10 [1950], pp. 16-26), in Stanton (ed.), *Interpretation*, pp. 30-41 (36); Jeremias, *Promise*, pp. 38-39. F. Hahn, *Mission in the New Testament* (SBT, 47; London: SCM Press, 1965), p. 65, and Barth, in Bornkamm, Barth and Held, *Tradition*, pp. 131-35, are more cautious; the enthronement has taken place, but the scene does not depict it. Cf. Frankemölle, *Jahwebund*, pp. 61-66.

321. For Matthew's text see n. 285 above.

322. We are not concerned here with the history of the saying (if it had one) in the tradition behind Mark, or with its possible authenticity as a saying of Jesus, which are the questions that dominate most scholarly discussion of the text: e.g. Perrin, *Rediscovering*, pp. 179-85. To that category belong also T.F. Glasson, *The Second Advent* (London: Epworth Press, 1947), pp. 63-68, and J.A.T. Robinson, *Jesus and his Coming* (London: SCM Press, 1957), pp. 43-48, who sought to

ject of the final Christophany is the ascended and glorified Christ. Some
have seen it as a 'proleptic parousia',[323] and in so far as it depicts a
'return' of the Lord to his own in majesty this has force; but because it
is given only to a select few it lacks the public and ineluctable character
with which Matthew, following his sources, elsewhere invests the
parousia.[324] The temporal expression at 26.64 has meanwhile shifted
the emphasis from the final coming to the present glorification of Jesus.

ἐν οὐρανῷ καὶ ἐπὶ γῆς corresponds virtually word for word with the
Lord's Prayer (6.10),[325] and indicates that the kingdom for which the

eliminate the idea of an early return of Jesus from his personal teaching with the
argument that the 'coming' in Mk 14.62 originally meant a coming *to* God, as it
evidently does in Dan. 7.13. This is impossible for Mark if the saying is read in
context. Those addressed (the Sanhedrin) are not persons with a privileged access to
what goes on in the heavenly places; the 'seeing' which they are promised is not
distinct from that which will be the general lot of non-believers at the parousia (cf.
Mk 13.26). All the elements of Mk 14.62 are retained by Matthew in his parallel at
26.64 (cf. also 24.30), and what ἀπ' ἄρτι adds was already implicit in Mark. It is
left for Luke to separate the two halves of the Markan saying, and by eliminating
the thought of 'seeing' from his version at 22.69 to convey in plain language the
point of Matthew's redaction (cf. Goulder, *Luke*, p. 754); and it is at least possible
that the cloud that receives the ascending Jesus out of the apostles' sight at Acts 1.9
is that of Dan. 7.13 in its original meaning; so Hartman, 'Exegesis', p. 143. In Matthew this 'Godward' movement of the Son of man is assumed to have taken place
before 28.16 (Hartman, 'Exegesis', pp. 144-45).

323. Originally R.H. Lightfoot, *Locality and Doctrine in the Gospels* (London:
Hodder & Stoughton, 1938), pp. 67-72; followed by Meier, *Vision*, pp. 37, 142,
212, who sees it as the inauguration of the abiding presence of Jesus with his
Church. Matthew's redaction of Mk 9.1 at 16.28 may be connected.

324. Cf. 24.29-31, 37; 25.13; 13.37-43. Matthew, alone among the Evangelists,
uses the technical term παρουσία (4 times in ch. 24). He also expands the catena of
Old Testament texts quoted or alluded to: note esp. the allusion to Zech. 12.10-14 at
24.30.

325. Both 6.10 and 28.18 have ἐν οὐρανῷ (anarthrous); in both the MS tradition
varies between an anarthrous γῆς and one with the article (though very few witnesses have the same for both texts). A quick review of the evidence suggests that
(1) for heaven as the dwelling place of God, or the reverential circumlocution for
his name, Matthew prefers the plural (usually with article); (2) he sometimes uses
the anarthrous singular as equivalent for this, whereas with the article it usually
denotes the created firmament, the sky; (3) where he speaks of heaven and earth
together he is not concerned to match an anarthrous οὐρανός with an anarthrous γῆ
(or the converse). There are exceptions to all three statements, some of them possibly attributable to the confusions of the MS tradition (of which Meier takes no

Prayer prays is now the kingdom of the Son of man (cf. 13.41) as well as of the Father.

The position of πορευθέντες, referred to above, indicates emphasis; it is not to be understood here as 'having no independent syntactical function',[326] like the participle in ἀποκριθεὶς εἶπεν. The word is twice used non-participially in the words from Joshua 1 quoted above, clearly in connection with entering the promised land to take possession of it.

πάντα τὰ ἔθνη recalls not only the authority given to the Son of man in Dan. 7.14 but the promise to Abraham in Gen. 18.18, repeated to his son Isaac at Gen. 26.4 and frequently alluded to elsewhere;[327] cf. the references to Abraham at Mt. 1.1; 3.9. The addition of τῆς γῆς in all of the first three texts above makes a further catchword connection with 2 Chron. 36.23.

ἐν τῷ ὀνόματί μου (so Eusebius) is best understood not with reference to 7.22 (where the preposition is missing and the actions thus qualified are in any case repudiated) but to 23.8, where the audience are instructed not to allow themselves to be called 'rabbi', since they all remain disciples of the one true teacher. μαθητεύειν means to make disciples for him, and not for themselves as the rabbis did.

The teacher has however been named in the first chapter of the Gospel, and that not once but twice. Through his (foster) father, but in reality from God by a dream direction, he has been given the name Jesus (= Joshua).[328] It is no coincidence that Joshua 1 is more heavily

---

account in his attempt to sort out tradition from redaction in the occurrences of the double expression; cf. 'Two Disputed Questions', p. 410). All that can be confidently asserted on that front is that 24.34 (and 5.18a which seems to be dependent on it) reproduces the usage of Mk 13.31 (2 articles; heaven = the sky), and 11.25 that of Tob. 7.17 (again 2 articles; see §7b, above). Cf. Traub, 'οὐρανός', pp. 514-20; G. Schneider, 'Im Himmel—auf Erde: Ein Perspektiv matthäischer Theologie', in L. Schenke (ed.), *Studien zur Matthäusevangelium* (Festschrift W. Pesch; SBS; Stuttgart: Katholisches Bibelwerk, 1988), pp. 285-97 (292-93); contra Strecker, *Weg*, p. 209; Trilling, *Israel*, p. 24 n. 19.

326. Contra Donaldson, *Mountain*, p. 184; see n. 336 below.

327. E.g. Gen. 15.5; 22.17; Exod. 32.13; Deut. 1.8; 2 Kgdms 7.12; Neh. 9.23.

328. 1.21; see §1 above. My failure in 'Solomon', p. 227, to find typological allusion in Matthew to the original Joshua was thus an error. The allusion of 28.20 to the name Emmanuel at 1.23 is generally recognized; it is the substitution of the baptismal triad, with its entirely different use of 'name' (see Green, 'Matthew 28.19', p. 126, and cf. Strecker, *Weg*, p. 209) that has obscured the double reference to the given names of Christ.

drawn on for the content of these verses of Matthew than any other single Old Testament source.[329] In its context it reads like an epilogue to the final chapters of Deuteronomy, in which Moses finishes all his instructions (καὶ συνετέλεσεν Μωϋσῆς λαλῶν πάντας τοὺς λογοὺς τούτους: Deut. 31.1; cf. Mt. 26.1[330]), associates Joshua with his authority (31.7; 32.44), and dies, not having entered the promised land (ch. 34). Jesus has also completed his instructions (26.1), associated his disciples with himself (26.26-32), and died (ch. 27). As the true anti-

---

329. I had independently reached this conclusion (cf. 'Matthew 28.19', p. 134 and n. 63) before the appearance of Allison, *New Moses* or its pilot study, W.D. Davies and D.C. Allison, 'Matt 28.16-20: Texts Behind the Text', *RHPR* 72 (1992), pp. 89-98. Most of the evidence can be found in Josh. 1.1-9, but the vocabulary statistics of the whole chapter are even more striking:

δίδωμι	4
πορεύομαι	2
γῆ	6
πᾶς (all inflections)	8
πάντα ὅσα	2
πάντα ὅσα ἐντείλη ἡμῖν	1
ἐντέλλομαι (all inflections)	6
ἐνετείλατο	2
ἰδού	1
μετά σου (ὑμῶν) εἶναι	3
ἡμέρα	2
πάσας τὰς ἡμέρας	1

Allison's reduction of all the Old Testament allusions in the commission to Moses-typology requires, as we have seen (n. 319 above), the assumption of a pre-Matthaean *Vorlage* to which the echoes of Daniel can be assigned. These extend further, however, than the first distich; see Frankemölle, *Jahwebund*, p. 66 and nn. 259, 261 for evidence of the last four items in the above list in the final chapters of Daniel as well.

330. 26.1 is Matthew's fullest parallel to Deut. 31.1, 24; 32.4-5, yet it is only the final item in a series (7.28; 11.1; 13.53; 19.1; 26.1) in matching wording. If Deuteronomy is in fact the model (so Frankemölle, *Jahwebund*, pp. 339-41; N.A. Dahl, 'The Passion Narrative in Matthew', in Stanton [ed.], *Interpretation*, pp. 42-55 [52]), Lk. 7.1 can only be a paraphrase of Mt. 7.28, since Luke, though he may vary the extent of a scriptural quotation (e.g., 4.4 [diffMt. 4.4]), and even alter some of its wording by following an alternative version (e.g., 13.27 [diffMt. 7.23]), never changes *all* its significant words, as he is sometimes close to doing with his contemporary sources (e.g., 11.21-22 [diffMark 3.27//Mt. 12.29]). Cf. Goulder, *Luke*, p. 376.

type to Moses he does both what Moses did (hence the echo of Deut. 4.14, Moses' instructions in preparation for life in the promised land), and what he could not do but his historical successor did, that is, enter into possession of the land; the latter however is to be accomplished only through the mission of his disciples who, as it were, play Joshua to his Moses as he plays Joshua to the original Moses—but with this difference, that he is not absent from them as Moses was from the original Joshua, but is with them as the Lord was with both his prototypes,[331] and will be so until the parousia. Hence his other name, Emmanuel, and the final couplet of the commission.

At this point we can return to the theme of the replacement of the temple. At 18.20 Jesus is represented as saying that where two or three are assembled in his name, there he is in their midst. I have previously drawn attention to the early rabbinic parallels to this, particularly the saying at *m. Ab.* 3.2,[332] which offers an alternative locus for the Shekinah, after the destruction of the temple, in the shared study of Torah. As we saw then, the saying put in Jesus' mouth identifies him with both Torah and Shekinah, and makes a final link between 11.28-30, where the yoke of Jesus is offered in place of the Mosaic Torah, and 28.18-20, where his disciples are authorized to teach what *he* has commanded them, and his presence with them as they do so is the equivalent of the Shekinah.

The substantival expression συντελεία τοῦ αἰῶνος which Matthew has substituted at 24.3 for Mark's ὅταν μέλλῃ ταῦτα συντελεῖσθαι πάντα (Mk 13.4), though not found in the LXX, nor, with one exception,[333] in the New Testament outside this Gospel, has close parallels in contemporary Jewish literature, including that of Qumran.[334] Moreover συντελεία with a dependent genitive is found repeatedly in the closing chapters of Daniel, including the final verse quoted above. An allusion to it here will indicate that Matthew has linked the conclusion of his book to those of the Pentateuch (Deuteronomy), the history of the kingdoms of Israel (2 Chronicles) and the prophetic canon (Daniel). This is

331. Cf. Josh. 1.5.

332. Note 145 above.

333. Heb. 9.27, where the possibility of dependence on Matthew cannot be ruled out; see Green, 'Clement', p. 24.

334. Found frequently in *2 Baruch*; also 1QpHab 7.1-2. See list in Gundry, *Matthew*, p. 477.

part of what is meant by saying that Jesus fulfils the law and the prophets (cf. 5.17-18).[335]

There is then a fundamental unity of theme running through the last four examples of Matthew's poetic composition that we have been examining: the supersession of the Mosaic law in its original form by Jesus' messianic interpretation of it, that of the old Israel centred on the temple by the Church, and that of the occupation of the promised land by the mission to the new land of promise, the world of the Gentiles.[336] In each of them the part of Jesus is indicated by a type figure: in the first the wisdom of Jesus ben-Sira as contrasted with that of Solomon; in the second Joshua the high priest, again as contrasted with Solomon; and in the third Joshua the son of Nun as contrasted with Moses.[337]

335. See J.P. Meier, *Law and History in Matthew's Gospel* (AnBib, 71; Rome: Pontifical Biblical Institute, 1976), p. 88; *Vision*, pp. 227-34.

336. Donaldson, *Mountain*, pp. 179-88, includes these motifs in an extended argument (following K.H. Rengstorf, 'Old and New Testament Traces of a Formula of the Judaean Royal Ritual', *NovT* 5 [1962], pp. 229-44) for interpreting the whole passage in terms of 'Zion-eschatology'. While much of this is illuminating, not least for the understanding of the mountain setting ('the mountain motif in Matthew acts as a vehicle by which Zion expectations are transferred to Christ' [p. 184]), I have to take issue at two points: (1) the arguments for basing the opening distich on Ps. 2 rather than on Dan. 7.14 pay too little attention to Matthew's own allusions (see n. 322 above), and too much to other first-century writing; (2) the function envisaged for Jesus as the transcended Mount Zion retains too much of the static character of its Old Testament type. The thrust of the final commission is clearly in the direction of a 'going out' to the nations rather than of their 'coming in' (though that is doubtless envisaged as its result), and it is to this 'going out' that the promise to 'be with' the disciples is attached. Donaldson also, in my judgment, misses the contrast between the temple and the 'high mountain' in the temptation narrative, and its significance for the Matthaean *Heilsgeschichte* (see Green, *Matthew*, p. 68 onwards, and cf. Freyne, *Galilee*, p. 189).

337. Solomon need not however be entirely excluded from this stage of the comparison. He was, as I have argued elsewhere ('Solomon', p. 230), not only the archetypal wise man and the builder of the original temple, but the posthumous divider of the nation by his 'heavy yoke' (cf. §7a, above). But whereas after the original break the future of the chosen people lay with the southern kingdom, the Davidic line and the temple at Jerusalem, this time it will lie with the counterpart of the northern territory, first literally (Galilee) and then symbolically as that of the Gentiles (cf. 4.15-16; 28.18-19 [with nn. 327, 336 above]), with the true son of David who will have no need of successors, and with the Church as the true *locus* of his abiding presence.

Chapter 5

CONCLUSION: ONE WRITER

I have identified a total of thirteen[1] Matthaean texts composed (in Greek) according to certain canons of Hebrew prosody, with (usually extensive) influence from the Greek Bible. They fall into three recognizable categories:

(a) those for which evidence of redaction or of a certain dissonance with their present context suggests that they antedate the composition of the Gospel itself: 6.9-13 (the Lord's Prayer); 11.7-9, 11, 13; 11.16-19b;[2] 11.21-24; 23.37-38;

(b) those whose position in the Gospel, as well as their more carefully crafted character, suggest an integral relation to its total structure and a significant part in the organization of its contents: 11.5; 11.28-30; 28.18-20;

(c) those whose relatively unpolished state suggests that they took shape in the course of actually writing the book: 1.20b-21; 10.8; 11.25-26; 11.27; 16.17-19.

The distribution of the poetic characteristics of these texts is set out in the accompanying Table 5.1. It should be noted that it records their presence, not their total incidence, within any one text. Old Testament allusion, for example, may be limited to a single word, as in 11.27, or

1.   Exclusive of 15.30, which is not actually verse, and 23.39, which for me is a redactional addition to a verse that originally lacked it.

2.   Strictly speaking, this pericope is not verse all through, but contains two snatches of it in *oratio recta*. I have hesitated about including it in the first category. As it stands it was clearly composed with knowledge of Mark's Gospel; yet it appears to reflect the 'high' view of the Baptist in relation to Jesus which the Evangelist, partly under Markan influence, felt constrained to modify in his final version (see Chapter 4 §§4 and 7b, above, and Appendix B, below). It could however be transferred to category (c) without great disturbance to the findings of this chapter.

embrace a whole catena, as in the texts that immediately precede and follow it. The half mark, recorded in two instances only,[3] indicates not a smaller incidence but a more doubtful case. The metrical data, on the other hand, are specified; only thus can the range and distribution of the writer's prosodic preferences be recorded.[4]

	single distichs	4-line	3-distich	4-distich	tristich	qinah	2 strophes	5-line concentric	other chiasmus	inclusio	parallelism of alternate lines	rhyme	π-alliteration	other allit. and assonance	quantitative scansion	enjambment	anaphora	word count	multiple meaning	word play and paronomasia	OT allusion	Totals
6.9-13 (LP)			1					1	1	1	1	1	1	1	1	1		1	1		1	13
11.7-9, 11a, 13							1	1					1	1							½	4½
11.16-19b	1											1		1	1			1		1	1	7
11.21-24			1									1		1		1			1		1	6
23.37-38						1		1		1		1				1		1			1	7
a	1	–	1	–	–	1	1	2	–	1	–	3	1	3	1	2	–	2	1	1	3½	24½
11.5			1						1	1	1	1			1						1	7
11.28-30				1					1	1	1		½	1		1			1		1	8½
28.18-20				1					1			1	1	1	1	1					1	8
b	–	–	1	2	–	–	–	–	3	2	2	2	1½	2	2	2	–	–	1	–	3	23½
1.20-21			1															1	1	1	1	5
10.8		1										1	1	1								4
11.25-26			1									1				1					1	4
11.27					1				1					1			1	1	1		1	7
16.17-19				1									1		1	1				1	1	6
c	–	1	2	1	1	–	–	–	1	–	–	2	2	2	1	2	1	2	2	2	4	26
Total	1	1	5	3	1	1	1	3	5	4	3	8	5½	8	5	7	1	5	5	3	11½	87
5.3-10 (Beatitudes)				1				1	1	1	1	1	1	1		1		1	1		1	12

Table 5.1. *Distribution of poetic characteristics in Matthaean texts*

3.   Of Old Testament allusion in 11.11a: γεννητοῖς γυναικῶν, an expression apparently borrowed from the LXX of Job (see n. 86 to Chapter 4), carries no reference to the content of those passages. Of π-alliteration in 11.28-30: here so mixed up with alliteration of other letters (κ in particular) that it does not readily stand out as distinctive.

4.   In some instances there is a change of metre within the piece; in others a

The Lord's Prayer, although correctly classified with pieces that ante-date the Gospel, nevertheless, by virtue of its highly wrought composition, stands somewhat apart from the others in that category. To include it with them in calculating averages would therefore have a distorting effect on the result. Without it, the remaining items in group (a) score an average of 6.1, as against 7.9 for (b) and 5.2 for (c). A high score for (b) is what we should expect, given the part these compositions play in the structuring of the Gospel. We should also expect items composed in the course of actually writing the book to be stylistically less considered creations than those composed independently. It is thus noteworthy that the average score in (c) is so close to that in (a), and the spread of poetic characteristics, if anything, slightly wider.

The texts in categories (b) and (c) came into being, it was suggested, as part of the actual writing of the Gospel. This implies a single author for them, as distinct from a 'school'[5] or a mere 'redactor'.[6] For those in (a) the case is less clear-cut; these pre-existent texts could in theory be the work of other writers, and two of them, as has been argued,[7] have undergone redaction to reach their present form in the Gospel. Yet these two, if my analysis is right, contain, in common with the Lord's Prayer,[8] an example of the striking 5-line concentric construction; and the presence in all of them of rhyme and/or alliteration, which cannot be carried over from another language,[9] points to a writer or writers versifying in Greek. We know of one such; is it necessary to postulate others?

An adequate answer to this question will involve some reference to the incidence of Semitic-style poetry elsewhere in the Greek New Testament. Four areas call for consideration.

---

further prosodic feature (e.g. strophe division) is superimposed on the basic metre.

5.   Stendahl's case for a Matthaean 'school' has not won lasting acceptance (except from B. Gerhardsson; see n. 9 to Chapter 10 below), and I am not concerned to revive it.

6.   On this often question-begging term, much favoured by synoptic critics, see the conclusion to Appendix B.

7.   11.7-9, 11, 13 (Chapter 4 §4, above); 23.37-38 (Chapter 4 §9b, above).

8.   See Chapter 4 §2a, above, and cf. Green, 'Matthew 11.7-15', pp. 463-64.

9.   See Chapter 2 above.

1. *The Pauline and Deutero-Pauline Letters*

a. It has been widely recognized since the pioneering work of Ernst Lohmeyer[10] that Phil. 2.6-11 embodies a hymn adapted but not originally composed by the apostle.[11] Lohmeyer's own analysis of it remains the most coherent and convincing,[12] though his speculations about its origins have slightly clouded the picture.[13] He saw it as a poem in two strophes of three tristichs each in 3-3-3 rhythm;[14] this required the excision of θανάτου δὲ σταυροῦ as a Pauline gloss, but no other surgery was called for. The tristich stanzas are carefully linked by particles, and each, with one exception, contains only a single main verb, with multiple dependent participles. Lohmeyer concluded for a composition in Greek by an author whose first language was Aramaic.[15] He recognized that the line ἐπουρανίων καὶ ἐπιζείων καὶ καταχθονίων

---

10. See especially his *Kyrios Jesus: Eine Untersuchung zu Phil. 2, 5-11* (Sitzungsberichte der Heidelberger Akademie der Wissenschaft, Phil.-hist. Klasse, Jahr. 1927–28, 4 Abh.; Heidelberg: Winter, 1928); cf. *Die Briefe an die Philipper, an die Kolosser und an Philemon* (KEKNT; Göttingen: Vandenhoeck & Ruprecht, 1930), p. 90.

11. For subsequent discussion in the light of his hypothesis see R.P. Martin, *Carmen Christi* (SNTSMS, 4; Cambridge: Cambridge University Press, 1967), pp. 25-38.

12. See *Kyrios*, pp. 5-6; cf. Martin, *Carmen*, pp. 29-30, 38-40. The best of the alternatives is that of Jeremias, 'Zu Gedankenführung in den paulinischen Briefen', in J.W. Sevenster and W.C. Van Unnik (eds.), *Studia Paulina in honorem J. de Zwaan* (Haarlem: Bohn, 1953), pp. 146-54 (153), which by eliminating ἐπουρανίων κτλ. from v. 10 and εἰς...πατρός from v. 11 arrives at a composition in 4 tetrastichs. This lacks the connectedness of Lohmeyer's version, and some of the lines are excessively long (his final line would contain 6 stresses!). And while his proposal (following Dibelius and Cerfaux) to bring together vv. 7c and 7d in synonymous parallelism is initially attractive, elsewhere in the hymn parallelism is never simply repetitive, but progressive (see n. 19 below). Martin's analysis (*Carmen*, pp. 36-38) simply breaks down Jeremias' quatrains into couplets for antiphonal recitation.

13. His suggestion that the hymn had its origin in the worship of the Christian community in Jerusalem encouraged the supposition (cf., e.g., Martin, *Carmen*, pp. 40, 60 n. 60) that it had been originally composed in Aramaic. But see nn. 16, 17 below.

14. A few lines are actually 2-stress, e.g. the first in v. 8.

15. See *Kyrios*, p. 9.

cannot represent a Semitic original;[16] yet it cannot be excised without violence to the metrical scheme. He could have added that the rhyming endings of the pivotal verbs ἐκένωσεν, ἐταπείνωσεν, ὑπερύψωσεν, and of the noun forms ὁμοιώματι, σχήματι, ὀνόματι, do not correspond to anything in the retroversions into Aramaic proposed by other scholars.[17] Though there is no alliteration, there is integral enjambment[18] in three of the stanzas, and the evidence of anaphora[19] between lines and between stanzas is unmistakable.[20]

b. It is easier to recognize the lyrical quality of 1 Corinthians 13 than to reduce it to any regular prosodic pattern. It is thus too far removed from what we have found in Matthew for any detailed analysis to be illuminating.

c. N.T. Wright's analysis of Col. 1.15-20[21] (which I take to be deutero-Pauline, though he does not), has yielded two matched strophes of 55 words each[22] (cf. the Beatitudes, and Mt. 11.21-24). I have suggested that the word count in the two latter texts compensates for unevenness in the length (and even, in the latter case, of the number) of the lines; but the matching in the Colossians poem is markedly more flexible even than this, and has evidently moved further from Old Testament exemplars.

d. The hymn quoted at 1 Tim. 3.16 shows signs of a dovetailed arrangement based on slight variations in the rhyming forms of the aorist passives (AABCCB):

16. P.P. Levertoff, who attempted a retroversion of Lohmeyer's version of the hymn into Aramaic (see W.K. Lowther Clarke, *New Testament Problems* [London: SPCK, 1929], p. 148), noted that it broke down metrically in the last two stanzas. He connected this with the allusion to Isa. 45.23 LXX—a further reason for questioning an Aramaic original.

17. This can be checked against Levertoff's attempt (see previous note).

18. See n. 306 to Chapter 4.

19. See Chapter 4 §7c *ad fin.*, and cf. Martin, *Carmen*, p. 27.

20. The composition as analysed by Lohmeyer would rate a count of 7 on the scale used for Matthew in Table 5.1.

21. N.T. Wright, *The Climax of the Covenant* (Edinburgh: T. & T. Clark, 1991), pp. 99-118 (= *NTS* 36 [1990], pp. 444-68).

22. *Climax*, p. 103 n. 19.

<ὃς>
ἐφανερώθη ἐν σαρκί,
  ἐδικαιώθη ἐν πνεύματι,
  ὤφθη ἀγγέλοις,
  ἐκηρύχθη ἐν ἔθνεσιν,
  ἐπιστεύθη ἐν κόσμῳ,
    ἀνελήμφθη δόξῃ.[23]

e. The first two lines of the hymn fragment at 1 Tim. 6.15 rhyme terminally and have matching quantitative scansion (apart from the initial syllable of each line):

ὁ βασιλεὺς τῶν βασιλευόντων
καὶ κύριος τῶν κυριευόντων·

and the next two also have parallel scansion if the convention that two short syllables are equivalent to one long is allowed to operate:

ὁ μόνος ἔχων ἀθανασίαν,
φῶς οἰκῶν ἀπρόσιτον·

The Pauline literature thus contains one early, and unique, precursor of Matthew's poetic style, though the formal parallels are limited and the content quite different. Otherwise there are only late and scattered parallels to the details of his literary practice. It is an unimpressively small catchment for the phenomenon we are considering.

2. *The Johannine Apocalypse*

This document, as will be familiar, contains a number of songs or hymns sung by figures or groups within the vision.[24] The density of Old Testament quotation and allusion in them does not mark them off from the surrounding prose; there is no reason to attribute them as a whole to

23. For this arrangement see Lohmeyer, *Kyrios*, p. 63 and n. 1. E. Schweizer, 'πνεῦμα, πνευματικός', *TDNT*, VI, pp. 415-16 (followed by M. Dibelius, *The Pastoral Epistles* [ed. H. Conzelmann; Hermeneia; Philadelphia: Fortress Press, 1972], p. 62; J.T. Sanders, *The Christological Hymns of the New Testament* [SNTSMS, 15; Cambridge: Cambridge University Press, 1971], p. 15), argues from the meaning of the words for a double chiastic arrangement, ab-ba-ab (where a indicates events in the earthly sphere, b events in the heavenly). If this is the case, it remains for all that subordinate to the basic formal structure, and shows evidence of tension between form and meaning.

24. On the poetic analysis of these the commentaries are mostly unhelpful.

earlier hands in the tradition. They are rhythmically loose, with wide variation as a rule in the length of the lines. In two places only can a more regular pattern be discerned: 12.12, three distichs which form the conclusion of a longer and rather freer piece, and 15.3b-4, four distichs constructed from LXX texts, with the rhythm of the last apparently disturbed by two non-LXX and non-rhythmical insertions.[25] The way the Old Testament is used constitutes a real parallel with Matthew, but there is no evidence of the other poetic devices which I have identified in his Gospel.

3. *The Gospel of John*

While a number of scholars—and translators[26]—have seen poetic rhythms in the discourses of the fourth Gospel, this, as Raymond Brown admits,[27] is impressionistic rather than based on systematic analysis. Only the prologue has attracted the latter, and there the effort to distinguish poetry (the Logos hymn) from prose (Evangelist's comment and/or an earlier and simpler introduction to the book[28]) has not yielded even a minimum of agreed findings,[29] let alone parallels to the features identified in Matthew. As an utterance of the implied author of the book its content has more in common with the hymn in Philippians 2, and this may conceivably extend to its form, if Lohmeyer's two-strophe account of the latter is sustained.[30]

25. ὅτι μόνος ὅσιος and ὅτι τὰ δικαιώματά σου ἐφανερώθησαν.

26. JB and NJB follow D. Mollat's French version (BJ) in printing extended sections of the Johannine discourses in lines to indicate verse, a practice followed independently by Brown in his commentary (see next note).

27. R.E. Brown, *The Gospel according to John* (AB, 29; New York: Doubleday; London: Chapman, 1971), p. cxxxiv; cf. pp. cxxxii-cxxxv on the whole subject.

28. The latter alternative is the contribution of J.A.T. Robinson, *Twelve More New Testament Studies* (London: SCM Press, 1984), pp. 65-76 (= *NTS* 9 [1962–63], pp. 120-29).

29. For a survey of attempts at a verse analysis of John's prologue down to 1971 see Brown, *John*, p. 22; bibliography, pp. 36-37. Of subsequent work in this category, strictly understood, there has been little or nothing. The valuable essay of J. Ashton, 'The Transformation of Wisdom', in *Studying John* (Oxford: Clarendon Press, 1994), pp. 5-35, neither presents nor cites any analysis of the prosody.

30. Brown, *John*, p. 20, notes the parallel, and accepts (p. 22) from previous analysts of the prologue (including an early effort of my own) the possibility of a strophic arrangement.

4. *The Gospel of Luke*

The questions raised by the Third Gospel are whether the examples of verse composition which it undoubtedly contains (and puts in the mouths of its characters) are earlier than the Evangelist (and could therefore have had independent circulation), and whether they provide independent evidence of the characteristics that we have recognized in Matthew.

a. I consider first the hymns of Luke's infancy narrative: the Magnificat (1.46-55), Benedictus (1.68-79), and Nunc Dimittis (2.29-32).[31] Were these (a) translations from Hebrew or Aramaic,[32] or (b) originally composed in Greek?—and if (b), were they (c) received from earlier tradition by the Evangelist and adapted by him,[33] or (d) his own creation?[34]

---

31. The Gloria in excelsis (2.14) is so close to Luke's redactional alterations to the acclamation of Mk 11.10 at 19.38b that its Lukan provenance is hardly in question (so, e.g., J.A. Fitzmyer, *The Gospel according to Luke* [AB; New York: Doubleday; London: Chapman, 1981], p. 397).

32. So P. Winter, 'Magnificat and Benedictus—Maccabaean Psalms?', *BJRL* 37 (1955), pp. 328-47; D.R. Jones, 'The Background and Character of the Lukan Psalms', *JTS* NS 19 (1968), pp. 19-50; H. Schürmann, *Das Lukasevangelium* (Freiburg: Herder, 1969), I, pp. 77-83, 93-94; S. Farris, *The Hymns of Luke's Infancy Narratives* (JSNTSup, 9; Sheffield: JSOT Press, 1985), pp. 14-26. P. Benoit, 'L'enfance de Jean-Baptiste selon Luc', *NTS* 3 (1956–57), pp. 169-94 (182-84) (on the Benedictus) and R.E. Brown, *The Birth of the Messiah* (London: Chapman, 2nd edn, 1993), pp. 350-55, cf. p. 644, keep an open mind about the language of the original. Jones, who argues effectively for a Christian origin of the canticles and for a single author of all three, and against theories of redactional additions to their original content, seems to rest his case less on strictly linguistic evidence than on literary affinities with post-biblical writings, some of which (e.g., *Test. XII Patr.*; *Pss. Sol.*) are known to us, and could have been known to Luke, in Greek translations.

33. So Fitzmyer, *Luke*, pp. 358-62, 376-79; C.F. Evans, *Saint Luke* (TPI; London: SCM Press, 1990), p. 172. Brown, *Birth*, pp. 349-50, 354-55, holds that they came to Luke in Greek, whatever their original language. Horgan and Kobielski, 'Hodayot', p. 182, in practice assume a pre-Lukan Greek source, while not absolutely ruling out a Semitic one.

34. So A. Harnack, *Luke the Physician* (trzns. J.R. Wilkinson; London: Williams & Norgate, 1907), pp. 215-17; Creed, *Luke*, pp. 306-307; M.D. Goulder and M.L. Sanderson, 'St Luke's Genesis', *JTS* NS 8 (1957), pp. 12-30; Goulder, *Luke*, pp. 225-33, 239-44; for the Magnificat, R.C. Tannehill, 'The Magnificat as a Poem',

If (a) they need not detain us further, since what we seek is evidence of Hebrew-style versifying in Greek, and in extant translations, as already noted,[35] this is not forthcoming. In fact no fully convincing evidence from these hymns of translation or of an underlying familiarity with Aramaic or Hebrew has been produced;[36] and the presence in them of rhyme, assonance and alliteration, though not in any great profusion,[37] must indicate, as it does in Matthew, a Greek-language original. If then (d), further exploration will be equally unnecessary; what proceeded from the mind of the Evangelist will not have circulated as independent material.

How strong then is the case for (c)? It rests on two main props: (1) the modifications which the two longer canticles have allegedly undergone in order to fit them to their present contexts (1.48 for Magnificat, and 1.70, 76-77 for Benedictus), and (2) the supposedly 'primitive' ambience evoked by the texts themselves.

(1) is a hypothesis entailed by the assumption that these canticles are pre-Lukan; if Luke himself composed them for their present contexts, there is nothing to explain. No change in style or vocabulary has been demonstrated in the presumed redactional additions,[38] and the devices noted above are present here too.[39]

(2), where not simply subjective, is argued on the basis of the poverty and simplicity attributed to the primitive apostolic community in Jerusalem in the early chapters of Acts.[40] But this too is Lukan testimony, uncorroborated and widely believed to idealize the historical situation; if to demonstrate the independence of these hymns could undermine

---

JBL 93 (1974), pp. 263-75, whose case on poetic grounds for the integrity of the composition (and by implication for its having been composed in Greek) is compelling. The two uneven strophes that he identifies are characteristic of later Jewish poetic style; cf. n. 42 below.

35. Chapter 2, above.

36. So, with the authority of a Semitics specialist, Fitzmyer, *Luke*, pp. 358, 378.

37. Cf. Tannehill, 'Poem', p. 273; Horgan and Kobielski, 'Hodayot', pp. 191-92. In the Nunc Dimittis, which neither article analyses, cf. δοῦλον-δέσποτα and ῥῆμα-εἰρήνη in 2.29.

38. This is admitted by Horgan and Kobielski, 'Hodayot', p. 193. See also Jones, 'Lukan Psalms', p. 49, cf. pp. 35-37; Goulder, *Luke*, pp. 231-33.

39. Note in 1.48 the verbal reminiscence (ταπείνωσιν) of the Song of Hannah (the primary model for the whole canticle [cf. Goulder, *Luke*, pp. 225-27, 233]), and the π-alliteration and cumulative infinitives in 1.76-77.

40. Thus Brown, *Birth*, pp. 349-55; Fitzmyer, *Luke*, pp. 361-62.

that verdict, the demonstration requires evidence from another quarter and is still awaited.[41] A stronger argument lies in the resemblances that have been noted between the style of the Lukan hymns and the Qumran *Hodayôt*, particularly in their variation of the length of lines and strophes, in their liking for cumulative infinitives and suppression of the predicative copula, to say nothing of their pervasive allusions to the Old Testament. The essay of Horgan and Kobielski[42] which draws attention to this does not argue for original composition in Hebrew; but if that style was able to cross the language barrier, whether under the auspices of Hellenistic Judaism or Christianity, its wider dissemination is not necessarily a problem.[43]

All three hymns display an ability for free poetic composition on Old Testament models,[44] in a context in which Luke is already exercising his gift for writing Septuagintal pastiche. The inspiration is of course uneven; if the first of them, the Magnificat, as Tannehill has impressively shown,[45] is, poetically speaking, his masterpiece, the fact that there is some falling off in the others is no reason to deny him authorship or to posit earlier sources; it simply shows the unevenness we have found in Matthew's poetic *oeuvre* to be no less true of Luke's.[46]

41. M. Dibelius, *James* (ed. H. Greeven; Hermeneia: Philadelphia: Fortress Press, 1976), pp. 39-45, offered an extended account of how the tradition of devout poverty might have passed from Palestinian Judaism to primitive Christianity which falls well short of a demonstration that it actually did so. But, interestingly, he saw the strand in late first-century Christianity which Bousset called 'liberated Diaspora Judaism' (James, the Pastoral Epistles, 1 Clement) as the likeliest context for its survival. This is not far from where some recent studies have located Luke; cf. Ravens, *Luke*, pp. 254-55; M. Pettem, 'Luke's Great Omission and his View of the Law', *NTS* 42 (1996), pp. 35-54.

42. 'Hodayot', pp. 184-88.

43. Cf. Chapter 2 above on the hypothesis of J. Irigoin.

44. See Horgan and Kobielski, 'Hodayot', pp. 188-92; Goulder, *Luke*, pp. 225-33; 239-44.

45. As analysed by him, the Magnificat fully shares the rhythmical unevenness that characterizes so much post-biblical Hebrew poetry; what makes it exceptional is the subtlety with which the medium is handled and the sustained tension between the parts which results: see 'Poem', esp. pp. 272-74.

46. Farris' argument (*Hymns*, pp. 17-20), that if Luke was himself responsible for these hymns he would have composed others at subsequent points in his Gospel, does not allow for the constraints of his subject matter upon him (cf. Goulder, *Luke*, p. 233), nor for the possibility (to call it no more) that the infancy narrative was added when his project was in an advanced state of preparation (in my view, after

b. Next to be considered is the Sermon on the Plain (6.20-49). The consensus of Q adherents is that this largely represents the earlier version of the Sermon altered and enlarged by Matthew. That it contains material from an earlier version (in my view that of Matthew) is not in question. But its final form displays a unique blend of Hebrew poetic and Greek rhetorical characteristics, and bears the imprint of a single author.[47] The insistent four-beat rhythm has often been pointed out:[48] four beatitudes followed by four woes (the last item in each markedly longer than the rest); the two-line injunction of Mt. 5.44 expanded into four stately lines (6.27-28), followed by the compression of Mt. 5.39-42 into four pedestrian ones (6.29-30); then, after a brief diversion into a three-beat pattern (6.32-35; Luke's habit of variation again!), a return to the original rhythm for the climax, in which four short lines beginning with an imperative verb (6.37-38a) build up to a coda in which the four stresses fall on single words:

μέτρον καλὸν πεπιεσμένον
σεσαλευμένον ὑπερεκχυννόμενον
δώσουσιν εἰς τὸν κόλπον ὑμῶν (6.38b).

This is clearly the climax of the Sermon; the parables that form its conclusion (6.39-49) also number four.[49] Here is further evidence that the fourfold pattern derives from the conscious literary art of the Evangelist himself. Without that there would be little in the underlying material to compare, formally speaking, with what we have discovered in Matthew.

c. The only other text in Luke which displays verse characteristics independently of what we have in Matthew is the two-strophe poem at 17.26-29.[50] The parallel to the first strophe at Mt. 24.37-39 is not verse as it stands, though the balance between the four participles offers an

his discovery of Matthew; see 'Credibility', pp. 133, 144-45; cf. Franklin, *Luke*, pp. 353-64).

47. See esp. Morgenthaler, *Quintilian*, pp. 260-73.

48. Notably by R. Morgenthaler, *Die lukanishe Geschichtesschreibung als Zeugnis* (Zürich: Zwingli, 1948), I, pp. 83-84; cf. Green, 'Clement', pp. 7-11.

49. There are also four detached sayings which serve as 'markers': 6.27a, 31, 36, 38c: see Green, 'Clement', p. 8.

50. The two strophes are clearly composed in lines, with a swinging if irregular rhythm. Something of the style identified in the Sermon on the Plain is to be found here too.

invitation to it for a redactor; the second is without parallel. If both had stood in a common source, it would be uncharacteristic of Matthew, since he is much happier with repetition than is Luke, to have omitted one of them. Whoever added the second strophe was thus familiar with either Matthew's text or his source for the first.[51] Two features in particular indicate that it was the work of Luke himself.[52]

(1) The duplication is comparable with two other passages in his Gospel,[53] though neither is to be classified as verse: the reference to two Old Testament figures is reminiscent of 4.25-27, and the matching of what is said of them recalls the paired parables in 15.4-10, where the first member is again paralleled in Matthew. These combine a very close correspondence of content with a marked variation of incidental wording.

(2) The four asyndetic words ἤσθιον, ἔπινον, ἐγάμουν, ἐγαμίζοντο (17.27) are a characteristic of his style (cf. 7.22 [diffMt. 11.5]; 12.19; 14.13).[54] But it is striking how he avoids directly repeating this pattern in his second strophe. By themselves the words ἠγόραζον, ἐπώλουν, ἐφύτευον, ᾠκοδόμουν (17.28)[55] would have offered a succinct summary of the elements of economic life to balance those of physical life in the first strophe (and a suitable run-up to a judgment on a *city*). The repetition of ἤσθιον, ἔπινον confuses the picture as well as upsetting the symmetry. But Luke's 'habit of variation' abhors exact symmetry, and the intrusion of the two additional words finally stamps the whole piece as his composition.

Thus the New Testament contains a single early example, preserved in, if not necessarily deriving from, the Pauline churches of the Aegean, of Hebrew-style verse composition in Greek, but little evidence, and that mostly late, of continuous practice of it. The examples in Luke can plausibly be regarded, like those in Matthew, as the work of a single mind. Nor is there, even in the Magnificat, anything to compare with the range of metrical form and poetic devices that we have found in

---

51. Schulz, *Q*, pp. 279-80, treats the addition as post-Q but pre-Lukan.

52. P. Vielhauer, *Aufsätze zum Neuen Testament* (Munich: Chr. Kaiser Verlag, 1965), p. 67, takes this position.

53. See Goulder, *Luke*, pp. 653, 656-57.

54. Cf. Goulder, *Luke*, p. 652.

55. Goulder suggests (*Luke*, p. 653) that Luke dropped ἐγάμουν, ἐγαμίζοντο bcause of the city's deviation from this norm. As on this account he replaced two words with four, the problem of the asymmetry remains.

Matthew, and which can only be attributed to first-hand knowledge of Old Testament poetry and access to a living tradition deriving from it.[56]

At the foot of Table 5.1 I have added the count for the Beatitudes.[57] It indicates that they belong with the Lord's Prayer as an outstanding example of the range of the Evangelist's poetic art. The further question, whether, like the Lord's Prayer, they antedated the composition of the Gospel or were composed for their present position in it, must await the detailed analysis of their content which will occupy us next.

56. On post-biblical developments in Hebrew verse (beginning with Ben-Sira) see also Hrushovski, 'Prosody', pp. 1208-10.

57. All the items entered in this line can be justified from what has been noted in Chapter 2, with the exception of *multiple meanings*, which will be argued in Part II.

Part II

POETRY AND THE MEANING OF THE BEATITUDES

Chapter 6

STRUCTURE AND MEANING

We now take up the formal characteristics of the Beatitudes poem as identified in Part I, Chapter 2, and consider their significance for the meaning of the individual beatitudes in relation to the whole composition. My analysis there disclosed a two-strophe structure with an *inclusio* linking the last beatitude with the first; and within this a pairing of alternate beatitudes. Words can be paired according to their basic meaning, which can survive, yet still be affected by, translation into another language; or according to their associations, which covers both the diverse ways a single vocable is used (literally and metaphorically) and the synonyms and approximations which a particular usage may throw up. A pair may express converse relations to a single process, for instance, active-passive, or negative-positive. All these distinctions will be found relevant to the discussion that follows. But whereas in construing a prose text the normal assumption is that it will have a single exclusive meaning, this, as we have already seen, is emphatically not the case in poetry. Multiple meanings are part of its stock in trade;[1] and a concentration of them, as A.C. Graham suggested in connection with Chinese poetry of the late T'ang period, seems to be characteristic of times of cultural upheaval in which a 'new sensibility' emerges.[2] The Dominican theologian Cornelius Ernst, who drew attention to this judgment, suggested that the period of the later New Testament writings was just such a time.[3] He argued primarily from the evidence of the Fourth Gospel (and the affinities with, for instance, the Hermetic writings and the *Odes of Solomon* which have been claimed for it). The

1. See discussion in Chapter 1, with n. 19.
2. A.C. Graham (trans. and intr.), *Poems of the Late T'ang* (Penguin Classics; Harmondsworth: Penguin Books, 1968), pp. 19-20.
3. C. Ernst, *Multiple Echo* (London: Darton, Longman & Todd, 1979), pp. 141-42.

presence of *double entendres* in John is beyond dispute; but they normally take the form of irony in the comments of the Evangelist in the course of his narratives, or in the pronouncements of Jesus or other actors in the story in dialogue within them.[4] In this he is partly anticipated by Mark,[5] and the practice is not wholly foreign to Matthew.[6] But the practice of poetic ambiguity covers much more than this,[7] and the incidence of it in Matthew's poetry is unparalleled elsewhere in the New Testament.

The starting point of the exploration is necessarily the Greek word; but while its everyday meaning for a Koine Greek speaker of the period must not be ignored, Dupont was right to insist on the priority of the Semitic substratum,[8] especially as mediated through the LXX. There will often be tensions between this and the ordinary Greek sense, as there will sometimes be also between the Hebrew and the LXX (or other versions) of a text, as we have already found in Part I.[9] These would have been seen, by one who practised exegesis in the contemporary Jewish manner, not as contradictions, but as opportunities to widen the application of a text.[10] The words will therefore be examined against their Old Testament background (taking the LXX as starting point), both by the concordance method (since the second of the *middôt*[11] encouraged the comparison of texts on the basis of shared words), and by identifying clusters of words closely related in Hebrew usage, and their Greek equivalents. Particular attention will be given to books which are

4.   See P. Duke, *Irony in the Fourth Gospel* (Atlanta: John Knox Press, 1985); also M.W.G. Stibbe, *John as Storyteller* (SNTSMS, 73; Cambridge: Cambridge University Press, 1992), pp. 18, 27-28, 49.

5.   See J. Camery-Hoggatt, *Irony in Mark's Gospel* (SNTSMS, 72; Cambridge: Cambridge University Press, 1992), which, if anything, understates the case.

6.   E.g. 27.4, 15-23 (note Matthew's Ἰησοῦς Βαραββᾶς).

7.   The classical account of this (though written before the influence of Roman Jakobson became dominant) is W. Empson, *Seven Types of Ambiguity* (London: Chatto, 2nd edn, 1947 [1935]). Though his subject matter is confined to English poetry, Graham found his insights illuminating for Chinese, and I have found more than one of his distinctions relevant to Matthew.

8.   Dupont, *Béatitudes*, III, pp. 470, 495-502.

9.   For tensions between the LXX and the MT cf. on 1.23; 2.18; 4.15-16; 12.18-21 (Chapter 4 §1, Chapter 3 §§2, 3, 4 above).

10. See R. Bloch, 'Midrash', in W.S. Green (ed.), *Approaches to Ancient Judaism* (BJS, 1; Missoula, MT: Scholars Press, 1978), pp. 29-49 (46-48).

11. See n. 6 to Chapter 3.

known to have had a special importance for Matthew: Deuteronomy,[12] Chronicles,[13] Isaiah,[14] Jeremiah,[15] Daniel,[16] Hosea,[17] the Psalter[18] and Ben-Sira.[19] Three of these, it may be noted (Deuteronomy, Isaiah and the Psalter), had a special prominence in the library of Qumran.

When a provisional account of the meaning(s) of a beatitude has been arrived at, this will then be tested, first against the rest of the Sermon on the Mount, because if the Beatitudes stand at the head of the Sermon (as the Decalogue stands at the head of the Old Testament Law), we should expect them to have some bearing on the content of the latter; and secondly against the rest of the Gospel, to which the Sermon in its strategic position as the first of the Five Discourses must be seen as integral.[20] A coherent account of the structure of the Sermon will be of some importance here. Many authorities agree that its central core runs from 5.17 ('do not think that I have come to abolish the law and the prophets') to the *inclusio* at 7.12 ('this is the law and the prophets'),[21]

12. Cf. n. 330 to Chapter 4; and see in general Steck, *Israel*, esp. pp. 304-16; Frankemölle, *Jahwebund*, pp. 325-30, 391-400; Knowles, *Jeremiah*, pp. 319-23.

13. See Frankemölle, *Jahwebund*, pp. 314-15, 391-400; Goulder, *Midrash*, pp. 29-46; Green, *Matthew*, pp. 11-12, 17.

14. See Davies and Allison, *Matthew*, I, pp. 211-12, 293; Luz, *Matthew*, I, p. 157; Van Segbroeck, 'Verheissung', pp. 125-28; Kahmann, 'Les citations', pp. 264-68; Nolan, *Royal Son*, pp. 21 n. 3, 44-46, 189-90, 202, 206-208.

15. See Knowles, *Jeremiah*; cf. M.J.J. Menken, 'The References to Jeremiah in the Gospel according to Matthew, *ETL* 60 (1984), pp. 5-24; Orton, *Scribe*, pp. 154-55; L.Vouga, 'La séconde passion de Jérémie', *LumV* 32 (1983), pp. 71-82; Davies and Allison, *Matthew*, I, pp. 266-67; Nolan, *Royal Son*, pp. 136-39.

16. See Frankemölle, *Jahwebund*, pp. 62-67; Orton, *Scribe*, pp. 145-48; and cf. Chapter 4 §§7b and 10c.

17. Quoted at 2.15; 9.13; 12.7; cf. 11.27 (see Chapter 4 §7c above).

18. See above, Chapter 3 with n. 8.

19. See Orton, *Scribe*, especially pp. 145, 161, 175; Goulder, *Midrash*, pp. 10, 12-13. Cf. Chapter 4 §7a, b.

20. Even if the basic thesis of Betz, *Sermon on the Mount* were established, this would still hold good for the Gospel in relation to the Sermon, though in that case not vice versa. Betz claims to find discrepancies between Matthew's theology and that of the Sermon; but the Evangelist, even on Betz's assumptions, could hardly have incorporated the Sermon without general approval of its content.

21. E.g. Betz, *Sermon on the Mount*, pp. 50-58; J. Lambrecht, *The Sermon on the Mount: Proclamation and Exhortation* (Wilmington, DE: Michael Glazier, 1985), p. 28. D.C. Allison, 'The Structure of the Sermon on the Mount', *JBL* 106

with the Beatitudes and the material immediately following them forming a preparatory prologue, and 7.13-27 a cautionary epilogue uttered
with special reference to the Evangelist's contemporary Christians, and
to the coming judgment.[22] Within the central core the antitheses of
5.21-48 and the threefold injunction on true and false piety (6.1-18,
incorporating the Lord's Prayer) comprise two well defined sections.
But few exegetes make comparable sense of the third (6.19–7.12). The
majority treat it, either explicitly[23] or by their silence, as a miscellany
without any coherent theme or pattern. Bornkamm[24] saw the inade-
quacy of this as an account of Matthew's literary practice, and proposed
an arrangement based on the Lord's Prayer; but despite one or two illuminating connections neither he nor his principal supporter in this ini-
tiative, R.A. Guelich,[25] was able to offer a convincing systematic
justification of it. There has been a strange reluctance on the part of
scholars to take seriously the suggestion of W.D. Davies,[26] that the cen-

(1987), pp. 423-45, makes 5.13 the beginning of the central section; against this see
Chapter 8 §3 below.

22. Each of the Five Discourses ends with a section relating its content to the
coming judgment and addressed quite specifically to Matthew's contemporary
Christians; cf. G. Bornkamm, 'End-Expectation and Church in Matthew', in Bornkamm, Barth and Held, *Tradition*, pp. 15-51 (15-24); Green, *Matthew*, pp. 19-20.

23. E.g. McNeile, *Matthew*, p. 90; F.W. Beare, *The Gospel according to
Matthew* (Oxford: Basil Blackwell, 1981), pp. 180, 188; Meier, *Vision*, p. 64;
Strecker, *Sermon on the Mount*, p. 130.

24. G. Bornkamm, 'Der Aufbau der Bergpredigt', *NTS* 24 (1977–78), pp. 419-
31, following some suggestions of W. Grundmann, *Das Evangelium nach Matthäus*
(Berlin: Evangelische Verlagsanstalt, 1968), pp. 206, 217. Luz, *Matthew*, I, pp.
212-13, following J. Kürzinger, 'Zur Komposition der Bergpredigt', *Bib* 40 (1959),
pp. 569-89, and R. Riesner, 'Der Aufbau der Reden im Matthäus-Evangelium',
Theologische Beiträge 9 (1978), pp. 173-76, sees the Sermon as a concentric construction pivoted on the Lord's Prayer. Though formally impressive, this offers no
thematic clue to the arrangement of 6.19–7.12.

25. *The Sermon on the Mount* (Waco, TX: Word Books, 1982), pp. 324-25; cf.
van Tilborg, *Intervention*, p. 161 n. 1: 'Guelich has worked out (Bornkamm's) suggestions consequently (*sic*) with enormous consequences for the interpretation'.

26. *Setting*, pp. 305-15. Before this appeared, T.W. Manson had made use of the
hypothesis in *Ethics and the Gospel* (London: SCM Press, 1961), pp. 34-39; but
Davies confirms Manson's dependence on him here (cf. *Setting*, p. 307 n. 1; Davies
and Allison, *Matthew*, I, p. 134 n. 107). Betz, *Sermon on the Mount*, pp. 62-64,
takes the suggested tripartite division seriously, but the demands of his own dating
of the Sermon lead him to seek an alternative inspiration for it.

tral core of the Sermon is organized in accordance with the 'three pillars' ascribed to R. Simeon the Just (third century BCE): Torah, cult, and 'acts of mercy'.[27] A fresh interpretation of this in the light of the disappearance of the temple cult, attributed to R. Johanan b. Zakkai and thus contemporary with Matthew, understood it to mean: *study of* the Torah, prayer, and observance of the commandments.[28] The first two sections of the Sermon correspond closely with this; the third parts company with it, as can be seen both from its content and from the applications further on in the Gospel of Hos. 6.6 (9.13; 12.7), which are different from R. Johanan's and reflect a more inclusive understanding of the meaning of *ḥesed*.[29] The two matching sections into which 6.19–7.11 falls (both consisting of three short logia, a more extended poem, and a concluding epigram)[30] each cover different aspects of it.

We therefore now proceed to the examination of the four pairs of beatitudes.

27. *m. Ab.* 1.2. Manson's rendering of the third item is 'the imparting of kindness'.

28. Davies, *Setting*, p. 307.

29. *Setting*, pp. 306-308. C. Burchard, 'Versuch, das Thema der Bergpredigt zu finden', in G. Strecker (ed.), *Jesus Christus in Historie und Theologie* (Festschrift H. Conzelmann; Tübingen: J.C.B. Mohr, 1975), pp. 409-32 (428), goes so far as to say that Davies' theory breaks down on 6.19 onwards. But see further n. 104 below.

30. Cf. Green, *Matthew*, pp. 92-95; Allison, 'Structure', pp. 434-38; Davies and Allison, *Matthew*, I, pp. 626-67. Betz, *Sermon on the Mount*, p. 65, gives qualified support to Allison, though he finds some of the classification too rigid and artificial. I concur with this, though not with his approval of 'social issues' as the overall theme of the two sections, which is still too vague to serve as a version of 'acts of mercy'.

Chapter 7

THE MATCHED PAIRS

1. *I. The Poor in Spirit (πτωχοὶ τῷ πνεύματι)*
III. The Meek (πραεῖς)

a. *The Semitic Substratum*

The parallelism between these two beatitudes, as has already been observed,[1] was not lost on the early Church, and sufficiently explains the closer juxtaposition of them found in some MS authorities and supported by many modern exegetes.[2] But the alternating pattern which has been detected in the formal arrangement of the total composition favours the conclusion that the *prima facie* more difficult (and therefore text-critically preferable) order is in fact the true one. The parallelism is there nevertheless, and must be elucidated from the biblical background of the two words.

Some scholars[3] have sought to rest it on the affinity in sound, etymology and meaning between the Hebrew cognates *'ānî* and *'ānāw*. Certainly *'ānāw* lies behind πραεῖς, since III is a direct quotation of Ps. 36.11, where the Hebrew has *ᵃnāwîm*. But the Hebrew of Isa. 61.1 also has *ᵃnāwîm* (here rendered, untypically, by πτωχοί in the LXX); and the sequence of πτωχοῖς...πενθοῦντας...γῆν...κληρονομήσουσιτγὺ makes

---

1. Note 1 to Chapter 2.
2. See n. 2 to Chapter 2. Some who do not adopt that position hold that the two beatitudes were linked in the tradition before Matthew separated them; see Dupont, *Béatitudes*, III, p. 474 n. 1.; Guelich, *Sermon*, pp. 81-82. Cf. Broer, *Selig-preisungen*, p. 80.
3. E.g. Schniewind, *Matthäus*, p. 43; E. Lohmeyer, *Das Evangelium des Matthäus* (ed. W. Schmauch; KEKNT; Göttingen: Vandenhoeck & Ruprecht, 1956), pp. 81, 84; Grundmann, *Matthäus*, p. 123; Frankemölle, 'Makarismen', p. 59; G. Jacob, 'Die Proklamation der messianische Gemeinde: Zur Auslegung der Makarismen in der Bergpredigt', *ThV* 12 (1981), pp. 47-75: Guelich, 'Matthean Beatitudes', pp. 425-26.

it virtually certain that the text underlying I and linking it to what immediately follows it in the Matthaean composition is Isa. 61.1-7.[4] It is also the case that in 1QM 14.7, the first known Hebrew parallel to Matthew's πτωχοὶ τῷ πνεύματι, the evidence, though the text is fragmentary, favours *'ānāw* rather than *'ānî*.[5]

It would seem therefore that the two Greek words have a common substratum in the Hebrew *'ānāw*. But, for all that, the fact that the two beatitudes are in synonymous parallelism does not make them identical twins, as the distinction in the promised reward in any case makes clear. There is actually evidence, from a date considerably later than Matthew, that rabbinic exegesis working from Hebrew alone was capable of offering significantly different interpretations of the one word in the same two contexts.[6] Matthew was able in addition to draw on the translation variants in the LXX; he was certainly familiar with, and himself sometimes practised,[7] the type of exegesis which sought additional light on the meaning (or relevance) of a text from renderings of it into other languages. For this reason the regular meaning of the Greek words, while it is to be kept subordinate to the Hebrew substratum, is not to be simply disregarded.

The history of the usage of the Hebrew words for 'poor'[8] is complex, and reveals a process of development and a hospitality to fresh thinking which were not necessarily exhausted by the beginning of the Christian

---

4. So Dupont, *Béatitudes*, III, *passim*; Frankemölle, 'Makarismen', pp. 59-60, 69-70.

5. See J. Dupont, 'Les πτωχοὶ τῷ πνεύματι et les *'nwy rwh* de Qumran', in J. Blinzler, O. Kuss and F. Mussner (eds.), *Neutestamentliche Aufsätze* (Festschrift J. Schmid; Regensburg: Regensburger, 1963), pp. 53-64 (54-56).

6. See F. Böhl, 'Die Demut (*'nwh*) als höchste der Tugenden: Bemerkungen zu Mt 5,3.5', *BZ* NS 20 (1976), pp. 217-23. Rather strikingly in view of my own findings (below, §§1b, e *ad fin.*), the interpretations that he discovers are (for Ps. 37.11) 'Streitverzicht und Versöhnungswille', and (for Isa. 61.1) 'glaubiges Vertrauen'.

7. See n. 10 to Chapter 6 above.

8. See F. Hauck and S. Schulz, 'πραΰς κτλ.', *TDNT*, VI, pp. 647-51; E. Bammel, 'πτωχός', *TDNT*, VI, pp. 885-902; W. Grundmann, 'ταπεινός κτλ.', *TDNT*, VIII, pp. 1-26; H. Birkeland, *'Ani und 'anaw in der Psalmen* (Skriften utgitt av Det Norske Videnskaps-Akademie i Oslo, II. Hist.-Filos. Klasse 1932, No. 4; Oslo: Dybwad, 1933); *idem, Der Feinde des Individuums in der israelitischen Psalmenliteratur* (Oslo: Grondahl, 1933), pp. 317-20; Percy, *Botschaft*, pp. 45-63; R. Leivestad, 'ΤΑΠΕΙΝΟΣ–ΤΑΠΕΙΝΟΦΡΩΝ', *NovT* 8 (1966), pp. 36-47; Dupont, *Béatitudes*, II, pp. 24-34.

era. In pre-exilic times they were applied especially to the situation of Israelites suffering economic exploitation at the hands of their fellow Israelites (which deprived them of their rights as members of the covenant people, and thus cried out for the intervention of God). The experience of exile widened this application to cover the nation as a whole, or rather that remnant of it which remained faithful in captivity and looked for restoration to its own land; but after the return the evidence from the Psalter[9] in particular suggests that the vicissitudes of life in the restored community tended to narrow it once more, so that the remnant is now commonly an oppressed but faithful group (or groups) within the nation as a whole. Eventually the faithfulness comes to be seen in terms of obedience to the Torah. The most logical expression of this development is to be found at Qumran, a community which has separated itself from the rest of Israel to observe the Torah in its full rigour,[10] and which speaks of itself regularly as 'the poor';[11] a self-designation which apparently reflects neither its practice of community of goods nor its awareness of the dangers of wealth, but a corporate submission to the will of God.[12]

All the words for 'poor' were affected by this development, but the relatively late coinage *'ānāw* seems to have moved more rapidly and more predominantly than its older cognate *'ānî* from an originally sociological connotation to an ethical and religious one.[13] Whereas in the Psalter *'ānî* is more commonly used, especially when linked with *'ebyôn* (the pair being rendered πτωχὸς καὶ πενής in the LXX[14]), to convey the

9.   Birkeland, *'Ani*, pp. 223-32; Leivestad, 'ΤΑΠΕΙΝΟΣ', pp. 37-39; Dupont, *Béatitudes*, II, p. 27.

10.   Cf. 1QS 5.7-11; and see G. Vermes, *The Dead Sea Scrolls in English* (Harmondsworth: Penguin, 4th edn, 1995), pp. 42-64, on the place of the covenant in Essene thinking.

11.   See J. Maier, *Die Texte vom Toten Meer* (Basel: Reinhardt, 1960), pp. 83-87.

12.   See Dupont, *Béatitudes*, III, pp. 462-65.

13.   On this see esp. Leivestad's nuancing of Grundmann's too clear-cut distinctions, 'ΤΑΠΕΙΝΟΣ', pp. 36-37; cf. Dupont, *Béatitudes*, II, p. 27. The fact that, with the single exception of its application to Moses at Num. 12.3 (possibly a slip), *'ānāw* is always found in the plural may indicate that those of whom it was used already saw themselves as some sort of defined group; see n. 62 below.

14.   The choice of equivalents illustrates both the problems faced by the LXX translators and the hazard of over-reliance on Greek lexicography. In secular Greek

oppression of the remnant, *ʿānāw* expresses rather its faithfulness under oppression. A parallel shift of meaning from subjection to submissiveness has often been observed in the etymological history of the word 'humble',[15] its nearest English equivalent.

If then *ʿānāw* lies behind both beatitudes, the root meaning of both will be 'humble'. It remains to be seen what nuances, if any, are added to either by the semantic and other associations of the different words chosen to render it in Greek. Since this is by general consent a less contentious matter to establish in the case of the πραεῖς than in that of the πτωχοὶ τῷ πνεύματι, and since the former is the more usual LXX rendering of *ʿnāwîm*, it will be convenient to take that first, and then to examine the latter in the light of our findings.[16]

b. *The Meaning of 'Meek'*

What the Greek πραΰς conveys in common speech is basically gentleness, unassertiveness, non-resistance and non-violence.[17] As Dupont has shown,[18] these elements are already present in the later Jewish understanding of *ʿānāw* alongside its basic connotation of humility, and this not only justifies the LXX translators' preference for it in rendering the Hebrew word, but is reflected in early Greek-speaking Christian usage both within and outside the New Testament.[19] This is evidently true of the two passages in which the word recurs in Matthew. The two texts are formally parallel, with a suggestion of hendiadys in each:

πραΰς...καὶ ταπεινὸς τῇ καρδίᾳ (11.29):
πραΰς καὶ ἐπιβεβηκὼς ἐπὶ ὄνον (21.5).

Though one of these is found in words uttered in this Gospel by Jesus himself, while the other forms part of a prophecy quoted by the Evan-

---

usage πενής denotes one who needs to work (manually) for his living, πτωχός one who has to beg for it.

15. Dupont, 'Les πτωχοὶ', p. 62, notes that the true Hebrew counterpart to the etymology of 'humble' is *šāpel*. The usefulness of the looser analogy is not necessarily affected, however.

16. This is undertaken with the expectation of finding some *differentia* in III and not having to treat it, with Dupont (and others), as a virtual clone of I. On I as the heading and base text for the whole poem see Chapter 8 below.

17. Hauck and Schulz, 'πραΰς', p. 649.

18. *Béatitudes*, III, pp. 496-502.

19. *Béatitudes*, III, pp. 502-509.

gelist as fulfilled in him, both, as we have already seen,[20] are actually the product of Matthew's own exegesis. Both use the word of Jesus personally, and each combines it with another epithet carrying a significant overlap of meaning.

(1)   πραΰς εἰμι καὶ ταπεινὸς τῇ καρδίᾳ,
             καὶ εὑρήσετε ἀνάπαυσιν ταῖς ψυχαῖς ὑμῶν.

For general commentary on the poem of the Easy Yoke, see Chapter 4 §7a above. The poem leads in to the controversies with the Pharisees over the requirements of the law in ch. 12, in which these latter are depicted as overbearing in their personal attitude and harsh in the demands they make on their people in the name of the Torah and its strict observance; whereas Jesus, by contrast, is not only humble and unassertive in his own bearing, but gentle and considerate of human frailty in what he requires of disciples.

These then are what the context suggests as the qualities conveyed by πραΰς...καὶ ταπεινὸς τῇ καρδίᾳ.[21] It would be possible to take the expression as a straightforward hendiadys: in that case ταπεινὸς (which is occasionally used to translate 'ānāw in the LXX[22]) would not add what πραΰς by itself lacks, but would reinforce the basic sense of the latter, which is nevertheless the more inclusive word and determines the force of the combined expression. On the other hand the two words may be intended to convey distinct nuancings of the underlying 'ānāw. ταπεινὸς τῇ καρδίᾳ is reminiscent of texts which will be found to have associations with πτωχοὶ τῷ πνεύματι; it may therefore (to anticipate certain conclusions of the next section) introduce the thought of Jesus as 'identified with sinners'[23] (and therefore not one to make harsh judgments of them or to refuse them the benefit of any doubt in difficult cases)—a possible target of the appeal to Hos. 6.6 at 12.7.

20. Chapter 3 §6 and Chapter 4 §7a, above.
21. For the combined expression cf. Zeph. 3.12. Although πραΰς there represents 'ānî (note the singular; similarly in Zech. 9.9 [below]), the context (of a restored Israel) makes clear that the words are to be understood qualitatively. There could thus be influence at the level of the Greek text.
22. Amos 2.7; Zech. 2.3; Isa. 11.4; 61.1 (with S[1]). Both meanings are covered. Cf. nn. 64, 66 below.
23. See §1d below.

On either interpretation gentleness towards others is a significant constituent of the total meaning of πραΰς for Matthew.[24] Both the unassertiveness and the gentleness are taken up a little further on in ch. 12 in his version of Isa. 42.1-4 at 12.18-21, especially vv. 19-20.[25]

(2)   πραΰς καὶ ἐπιβεβηκὼς ἐπὶ ὄνον,
        καὶ ἐπὶ πῶλον υἱὸν ὑποζυγίου.

The composite formula quotation of Isa. 62.2 and Zech. 9.9 (only the latter is discussed here) at 21.5 has been briefly introduced in Chapter 3.[26] At two points it differs remarkably from both the LXX and the MT:

(a)   the omission of the words represented in LXX by δίκαιος and σώζων. As neither of these are words that Matthew would normally seek to avoid, it would seem that his purpose in suppressing them here was to give special emphasis to πραΰς;

(b)   the rearrangement of the words for 'ass'. MT has three: *ḥᵃmôr* (he-ass), *'ayîr* (young ass), *'āṯôn* (she-ass), in that order, the first two, in parallelism, denoting one animal, the third its (off-stage) mother. The LXX, doubtless reflecting the limitations of Greek vocabulary, reduces these to two, ὑποζύγιον καὶ πῶλον νέον, again denoting one animal. Matthew increases the words to three again and the animals to two, adding ὄνον and placing it first, but retaining ὑποζύγιον in third place and using both words to denote the female, the colt's mother.

These alterations are clearly deliberate, and Stendahl[27] is right, so far as he goes, in connecting them with the implication that Jesus rode in on both animals. But he stops short of explaining why even Matthew would want to imply anything so visually grotesque.[28] That question

24. Cf. Luz, *Matthew*, I, pp. 241-42: 'in Jewish parenesis humility and kindness are inseparable'.
25. See Chapter 3 §4 above.
26. Chapter 3 §6 above.
27. *School*, p. 119. He points out that rabbinic commentators on Zech. 9.9 also lay most stress on the word *'ānî* and on the ass.
28. Cf. Dupont's observations (*Béatitudes*, III, p. 540) on Matthew's general lack of visual imagination. Against the argument of Strecker (*Weg*, p. 76, followed by Meier, *Law*, pp. 16-18, *Vision*, p. 22, and Broer, *Seligpreisungen*, p. 79 n. 53) that the final redactor of Matthew was unfamiliar with Hebrew poetic parallelism, see especially M. Hengel, 'Zur matthäischen Bergpredigt und ihrem jüdischen

must be answered on a symbolic and prefigurative rather than a literal level, and his retention of ὑποζύγιον, which has no obvious literal relevance, may offer the clue. Though Jesus is acclaimed here (by his disciples) as king, his rule on earth will not be exercised by himself in his earthly life, but claimed in his name by those and other disciples, the meek who are to inherit the earth. These will be 'under the yoke' in the sense of 11.28-30;[29] but since the purpose of a yoke in its literal meaning is to control two working animals, the interpretation early proposed by Justin Martyr,[30] that it also signifies a Church recruited both from those previously 'under the yoke' of the Torah and from the hitherto unharnessed Gentiles, may well not be foreign to the Evangelist's own mind. No other suggestion makes any satisfactory sense of the double mount.

It remains to consider the position of ὄνον and the way in which πραΰς is linked with it in the quotation. That Matthew draws attention as he does to the species of the mount is to be connected, as some commentators recognize,[31] with its function in the original prophecy, that of signifying that the rider's intentions were peaceable.[32] The sense of πραΰς which fits most naturally with this is 'non-violent'; 'non-violent and pacific' would be an accurate paraphrase of the combined expression, which is not quite a hendiadys, but links the beatitude on

Hintergrund', *TRu* 52 (1987), pp. 327-400 (342-45) and nn. 28, 31-33; also Gundry, *Matthew*, p. 409, as well as the evidence of the present study.

29. Zeph. 3.9-12 speaks of a single yoke for Jews and Gentiles, and links this with the prospect of a people that will be πραΰς καὶ ταπεινός; see on 11.28-30 (Chapter 4 §7a, above), and cf. Charette, *Recompense*, p. 86. Allison, *New Moses*, pp. 248-53, with some support from later rabbinic tradition, sees in ὑποζύγιον a reference to Exod. 4.20, i.e. to Moses as a type of Christ. Matthew certainly alludes to the latter text at 2.19, and we shall find reason to suspect that, like Rev. 11.8, he thinks of Jerusalem as 'Egypt' (see §3a.1, on 2.15). But while 21.11 may well allude to Deut. 18.15, the predominant type in 21.1-17 is David rather than Moses. Hence the suggestion of M.J.J. Menken, 'The Quotations from Zech 9,9 in Mt 21,5 and in John 12,15', in Denaux (ed.), *John and the Synoptics*, pp. 571-78 (574), that Matthew is thinking of 2 Kgdms 16.2, which however can be at most only a minor contributor to the text.

30. *Dialogue against Trypho*, 53; cf. Lindars, *Apologetic*, pp. 115; for attribution to Matthew, Green, *Matthew*, p. 176.

31. E.g. McNeile, *Matthew*, p. 295; Schweizer, *Matthew*, p. 404; Jacob, 'Proklamation', p. 72.

32. See n. 85 to Chapter 3. In view of the associations noted there, a reference to the domestic donkey as a 'humble beast' seems less probable.

the meek with that on the peacemakers as 11.29 (on my second interpretation) linked it with that on the poor in spirit. This aspect of the
meaning of πραΰς is spelled out, though without the word, in the command not to resist the aggressor at 5.38-42, and Jesus is depicted as
himself acting upon it at the time of his arrest at 26.47-50.

The humility which III commends is thus to be seen as in general a
humility towards people, which can be qualified as gentle, non-assertive
and non-violent.

It is promised that the πραεῖς will inherit τὴν γῆν. That this means
the earth and not just the territory of Israel[33] can be confirmed by an
examination of Matthew's word usage. Apart from the contexts in
which it simply means 'ground' or 'soil'[34] (which are irrelevant here),
the word when used absolutely means the whole earth;[35] when used of a
particular territory it is always qualified by the addition of the appropriate name[36] (with the exception of one passage where the demonstrative pronoun does duty [twice] for this[37]). It will be recalled that the
last of the three temptations of Jesus in the wilderness (4.8-10) offers
him 'all the kingdoms of the world'. His investment with 'all authority
in heaven and earth' (28.18), by contrast, is the consequence not of the
exercise of power as the world understands it, but of his meek submission to death; his kingdom in its earthly aspect is to be claimed, as we
saw above,[38] by his missionary disciples (28.19-20), using the same
methods and exhibiting the same qualities. It is not wholly distinct from
what Matthew calls the 'kingdom of heaven', nor as yet fully coextensive with it; rather it is that proleptic and provisional form in which
that kingdom already exists and is at work on earth in the interim period

33. Cf. W.D. Davies, *The Gospel and the Land* (Berkeley: University of California Press, 1974), pp. 360-62; Beare, *Records*, p. 55. Strecker, *Sermon on the
Mount*, p. 36, thinks of a spiritualized rather than a universalized 'land'. Dupont,
Béatitudes, III, pp. 485-86 argues for a transfigured earth as the locus of the final
eschatological reign as understood by Matthew; cf. Charette, *Recompense*, pp. 86-
87.

34. 13.5, 18, 23; 15.35; 23.35; 25.18, 25; possibly also 27.51, but cf. next note.

35. 21 times in Matthew, including 27.45 which clearly depicts a cosmic event
(note also the allusion to Amos 8.9, already in Mark). For the expression 'heaven
and earth' cf. n. 325 to Chapter 4).

36. 2.6; 4.15 (MtR of LXX); 2.21, 22 (γῆ Ἰσραήλ); 10.15=11.24.

37. 9.26, 31.

38. In Chapter 4 §10c, above.

before the final eschatological reign.[39] But the full inheritance of the earth belongs to the latter.

c. *The Poor in Spirit: Dupont and After*

Whatever may finally need to be said in criticism of his conclusions, Dupont's review of the history of the interpretation of this expression,[40] and the subtle and extended argument which he bases on it[41] and to which it is impossible to do justice in a bare summary, are the indispensable starting point for any subsequent discussion. He establishes, first of all, that in this kind of expression it is the nominal suffix that qualifies the adjective, and not the adjective the noun, and is thus able to dispose effectively of interpretations that construe πτωχοὶ negatively, in the sense of a deficiency in whatever πνεῦμα is taken to mean—whether courage, native wit, or the Holy Spirit.[42] Next, he argues that what a suffix such as τῷ πνεύματι does for the adjective it qualifies is to effect a *transposition* from an exterior situation (where the adjective by itself would convey that) to an interior quality or attitude. Where the adjective by itself already expresses the interior attitude, it is not further modified, though it may be clarified, by the suffix. On the basis of this he rejects, on the one hand, those interpretations for which τῷ πνεύματι simply expresses an inner attitude to a real, literal poverty, whether chronic and endured or voluntarily undertaken,[43] as not effecting a full transposition; and on the other hand that line of interpretation (on whose historical roots and theological *Tendenz* he puts his finger very acutely[44]), which can be summed up in the NEB rendering 'how blest are those who know their need of God',[45] as requiring a 'double trans-

---

39. Cf. 13.41.
40. *Béatitudes*, III, pp. 385-450.
41. *Béatitudes*, III, pp. 450-71.
42. *Béatitudes*, III, p. 396.
43. E.g. Lohmeyer, *Matthäus*, pp. 82-83; Gaechter, *Matthäus-Evangelium*, p. 147; K. Schubert, 'The Sermon on the Mount', in K. Stendahl (ed.), *The Scrolls and the New Testament* (London: SCM Press, 1958), pp. 118-28 (122-23); cf. Dupont, *Béatitudes*, III, pp. 424-27.
44. *Béatitudes*, III, pp. 442-50, but subsuming also (pp. 429-42) the application of the beatitude to the condition of the despised *ʿām ha-ʾāreṣ* proposed by J. Weiss. For associations with the interpretation of Luther cf. *Béatitudes*, III, pp. 438, 445.
45. Dupont does not quote this rendering (nor its earlier form of 1961 'who know that they are poor'), but its affinities with that which he quotes (p. 445 n. 6) from A.M. Hunter, *Design for Life* (London: SCM Press, 1953), p. 31, 'those who

position' from a literal to a metaphorical understanding of poverty, and from the exterior condition to an interior attitude towards it. He then leaves himself with a straight choice between two interpretations of 'poor in spirit' not excluded by this principle (both, as he shows,[46] well represented in the tradition of patristic exegesis): 'humble' and 'detached from wealth'. The second of these he rejects as insufficiently grounded in the usage of the New Testament and its Semitic background,[47] and he therefore settles for the first.[48] The notion of humility for which he argues is just sufficiently nuanced to distinguish it from the self-abasement of 18.4; 23.12,[49] but hardly from the unassertiveness conveyed by III (see below).

Dupont has made an impressive and formidable case. There remain nevertheless certain difficulties which his treatment has not resolved.

(1) He seems to begin by assuming that the Evangelist intended his expression to have a single unambiguous meaning, which can be established by a process of elimination. This disregards not only the poetic character of Matthew's writing to which I have drawn attention, but the 'inclusive' tendency of the tradition of scriptural exegesis to which he undoubtedly belongs.[50]

(2) Dupont does not really explain why, if Matthew understood the first Beatitude, as reformulated by him, in this way, he went out of his way to introduce another, its wording lifted straight out of the LXX, to convey an almost identical meaning. At times Dupont writes as if there were no nuancing on either side to distinguish between them. What finally emerges, however, is that there is some nuancing, but it is all on the side of the 'meek'; the meaning of the Greek πραΰς is allowed some slight influence,[51] that of πτωχός none. The impression given (if not actually stated) is that the πραεῖς have been introduced as a control on the interpretation of πτωχοί; no sense of the latter word which is not valid also for the former will be admissible.

---

feel their spiritual poverty', are clear enough. Broer, *Seligpreisungen*, p. 68, has picked up the 1961 version with his 'Wohl denen, die arm sind und es wissen'. REB has wisely reverted to a literal rendering. But see further n. 63, below.

46. *Béatitudes*, III, pp. 399-411 and 411-17 respectively.
47. *Béatitudes*, III, pp. 451-57.
48. *Béatitudes*, III, pp. 457-69.
49. *Béatitudes*, III, p. 470. On 18.4; 23.12 see §1d, below.
50. See Chapter 3, *passim*.
51. *Béatitudes*, III, pp. 509-10.

(3) A transposition from literal to metaphorical is not strictly the same as one from exterior to interior, and the suffix 'in spirit', more or less by definition, conveys that the transposition is of the latter kind, whether or not it also involves, as it commonly does, the former. Dupont is right to say that when an adjective already has an 'interior' sense the suffix adds nothing new to this.[52] But it does not follow from that that if it has a metaphorical but not an interior sense the suffix will still add nothing. The combination of metaphorical and exterior is not very common, but its presence is not to be ruled out *a priori*. An example from the Matthaean vocabulary (though not found with a suffix) is his use of μικρός at 10.42; 18.5-14, of which more will be said below.

(4) The root of the difficulty can be identified as the genetic method on which Dupont relies, and the source hypothesis from which he starts. This postulates a tradition of beatitude material behind Matthew (and Luke) going back, in part at least, to Jesus himself. Matthew's 'in spirit' is presumed to qualify Jesus' 'Blessed are the poor'; it only needs to be determined in what sense. Either Jesus meant the materially poor and Matthew 'transposed' this,[53] or he was using 'poor' in a 'religious' (i.e., for Dupont, already transposed) sense and Matthew rescued it from the ambiguity consequent on its translation into Greek (which misled Luke).[54] But in the light of the oscillations in the significance of the Hebrew words for 'poor', to speak of a 'religious' sense for them is itself ambiguous. The true contrast is between those who are poor in an exterior sense, whether understood materially or figuratively (e.g. of 'God's downtrodden people'), and those who have the corresponding interior qualities or self-awareness; only the latter can be denoted by the suffix 'in spirit'.

Dupont's source-critical assumptions, it will be evident, are not mine. A study that does not begin by assuming Q is free to prescind from the dilemma to which the genetic approach leads, and can start instead from an examination of the Evangelist's own word usage. The lessons learned from a critical evaluation of Dupont's findings can still have a substantial influence on the direction of this.

---

52. *Béatitudes*, III, pp. 392-93.
53. So, e.g., Percy, *Botschaft*, pp. 45-84, esp. pp. 81-82; L.E. Keck, 'The Poor among the Saints in the New Testament', *ZNW* 56 (1965), pp. 100-29 (113).
54. So Manson, *Sayings*, p. 47; Davies, *Setting*, p. 253; Dupont, *Béatitudes*, I, pp. 216-17.

d. *Poor in Spirit: The Poor as Sinners*

Apart from this beatitude the word πτωχός is found four times in this Gospel (11.5; 19.21; 26.6, 11), always in the plural. In the three latter (all derived from Mark) the word is used in its material sense (always of the poor as objects of charity); these will be considered in their turn. 11.5 evidently gives it, in some sense, a 'religious' meaning, and like 5.3 it carries a clear allusion to Isa. 61.1.[55]

11.5 has already been examined in relation both to its Old Testament background and to its context in this Gospel.[56] It was seen then that every item is a fulfilment of prophecy, and that each of them has its counterpart in chs. 8–9 of the Gospel (in every case drawn from Mark, though without regard for the latter's context or order). The climax of the list of messianic wonders is the proclamation of the good news to the poor. We therefore expect some counterpart to this too in the previous narrative section, and it is to be found at 9.1-14, which comprises: (a) the association of the healing of the paralytic with the forgiveness of sins (which receives all the emphasis);[57] (b) the call of Matthew the tax-collector (the alteration of his name from Mark's 'Levi' implying that the inner circle around Jesus included reclaimed public sinners from the beginning);[58] (c) the controversy over Jesus' entertainment of tax-collectors and other outcasts, with the proverbial saying that it is the sick who need the doctor interpreted, with a sideways glance at Hos. 6.6, of the gospel call to sinners. The 'poor' of 11.5 are thus identified not as materially poor (far from it, in some cases!), but as sinners, those whose way of life has put them outside the pale of observant Judaism.[59] They

---

55. On the connection of 11.5 with 5.3 cf. Bammel, 'πτωχός', p. 904 (who allows an element of self-awareness in the meaning of τῷ πνεύματι; p. 904 n. 171); Gnilka, *Matthäusevangelium*, I, p. 408; Catchpole, *Quest*, p. 17.

56. Chapter 4 §3, above.

57. See Strecker, *Weg*, pp. 220-26.

58. So Green, *Matthew*, p. 103, on 9.9.

59. The recent study of F. Herrenbrück, *Jesus und die Zöllner* (WUNT, 2.41; Tübingen: J.C.B. Mohr, 1990), pp. 162-225, by establishing that in the former territory of the Seleucids their system of revenue-raising remained substantially unchanged under the Romans, will compel scholars to modify their account of the social and religious status of the τελῶναι in first-century Palestine. Their function was that of revenue-contractors, who did business directly with the administration, and the evidence is that they were generally well integrated socially, and to a considerable extent even religiously, with contemporary Jewish society. See the discussion of Herrenbrück's case in Chilton, *Feast*, pp. 26-31: he sees the linking of them

reappear in the mission discourse, which extends to the disciples the work of proclamation inaugurated by Jesus, as 'the lost sheep of the house of Israel' (10.6),[60] an expression which echoes, among other texts,[61] Ps. 118.176, the cry of the Psalmist that he has transgressed the Law for which he has been professing his love at such length.

That the 'poor' of Isa. 61.1 can be understood here not of the oppressed faithful but of the marginalized backsliders is a striking divergence from the *'^{a}nāwîm*-piety of post-exilic Judaism,[62] without doubt to be attributed to the influence of the remembered attitude of Jesus himself, the impact of which reverberates unmistakably in all the Synoptic Gospels, whatever view is taken of their origin and sources.

'Poor' then denotes a situation which the gospel of the kingdom reverses: as the blind and the lame are healed and the dead restored to life, so the sinner is called to repentance and/or forgiven. It cannot therefore stand unmodified in a list of the qualities or attitudes characteristic of the converted and committed disciple; a transposition of some kind is called for. This is presumably what the suffix τῷ πνεύματι effects.[63] If those who have accepted the way of a disciple are no longer

---

with 'sinners' as reflecting a combination of the traditional suspicion of the tax-collector, a genuine awareness that many of them were corrupt or extortionate, and the concern of certain Pharisaic groups for an understanding of ethnic and legal purity which the conditions of his work required the collector to transgress. Cf. nn. 83, 84 below.

60. So Bammel, 'πτωχός', p. 898 n. 108; cf. 15.24 (MtR of Mk).

61. E.g. Ezek. 34.4, 8, 16; Mic. 4.6; 3 Kgdms 22.17.

62. As found in the Psalter; see §1a and notes. Later movements within a still pluralist Judaism continued to use this language of themselves: the *h^{a}sîdîm* of the Maccabaean period, the Qumran covenanters, the (probably) Pharisaic group that composed the *Psalms of Solomon*; if the name given to those later survivors from Jewish Christianity, the Ebionites, was of their own choosing, they could be added to the list. See Bammel, 'πτωχός', pp. 896-98. But to postulate a single continuing movement within Judaism from which some of the earliest Christian converts could have been recruited (so Brown, *Birth*, pp. 350-55) begs too many questions. Cf. Percy, *Botschaft*, pp. 68-70.

63. Cf. T. Soiron, *Die Bergpredigt Jesu* (Freiburg: Herder, 1941), p. 159: 'Die Armut in Geiste, die Demut des Sünderbewusstseins...' The difference between this and the 'Lutheran' understanding discounted above (cf. n. 45) may not seem very great. Here however the suffix expresses not just an awareness of a universal condition conveyed by πτωχός (for which cf. also Betz, *Sermon on the Mount*, p. 115: 'an intellectual insight into the human condition'), but a positive and continuing self-identification with those to whose situation the good news (Isa. 61.1) is

public and unrepentant sinners, 'poor' in the already metaphorical but as yet exterior sense of 11.5, true humility before God will require them nevertheless to see themselves as sinners still.

What will this mean in practice? First, naturally, contrition, an awareness of the need for forgiveness and a readiness to seek it. This will be taken up in the petition for forgiveness in the Lord's Prayer. But it is already present in germ in the Old Testament background, beginning with the text which has already been identified as the starting point of the Beatitudes:

> Isa. 61.1: ...εὐαγγελίσασθαι πτωχοῖς ἀπέσταλκέν με, ἰάσασθαι τοὺς συντετριμμένους τῇ καρδίᾳ,

> cf. Ps. 33.19: ἐγγὺς Κύριος τοῖς συντετριμμένοις τὴν καρδίαν, καὶ τοὺς ταπεινοὺς τῷ πνεύματι σώσει.

Ps. 50.19 sets these expressions firmly in the context of penitence and contrition:

> θυσία τῷ θεῷ πνεῦμα συντετριμμένον·
> καρδίαν συντετριμμένην καὶ τεταπεινωμένην ὁ θεὸς οὐκ ἐξου-
> θενώσει.[64]

Secondly, the reclaimed sinner is to remain identified, in his own estimation, with sinners in (not his but) their sinfulness. The probable reason for the change of the converted tax-collector's name has already been noted. It is also possible that the reply of Jesus to the Baptist's disclaimer at 3.16, 'thus it is fitting for us to fulfil all righteousness', which G. Barth[65] sought to connect, as an expression of his acceptance of humiliation, with Beatitude III,[66] is after all concerned not only with the

---

addressed. Cf. E. Cothenet, 'La baptême selon saint Matthieu', *SNTU*(L) 9 (1984) pp. 79-94 (93): 'En se solidarisant avec la foule des pénitents Jésus avait montré que la "voie de justice" consistait à rejoindre les pécheurs pour leur apporter la bonne nouvelle de la miséricorde de Dieu'. If the subject of that observation is Jesus himself, it should not be forgotten that the Beatitudes serve as a portrait of the Master as well as a model for his disciples. See below, Chapter 10.

64. Leivestad, 'ΤΑΠΕΙΝΟΣ', p. 44, contends that 'meek' ('demütig') is too weak a rendering for ταπεινός in this context.

65. Barth, in Bornkamm, Barth and Held, *Tradition*, pp. 123, 129, 137-41.

66. Thus p. 140: 'Jesus fulfils all righteousness by his humiliation [better: 'humbling of himself'; cf. p. 141] in that he enters the ranks of sinners'. Cf. n. 63 above. On the residual Paulinism in Barth's understanding of 'righteousness' in

problem of the Messiah's baptism by the forerunner, but also with his acceptance of a baptism of repentance,[67] and is thus an example of what, on this interpretation, is meant by I. There is an interesting Pauline parallel to this in 2 Cor. 8.9: 'For you know the grace of our Lord Jesus Christ, how though he was rich, yet for your sakes he became poor, that you through his poverty might be rich'. This usually gets a purely incarnational interpretation, but the thought of the exchange between Christ and the redeemed has already been anticipated, in terms which, if different, are complementary to it rather than exclusive, at 5.21: 'God made him who had known no sin to be sin on our behalf, that in him we might become the righteousness of God'. If 'becoming poor' and 'being made sin' are speaking of the same process, as seems to be the case,[68] then we have here a parallel to the association of 'poverty' and sinfulness. In view of what will be said below, it is striking that Paul introduces the thought into an appeal for generosity with money.

This approach to discipleship has reverberations elsewhere in Matthew. In the Sermon on the Mount disciples are commanded not to judge, since they are themselves under judgment (7.1-2, with its sequel in 7.3-5). Outside it there are the conclusions to the parable of the wedding feast (the wedding garment, 22.11-14)[69] and the Great Assize (25.41-45),[70] which seem to be warnings to Christian converts not to regard themselves as *ipso facto* exempt from the judgment that has already overtaken the old Israel. There is also a counterpart to the suggested understanding of 'poor' in the teaching on humility in ch. 18. In 18.4 the disciples who have been disputing about greatness are shown a

Matthew cf. B. Przybylski, *Righteousness in Matthew and his World of Thought* (SNTSMS, 41; Cambridge: Cambridge University Press, 1980), pp. 91-94.

67. For Matthew John's baptism is a sign of repentance (3.1-2), not (as in Mark and Luke) a means of forgiveness, which for him is rooted in the death of Christ (26.28; cf. 1.21).

68. The majority of commentators refer to Phil. 2.5-11 (as traditionally interpreted): for details see Thrall, *II Corinthians*, II (published 2000; I am obliged to Dr Thrall for allowing me a preview of her comment on this verse). The parallel with 2 Cor. 5.21 is recognized by H. Windisch, C.K. Barrett, V.P. Furnish, R.P. Martin, C. Wolff, and by Thrall herself.

69. For the meaning of this (the Matthaean conclusion to an arguably Matthaean parable) see J.D.M. Derrett, *Law in the New Testament* (London: Darton, Longman & Todd, 1970), pp. 126-55 (142-43, 155); Goulder, *Midrash*, pp. 415-18.

70. On the exegesis of this see §2c, with nn. 146-50 below.

child as a model of the humility in which true greatness consists;[71] in 18.5 they are told that to receive in the name of Christ a child thus (metaphorically!) understood is to receive Christ himself, and in 18.6 that to 'scandalize' one of the 'little ones' (μικρῶν: cf. 10.42) is a matter of infinite gravity, comparable (it is implied) to Judas' betrayal of Jesus.[72] The impression given by the warnings in 18.5-14 is that the word μικροί is being currently used to disparage a particular group or category of church members,[73] it would seem for their moral shortcomings;[74] the injunctions to disciples with which the chapter opens (18.1-4) convey, on the other hand, the Evangelist's determination to defend or reclaim 'littleness' as an esential element in the self-understanding of every disciple.[75] If they continue through life to see them-

71. Dupont (*Béatitudes*, III, pp. 465-66) himself draws attention to the correspondence of the themes with which the Sermon on the Mount and ch. 18 open (though he qualifies this on p. 470). See further Schniewind, *Matthäus*, p. 193; O. Michel, 'μικρός', *TDNT*, IV, pp. 650-61, esp. n. 22; S. Légasse, *Jésus et l'enfant* (Paris: Gabalda, 1969), pp. 35-36, 65-67, 223-24; W.G. Thompson, *Matthew's Advice to a Divided Community* (AnBib, 44; Rome: Pontifical Biblical Institute, 1970), pp. 69-84, 108-11, 119-20, 133-39, 153-74; Frankemölle, *Jahwebund*, pp. 185-88.

72. Cf. 26.24. This connection is due to MtR, and was picked up by *1 Clem.* 46.8; cf. Thompson, *Advice*, pp. 110-11; Green, 'Clement', pp. 13-14.

73. W. Pesch, *Matthäus der Seelsorger* (SBS, 2; Stuttgart: Katholisches Bibelwerk, 1966), pp. 20-21, assumes two groups within the Matthaean community: those little in others' eyes (and often in their own), and those who see themselves as great in terms of religious performance or standing in the community. Thompson, *Advice*, p. 119, resists identification of the μικροί with a particular defined group (e.g., recent converts), but sees (pp. 153, 163) a close connection between them and sheep going astray (cf. 18.10, 14), which of course can happen to any disciple. The language nevertheless indicates a current pastoral problem in the church, in which the Evangelist sees a parallel to the situation of the 'lost sheep' of 10.7; 15.24 in the context of Jesus' own ministry.

74. A possible clue to the meaning is the use of ἐλάχιστος at 5.19 to belittle those who sit lightly to the details of the law. In its present context it is possible to understand this of the law as newly interpreted by Jesus (cf. 28.20); but it is unlikely that that was the original force of the saying, which could have become, in the wrong hands, a stick to beat Christians who lived ἐθνικῶς. ἐλαχίστων at 25.40, 45 is clearly the counterpart of μικρῶν at 10.42; so, rightly, Stanton, *Gospel*, p. 215.

75. So Frankemölle, *Jahwebund*, p. 186 (following Schniewind, *Matthäus*, and Michel, 'μικρός'): 'Die *qtnym*-μικροί sind eine neue Variation zu den '*nwym*-πτωχοὶ τῷ πνεύματι und den Kontextbegriffen in 5,3-10'; contra Légasse, *Enfant*, p. 65.

selves as 'little ones', they will not be able at the same time to despise or write off those in whom they should be recognizing Christ. This is little more than the message of 7.1-2 in different language. There is a looser parallel in the instruction at 23.8 not to accept the designation 'rabbi', which implies that all, whatever their gifts or responsibilities, are to continue to look upon themselves as learners. The need to 'humble' (ταπεινοῦν) oneself is stressed in both contexts (18.4; 23.12).[76]

Finally, it may be observed that the 'spirit of poverty' (i.e., humility) inculcated at Qumran, which, as we have seen, has little to do with material poverty or community of goods, is associated in the *Community Rule* with the forgiveness of sins:

> He shall be cleansed from all his sins by the spirit of holiness uniting him to his truth, and his iniquity shall be expiated by the spirit of uprightness and humility. And when his flesh is sprinkled with purifying water and sanctified by cleansing water, it shall be made clean by the humble submission of his soul to all the precepts of God.[77]

Since the practice at Qumran, in contrast with the Christian Church, was to baptize repeatedly for renewed transgressions, it is fair to infer that the ongoing 'spirit of humility' included a readiness to seek forgiveness, and thus a penitential component.[78]

e. *Poor in Spirit: The Poor as Needy*
The above account of the meaning of 'poor in spirit' would not seem at first sight to leave much room for a supplementary exegesis based on the literal meaning of πτωχός as it is used at 19.21; 26.9, 11. Such an interpretation can claim no support from Qumran, but it is not therefore simply ruled out for Matthew, who was not writing for a community organized on the lines of Qumran, and was moreover writing in Greek. Nor can a consistent application of the method of analyzing his own word usage stop short of the literal meaning of a word. 19.21, both in its immediate and in its wider context, will have important and relevant things to say in this connection. It will need to be studied, however, in relation to Matthew's general attitude to wealth.[79]

76. Charette, *Recompense*, p. 86 n. 2, notes the echo of Ps. 36.34 (ὑψώσει) in 23.12.

77. 1QS 3.8; (trans. Vermes, *Scrolls*, p. 72).

78. See M. Newton, *The Concept of Purity at Qumran and in the Letters of Paul* (SNTSMS, 53; Cambridge: Cambridge University Press, 1985), pp. 29, 49.

79. For what has been the prevailing and, until recently, practically unques-

Two issues must be distinguished here: that of social and economic injustice, and the call to be identified with the victims of it (the 'preferential option for the poor', as it is called in some modern Christian circles); and that of the spiritual dangers for the individual disciple inherent in the possession of wealth. Strenuous efforts are being made in our time, and from the best of motives, to enlist the original gospel programme of Jesus on the side of the first of these;[80] but it has to be said, however regretfully, that the evidence for it is not really substantial, and presumes a continuity between the known outlook of Luke[81] and the assumed attitude of Jesus[82] to which the rest of the tradition

tioned account of Matthew's attitude to wealth, see n. 88 below. It has been challenged in three recent works, each with its share of ideological loading, but in different directions which tend to cancel each other out. Van Tilborg, *Intervention*, offers an explicitly Marxist reading of Matthew, and an occasionally salutary caution against over-ready spiritualizing of its outlook (endorsed by Freyne, *Galilee*, p. 72). M.H. Crosby, *House of Disciples: Church, Economics and Justice in Matthew* (Maryknoll, NY: Orbis Books, 1987), makes Matthew the starting point for a contemporary programme of redress for the world's poor, interpreting its understanding of δικαιοσύνη, by an appeal to the message of the pre-exilic prophets over the head of later Jewish thinking, as social and economic justice. As far as success in undermining the previous consensus goes, this is the least effective of the three. T.E. Schmidt, *Hostility to Wealth in the Synoptic Gospels* (JSNTSup, 15; Sheffield: JSOT Press, 1987) challenges (apparently in defence of the reliability and authenticity of the synoptic tradition [cf. pp. 17-18, 170 n. 5], but not ineffectively) both presuppositions and conclusions of some recent work on the socio-economic background of the New Testament. His redaction criticism of relevant texts in Matthew is, as will be indicated, valid and useful.

80. E.g. L. Schottroff and W. Stegemann, *Jesus von Nazareth—Hoffnung der Armen* (Stuttgart: Kohlhammer, 3rd edn, 1990).

81. For this see, e.g., Bammel, 'πτωχός', pp. 905-907; H. von Campenhausen, *Tradition and Life in the Church* (trans. A.V. Littledale; London: Collins, 1968), pp. 98-100; H.J. Degenhardt, *Lukas: Evangelist der Armen* (Stuttgart: Katholisches Bibelwerk, 1965); R.C. Tannehill, *The Narrative Unity of Luke–Acts*, I (Philadelphia: Fortress Press, 1986), pp. 127-32. Schmidt's challenge to this account (*Hostility*, pp. 135-62) requires him to drive a wedge between Luke's sources and his redaction (note his indebtedness to Bammel here; cf. 'πτωχός', p. 907), and between Gospel and Acts. This does not fully convince, though he is right to conclude that Luke's wealth-ascetic for practising Christians does not differ fundamentally from those of Mark and Matthew (on this cf. Keck, 'Poor', p. 109).

82. Schottroff and Stegemann, *Hoffnung*, pp. 34, 38-46 only sustain their position by treating the Lukan Woes (Lk. 6.24-26; see Chapter 9 §3a below), the Magnificat (Lk. 1.46-55; see Chapter 5 §3a above) and the parable of Dives and

offers small support. Jesus did indeed associate with marginalized elements of Jewish society, and gave priority to them in the direction of his message; but the most prominent of these were the tax-collectors, some of whom (unless the reference is restricted to their minor agents[83]) not only enjoyed considerable affluence but often owed it to unjust extortion from the people least able to defend themselves. Nor do we know what, if anything, was asked of these by way of repentance or restitution.[84] There is an ambivalence, in its present context, even about the logion with the best claim to be an authentic expression of hostility to wealth on the part of Jesus, Mk 10.25:[85] does it speak, like the rest of its context in Mark, of the divisive effect of the possession of wealth on a person's response to God, or is it a challenge to the system under which that wealth would have been acquired in the first place?

This remains a disputed question, to which the available evidence is insufficient for a confident answer. What is clear is that by the time that Mark wrote there was already emphasis on the spiritual dangers of wealth, and that if Matthew developed this, as redaction criticism of 19.16-26 and other passages[86] confirms that he did, the development was in a direction in which the material in his *Vorlage* was already pointing. The converse conclusion that (to quote the judgment of E. Bammel) 'Matthew was not greatly interested in the problems of actual want'[87] would seem to apply to Mark as well, even if the proportion between eschatological urgency and surrounding affluence in

---

Lazarus (Lk. 16.19-31; see Chapter 9 §3b below) as part of the primitive tradition. Against this, see J.O. York, *The Last Shall be First: The Rhetoric of Reversal in Luke* (JSNTSup, 46; Sheffield: JSOT Press, 1991).

83. This distinction (assumed both by Schottroff and Stegemann, *Hoffnung*, p. 18, and van Tilborg, *Intervention*, p. 140) presupposed the presence of the Roman *publicani* and the two-tier system which that involved (e.g., in Asia Minor). Herrenbrück, *Zöllner*, has now shown that this was not true of Palestine. The τελῶναι of the Gospels are apparently self-employed and comfortably off.

84. It is unsafe to take the story of Zacchaeus (Lk. 19.1-10) as evidence of what Jesus required, rather than of what Luke thought appropriate.

85. The *Kamelspruch* of Mk 10.25 has parallels in the rabbinic tradition (*b. Ber.* 55b; *b. B. Meṣ.* 38a; see McNeile, *Matthew*, p. 280), and Schottroff and Stegemann, *Hoffnung*, pp. 34-36, make a strong case for the foreignness of what it says to its present context in Mark.

86. See Schmidt, *Hostility*, pp. 122-34, and summary on p. 134. On 19.16-22 (Schmidt, pp. 132-33) see §3b below.

87. 'πτωχός', p. 904.

the factors contributing to their respective positions did not remain static. The milieu of Matthew's church may well have been the more affluent of the two. But the widespread (and by no means exhausted) assumption[88] that his attitude to this was one of complacency is not borne out by the evidence of his Gospel, if this is considered as a whole and not simply in terms of his treatment of putative sources.[89] There are a number of indications that he saw the possession of wealth as a serious danger to the spiritual progress of the disciple and its elimination as an element in his striving for perfection.

(1) Matthew takes a consistently radical stance on other ethical issues, notably those listed in the antitheses of the Sermon on the Mount: anger, lust, swearing of oaths, non-resistance, love of enemies (the modification of the saying on divorce is not necessarily an exception to this[90]). It would have been inconsistent with his general outlook for him to take a lax view of the dangers of wealth, especially with the tradition of Jesus' own severity before him in his sources.

(2) Matthew's version of the *Shema'* at 22.37 restores the 'three-tone' form of it found at Deut. 6.5 MT and LXX, as against the 'four-tone'

88. Cf. G.D. Kilpatrick, *The Origins of the Gospel according to St Matthew* (Oxford: Clarendon Press, 1947), pp. 125-26; Barth, in Bornkamm, Barth and Held, *Tradition*, p. 96: 'Matthew shows no kind of ascetic tendency in respect of property and wealth'; similarly Davies, *Setting*, p. 213; W. Trilling, *Christusverkundigung in den synoptischen Evangelien* (Munich: Kösel, 1969), p. 80; D.L. Mealand, *Poverty and Expectation in the Gospels* (London: SPCK, 1977); Catchpole, *Quest*, pp. 23 (with reference to MtR of Mk 14.7 at 26.11), 87.

89. I think particularly of Mealand, *Poverty*, pp. 13-16, 21-22, 37; Catchpole, *Quest*, pp. 23, 87.

90. There are three alternative possibilities: (1) Matthew's exceptive clause is no real exception but a truism: a wife who is already an adulteress cannot be made one by the action of her husband (this however fits 5.32 better than 19.9). So, most recently, Betz, *Sermon on the Mount*, pp. 251-52, 258. (2) J. Dupont, *Mariage et divorce dans l'Evangile* (Bruges: Abbaye Saint-André, 1959), pp. 170-75, 221-22, interprets 19.9 in conjunction with the hard saying at 19.10-12; if this is accepted it is impossible to understand the exceptive clause as a concession. (3) According to the argument of H. Baltesweiler, *Die Ehe im Neuen Testament* (Zürich: Zwingli, 1967), pp. 87-102, the reference of πορνεία in Mt. 5.32; 19.9 is not to adultery or other forms of unchastity but to marriage within the prohibited degrees, a situation in which dismissal of the wife would not be breaking up the marriage but a recognition that none existed.

version of the parallel at Mk 12.33, but does so, remarkably, by drop-ping not Mark's apparently intrusive and repetitious διανοία, but his ἰσχύς which is integral to the original text. No fully satisfactory expla-nation of this on textual or source-critical grounds has so far been offered.[91] But Birger Gerhardsson, who has drawn attention in a num-ber of places[92] to the rabbinic exegesis of Deut. 6.5 which understood 'strength' as wealth (the *Mishnah* and *Sifre* actually use the word *mamôn* for it[93]), also notes the tendency to make the third term used 'congruent' with the other two which denote human faculties.[94] The emphasis is thus shifted from the external resources to 'that which deter-mines one's attitude'[95] to them. At Mt. 6.24 a saying in gnomic form about the general impossibility of being slave to two masters is applied to the specific case of God and mammon.[96] The radical view of wealth that this conveys calls for a modification of the traditional exegesis: if the ownership of riches involves enslavement to them, then one cannot serve one master with that which binds one to another. One cannot love God *with* one's mammon, but only by letting go of it. Those who do this can be called poor in spirit.[97]

(3) The thought of treasure and where it is truly to be found links three passages in different parts of the Gospel (and stemming, according to conventional source analysis, from different strands in the synoptic tradition):

91. Gundry, *Use*, pp. 22-24, makes eleven different suggestions but no choice between them. That numbered (d) (p. 24) approximates to B. Gerhardsson's (*The Ethos of the Bible* [trans. S. Westerholm; London: Darton, Longman & Todd, 1982], p. 45).

92. See Gerhardsson, *Testing*, pp. 71-83; *Ethos*, pp. 27-62; and the papers now collected in *Shema*.

93. *m. Ber.* 9.5; *Sifre* on Deut. 6.5. Gerhardsson himself (*Shema*, p. 303) prefers the rendering 'resources', which can be understood more inclusively than wealth alone. Cf. §3, below. The LXX of Deut. 6.5 renders with δύναμις; at 4 Kgdms 23.25 (which has also influenced Matthew's text) it has ἰσχύς (cf. Mk 12.30).

94. See *Shema*, pp. 27-29 (= *NTS* 14 [1967–68], pp. 168-70; p. 209 (= R.G. Hamerton-Kelly and R. Scroggs [eds.], *Jews, Greeks and Christians* [Festschrift W.D. Davies; Leiden: E.J. Brill, 1976], p. 136).

95. Gerhardsson, *Ethos*, p. 45.

96. See n. 104 below.

97. See further Chapter 10, below.

(a) 13.44-46 (Matthew only): the little pair of parables here compare the kingdom to men who, starting from very different lifestyles, both sell everything they have to acquire that on which they have set their heart. While the hidden treasure and the pearl serve here as images of the kingdom, the connection between selling all and 'treasure in heaven' at 19.21 (see below) should be a warning against completely spiritualizing the meaning of selling up in this context.[98]

(b) 19.16-22 (//Mk 10.17-22): not only is Matthew careful to reproduce in the following paragraph the very severe assessment of the situation of a rich man vis-à-vis the kingdom which he found in Mk 10.23-27, but here in the encounter with the young man which precedes it the challenge to sell his possessions and follow Jesus is no longer a mark of special favour ('Jesus...loved him':[99] Mk 10.21), but an implication of the 'perfection' urged on all disciples (19.21; cf. 5.48).[100] Matthew clearly sees wealth as competing with God for the possession of a man's heart, and the retention of it as a grave threat to his salvation over which he must be challenged. Much better to dispose of it and invest the proceeds where they can be of most profit, not just to the poor but to himself.

(c) 6.19-21 (//Lk 12.33-34): the understanding of 'treasure in heaven' outlined above is here spelled out in greater detail.[101] According to the conventional Jewish approach to almsgiving in Matthew's day,[102] to

98. Cf. van Tilborg, *Intervention*, p. 16.

99. Green, *Matthew*, p. 171. This seems a more credible reading of Mark than Morton Smith's suggestion of a residual survival from 'Secret Mark' (see n. 47 to Chapter 1).

100. It is now generally recognized that Matthew does not teach a 'two-level' ethic; the command to be τέλειος in 5.48 is addressed to all disciples. Cf. Dupont, *Béatitudes*, III, p. 653 n. 2; A. Sand, *Das Gesetz und die Propheten* (BU, 11; Regensburg: Regensburger, 1974), pp. 54-58; H. Giesen, *Christliche Handeln* (Frankfurt: Peter Lang, 1982), p. 141 and n. 346; contra the older position of Bammel, 'πτωχός', p. 903; G. Kretschmar, 'Ein Beitrag zur Frage nach der Ursprung frühchristlicher Askese', *ZTK* 61 (1964), pp. 27-67 (57-61); H. Braun, 'Qumran and the New Testament', *TRu* NS 33 (1963), pp. 91-234 (136); Cope, *A Scribe*, p. 116 n. 53.

101. See Goulder, *Midrash*, pp. 301-302, 309-10, for evidence of Markan influence on the Sermon on the Mount; for the meaning, W. Pesch, 'Zur Exegese von Mt 6,19-20/Lk 12, 33-34', *Bib* 41 (1960) pp. 356-78.

102. The fullest and best known statement of this is at Tob. 4.7-11, but it is widely attested throughout the intertestamental literature; see F. Staudinger, 'ἐλε-

possess 'treasure on earth' offered an opportunity to acquire 'treasure in heaven' (i.e., merit), money given to charity being the equivalent of property wisely stored or invested. Matthew radicalizes this principle, and in doing so polarizes the alternatives: either treasure on earth, with both the material risk of loss or depreciation and the spiritual hazard of a heart diverted from God, or treasure in heaven (*all* given away).[103] The thrust of the argument is carried further in the logia that follow:[104] either total generosity (the single eye) or utter meanness or greed (the evil eye) (6.22-23).[105] To refuse the choice is to attempt to serve two

ημοσύνη', *EDNT*, I, pp. 428-29; Schmidt, *Hostility*, pp. 65-76. All these texts, however, think in terms of this-worldly reward; cf. Pesch, 'Exegese', pp. 362-63.

103. Pesch, 'Exegese', p. 366, finds no parallel to this total renunciation in post-biblical Jewish literature. Cf. Schmidt, *Hostility*, p. 125: 'To spiritualize the saying into a command to submit one's heart to God's sovereign rule is to reverse the order of treasure and heart'.

104. Schmidt, *Hostility*, p. 126, notes that vv. 20-21 offer 'the strongest indication of reward in the entire section 6.19-34', and thus 'should probably be understood to apply to the following sections [*sic*] as well'. For generosity with money as the connecting theme of 6.19-34, cf. Manson, *Ethics*, pp. 55-56; Schweizer, *Matthew*, pp. 160-64; Gundry, *Matthew*, pp. 113-14; van Tilborg, *Intervention*, pp. 142, 144-45, 154, 161-62; Burchard, 'Versuch', p. 427 (rejected by Betz, *Sermon on the Mount*, p. 424, who thus misses the sequential connection); Strecker, *Sermon on the Mount*, pp. 130-31; J.H. Elliott, 'The Evil Eye and the Sermon on the Mount: Contours of a Pervasive Belief in Social Scientific Perspective', *BibInt* 11 (1994) pp. 51-84, esp. 78.

105. Matthew here uses a very basic account of the nature of ocular vision as understood in contemporary optics as a metaphor for a person's moral and spiritual condition, with particular reference to material possessions. Its interpretation is not made easier by the familiar tendency in his use of parables to allow the 'reality' part to press into the 'picture' part (so, with examples, E. Linnemann, *Parables of Jesus* [trans. J. Sturdy; London: SPCK, 1966], p. 97). It presupposes the 'extramission' theory of vision (light proceeding from the eye upon its object); but since a lamp, properly speaking, is only a secondary source of light, the latter must be understood as coming from within. At this point there is a choice between two options: either, following Betz (*Sermon on the Mount*, pp. 450-53) the light that the eye transmits originates at a specific point in a person's inner self (the ψυχή?), and the illumination of the body (i.e., the whole person) is the effect of the activity of seeing; or, as argued by D.C. Allison in a critique of Betz's earlier treatment ('The Eye is the Lamp of the Body [Matthew 6.22-23: Luke 11.34-36]', *NTS* 37 [1987], pp. 61-83), the illumination of the whole person is itself the source of the light transmitted by the eye and is thus prior to it. For Allison (see esp. pp. 74-76) the condition of the eye is evidence, not cause, of a person's illumination (or want of it). It will be

masters (6.24);[106] a likely motive will be anxiety over the possibility of finding oneself without provision (6.25-33).[107] At 8.20 a would-be disciple is told that 'the Son of man has nowhere to lay his head'. Since the disciple is to be 'like his teacher' (10.24), an insecurity which wealth would insure against is assumed as his lot. Here (6.25-33: cf. v. 33) he is urged to rely instead on God's providential care while he makes

seen that this is an unsatisfactory account of ancient optics if the case of a man totally blind is considered. On Allison's view the state of his eyes would have no causal connection with his inability to see; it would only be evidence of unexplained 'darkness within'. This is clearly not how, e.g., Greek medical writers saw the matter; and if taken as the basis of Matthew's metaphorical treatment it will undermine its practical application, which is concerned not with the theoretical sources of certain moral attitudes but with their spiritual consequences. Matthew's epithets can be understood both at the literal and metaphorical level; but while the primary meaning of πονηρός is a physical, not a moral one (cf. 7.17-18, and see LSJ s.v.), ἁπλοῦς can only mean 'sound' or 'undamaged' in so far as it represents the Hebrew *tamîm* (see on VI, §4a, below), which belongs to a word group itself predominantly metaphorical in use. And ἁπλοῦς is the key word here, with a range of related meanings that link it to the wider context (see J. Amstutz, *ΑΠΛΟΤΗΣ* [Theophaneia, 19; Bonn: Peter Hanstein, 1968], esp. pp. 96-102). As contrasted here with πονηρός (= mean, niggardly, greedy, envious—all connotations associated with the 'evil eye'; cf. 7.11; 20.15) it means 'generous', 'ungrudging' (for ἁπλότης = generosity cf. 2 Cor. 8.2; 9.11, 13). But, equally, it connotes the singleness of heart commanded in 6.19-21, and the undivided service required at 6.24. (For literature on these verses see Betz, *Sermon on the Mount*, pp. 437-38; add van Tilborg, *Intervention*, pp. 138-42; Elliott, 'Evil Eye', pp. 74-80.)

106. S-B, I, p. 433 offers evidence that dual ownership of slaves was a legal and practical possibility; cf. van Tilborg, *Intervention*, pp. 148-54; Strecker, *Sermon on the Mount*, p. 134. In the light of this it is unlikely that Matthew is quoting a current proverb. He says in effect: 'No slave can *really*, with total commitment, serve two owners: he will always like B better than A, or respect A more than B'. Whether or not the argument is, as van Tilborg maintains (p. 153), addressed to slave-owners, it presupposes, as he says, a freedom to choose which the slave has not—and the free person will not long retain, if he or she chooses mammon. There are analogies here with what Paul says about the flesh in Rom. 7.

107. 6.25-33, if in some form it antedated the composition of the Gospel, could conceivably have had its origin in instructions to missionaries carrying out a programme of the sort offered at 10.5-15 par. (cf. Jeremias, *Parables*, p. 215). In its present context, however, it concerns all disciples, and assumes a measure of economic insecurity as inseparable from the Christian calling.

God's kingdom and righteousness (the overall theme of the Beatitudes) his absolute priority.[108]

The logic of this is that true disciples should not retain any wealth for themselves while the claims of the needy give them opportunity to dispose of it.[109] The rich can expect to join the ranks of the poor.[110]

The cumulative impression left by these texts is one of hostility to material wealth, which is seen as a grave hazard (19.23) if not an actual bar (19.24) to entrance into the kingdom. In the circumstances it would be remarkable if a beatitude framed in the Greek language and promising the kingdom of heaven to the inwardly poor did not carry even a secondary reference to it. But if it does, how is it to be understood? Dupont, as we have seen, rules out 'spiritual' attitudes to real poverty as involving an 'incomplete transposition';[111] he includes in this the formal renunciation of personal property, as at Qumran.[112] He also rejects an attitude of detachment from real wealth where the ownership of it is retained, as lacking evidential support in contemporary literature;[113] so far as it goes, the evidence that we have been examining bears him out. Both kinds of attitude may be called static; they relate to steady states, whether of wealth or poverty, in a uniform way. The attitude that the evidence seems rather to call for is a dynamic one, an active engaging with the pressures and the dangers of wealth and the threat that they pose to the 'perfection' for which disciples are to strive, which may not begin with their divesting themselves of their possessions, but is very likely, if love does not grow cold (24.12), to lead them to it sooner rather than later.

If these two meanings can cohere in the expression 'poor in spirit',[114]

---

108. Orton, *Scribe*, p. 141, observes that 'the phrase διὰ τοῦτο in Matthew is used most frequently *in a position of climax*' (his emphasis), but excepts 6.25 from the scope of this on the grounds that it is not a warning to disciples like 18.23-35 or 24.44, but a reassurance (p. 142). In my reading of the context it *is* the climax of the sayings about giving away one's wealth.

109. See Schmidt, *Hostility*, pp. 128, 130, 134; van Tilborg, *Intervention*, p. 161.

110. Cf. van Tilborg, *Intervention*, p. 14: 'Is it possible to be poor in spirit without being poor? I do not think so.' (He compares 5.27.) Freyne, *Galilee*, pp. 72-73, follows him.

111. *Béatitudes*, III, pp. 422-29.

112. *Béatitudes*, III, pp. 425-27.

113. *Béatitudes*, III, pp. 451-57.

114. S. de Diétrich, *St Matthew* (Layman's Bible Commentaries; London: SCM Press, 1961), p. 28, recognizes the double meaning.

is it possible to do justice to both of them in a single articulation of it? What I am moved to propose is 'humble before God, and relying on his mercy[115] for forgiveness and for sustenance'.[116] This suggests that in the overall scheme of the Beatitudes I is not only the counterpart of III, but the converse of V, which occupies the corresponding position in the second quatrain to that of I in the first. We have already found traces of a comparable relation between III and VII. With this in mind we now examine V and VII in detail.[117]

2. *V. The Merciful (ἐλεήμονες)*
VII. The Peacemakers (εἰρηνοποιοί)

These are both, in their different ways, rare words. ἐλεήμων, where it translates the Hebrew *ḥannûn* in the LXX, is used once of a human subject, at Ps. 111.4, which I shall show reason to regard as a text behind this beatitude.[118] εἰρηνοποιός is a New Testament *hapax*, and a form not found in the LXX; its cognate εἰρηνοποιεῖν occurs there once, at Prov. 10.10, where it does not represent the present Hebrew text. In neither case is the basic idea in the Hebrew substratum most naturally conveyed by an adjective: in place of 'merciful' it would be more natural to use the cognate verb, and in place of 'peacemakers' the abstract noun *šālôm*—as is shown by the form of the Aaronic blessing at Num. 6.25-26:

> The Lord make his face to shine upon you and be gracious to
> (LXX ἐλεήσαι) you;
> The Lord lift up his countenance upon you and give you
> peace (LXX εἰρήνην).

Matthew's poetic choice of vocabulary thus strains ordinary word usage. It creates a formal parallel between the two, which draws attention to

---

115. Cf. Broer, *Seligpreisungen*, p. 74: 'diejenigen, die auf Jahwe vertrauen'; contra Dupont, *Béatitudes*, III, pp. 470-71, who objects to any exegesis of the expression which takes it as directed primarily towards God, apparently on the grounds of its inapplicability to the (for him) virtually synonymous πραεῖς.

116. Cf. Böhl, 'Demut', p. 222; for parallels in the Dead Sea Scrolls, J. Gnilka, 'Die Kirche des Matthäus und die Gemeinde von Qumran', *BZ* NS 7 (1963), pp. 43-63: 58, citing 1QH 5.22, 1QM 11.9.

117. For discussion of the apodosis 'for theirs is the kingdom of heaven' see §5, below.

118. See n. 125, below.

the correspondence (once more, not the identity) of the underlying ideas. This is sustained in the apodoses, the wording of which reflects, though in inverse order, two lines in the same context of Hosea:

Hos. 2.3 (Heb. 2.1): Say to your brother, My people, and to your sister, She has obtained mercy (Ἠλεημένη).

2.1 (Heb. 1.10): And it shall be in the place where it was said to them, Not my people, there they shall be called sons of the living God (κληθήσονται υἱοὶ θεοῦ ζῶντος).

The parallels with Matthew's wording will be evident.[119]

The association of mercy and peace in the Aaronic blessing seems to have left little mark on the rest of the Old Testament.[120] But the fact of its continuing liturgical use may have contributed to the form of the initial greeting of official pastoral letters. 'Mercy and peace' is found (with ἀγαπή added) in the opening of the (Jewish-Christian) Letter of Jude (1.2). The Pauline form 'grace (χάρις) and peace'[121] may have been influenced by a word-play on the verb χαίρειν normally used in the exordium of Greek letters, or (irrespective of that) by a more general tendency in the centuries immediately subsequent to the production of the LXX to prefer χάρις to ἔλεος as a Greek equivalent to the Hebrew *ḥesed*.[122] (Interestingly, in his final handwritten conclusion at Gal. 6.16, Paul reverts to ἔλεος—perhaps a more direct echo of the Aaronic blessing.) Some later New Testament letters conflate the two forms.[123]

The significance of this for our present purpose is that mercy and peace are seen as divine gifts, and the exercise of them as an aspect of the activity of God.[124] Aaron blesses in the name of Yahweh, and Paul salutes his readers 'from God our Father and the Lord Jesus Christ'. To require of men and women that they shall be merciful and peacemakers

---

119. See nn. 173, 174 below.

120. Isa. 54.10; Ps. 84.15; Tob. 7.12 only.

121. Cf. Rom. 1.7; 1 Cor. 1.3; 2 Cor. 1.2; Gal. 1.2; Phil. 1.2; Col. 1.2; Eph. 1.2, etc.; also 1 Pet. 1.2; 2 Pet. 1.2; Rev. 1.4.

122. Cf. H. Conzelmann, 'χάρις κτλ.', *TDNT*, IX, pp. 372-415 (394); for the second possibility J.A. Montgomery, 'Hebrew *ḥesed* and Greek *charis*', *HTR* 32 (1939), pp. 97-102 (100); C.H. Dodd, *The Bible and the Greeks* (London: Hodder & Stoughton, 1935), p. 61.

123. 1 Tim. 1.2; 2 Tim. 1.2; 2 Jn 1.2.

124. Cf., for mercy, R. Bultmann, 'ἔλεος κτλ.', *TDNT*, II, pp. 473-87 (479-80); for peace, W. Foerster, 'εἰρήνη κτλ.', *TDNT*, II, pp. 400-20 (403-404).

is an invitation to the *imitatio Dei*. Not only these two beatitudes, but all those of the second quatrain, as will be shown, are in some sense concerned with this.

a. *The Quality of Mercy*
The nearest that the LXX comes to the wording of V in its totality is Prov. 17.5: ὁ δὲ ἐπισπλαγχνιζόμενος ἐλεηθήσεται. But there are other texts which actually convey the thought of reciprocal mercy in the form of a macarism: Ps. 111.4 enumerates the attributes (ἐλεήμων καὶ οἰκτίρμων καὶ δίκαιος) of the God-fearing man, the subject of the beatitude with which the psalm opens. The first two of these are the counterpart of the attributes of God in the corresponding verse of the paired previous psalm (Ps. 110.4).[125] Matthew's beatitude compresses the meaning of the two parallel texts into a single statement. There is also a quasi-beatitude at Prov. 14.21 (ἐλεῶν δὲ πτωχοὺς μακαριστός), and a full one at Ps. 40.2:

μακάριος ὁ συνίων ἐπὶ πτωχὸν καὶ πένητα·
ἐν ἡμέρᾳ πονηρᾷ ῥύσεται αὐτὸν ὁ κύριος.

This psalm continues at v. 5 with the words:

ἐγὼ εἶπα Κύριε, ἐλέησόν με·
ἴασαι τὴν ψυχήν μου, ὅτι ἥμαρτόν σοι.

There are verbal links here with the great psalm of repentance, Ps. 50.3:

ἐλέησόν με, ὁ θεός, κατὰ τὸ μέγα ἔλεός σου;
καὶ κατὰ τὸ πλῆθος τῶν οἰκτιρμῶν σου ἐξάλειψον τὸ
    ἀνόμημά μου

---

125. These two alphabetical psalms are composed as a kind of diptych, with the attributes of Yahweh in the first mirrored in those of the God-fearer in the second; cf. W. Zimmerli, 'Zwillingpsalmen', in J. Schreiner (ed.), *Wort, Lied und Gottesspruch* (Festschrift J. Ziegler; Würzburg: Echter, 1972), pp. 105-13; P. Auffret, 'Essai sur la structure littéraire des Psaumes CXI et CXII', *VT* 30 (1980), pp. 257-79. Gunkel (see Zimmerli, 'Zwillingpsalmen', p. 107 n. 8) suggested emending the Hebrew text of Ps. 112.4 (MT) to make 'the righteous' the subject, which would give an exact parallel at this point (followed by James Moffatt, *A New Translation of the Old Testament* (London: Hodder & Stoughton, 1920], *ad loc.* and by the Psalter of the ECUSA Book of Common Prayer [1979]). But if he was right, the corruption pre-dated the LXX, and the true text would have been unknown to Matthew.

The thought of mercy thus covers two distinct areas: the relief of need and the forgiveness of sin.

b. *Mercy and Forgiveness*

ἐλεήμων does not recur in Matthew, nor elsewhere in the New Testament apart from Heb. 2.17, where it is used of Christ the compassionate high priest. Of its cognates, ἐλεημοσύνη is found in this Gospel only in the instruction on almsgiving at 6.2-4, and elsewhere in the New Testament only in two texts (both redactional) in Luke,[126] and in four contexts in Acts.[127] ἔλεος occurs in three passages in this Gospel, two of them quotations of the same Old Testament text (Hos. 6.6; see 9.13; 12.7), and the third an allusion to another Old Testament text (Mic. 6.8; see 23.23); the two former will be found to be of considerable significance in their contexts. The verb ἐλεεῖν is commoner; it is found in one context in Mark (10.47-48) to which Matthew has two counterparts (9.27; 20.30-31), and in addition to these he has introduced it redactionally into two Markan contexts (15.22; 17.15), as well as his own parable of the unmerciful servant (see below) and this beatitude.

These bare statistics do less than justice to the part played by the thought of mercy in Matthew's version of the Christian message. It is a thread running right through the Gospel,[128] and an important counterweight to his perfectionist strain of which those who habitually speak of, for instance, his 'ferocity'[129] have perhaps not taken sufficient account. The following paragraphs will attempt to trace it, first in the Sermon on the Mount and then in the rest of the Gospel.

---

126. Lk. 11.41; 12.33. In both places Luke appears to have gone out of his way to introduce it; cf. Tuckett, *Q*, p. 88.

127. Acts 3.2, 3, 10; 9.36; 19.4, 31; 24.17.

128. See E. Neuhäusler, *Anspruch und Antwort Gottes* (Dusseldorf: Patmos, 1962), p. 263; Bornkamm, in Bornkamm, Barth and Held, *Tradition*, p. 37; Frankemölle, 'Makarismen', p. 71; Dupont, *Béatitudes*, III, pp. 616-32, 665-66; J. Zumstein, *La condition du croyant dans l'Evangile selon Matthieu* (OBO, 16; Fribourg: Presses Universitaires; Göttingen: Vandenhoeck & Ruprecht, 1977), p. 290; Przbylski, *Righteousness*, pp. 70-72, 99-101; Pamment, 'Kingdom', p. 215; R. Schnackenburg, 'Die Seligpreisung der Friedenstiften (Mt. 5,9)', *BZ* NS 26 (1982), pp. 161-79 (169); Green, 'Clement', pp. 4-7; Catchpole, *Quest*, p. 82: 'The supremacy of mercy over all other commitments, however good in themselves, is a deep-seated Matthaean principle expressed in 9.13, 12.7, 23.23'.

129. E.g. Drury, *Tradition and Design*, pp. 154, 157; cf. Goulder, *Midrash*, p. 63.

Attention was drawn above to the 'three pillars' of R. Simeon the Just as the key to the arrangement of the Sermon, and to the content of 6.19–7.12 as corresponding to 'acts of mercy'.[130] The subject matter of that section, however, casts its shadow before. It is true that the instruction on almsgiving, prayer and fasting (6.1-18) seems, with one exception, less concerned with the positive values of those exercises than with the danger of practising them with ostentation or insincerity; Matthew's real views on financial generosity are given, as I have argued,[131] at 6.19-24, and he does not linger over fasting, of which more will be said at 9.14-15. The single exception is the reinforcement of the item on prayer by the insertion of the Lord's Prayer. But, significantly, the clause in that which is singled out for further comment is the petition for forgiveness with its qualifying condition. What links this with its immediate context is the implied insincerity of praying for forgiveness without being prepared to forgive. Yet it is at the same time the first instalment of what Matthew understands by mercy—one which is not further developed in the Sermon on the Mount, but is picked up in the second half of ch. 18, where the duty of unlimited personal forgiveness (18.21-22) leads into the parable of the unmerciful servant (18.23-35): note especially v. 33: '...and should you not have had mercy on (ἐλε-ῆσαι) your fellow servant, as I had mercy on (ἠλέησα) you?'. Literally, at the level of the story, this speaks of the remission of the debt as an act of personal generosity, but figuratively, and essentially, of forgiving others as the condition of one's own forgiveness.[132]

The second section of the Sermon thus implicitly anticipates the third, that directly concerned with 'acts of mercy'. We have seen that the heavy weather that most commentators have made of the arrangement of this is uncalled for, and that the two sections into which it falls (6.19-34; 7.1-12) have a close formal correspondence with each other.[133] The first of them develops the theme of generosity with money; its contents and general drift have been outlined above in connection with I,[134] and we shall return to its implications. The subject of the second is succinctly stated in its opening saying: 'Judge not, that you be not

130. See Chapter 6.
131. Above, §1e.3.
132. Note the repetition of ὀφείλειν and its cognates, and cf. Chapter 4 §2b.3, above, on the Lord's Prayer.
133. Above, Chapter 6 *ad fin.*
134. Above, §1e.3 and nn. 104, 105.

judged...'; this is expanded in the parable of the splinter and the log (7.3-5: criticism begins with self-criticism), and presumably in the difficult saying about casting pearls before swine (7.6; see note).[135] The disciple must act as one who expects to receive mercy for himself, both from God in the judgment (the poem, 7.7-11) and from people (the Golden Rule, 7.12). The latter forms an *inclusio* with 5.17, and is thus to be taken as summing up not only its immediate section, nor even the total of instruction about 'acts of mercy', but the entire Sermon. 'Mercy' in this inclusive sense is the necessary complement of the intensive demands of 5.20-48. The ethical requirements of the gospel are pitched very high, but their stringency is counterbalanced by an understanding of human weakness and a pastoral concern for those most at risk to it.[136] It is not for nothing that in this beatitude alone there is an exact

135. There is no agreement among scholars about the application of the metaphor in 7.6, as Luz, *Matthew*, I, pp. 418-20, candidly admits. Suggestions of mistranslation from Aramaic have not won general support, and Gundry, *Matthew*, pp. 122-23, shows that vocabulary, rhythmic pattern and an Old Testament echo (Ps. 21.17; cf. the final petition of the Lord's Prayer) point to Matthaean composition. 'Dogs' must refer to persons outside the Christian fellowship, but not necessarily to Gentiles (Gundry cites Phil. 3.2); 'swine', on the other hand, has a definitely Gentile ring about it, and the double image ('trample...maul') seems to imply distinct responses. It may be (contra both Gundry and Goulder [*Midrash*, pp. 264-66]; see also van Tilborg, *Intervention*, pp. 182-88) that Matthew is simply being evenhanded in his criticisms (as he was in 6.5-8). What then is the referent of the 'holy thing' and the pearl? The context demands a third saying commending mercy = non-judgment (to correspond with the three short sayings of 6.19-24 which commend mercy = generosity with money). Goulder suggests that it is the 'honour' (cf. *m. Ab.* 2.10) of a fellow disciple, which is not to be exposed to criticism behind his back in the company of non-believers. While this has not a little to commend it (including an allusion to the malicious tongue to match the 'evil eye' of 6.22-23), it offers no answer to the question 'why only non-believers?'; and μαργαρίτης (found in this Gospel only) is at 13.46 an image of the kingdom. It therefore seems preferable to see the words as used of the gospel itself; not, however, as often in the past (and still endorsed by Davies and Allison, *Matthew*, I, p. 676), as an invitation to 'reserve in the communication of religious knowledge' (which does not fit the non-judgment sequence). As 7.3-5 warns against criticizing a fellow disciple from a stance of assumed superiority, so 7.6 warns against denouncing a non-disciple in the name of a gospel which he has not accepted: to a pagan it will make nonsense, and he will treat it with contempt, while to a Jew it will be offensive, and he will savage you for it. For the distinction cf. 1 Cor. 1.23. Prov. 9.7-8 offers an Old Testament precedent, though without direct verbal links.

136. This is the overall theme of ch. 18; cf. §1d above.

correspondence between the virtue commended and the promised reward, or that it has been designated 'the only beatitude that has been framed as a proposition of sacred law'.[137]

The recurrence of the theme in the rest of the Gospel bears out this conclusion. The quotation from Hos. 6.6, as we have seen, is used twice. At 9.13 it is part of the concluding comment on a section structured, as was noted, on the theme of the gospel call to sinners: the absolution of the paralytic (with the implication that the authority to do this has passed to the church of Jesus' disciples: 9.1-8),[138] the call of Matthew (9.9), and the Pharisees' criticism of Jesus' entertainment of sinners (9.10-13). The Pharisees appear to regard the tax-collectors and those bracketed with them as beyond the pale, and irretrievably so; they can neither conceive of themselves (or indeed of Jesus and his disciples) as on the same footing as these outcasts, nor accept the reality of the latter's pardon from God. Their attitude remains implacably judgmental, and Jesus, as depicted by Matthew, attributes it to a system which gives the literal observance of the ceremonial law priority over the claims and needs of persons. The same applies to the second occurrence of the text at 12.7; only here the Pharisees are accused of condemning the guiltless, that is, of unnecessary fault-finding, a determination to put people in the wrong, where a more compassionate approach could have found room for what they did within the permitted interpretation of the law's requirements.[139]

That these strictures are not reserved only for the external opponents of the gospel is clear from ch. 18, which is addressed to the community of disciples, and, it would appear, to a conflict situation within the Evangelist's own church. We have seen that the way in which μικροί is used there suggests that it has become a sobriquet for a particular category of Christians, whom their fellow disciples are tending to regard as so far from their own standards of Christian behaviour that their prospects of salvation can be discounted.[140] Matthew does not play down their

---

137. Zumstein, *Condition*, p. 290 n. 4 [*sic*: author's error for 5]; cf. de Diétrich, *St Matthew*, p. 29: 'the first [Beatitude] related to the judgment of God'.

138. See Held, in Bornkamm, Barth and Held, *Tradition*, pp. 249, 273-74; Strecker, *Weg*, pp. 221-22.

139. Cf. Barth, in Bornkamm, Barth and Held, *Tradition*, pp. 81-83; Gundry, *Matthew*, pp. 221-24. For mercy as a necessary component in the administration of justice in the later Tannaitic literature see Przbylski, *Righteousness*, pp. 71-72.

140. It could be argued (but cf. n. 73 above) that the μικροί are vulnerable recent

shortcomings, but he implies that such a judgmental view of their situation is liable to be self-fulfilling, and that the consequences of this for those who allowed it to happen will be infinitely grave (cf. 18.6).[141] Instead of despising the erring, established and responsible disciples are, first, to see themselves in the same light (under judgment, and in need of mercy), and, secondly, to be prepared to go to any lengths to reclaim the backsliders, and to extend the community's forgiveness (which is also God's; cf. 18.18b) to them if they repent. Even if a person's obstinacy in sin has to lead to the grave step of excommunication, this is nevertheless to be done with prayer that they may eventually be won back.[142] Judgment is thus a reluctant last resort of the community, undertaken in the hope that it may still not be final; it is inappropriate for the individual disciple, for whom the obligation to forgive personal injuries is unlimited (18.22). The requirement of mercy in the concluding parable sums up the teaching not just of the final section, but in a more general sense of the whole chapter.[143] Forgiveness, reclamation of the erring and the refusal to judge are all part of its definition.

c. *Mercy and the Relief of Need*
There remain for consideration those passages in which mercy is occupied not with sin but with exterior need. This is the main thrust of most of the Old Testament texts that have been identified as lying behind V,[144] and it is the meaning of ἐλεεῖν in the only passage where Matthew takes it over directly from Mark, the healing of Bartimaeus at Mk 10.46-52. That Matthew not only duplicates this episode but imports

converts, and that among the implied readers are antinomian elements who are leading them into sin; but (1) the implied readers of ch. 18 are the same as those of the Sermon on the Mount to whom the antinomian elements (if such they are) are denounced; (2) the identification of Matthew's 'false prophets' as antinomian has not gained general acceptance; cf. Davies and Allison, *Matthew*, I, p. 701; (3) the interpretation does not fit my connection of μικροί with 5.19 (n. 74 above).

141. Cf. §1d, above.

142. This is one suggested explanation for the proximity of 18.20 to the disciplinary procedure outlined in 18.15-17; so Ellis, *Mind and Message*, p. 71; Green, *Matthew*, p. 164. But there are other possibilities; cf. Chapter 4 §8e, above.

143. Note its links with the language of the Lord's Prayer; see previous section.

144. §2 *ad init.* Note in addition Ps. 36.21, 26.

the word into two others in which Jesus is approached with a request for healing, where Mark does not use it,[145] is an indication that this sense of the word was an important constituent in its meaning for him. Where this is spelled out most explicitly is in the scenario of the Great Assize at 25.31-46.[146] Although neither ἐλεεῖν nor its cognates are used in this passage, the practices over which persons are judged clearly form an extended list of the 'corporal works of mercy':[147] giving food and drink to the hungry and thirsty, clothing the naked, sheltering the homeless, tending the sick and visiting the prisoners. By whom and for whom these have, or have not, been performed is a complex and unfinished question, and a systematic examination of it is not feasible at this point.[148] But the surprise both of the 'sheep' at being told that they have ministered to Christ and of the 'goats' at hearing that they have failed to do so[149] would seem to imply that for Matthew faith (in the sense of formal commitment) without matching action will not admit to the final kingdom,[150] whereas acts of mercy without formal adherence in certain

145. 15.22; 17.15. See Held, in Bornkamm, Barth and Held, *Tradition*, pp. 261-62.

146. For a survey of past work on this see now S.W. Green, *The Least of my Brothers (Matthew 25:31-46): A History of Interpretation* (SBLDS, 114; Atlanta: Scholars Press, 1989); and for a recent fresh angle on it, Stanton, *Gospel*, pp. 207-31.

147. The ensemble of these is drawn (*pace* Stanton, *Gospel*, pp. 219-20) from Isa. 58.7 (supplemented by Sir. 7.35 for the visiting of the sick, and by the cup of cold water [10.42] for the thirsty). The words 'hide not yourself from your own flesh' in the Isaiah text confirm that Matthew's version warns against neglect of suffering fellow disciples (see following notes).

148. There are strong reasons for taking 'these my brothers who are least' [my translation; cf. *Matthew*, p. 207] to refer to Christian disciples rather than to sufferers in general; see Stanton, *Gospel*, pp. 214-21. But though Stanton rightly emphasizes that the *genre* of the passage is that of an apocalyptic discourse, I cannot accept as a corollary of this that the judgment is of nations rather than of individuals within their nations; see my review (n. 85 to Chapter 1), pp. 96-97.

149. In my opinion the scenario is mounted as a warning to potential 'goats', especially if the surprise of those characterized as 'sheep' can be taken to imply that they may be non-disciples and thus outside the assumed readership. The passage conveys essentially the same message to members of the Church as 21.31 did to the representatives of the old Israel. Comparable warnings to complacent Christians have already been sounded at 7.21-23; 22.11-14, and in the immediately preceding 25.1-13, 14-30.

150. See esp. 7.21-23.

circumstances will. Those whose actions, even in ignorance, reflect the activity of God, will not be rejected by him in the day of reckoning.

How closely for Matthew is this aspect of 'merciful' (ἐλεήμων) related to the practice of almsgiving (ἐλεημοσύνη)? He passes swiftly over the practice in 6.2-4, and never uses the word again. While the language of the threefold instruction in 6.2-18 is broadly Matthaean, the fact that the Lord's Prayer has been worked into the paragraph on prayer indicates that the section as a whole, whether attributable to a predecessor in the same tradition or to an earlier phase in the Evangelist's own history,[151] allows of some distancing between its assumption of conventional almsgiving as an aspect of Christian piety and Matthew's considered attitude to it, which is set out in 6.19-33.[152] If my interpretation of that is sound, the Evangelist would have had reason to avoid a word associated with the stereotype of almsgiving as something practised by the well-to-do (who remain rich) towards the impoverished (who remain poor). His probable reasons for rejecting this, as has been shown,[153] have less to do with relief of need as an end in itself than with the total generosity that he insists on in this as in other areas of the life of the Christian disciple. It does not however follow (as Dupont's silence on the matter seems to imply[154]) that money, where available, plays no part; the build-up of 6.19-34 is not really intelligible without that.[155] But the logic of the situation that Matthew seems to envisage is that it will not go on being available indefinitely; it will run out sooner rather than later, yet the obligation to perform corporal acts of mercy (through sharing and personal contact) will still continue.

When the different meanings that we have distinguished for the word 'merciful' and its cognates are set alongside those previously distinguished for the expression 'poor in spirit', we find a paradoxical convergence of opposites. It is those who continue to see themselves as sinners who will not judge others; those who genuinely seek forgive-

151. See n. 8 to Chapter 4.

152. See §1e.3, above.

153. Above, §1e. See also the distinction between almsgiving and 'deeds of lovingkindness' in *t. Pe'ah* 4.19: '...almsgiving is done with a man's money, deeds of lovingkindness either with money or personally' (trans. G.F. Moore, *Judaism* [Cambridge, MA: Harvard University Press, 1927], II, p. 172; quoted in Przbylski, *Righteousness*, p. 67).

154. *Béatitudes*, III, pp. 626-32.

155. See §1e.3, above.

ness for their own sins who will not withhold it from others; the injunction to total generosity with this world's goods is at the same time an invitation to poverty. The practice of mercy begins with dependence on God's mercy;[156] those who aspire to the imitation of God have human frailty as their starting point.

d. *Peacemaking and Sonship*

The meaning of 'peace' (*šālôm*) had undergone a process of domestication in post-canonical Judaism.[157] While it continued to be thought of as the gift of God, and as a condition that would characterize the restored Davidic kingdom of current messianic expectation,[158] its emphasis had shifted from the total well-being of Israel to good social relationships and an absence of strife within the Jewish nation. Rabbinic sources, which offer the clearest evidence of this transformation, speak of one who promotes peace (whether on his or her own account or as a reconciler of others) as *'āśāh šālôm*, a maker of peace. This understanding of 'peace' has been compared to that of *agape* in the New Testament,[159] though it lacks both the universal scope of the latter and its concern for the final welfare (i.e., salvation) of the recipient.

Matthew's εἰρηνοποιός, as we have seen,[160] is found nowhere else in the New Testament or the LXX. Its cognate εἰρηνοποιεῖν occurs at Prov. 10.10, where, as noted, it does not represent the present Hebrew text, but may well render an earlier and sounder form of it: 'he who rebukes with boldness makes peace'.[161] In the LXX the adjective εἰρηνικός is used of people and their words to characterize them as 'peaceable' or friendly. In Ps. 36.37 it denotes the same persons that have

---

156. 6.25-33 and 7.7-11 are both invitations to trust in this, at corresponding points in their sections, in the light of the sayings that precede them.

157. See Foerster, 'εἰρήνη κτλ.', pp. 408-11.

158. See previous note, and cf. Guelich, *Sermon*, pp. 90-92.

159. So Foerster, 'εἰρήνη κτλ.', p. 409.

160. Above, §2 *ad init*. On the contemporary Greek background see Betz, *Sermon on the Mount*, pp. 137-38.

161. In the same Old Testament context two verses further on we meet the inverse phenomenon: the sense of the Hebrew, 'love covers all offences' (so RSV), is largely obscured in the LXX. But a Greek version closer to the Hebrew, ἀγάπη καλύπτει πλῆθος ἁμαρτιῶν, seems to have been current in the Greek-speaking churches (cf. 1 Pet. 4.8; Jas 5.20; *1 Clem.* 49.5), and may have been known to Matthew in view of 5.43-47.

already been categorized as πραεῖς (v. 11; see on III),[162] δίκαιοι (vv. 12, 17, 21, 29 etc.) and ἄμωμοι (vv. 18, 28).[163] Finally, at Ps. 33.15 would-be God-fearers are enjoined to 'seek peace (εἰρήνην) and pursue (δίωξον) it'—meaning the active pursuit of peace: 'pacific' rather than 'peaceable'.[164] It is likely that Matthew made a catchword connection between this verse and Ps. 36.37, and that in doing so he interpreted the weaker expression in the latter text in terms of the stronger.

His lexical usage thus gives the impression that the background assumptions from which he worked were not dissimilar to those afterwards typical of the rabbis. Does that make his εἰρηνοποιός equivalent to '*āśāh šālôm*?

If the latter part of the central section of the Sermon on the Mount, from ch. 6 onwards and especially from 6.19, is dominated by the thought of mercy, the first part of it begins and ends with that of peacemaking. The first antithesis (5.21-22), condemning angry words (and the aggression from which they spring) is followed by injunctions to take positive steps to be reconciled not only with one's brother (in the religious sense, Jewish or Christian) (5.23-24), but with one's legal adversary (5.25-26). In both cases it is the disciple himself who is assumed to be at fault, and the duty to admit this is complementary to the requirement of forgiveness of the faults of others (6.14-15, etc.). The transcending of the distinction between 'brother' and (even hostile) outsider is made explicit in the final antithesis (5.43-47),[165] where the meaning of 'neighbour' (Lev. 19.18; cf. 22.39), the equivalent of 'brother' in its original context, is universalized. The beatitude is expressly linked with this antithesis by the clause 'that you may be the

---

162. Above, §1b. Note v. 11b: [πραεῖς]...κατατρυφήσουσιν ἐν πλήθει εἰρήνης.

163. On this word see below in the discussion of VI, §4a.

164. Cf. Foerster, 'εἰρήνη κτλ.', p. 409; Dupont, *Béatitudes*, III, pp. 636-37 (note that Dupont's 'pacifique' is equivalent to my 'peaceable', while my 'pacific' is nearer to his 'artisans de paix'). If, as is almost certain, εἰρηνοποιοί carries an allusion to Ps. 33.15, there is a possibility of word-play between δίωξον there and δεδιωγμένοι in the following beatitude, which is taken up at 5.44 (see following notes).

165. According to D. Lührmann, 'Liebet Eure Feinde', *ZTK* 69 (1972), pp. 412-38 (415), εἰρήνη is generally taken as the opposite of ἔχθρα (cf. ἐχθροὺς in 5.44), and is thus the subject of this antithesis. Cf. J. Piper, *Love Your Enemies* (SNTSMS, 38; Cambridge: Cambridge University Press, 1979), p. 189 n. 118 (to p. 55). See also next note.

sons of your Father in heaven' (5.45),[166] and the scope of the activity of peacemaking is correspondingly extended; it is now to cover not only those willing to be reconciled but those who remain hostile; their well-being is still to be sought through intercessory prayer (5.44). The parallel between this and the implied requirement of prayer for those whose obstinate persistence in sin has led to their formal excommunication (18.15-20; see above) should not be missed; both the merciful and the peacemakers practise forms of *agape*.[167] It seems that 'peace' has here recovered something of its original sense of fundamental well-being; for peace in the sense of mere absence of conflict the Matthaean Jesus is not specially concerned.[168]

This final antithesis follows another on non-resistance (5.38-42). While the affinities between the two are evident, the nuances are subtly different. 5.38-42 concerns the attitude of the weak and defenceless towards their aggressors, and the non-resistance and acceptance of imposition that it enjoins is the characteristic response of the *meek*.[169] The peacemakers represent the other side of the coin. 5.43-47, with its call to the *imitatio Dei* (v. 45), is addressed to those who have the power to do positive good, but the temptation to limit the scope of it. It is not always easy in practice to see where one ends and the other begins. This tension is reflected in the Matthaean account of Jesus' arrest (26.47-56).[170] In the first part of this (vv. 47-50, resumed in

166. The word means, and the activity predicated of them implies, 'adult sons'. Cf. Strecker, *Sermon on the Mount*, p. 42 (who notes that the speaker is himself Son of God and so the embodiment of what is promised to the peacemakers); Frankemölle, *Jahwebund*, pp. 171-72; Guelich, *Sermon*, pp. 92, 288. See further n. 173.

167. Interestingly, what Matthew here presents as an example of peacemaking, Luke in his version (with a sideways glance at Sir. 4.10) connects with the practice of mercy; cf. Dupont, *Béatitudes*, III, p. 660. On Lk. 6.36 as secondary to Mt. 5.48 see n. 235 below.

168. Cf. 10.34: '...not...peace, but a sword'.

169. The meek are thus not the 'powerless' *as such* (contra Schweizer, *Matthew*, pp. 89-90, followed by Davies and Allison, *Matthew*, I, p. 449), but those who respond to their powerlessness in a particular way—a counterpart to the poverty of the poor in spirit.

170. A. Descamps, 'Rédaction et Christologie dans le récit matthéen de la Passion', in Didier (ed.), *L'Evangile*, pp. 359-415 (405-409), understands this redactional insertion both christologically, as expressing Jesus' obedience to the Father's will, and ecclesiologically, as a warning to disciples against responding to persecution with violence. What is also true is that Jesus, whom the narrative represents as

vv. 55-56) Jesus allows himself to be arrested without resistance; in the second part (vv. 51-54), expanded from Mark's stark little episode of the severing of the high priest's slave's ear, he insists that he has the power to call angels in their thousands to his defence, but that it would not be in accordance with the divine will revealed in scripture. His action here is the fulfilment of the prophecy at 21.5 that he is to come as the king who is meek and mounted on an ass, i.e., as we have seen, non-violent and pacific: distinct and converse qualities which nevertheless shade off into one another, like those of humility and non-judgment, or acknowledgment of sinfulness and readiness to forgive others, or indifference to wealth and generosity with it.

The relation of VII to III is thus parallel to that of V to I; and as there is a certain overlap of meaning between I and III, we shall expect to find the same between V and VII. I noted in the previous section the tendency in later and particularly rabbinic Judaism to understand 'strength' in the *Shema'* as wealth—a significant form of power in any society, and the only one practically available to a dispossessed and dispersed, and thus effectively de-politicized people such as Judaism was to be after 135 CE—and the influence of the earlier phase of this on Matthew's own attitude. The beatitude on the peacemakers recognizes that Christians may have access to power in another form (e.g., that of influence in public affairs); it sets this in parallel with wealth and inculcates a corresponding attitude to its exercise: it must not be held on to for its own sake, and it must be seen and used exclusively as the power to promote the good of others, to the point of forgoing it, if necessary, for oneself.

This brings us to the meaning of the apodosis. The clues that we have already discovered to the association of peacemaking and sonship (a matter that has remained obscure to most commentators, including, formerly, this one[171]) are these: peacemaking as a form of *imitatio Dei* (5.45); peacemaking as an aspect of messianic expectation (see, e.g., Isa. 9.4-6; Zech. 9.9; Ps. 71);[172] and the clear allusion in 5.9 to Hos. 2.1.[173] The most explicit, if late and idealized, Old Testament account

---

in full command of the action, declines to make any use of the power at his disposal to prevail by force. This is more than passive non-resistance; it is a positive choice to act pacifically.

171. *Matthew*, p. 78.
172. See nn. 157, 158 above.
173. Recognized by Dupont, *Béatitudes*, III, p. 656. The rendering 'children'

of the messianic expectation is to be found in God's promise to David concerning his son Solomon at 1 Chron. 22.8-10,[174] in which David explains to the young Solomon how his own past history of violence and bloodshed has disqualified him from building the temple as he had wished, but that God has promised that his son, a man of peace as his name implies, will do it in his place, and that 'he shall be my son, and I will be his father'. It is as this pacific son of David, of whom the historical Solomon was in the end but an imperfect prototype,[175] that Jesus is acclaimed in 21.1-16.[176]

This will explain why, though the reference to Hos. 2.1 in the apodosis is in the plural, the only other direct use of the text in Matthew is in the singular, in Peter's confession 'You are the Christ, ὁ υἱὸς τοῦ θεοῦ ζῶντος' (16.16). We have already seen[177] that the imagery of Jesus' response to this carries a strong suggestion of association in this sonship, made more explicit in the next 'Petrine supplement' at 17.24-27, where Peter (as I have argued,[178] in a representative capacity) shares in the exemption proper to sons—but is expected, appropriately, not to claim it in a manner likely to cause contention and discord.[179]

Thus the sonship of the peacemakers depends on their relationship to the Son who fulfils the prophecies concerning the peacemaker Messiah. Their own impartial practice of *agape* will not be the *cause* of their

---

(Luther, AV, revived in the interests of inclusive language by RSV, NRSV, NJB, REB [NIV retains 'sons']), obscures this allusion; so, rightly, Strecker, *Sermon on the Mount*, p. 41. For the darker associations of 'children' (τέκνα) in Matthew see Chapter 3 §2, Chapter 4 §9b, above; §3a.1, below.

174. H. Windisch, 'Friedensbringer–Gottessöhne', *ZNW* 24 (1925) pp. 240-60, drew attention in passing to this text, but was evidently disinclined to follow it up (see Betz, *Sermon on the Mount*, p. 138, for the context of his argument). Lohmeyer, *Matthäus*, pp. 91-93, was the first (to my knowledge) to see the point. Cf. now Gnilka, *Matthäusevangelium*, I, p. 127.

175. For the deterioration of Solomon's character and its posthumous consequences for the nation see 3 Kgdms 11–14 (cf. Deut. 17.14-20); and for the implications for Matthew's typology cf. Chapter 4 §7a, above, and n. 337 to Chapter 4.

176. For the significance of the ass, and the emphasis on it in Matthew's reduced quotation of Zech. 9.9, see on III, §1b, above.

177. Above, Chapter 4 §8b.

178. Above, Chapter 4 §8b.

179. Cf. 17.27a: 'so as not to give offence to them'; on this, Thompson, *Advice*, p. 61.

being sons, but it will reveal their right to be called sons, i.e., by God;[180] they will be known by their fruits.

Finally, what is foretold in the prophecy of Hos. 2.1 is to be located 'in the place where it was said to them "You are not my people" ': historically the northern kingdom, geographically equivalent in part to Galilee, and for Matthew symbolic of the Gentile world in which the Church's mission and the kingdom's earthly future lie. This, as we have seen,[181] is the force of τὴν γῆν, which the meek are to inherit, in III, and furnishes a last item of correspondence between III and VII.

e. *The Pattern So Far*

My examination discloses that not only are I and III and V and VII treated, respectively, as pairs, but that V is seen as the converse of I, and VII, correspondingly, of III. The four beatitudes of the 'left-hand column' have thus what may be called a 'quadrilateral' relationship. We cannot however assume in advance that the same holds good for those of the 'right-hand column'.

3. *II. Those who Mourn (πενθοῦντες)*
IV. Those who Hunger and Thirst for Righteousness (πεινῶντες καὶ διψῶντες τὴν δικαιοσύνην)

a. *Mourning*

II is linked with I by their common background in Isa. 61.1-3, and there is nothing in the wording (with the exception of the actual macarism) that cannot be derived from this text.

They are linked also by the penitential associations of mourning: if the poor in spirit are the humble-and-aware of sinfulness, the mourners are those who humble themselves to express their penitence. πενθεῖν in the LXX renders, in the great majority of instances, the Hebrew *'ābel*, the grief with which a community responds to a great natural or national disaster (or seeks to avert its worst consequences), and individuals to personal bereavement or to the recognition of their own or their nation's sinfulness.[182] Common to all these is their characteristic exterior

---

180. For the recognition (by God) of sonship as a reward, to be bestowed at the judgment, see Luz, *Matthew*, I, p. 343; Charette, *Recompense*, p. 93; Betz, *Sermon on the Mount*, p. 141; contra Catchpole, *Quest*, pp. 17, 83.

181. See above, §1b *ad fin.*

182. See R. Bultmann, 'πένθος, πενθέω', *TDNT*, VI, pp. 40-43; Strecker, *Sermon on the Mount*, p. 35.

aspect, which includes not only tears and lamentation, but fasting, abstinence from wine and from the use of oil, the wearing of sackcloth, and squalid surroundings (sitting in ashes)—not so much the experience as the expression of grief.[183]

Fasting is thus an integral part of mourning, and in the later Old Testament and intertestamental literature the usual motive for it is penitential, commonly in connection with the calamities that have come upon the nation in retribution for its sins (see especially the extended prayers, accompanied by fasting, in Neh. 9, Dan. 9). The events of 70 CE naturally produced a fresh wave of responses of this kind, which have left a permanent mark on the liturgy of the synagogue[184] as they have on some strains of Jewish popular piety (e.g., at the Wailing Wall), so that the restoration of Jerusalem, and especially of the temple, became and has remained a symbol of the messianic fulfilment for which the devout Jew prays and fasts.[185]

Matthew's Gospel was composed in fairly close proximity in time and place to those events, and he can be presumed both to have been aware of the neo-Pharisaic Jewish response to them and to have worked out his own in tension with it.[186] The clues that his Gospel offers to what this was are neither numerous nor explicit. The key words of this beatitude, πενθεῖν and παρακαλεῖν (in the sense of 'comfort') each recur only once elsewhere in the Gospel, at 9.15 and 2.18 respectively, both of them texts in which Matthew has made alterations to a *Vorlage*.

At 9.15a, in Jesus' answer to the question of John's disciples, Matthew has substituted πενθεῖν for Mark's νηστεύειν, while himself

---

183. Dupont, *Béatitudes*, II, p. 37. Luz, *Matthew*, I, p. 235, comments on the absence from contemporary Jewish literature of the use of πενθεῖν without qualification to convey penitence for sin. But in the case of Jas 4.9 he allows that the qualification is sufficiently supplied by the context. The same can be said of the word in its Old Testament associations, notably at Jer. 38(31).21 (on this see §3a.1, below, on 2.18). In any case Matthew's poetry sometimes demands the unexpected word (cf. §2 *ad init.*, above).

184. See S. Singer (ed.), *The Authorised Daily Prayer Book* (London: Eyre & Spottiswoode, 1962), pp. 105, 107, 110, 126, 130, 190, 193, 199, 214, 216, 303-304, 307, 319, 333, 344-45, 351, 370-71, 401.

185. See Hengel, 'Bergpredigt', pp. 354-55, for evidence from rabbinic sources (esp. *Pes. R.* 34) of a new wave of 'mourners for Zion' after 70 CE who made use of Isa. 61.2 and Zech. 9.9.

186. Cf. Chapter 4 §§8d-e, 10c, above.

retaining the latter word unaltered both in the question itself and in the second half of the verse which answers it. This establishes that the words are very close in meaning for him, though for all that not simply synonymous: πενθεῖν is the more inclusive and (despite its Hebrew background) the more appropriate word to use of an interior disposition, in line with other Beatitudes. There is a hint of this in the brief passage on fasting in the central section of the Sermon on the Mount (6.16-18), which contrasts the exterior motions of fasting, which can be gone through, unprofitably, to attract attention, with the secret interior disposition which is known only to God.

9.15 at the same time offers an indication of what Matthew (following his source) regarded as the proper motive for Christian fasting: 'the bridegroom will be taken away from them'. This invites two lines of interpretation: (a) *because the bridegroom has been taken away from them* (loss, mourning and repentance); (b) *in order that the bridegroom may be restored to them* (expectation, perseverance and prayer).

(1) *Loss, Mourning and Repentance.* For Matthew the destruction of Jerusalem and the terrible loss of innocent life that accompanied it are the consequence of Israel's rejection of its Messiah and its delivery of him to death forty years before. This is hinted at in the parables of chs. 21–22 (see especially 21.41-43; 22.7), spelled out at 23.37-39; 24.2, and explicitly accepted by the people at 27.25. Like so much of the later history, this is foreshadowed in Matthew 2, and particularly in the formula quotation of Jer. 38(31).15 at 2.18. I have examined in a previous chapter the divergences of Matthew's text of this from that of the LXX in its several recensions, and concluded that they are best understood as an independent revision of the latter by someone who was familiar with the Hebrew text but did not consider himself rigorously bound to it.[187] But it was also suggested there that certain of the differences in Matthew are due to interaction between the prophecy and its context in the Gospel, and are to be regarded as 'applied exegesis'.[188] These must now be examined further.

Of the words in question (τέκνα and παρακληθῆναι), τέκνον is a perfectly acceptable equivalent elsewhere in the LXX for the Hebrew

187. Above, Chapter 3 §2.
188. Note 22 to Chapter 3.

bēn,[189] but the LXX has υἱοῖς here; and in the previous formula quotation at 2.15 (Hos. 11.1) the opposite substitution has been made: for the LXX's ἐξ Αἰγύπτου μετεκάλεσα τὰ τέκνα αὐτοῦ [sc. Ισραήλ] Matthew has ἐξ Αἰγύπτου ἐκάλεσα τὸν υἱόν μου. The common element in the contexts of the two texts quoted is the figure of Ephraim and his need of repentance. Ephraim, of course, stands for Israel (explicitly at Hos. 11.1); Hosea's prophecy was addressed originally to the northern kingdom, and Jeremiah's, after the disappearance of the latter, to the remnant of Judah in captivity in Babylon. Neither has any suggestion of a contrast between the two kingdoms. Yet this is apparently what Matthew's typology derives from these texts. The associations of τέκνα in this Gospel are regularly with those caught up, without personal fault of their own, in the bloodshed that accompanied the fall of Jerusalem, the *children* of those who accept blood-guilt for the death of Jesus (27.25; cf. 23.37).[190] The fate of the Bethlehem innocents foreshadows this, and Rachel who weeps for them personifies Judaea, for Matthew the territory of the old Israel which rejected its Messiah and sent him to his death. At Jer. 38(31).21 there is an appeal to this Israel to repent: ὁδὸν ἥν ἐπορεύθης ἀποστράφητι, παρθένος Ἰσραήλ, ἀποστράφητι εἰς τὰς πόλεις σου **πενθοῦσα**. But Matthew's version of the Jeremiah prophecy implies that she has not heeded it. Though she weeps for her children, she does not *mourn* for them, for that would involve repentance, an acknowledgment of responsibility for the events that led to their death. Thus where the Hebrew says that she was inconsolable, and the LXX that she would not stop weeping, Matthew's οὐκ ἤθελεν παρακληθῆναι, though it takes something from both, means that she was *refusing* what alone would have brought her comfort, (not consolation, but) the forgiveness that follows repentance.

Ephraim, however, has repented. Between the Rachel text at Jer. 38(31).15 and the appeal to the daughter of Israel at v. 21 there stands his admission of sin, after bitter chastening, his plea for forgiveness in vv. 17-19, and God's promise of mercy (LXX ἐλεῶν ἐλεήσω αὐτόν) to him as a *son* in v. 20. What part has this in Matthew's meaning? Here too a distinction must be made between the level of the primary narrative and that of the prefiguration of future events. At the former, the reference of 'Out of Egypt have I called my son' must be to the child

189. 134 times in the LXX; see G. Fohrer, 'υἱός', B-C.1a, *TDNT*, VIII, pp. 340-55 (353).

190. See Green, *Matthew*, p. 221, cf. p. 60.

Jesus and his return from exile. It can hardly be the same where the thought is of events forty years after his death. If Rachel stands for Judaea, the homeland of organized Judaism, Ephraim's associations are with the northern territory, part of which had by this time become Galilee, the scene of Jesus' mission and ministry to 'tax-collectors and sinners' (9.9-13, etc.), and for Matthew also the symbol of the expansion of that mission into the countries of the Gentiles (4.12-16; cf. 5.5; 28.16-20). Here, as in the parable of the two sons, one of whom 're-pented and went' (21.28-32),[191] the former thought seems to be uppermost, without the latter being absolutely excluded. At this level Ephraim stands for those (originally Jewish, though often outcasts, and it may be predominantly Galilean) who have responded to the gospel call, and are to form the nucleus of the 'new nation' (21.43). In what sense, then, have they been 'called out of Egypt'? If the reference were simply to Gentile converts, there would be no difficulty: their deliverance from the domination of sin and pagan idolatry would be the typological counterpart of Israel's exodus, as indeed it is for much Gentile Christian exegesis, especially in a paschal context. This as it stands will not cover the situation of those converted from Judaism, even when it was no longer possible to be a Christian without ceasing to be, in the religious sense, a Jew. But the Johannine Apocalypse, from its strongly Jewish-Christian background, can speak of Jerusalem as 'the great city which is allegorically called Sodom and *Egypt*, where their Lord was crucified' (Rev. 11.8).[192] Even for disciples drawn from the Jewish matrix their conversion will involve a repudiation of the national and religious heart of the old Israel.[193]

---

191. G. Quell, 'πατήρ', B, *TDNT*, V, pp. 959-74 (973), suggested that Jer. 38(31).18-20 contains the germ of the Lukan parable of the prodigal son (Lk. 15.11-32). Goulder, *Midrash*, pp. 56, 59-60 (cf. *Luke*, pp. 609-15; Drury, *Parables*, p. 96) maintains that the parable is Luke's elaboration of Mt. 21.28-32; but in the light of Matthew's exegesis of the Jeremiah text the force of Quell's suggestion is not thereby excluded. Ravens, *Luke*, pp. 102-103, argues that for Luke the younger son stands for Ephraim, and Ephraim for the people of the northern territory whom he identifies with the Samaritans, a people despised by contemporary Jews but destined in the fulness of time to be reunited with them. Luke on this view diverges sharply from Matthew's *Heilsgeschichte*, for which the people for whom Ephraim stands are to supplant those represented by Rachel.

192. Cf. also Gal. 4.25: τῇ νῦν Ἰερουσαλήμ, δουλεύει γὰρ μετὰ τῶν τέκνων αὐτῆς. Egypt was Israel's 'house of bondage'.

193. On 23.39 see n. 286 to Chapter 4.

The likelihood that the Evangelist, in these opening chapters, was looking ahead to events closer to his own day does not mean, however, that he had nothing more to say, from his exegesis of these same texts, about the story of Jesus himself. Hos. 11.1 identifies Ephraim with Israel, and 11.3-4 speaks with great tenderness of God's care for him as a child; Jer. 38(31).20, in very similar language, calls him υἱὸς ἀγαπητός, the words in which the heavenly voice will proclaim Jesus after he has accepted a baptism of repentance 'to fulfil all righteousness' (3.17). It is significant that immediately after his acceptance of (and for) a representative role[194] in relation to the Israel that has been undergoing this baptism of repentance, he embarks on its behalf on a 'humiliating and testing hunger'.[195] Fasting not only expresses repentance but tests its reality, and that no less in the case of the innocent representative of the sinful nation than of those with sins of their own to repent of. The language of the temptation story, especially 4.1 ('led up by the Spirit...to be tempted') implies that the fast has been undertaken at the command of God:[196] that the temptation to abandon it under pressure of hunger is a real one, but that to do so would be both disobedience to God's expressed will and failure to trust the one who imposed it.[197] There may be some connection in Matthew's mind between the temptation to turn stones into bread and the little poem inviting trust in God at 7.7-11: 'What man of you, if his son asks him for a loaf, will he give him a stone?'.

That Jesus fasts is not, obviously, to be connected with the removal of the bridegroom; it is an aspect of his response to John's call to repentance (3.2, repeated in his own gospel message at 4.17 and that entrusted to his followers at 10.7). The bridegroom's removal is the consequence of the rejection of that. What his fasting does indicate is the possibility of penitential activity not just for personal sins of one's own but for the collective sins of those with whom one is personally identified; and this has a bearing on what Christians will do in a post-crucifixion situation.

---

194. For the 'Son of God' as representative of Israel in the temptation narrative, see Gerhardsson, *Testing*, pp. 20-24.

195. *Testing*, p. 40, cf. pp. 45-48.

196. *Testing*, pp. 36-40.

197. *Testing*, pp. 45-51.

(2) *Expectation, Perseverance and Prayer.* πενθεῖν in 9.15 is not to be understood as mourning for the dead, as Bultmann supposed.[198] The glorified Christ, in the thought of this Gospel, is no absentee Christ (cf. 18.20; 28.20), let alone a dead one, but he is not present in his role of bridegroom,[199] for the wedding feast is an image of the final eschatological reign which is is still to come (22.1-14; 25.1-13). It is in the context of longing for that, of prayer for its coming (and not for the restoration of the earthly Jerusalem[200]), and of perseverance in the face of widespread discouragement and of the obstacles still standing in the way of that prayer's fulfilment[201] that penitential humbling of oneself is still called for.

Mourning then is a penitential exercise, involving fasting, which follows the example of Jesus, and can express both personal repentance and penitence for the faults of one's spiritual community. The hunger which is the consequence of physical fasting is a real and literal hunger, i.e. a negative condition, and the 'comfort' promised is its final relief in the eschatological situation where fasting will be no more. The prophecy at Jer. 38(31).15 which, as has been suggested, underlies the formulation of this beatitude continues, shortly after the appeal to the virgin Israel (v. 21), with the words (v. 25):

ὅτι ἐμέθυσα πᾶσαν ψυχὴν **διψῶσαν**,
καὶ πᾶσαν ψυχὴν **πεινῶσαν** ἐνέπλησα.

And in Isa. 49.10, which Matthew would have every reason to see as a complementary text, we read:

οὐ **πεινάσουσιν**, οὐδέ **διψάσουσιν**...
ἀλλ᾽ ὁ ἐλεῶν αὐτοὺς **παρακαλέσει**.

The comfort of the mourners thus points forward to the satisfaction of the hungry which is the theme of IV.

198. 'πένθος', p. 42, apparently following A. Schlatter, *Der Evangelist Matthäus* (Stuttgart: Calwer, 1929), p. 134. Betz, *Sermon on the Mount*, pp. 119-24, continues this line of interpretation. His account of the origin of the Sermon precludes any reference to 9.15 or 2.18.

199. So Schlatter, *Matthäus*, p. 312.

200. Cf. n. 317 to Chapter 4.

201. See especially 24.9-14—best understood as alluding to the conditions of the Evangelist's own day; cf. Chapter 4 §9a, above, and n. 270 to Chapter 4.

b. *Hunger and Thirst for Righteousness*

The most significant clue to the connection between II and IV is the allusion we have already discovered to the first of Jesus' temptations in the wilderness. Jesus, after enduring a long fast at the command of God, is tempted to relieve his hunger by supernatural means; his response is an appeal to Deut. 8.3: 'man shall not live by bread alone, but by every word that proceeds frosm the mouth of God'. It is because his spiritual hunger for the word (i.e. the commandment, expressing the will) of God is stronger than his physical craving for food (great as that is) that the temptation is resisted.[202]

Two kinds of hunger are thus in play, the real physical hunger that fasting involves—a negative condition, to be endured as long as the declared will of God requires it, but destined finally to be relieved—and its positive counterpart, a transposed and metaphorical hunger, which will not be just relieved but satisfied, and that with nothing less than its final object.

Those who approach the text initially by the genetic method mostly start by assuming that the simpler form of it (i.e. that found in Lk. 6.21, which mentions only hunger) approximates to the original, and that Matthew (a) added thirst to hunger, and (b) spiritualized the whole expression by making δικαιοσύνη their object. (b) is undeniable, but does not require as its starting point a primitive beatitude on those who hunger only in the literal sense; II as interpreted above will serve equally well. As for (a), if Q is not assumed, there is no need to postulate an original in which hunger stood alone. The combined expression is common enough in the Old Testament background; we have already encountered it in the two texts quoted above. Closer than either of these to the wording of IV, indeed verbally identical as far as it goes, is Ps. 106.5: πεινῶντες καὶ διψῶντες (the only LXX text with the words in this inflection); the psalm goes on to speak of the relief of the condition at v. 9, using the word χορτάζειν. The form χορτασθήσονται is found at Ps. 36.19 (the psalm which has already contributed the wording of III, and will be shown to have verbal links with all the succeeding beatitudes[203]). Cross-referencing of these three words[204] in the LXX yields the following significant array of texts:

---

202. Gerhardsson, *Testing*, pp. 76-77.

203. See Chapter 9, with Table 9.1, below.

204. Since πεινᾶν has no cognate noun, λίμος had to do duty for this, and must therefore be included in the count.

Ps. 36.18-19: γινώσκει ὁ κύριος τὰς ὁδοὺς τῶν ἀμώμων,...
...καὶ ἐν ἡμέραις **λίμου χορτασθήσονται**.

Ps. 131.15: τοὺς πτωχοὺς αὐτῆς **χορτάσω** ἄρτων.

Deut. 8.3 ap. Mt. 4.4: οὐκ ἐπ᾽ ἄρτῳ μόνῳ ζήσεται ὁ ἄνθρωπος...

Ps. 106.5: **πεινῶντες καὶ διψῶντες**,
ἡ ψυχὴ αὐτῶν ἐν αὐτοῖς ἐξέλιπεν.

Ps. 106.9: ὅτι **ἐχόρτασεν** ψυχὴν κένην,
καὶ ψυχὴν **πεινῶσαν** ἐνέπλησεν ἀγαθῶν.

Ps. 33.11: πλούσιοι ἐπτώχευσαν καὶ **ἐπείνασαν**,
οἱ δὲ ἐκζητοῦντες τὸν κύριον οὐκ ἐλαττωθήσονται
παντὸς ἀγαθοῦ.

(Deut. 8.3 contd.): ἀλλ᾽ ἐπὶ παντὶ ῥήματι ἐκπορευομένῳ
διὰ στόματος θεοῦ.

Amos 8.11: ἐξαποστελῶ **λίμον** ἐπὶ τὴν γῆν,
οὐ **λίμον** ἄρτου οὐδὲ **δίψαν** ὕδατος,
ἀλλὰ **λίμον** τοῦ ἀκοῦσαι λόγον κυρίου.

Sir. 24.21: οἱ ἐσθίοντές με ἔτι **πεινάσουσιν**,
καὶ οἱ πίνοντές με ἔτι **διψήσουσιν**.

Ps. 41.3: **ἐδίψησεν** ἡ ψυχή μου πρὸς τὸν θεὸν τὸν ζῶντα·
πότε ἥξω καὶ ὀφθήσομαι τῷ προσώπῳ τοῦ θεοῦ;

Ps. 16.15: ἐγὼ δὲ ἐν **δικαιοσύνῃ** ὀφθήσομαι τῷ προσώπῳ σου,
χορτασθήσομαι ἐν τῷ ὀφθῆναι τὴν δόξαν σου.

In the light of these parallels an alternative account of the genesis of the beatitude and the thought that lies behind it can now be offered. With III, as we have seen already, the basic Old Testament background text for the Beatitudes has shifted from Isaiah 61 to Psalm 36. The πραεῖς of Ps. 36.11 (and, by derivation, of III) continue to be the subjects of its promises under other names, among them the δίκαιοι of vv. 17, 29, etc., and the ἄμωμοι of v. 18. Of the latter χορτάζειν is used absolutely, as indeed it is in all the instances quoted,[205] with the single exception of Ps. 131.15, which speaks of satisfying the poor with bread. 'Poor' makes the connection, which is otherwise missing, with I as the opening line of the Beatitudes composition; 'bread' asks to be con-

205. Contrast πίμπλαναι, which usually demands a secondary object; cf. Ps. 106.9b above.

tradicted, in the light of the quotation at 4.4; the hunger implied transcends physical hunger, and the satisfaction of it likewise. Ps. 106.9 and
Ps. 33.11 promise satisfactions of an inclusive but unspecific sort ('good
things'; cf. also Ps. 102.5), and the latter text drops the metaphor: those
who seek the Lord will go short of nothing good. This prepares the way
for a transposed, non-literal understanding of hunger, which is finally
specified in the Amos prophecy: it is hunger (and thirst) for hearing the
word of the Lord:[206] In the light of the warnings against hearing and not
doing elsewhere in this Gospel,[207] the text must mean for Matthew that
what a person lives by is *doing* the word, and that the hunger of which
the prophet speaks is hunger for hearing the word in order that one may
perform it. Although δικαιοσύνη has not been found in the background
texts that we have examined so far,[208] the meaning that we have ex-
tracted from these is in line with the general understanding of righteousness in this Gospel: doing the will of God (cf. 6.10; 7.21; 12.50;
21.31).[209] It is thus a matter of human behaviour;[210] in what sense it is at
the same time God's righteousness is a question which must occupy us
further.

---

206. The importance of this as a background text is noted by Dupont, *Béatitudes*,
III, p. 369.

207. E.g. 7.21-27; 21.28-32; 22.11-14.

208. Its occurrence three times in Isa. 61.1-11 has a general connection with the
theme of the Beatitudes rather than an obvious influence on any particular one;
contra Gundry, *Matthew*, p. 70; Hengel, 'Bergpredigt', p. 352.

209. J.A. Ziesler, *The Meaning of Righteousness in Paul* (SNTSMS, 20; Cambridge: Cambridge University Press, 1972), p. 133; Hare, *Persecution*, p. 131 n. 1.
Przbylski, *Righteousness*, pp. 106-15 (cf. p. 122) objects, on the grounds that (a)
Matthew's 'righteousness' language is confined to, and his 'will of God' language
excluded from, contexts which assume an interface between Christians and
observant Jews, and (b) the 'will of God' covers more than the behaviour required
of the disciple; in particular, it includes his or her salvation (cf. 18.14). The
methodology of the argument for (a) is very dubious in places (e.g. p. 110), and
21.31 is at variance with its conclusion, while that for (b) leaves the meaning of 'to
do the will of God' unaffected. 18.14 is actually a warning against attitudes that can
lead to the frustration of that will.

210. Luz, *Matthew*, I, pp. 237-38; so also Strecker, *Weg*, pp. 149-58; Ziesler,
Meaning, pp. 133-35; Dupont, *Béatitudes*, III, pp. 380-84 (for earlier authorities,
pp. 355-64); Przbylski, *Righteousness*, pp. 96-98; Davies and Allison, *Matthew*, I,
pp. 451-53; Hengel, 'Bergpredigt', pp. 357-62.

(1) *The Meaning of Righteousness.* Matthew speaks of righteousness, as it were, from two angles: in 5.20 and 6.1 of 'your' (i.e., disciples') righteousness (in the former text also of that of the scribes and Pharisees), and at 6.33 of God's. Does this mean that he alternates between two sorts of righteousness?[211] It may well be the case that his use of δικαιοσύνη covers two distinct Hebrew equivalents, *sedēq* (and its cognates) and *zekût*;[212] but this, if true, will still be no reason for reifying the concepts conveyed by them. If what Matthew means by 'God's righteousness' is that which he requires of human beings (an absolute), that which is specific to them ('*your* righteousness') is to be understood as the level of response to this that individuals or groups have settled for or to which they aspire (and so as empirical and relative). Thus at 5.20 disciples must aim for a higher standard than that exemplified by their Jewish rivals, and this 'greater righteousness' is spelled out at 5.48: they are to be whole, generous and irreproachable like God their Father.[213] It is not said that they are to be δίκαιοι as he is δίκαιος; nowhere in this Gospel, despite abundant LXX precedents, is the adjective used of God. The righteousness that is required of disciples is God's in the sense that it is he who requires it; his gift comes in the form of commandments to be obeyed.[214]

---

211. As suggested by those who understand the word to mean God's gift at 6.33: e.g. Soiron, *Bergpredigt*, pp. 169-70; Barth, in Bornkamm, Barth and Held, *Tradition*, p. 140; Meier, *Law*, pp. 77-78; Giesen, *Handeln*, pp. 166-79; Guelich, *Sermon*, pp. 85-87; also, but with a different understanding of its connotation, Schniewind, *Matthäus*, pp. 44-45, 94-95; G. Schrenk, 'δικαιοσύνη', *TDNT*, II, pp. 192-210 (198-99); P. Stuhlmacher, *Gerechtigkeit Gottes bei Paulus* (FRLANT, 87; Göttingen: Vandenhoeck & Ruprecht, 1966), p. 190; Gundry, *Matthew*, p. 70. See nn. 218, 220 below.

212. See Hengel, 'Bergpredigt', p. 359. Przybylski declined to include this word in his examination of the vocabulary of righteousness in the Tannaitic literature; see *Righteousness*, p. 41 and n. 22 (and for a possible explanation of his caution, E.P. Sanders, *Paul and Palestinian Judaism* [London: SCM Press, 1977], pp. 183-98). According to Hengel (citing Dalman and others), its Aramaic equivalent *zākû* regularly renders *ṣᵉdāqāh* in the Targums. The basic meaning seems to be 'good conduct of the sort that God is pleased to reward', i.e., something predicated of human beings. Cf. in the Sermon on the Mount 6.1 (on this, n. 217 below), 4, 6, 18, 19-21.

213. Both the *extension* of their righteousness (5.43-47) and its *intensiveness* (the whole section) are stretched as far as they will go. For further comment on the meaning of τέλειος see below on VI, §4a.

214. Strecker, 'Makarismen', p. 274; cf. *Weg*, p. 175. But see the reservations of Hengel, 'Bergpredigt', p. 362.

By the same token the acts of devotion that form the subject matter of 6.2-18 are introduced at 6.1 in terms which imply that they form part of a person's practice of 'righteousness'[215] even when done, as by the 'hypocrites', to impress the onlooker. Here the word is virtually equivalent to 'religion',[216] which, as the prophets knew, can be genuine or counterfeit; only that which God is pleased to reward can he, by definition, acknowledge as his.

Finally there is the injunction at 6.33 to 'seek first [God's] kingdom and his righteousness'. The links between the beatitude at 5.6 and the whole poem of which 6.33 forms the climax are unmistakable and significant. The theme of 6.25-33 takes its starting point from Ps. 36.25: 'I never saw the righteous forsaken, nor his seed begging bread' (LXX ζήτουν ἄρτους). Its assumptions are those of a subsistence economy, for which hunger (or the prospect of it) is the spur to greater effort, not an encouragement to wait for food to fall into one's mouth. The poem invites the transference of the effort from the struggle for physical survival to striving for the kingdom (the final satisfaction) by means of that rightness of life before God which he requires of those who seek admission to it,[217] and promises that those who make this their absolute priority will not lack material provision on the way; God, the universal provider, will supply all (πάντα) their material needs.[218] 6.33 itself is no more than an extended paraphrase of Ps. 33.11b (see above): note

215. See Przybylski, *Righteousness*, p. 78, for discussion of the text here. Neither the reading ἐλεημοσύνην for δικαιοσύνην in 6.1 nor the latter understood in the sense of the former makes an appropriate introduction to 6.2-18 as a whole.

216. So Davies, *Setting*, p. 307; Ziesler, *Meaning*, p. 134; cf. Przybylski, *Righteousness*, p. 88.

217. Przybylski, *Righteousness*, p. 90, understands this as essentially the imitation of God, and thus parallel with 5.48. While this interpretation is supported by my exegesis of Beatitudes V–VII, I am unconvinced by his structural argument that 6.33 is related to 6.1 in the same way as 5.48 is to 5.20 (see Chapter 6, above, on the structure of the Sermon on the Mount). God's righteousness is still what he requires, however grounded in his own essential nature.

218. It is thus not effort that is to be abandoned (cf. Broer, *Seligpreisungen*, p. 91; Strecker, *Sermon on the Mount*, p. 37; contra Jeremias, *Parables*, pp. 214-15), but *anxiety* (μεριμνᾶν: 6.25, 31), in view of the divine promise to provide all (6.32-33). This is indisputably gift, and linked (προστεθήσεται) with the kingdom seen as eschatological gift; but it does not require that God's righteousness be seen as gift in the same sense. The position of those cited in n. 211 makes righteousness essentially indistinguishable from the kingdom itself. Schrenk, 'δικαιοσύνη', p. 200, and Trilling, *Israel*, pp. 146-47, maintain this explicitly.

ἐκζητοῦντες/ζητεῖτε and πάντος ἀγαθοῦ²¹⁹/πάντα. The first of these connotes an active striving for righteousness, and makes it virtually certain that the hunger and thirst of IV is to be understood in the same sense, not as passive longing for a gift.²²⁰ Ps. 33.9 offers a beatitude on those who live by this rule:

> Taste and see that the Lord is kind;
> Blessed is the man who trusts in him.²²¹

It will be recalled²²² that the petition for daily bread in the Lord's Prayer follows 'your kingdom come' and 'your will be done', and can itself be prayed both as an expression of trust in God's daily provision, and of longing for the satisfaction of the heavenly banquet. All these themes are at work in 6.25-33 and summed up in its final verse.

c. *The Nature of the Satisfaction*

If righteousness is the object of hunger, is it then also the content of the promised satisfaction? The problem which this raises is well conveyed by what is said of wisdom, likewise the object of hunger (and thirst), at Sir. 24.21: those who feed on it can never have enough of it in this life. Wisdom as understood by Ben-Sira and righteousness as understood by Matthew are very closely related,²²³ and what Ben-Sira says of wisdom

---

219. Note ἀγαθὰ δόματα in the conclusion of the parallel poem at 7.11.

220. So, rightly, Dupont, *Béatitudes*, III, pp. 285-88; Broer, *Seligpreisungen*, p. 91; contra Meier, *Law*, p. 78. The anxieties of those who press for an element of 'gift' in Matthew's understanding of righteousness really concern the possibility of a major component of the New Testament canon not insisting on the primacy of grace (cf. Broer, *Seligpreisungen*, pp. 88-96). This is a problem for hermeneutics, not a justification for forced exegesis. For recent approaches to it see Stuhlmacher, *Gerechtigkeit*, p. 191: Matthew falls short of the full Pauline understanding of *sola gratia*; U. Luz, 'Die Bergpedigt im Spiegel ihre Wirkungsgeschichte', in J. Moltmann (ed.), *Nachfolge und Bergpredigt* (Munich: Chr. Kaiser Verlag, 1981), pp. 37-72: 42: Matthew's outlook affected by the need to combat 'cheap grace' (so also Green, *Matthew*, pp. 236-37; Broer, *Seligpreisungen*, p. 89; Hengel objects); Przbylski, *Righteousness*, pp. 106-107, 121-22: righteousness and salvation distinct concepts for Matthew (who on this account [to extend the terminology of E.P. Sanders] teaches a 'nomism of the new covenant'); Hengel, 'Bergpredigt', pp. 357-62, 395-400: conclusions similar to Stuhlmacher's.

221. This would be equally appropriate to I in its comprehensive meaning (cf. §1e *ad fin.*, above).

222. See Chapter 4 §§2a, 2b.2 above.

223. Cf. Orton, *Scribe*, p. 68: 'Wisdom and righteousness are two sides of the

in this text is equally applicable to the demands of righteousness in the First Gospel: there will always be more to be heard and done.[224] If then righteousness as thus defined were not only what is hungered for but what that hunger will be satisfied with, the satisfaction would by definition be only temporary, for on this side of the final eschatological reign there always remains the prospect of further opportunities of hearing and doing God's will. Nor can any form of the proposition that virtue is its own reward do justice to the eschatological dimension of the New Testament. The alternative view, that the satisfaction transcends the object of desire, is indeed to be identified with the kingdom itself,[225] is fully in line with Matthew's theology of the kingdom, and of righteousness as its correlative and the precondition of admission to it.[226]

Herein lies the significance of the two final texts quoted. Both are taken from psalms with a cultic background, a category to which Matthew gives a transcendental twist.[227] I include Ps. 41.3 to illustrate the extra dimension of intensity that the image of hunger receives from the addition of that of thirst, which conveys a keener quality of desire and one that perhaps lends itself more readily to the thought of ultimate satisfaction.[228] In Ps. 16.14-15[229] (the only one of our texts that actually names 'righteousness') the psalmist contrasts the physical satiety which his enemies have in this life, well-filled stomachs and abundance of sons to inherit their name and their wealth, with the transcendental satisfaction that he expects to receive when he stands face to face with God. Though it is likely that the author of this psalm understood his words in a cultic rather than an explicitly eschatological sense, they

same coin in much wisdom-influenced Jewish literature, and Ben Sira is the first writer who clearly identifies Wisdom and Torah'. See also above, Chapter 4 §7a.

224. See the fine paragraph of Dupont, *Béatitudes*, III, p. 370.

225. Dupont, *Béatitudes*, III, pp. 376-80. Meier'a attack on this (*Law*, p. 87) is as unfair as it is pedantic. Betz, *Sermon on the Mount*, p. 132, associates χορτασ-θήσονται with the eschatological banquet.

226. See esp. Dupont, *Béatitudes*, III, pp. 245-305.

227. See on VI, §4b, below.

228. Cf. A. Descamps, *Les justes et la justice dans les Evangiles et le christianisme primitif* (Gembloux: Ducoulot, 1950), p. 169: 'Le sens métaphorique du verbe διψᾶν est plus marqué, l'eau vivant ayant naturellement évoqué, mieux encore que le pain, les biens spirituels'.

229. On this text, and on the use of Isa. 49.10 (see above) and Ps. 22.1-2 in the context of final eschatological satisfaction at Rev. 7.16-17, see Légasse, *Les Pauvres*, p. 34; cf. Dupont, *Béatitudes*, III, pp. 372-74.

would certainly invite the latter interpretation from the Christian exegete that Matthew was. In that case the satisfaction promised to those who hunger and thirst for righteousness is nothing less than the sight of God in his kingdom. The apodosis of IV anticipates that of VI and is incomplete without it.

The suggestion that II, IV and VI thus form an ascending series with its climax in the beatitude on the pure in heart may throw some light on the fact that the two former, unlike the beatitudes previously considered, are taken up relatively little in the rest of the Gospel. The influence of VI on the other hand, as we shall shortly discover, is ubiquitous.[230] If the Evangelist saw the three as in some sense a single whole, with VI spelling out in plainer language a meaning which is hinted at and reached towards in the imagery and scriptural allusiveness of the other two, the phenomenon is sufficiently accounted for.

4. *VI. The Pure in Heart (καθαροὶ τῇ καρδίᾳ)*
VIII. Those Persecuted for Righteousness (δεδιωγμένοι ἕνεκεν δικαιοσύνης)

If, as noted above, there are indications that II, IV and VI form an ascending series, and if, as was observed in Chapter 2, VIII both corresponds with IV as the concluding line of a quatrain, with a reference to righteousness, and, by its apodosis, forms an *inclusio* with I, then VI and VIII are less self-evidently a pair than the beatitudes already examined, and the question of the relation between them is better deferred until they have been examined separately.

a. *The Pure in Heart*
It is generally agreed that the immediate literary antecedent of VI is Ps. 23.3-4:

> Who shall ascend the hill of the Lord,
> and who shall stand in his holy place?
> ἀθῷος χερσὶν καὶ **καθαρὸς τῇ καρδίᾳ**,...

The majority of commentators[231] seem content to work from this text alone, and thus to interpret the expression exclusively in terms of the

230. I find it extraordinary that Schnackenburg, 'Friedenstiften', p. 170, has difficulty in finding a place for VI in the remainder of the Sermon on the Mount. Cf. Chapter 8 §3, below.
231. E.g. McNeile, *Matthew*, p. 52; Dupont, *Béatitudes*, III, pp. 557-603;

implied contrast between the outward (clean hands) and the inward (pure heart): (as certain advertisements used to proclaim to an anxious public) 'inner cleanliness comes first'. While this nuance is undoubtedly present, it represents only the tip of the iceberg. Matthew's choice of words, governed as it is by poetic considerations, often offers only an indirect clue to a complex of word-associations which must be studied *in toto* if his meaning is to be fully understood.

καθαρός in Ps. 23.4 represents, unusually, the Hebrew *bar*. This relatively rare word reappears at Ps. 73.1 MT, where the LXX has εὐθής (the word normally used to render *yāšār* ['upright']),[232] and a later verse in the same psalm, v. 13, contains a verbal expression which corresponds closely to the adjectival one at Ps. 23.4:

> All in vain have I kept my heart clean (LXX ἐδικαίωσα)[233]
> And washed my hands in innocence.

The same Hebrew verb (*zākāh*) is found, with a different Greek equivalent, in Ps. 119.9-10MT:

> How shall a young man keep his way pure (LXX κατορθώσει)?
> By guarding it according to thy word.
> With my whole heart I seek thee;
> Let me not wander from thy commandments!

This couplet in its turn answers to the corresponding one (containing a double beatitude) in the opening stanza of the psalm, Ps. 119.1-2 MT:

Gundry, *Matthew*, p. 71; Beare, *Matthew*, p. 132; Gnilka, *Matthäusevangelium*, I, p. 126; Davies and Allison, *Matthew*, I, pp. 557-58; Strecker, *Sermon on the Mount*, pp. 39-40; Catchpole, *Quest*, p. 31; Betz, *Sermon on the Mount*, pp. 138-41. Schniewind, *Matthäus*, p. 49, is a shining exception; cf. also Lohmeyer, *Matthäus*, pp. 88-91; Luz, *Matthew*, I, pp. 238-39.

232. Dupont, *Béatitudes*, III, p. 570, notes: 'On peut penser que les deux formules sont plus ou moins équivalentes', but unaccountably fails to follow this up in his exegesis.

233. Cf. the expression at Gen. 20.5: ἐν καθαρᾷ (Hebrew *tām*) καρδίᾳ καὶ ἐν δικαιοσύνῃ χειρῶν (virtually equivalent to 'with a clear conscience'). The verb used at Ps. 51.4 (*tāhēr*: LXX καθάρισον) and its cognate adjective *tāhôr* (v. 12; LXX καθαράν), often cited by commentators on VI, carry somewhat different connotations: they are concerned with the restoration of purity, whereas *zākāh* signifies its preservation. While influence from this psalm on VI is not ruled out in principle at the level of the Greek text, its essential meaning is already associated in the Beatitudes with I and II (see §§1d, 3a, above).

Blessed are those who are blameless (Hebrew *tāmîm*) in the way,
  Who walk in the law of the Lord!
Blessed are those who keep his testimonies,
  Who seek him with their whole heart.

The LXX here renders *tāmîm* by ἄμωμος, as it usually does, including at Ps. 14.2 (a psalm with close affinities in its content to Ps. 23) and Ps. 36.18 (the psalm which links all the later Beatitudes from III onwards).[234] Another rendering, relatively seldom found, is τέλειος,[235] the word used by Matthew at a key point in the Sermon on the Mount (5.48) to convey the 'greater righteousness' of 5.20, and repeated, as we have seen,[236] in his version of the Markan story of the rich man (19.21). A third, ἁπλοῦς, represented in the LXX only by its cognate ἁπλότης,[237] was gaining ground by Matthew's time;[238] his use of it for the 'single eye' at 6.22 is clearly related.[239] Finally, the parallelism between 'blamelessness' (or 'purity') 'in the way' and seeking God with one's whole heart in Ps. 118.1-2 implies that the quality denoted by the former is that enjoined in the *Shema'*: 'you shall love the Lord your God

234. See also Ps. 17.24, 31, 33; 18.8, 14; 63.5; 118.1, 80; Ezek. 28.15 (of Adam); cf. Trilling, *Israel*, p. 194. The choice of it to render *tāmîm* reflects the sacrificial associations of the latter word ('without blemish'); hence its repeated use in Ezek. 43, 45–46 (but cf. Exod. 12.5, where it is rendered by τέλειος [which also has sacrificial associations in its etymology; cf. G. Delling, 'τέλειος', *TDNT*, VIII, pp. 67-78 (67)]). The related ἄμεμπτος renders *tām* at Gen. 17.1; Job 12.4 (and a variety of synonyms in the latter book).

235. Cf. Gen. 6.9 (and Sir. 44.17): δίκαιος τέλειος (of Noah); Deut. 18.13: τέλειος ἔσῃ. The principal text behind 5.48, however, is Lev. 19.2 (cf. 11.44): ἅγιοι ἔσεσθε, ὅτι ἐγὼ ἅγιος. See Trilling, *Israel*, p. 195; contra Delling, 'τέλειος', p. 74 n. 36. Authorities favouring priority of 5.48 to Lk. 6.36 include Sand, *Gesetz*, p. 54; Giesen, *Handeln*, p. 127; Green, 'Clement', pp. 8-9; Goulder, *Luke*, p. 365; Franklin, *Luke*, p. 323; contra Catchpole, *Quest*, p. 116, who argues unconvincingly from Luke's liking for cognates of τέλειος; Jacobson, *First Gospel*, p. 102. For application of the word to God, Abrahams, *Studies*, II, p. 157: ' "perfection in love" as the aim of imitation is a fuller concept than the third gospel's "perfection in mercy" '; R. Schnackenburg, *Christliche Existenz* (Munich: Kösel, 1967), I, p. 137; C. Sabourin, 'Why is God Called "Perfect" in Mt 5,48?', *BZ* NS 24 (1980), pp. 266-68.

236. Above, §1e.3.

237. See H-R, s.v., and cf. Amstutz, *ΑΠΛΟΤΗΣ*, pp. 18-39.

238. Amstutz, *ΑΠΛΟΤΗΣ*, pp. 41-63; cf. pp. 64-83 on the incidence of it in the Greek version of *Test. XII Patr.*, esp. *T. Iss.*

239. See n. 105 above.

with all your heart' (Deut. 6.5), on which Psalm 119(118) is no more than an extended verse commentary.[240]

There are two conclusions to be drawn from this lexical evidence. First, the lack of consistency shown by the LXX translators in their choice of equivalents indicates that there is a large overlap of connotation between the various words used in the original. It is thus a mistake to concentrate too narrowly on the dictionary meaning or the immediate associations of καθαρός.[241] Secondly, the fact that the same adverbial suffix is used with a number of different adjectives to convey, if with varying imagery, the same essential meaning calls for some qualification in this case of Dupont's insistence[242] that in expressions of that sort it is invariably the suffix that qualifies the adjective and not vice versa. It is true that 'heart' is often found in parallelism with 'spirit'.[243] Yet it would be wrong in these instances to see the two only as alternative expressions of what is interior to a person. As Aubrey Johnson put it,[244] 'the heart in all its wide range of emotional, intellectual, and volitional activity is obviously found to be of supreme importance to the *ego* or unit of consciousness...as such it is ultimately regarded as specially subject to the influence of the *rûaḥ*'. Thus, of the two, 'heart' is both the more concrete and the more specific to the individual. Its connotation in rabbinic thinking is appositely summed up by Birger Gerhardsson.[245]

> It is well known that the 'heart' (*lēbāb*, *lēb*) is used as an inclusive term for man's inner nature, not only as the 'seat' of the animal instincts but also as the 'seat' of faith and knowledge of God. (It is necessary to place the word 'seat' in quotation marks since there is hardly a question of localizing these qualities to one part of the body.) Using the Old Testament terminology, the rabbis would speak of the righteous man as one who has a clean, whole and undivided, 'perfect' heart (*bar lēbāb*, *tām lēbāb* or *lēbāb šālem*), as one 'who seeks God with his whole heart' (*dōrēs et yy bekôl lēbāb*), as one 'who loves God with his whole heart'

---

240. For this psalm as a model for the Beatitudes composition see above, Chapter 2.

241. Cf. nn. 231, 232 above.

242. *Béatitudes*, III, pp. 385-99; cf. §1c, above.

243. E.g. Deut. 2.30; Ps. 33.19; 50.12, 19; 77.8; 142.4; Ezek. 18.31; 36.26.

244. A.R. Johnson, *The Vitality of the Individual in the Thought of Ancient Israel* (Cardiff: University of Wales Press, 1949), pp. 83-84.

245. *Testing*, p. 48 (Hebrew transliterated).

(*'ōhāb et yy bekôl l'bābô*). The ideal is the integrated and uncomplicated personality wholly consecrated to the service of God.

In the rich complex of meaning uncovered by these word-associations it is possible to distinguish three main strands that are significant for Matthew's own usage.

(1) The first is that of generous response to the total demands of God. The requirement that the disciples must be τέλειοι (5.48) sums up and concludes not just the final antithesis of 5.43-47 but the whole series.[246] There is to be a total suppression of aggressive impulses in oneself and a total and generous non-resistance to them in others, absolute sexual purity, lifelong commitment in marriage, unqualified truthfulness in speech, and unlimited application to all people of the command to love one's neighbour. 5.48 is itself a paraphrase of Lev. 19.2: 'you shall be holy, for I am holy',[247] and the beatitude on the pure in heart, as the equivalent of τέλειος, is an invitation, like those which immediately precede and follow it, to the *imitatio Dei*. This absoluteness of demand is reflected outside the Sermon on the Mount in Matthew's version of the Markan pericope concerning the great commandment of the Law (22.34-40), and particularly at 22.40 which treats Deut. 6.5, in conjunction with Lev. 19.18, as the interpretative principle of the whole revealed will of God (law *and* prophets).[248]

(2) Secondly, this response cannot remain on the level of external behaviour, let alone concern with the opinions of others, but must be rooted in, and proceed from, a person's inner self. This is spelled out in the injunctions to true piety in the Sermon on the Mount (6.1-18), and echoed in the denunciation of the Pharisees (23.3-7, 27-28); 'hypocrisy', which looms so large in the Evangelist's case against the latter throughout the Gospel, is its antithesis.[249] Conversely, it is from the heart and

---

246. Contra Delling, 'τέλειος', p. 74 n. 35.

247. Note 235 above.

248. Cf. 5.20 in relation to 5.17.

249. Van Tilborg, *Intervention*, p. 144, treats ὑπόκρισις as the contrary of ἁπλότης. The integrity of character conveyed by Ps. 23.4 is contrasted in the same verse with δόλος; cf. Ps. 33.13; see also verbal form at Pss. 14.3, 36.3. At Isa. 53.9 and Ps. 31.2 it is found in formal parallelism with words for sin. See also D.O. Via, *Self-Deception and Wholeness in Paul and Matthew* (Philadelphia: Fortress Press, 1990), pp. 92-98, who argues for self-deception rather than conscious insincerity as

not from external contamination that the things that threaten a person's relationship to God proceed; see 15.1-20 (especially vv. 18-20),[250] and cf. 12.33-35; 23.25-26. Matthew's redaction of Mk 14.24 at 26.28 makes clear that he has in mind the new covenant of Jer. 31.31-34, in which the forgiveness of sins is to be accompanied by the law written on the heart.

(3) The third strand is the integrity of the single, undivided heart, as contrasted with one that is divided by the cravings associated with the *yēṣer hā-rāʿ*:[251] hunger and thirst (see above on the first temptation of Jesus[252]), sexual desire (cf. 5.27-28), and (for Matthew, especially) avarice. The latter, as we have already seen,[253] is the connecting theme of 6.19-24 (note especially the relation of treasure and heart at 6.19-20, the emphasis on the 'single' eye at 6.22-23, and the application of the image of the slave with two masters to the demands of God and money). The lesson of the poem that follows is 'give priority to the demands of the kingdom (and your basic needs will be supplied)'. The theme is picked up outside the Sermon on the Mount, as we have seen,[254] in the episode of the rich young man,[255] who in Matthew's version is directed to sell all if he wishes to be τέλειος, and promised treasure in heaven. A comparable dividedness seems to obtain in the case of those who hear, pray, promise or preach without themselves taking the action required of them: see 6.14-15; 7.21-27; 21.28-30; 23.3-4.

the meaning here; Strecker, *Sermon on the Mount*, p. 99.

250. See Davies and Allison, *Matthew*, II, pp. 535-36, for the suggestion that διαλογισμοὶ πονηροί may be Matthew's Greek equivalent for the *yēṣer hārāʿ* (cf. following paragraph).

251. On this, Gerhardsson, *Testing*, pp. 48-51, and authorities cited there, esp. S. Schechter, *Some Aspects of Rabbinic Theology* (London: A. & C. Black, 1909), pp. 219-92; also W.D. Davies, *Paul and Rabbinic Judaism* (London: SPCK, 1948), pp. 20-35.

252. Section 3b, above; cf. Gerhardsson, *Testing*, pp. 43-48.

253. Above, §1e.3 (3).

254. Above, §1e.3 (2).

255. Only Matthew calls him this (19.20, 22). The word is MtR of Mk 10.20: ἐκ νεότητός μου. The alteration may be due to catchword connection with Lam. 3.27 (cited, Chapter 4 §7a above), read in conjunction with 11.28-29. But the introduction of τέλειος at 19.21 and its associations with the 'whole heart' suggest that despite his choice of a different word (νεανίσκος for νεώτερος) he is also thinking of Ps. 118.9-10 (see above); so Green, *Matthew*, p. 171.

We can now turn to the apodosis. Why, and in what sense, is the vision of God a fitting recompense for purity of heart?[256]

b. *The Vision of God*
The primitive and originally anthropomorphic belief that seeing God was a rare occurrence and potentially fatal to the beholder[257] was patient of reinterpretation in two directions: ethically, by emphasis on the moral unworthiness of humankind when confronted with the holiness of God; and theologically, by an intensified insistence on the divine transcendence. The first way is represented, uniquely, by the vision of Isaiah (Isa. 6.1-7). But it was the second that gradually prevailed in later Hebrew thought, which came to see the vision of God as something not so much dangerous as impossible for human beings in the conditions of earthly life.[258] This has left its mark on the developed text of the Old Testament; mediating figures like 'the angel of the Lord' and mediating concepts such as 'the glory of the Lord' or the Shekinah which embodies it are interposed between a human being and the direct apprehension of God. The process is not confined to primitive narratives. Texts with a cultic background (mostly from the Psalter) in which the temple worshipper describes his experience in terms of 'seeing' God were reinterpreted as meaning to 'appear before' God; so far as the Hebrew text was concerned it was possible to put this construction on it without disturbance of the characters (a standing problem for modern translators), but the consistent adoption of the latter construction by the LXX translators up to two centuries before the New Testament is a clear indication of the tradition of exegesis that would have obtained in the first century CE and been inherited by the New Testament writers.[259]

Post-biblical Judaism maintained the emphasis on the absolute transcendence of God (even angels are excluded from seeing him[260]—which

256. According to Soiron, *Bergpredigt*, p. 186, this condition for attaining the vision of God has no parallel in the entire rabbinic literature.
257. Gen. 32.31; Exod. 33.20; Deut. 5.26; Judg. 6.22; 13.22; Isa. 6.5.
258. See W. Michaelis, 'ὁράω κτλ.' *TDNT*, V, pp. 315-82 (339-40).
259. On the whole process see Michaelis, 'ὁράω', p. 325, and cf. A.T. Hanson, 'The Treatment in the LXX of the Theme of Seeing God', in G.J. Brooke and B. Lindars (eds.), *Septuagint, Scrolls, and Cognate Writings* (SBLSCS, 33; Atlanta: Scholars Press, 1992), pp. 557-68 (557-59).
260. Evidence in S-B, I, p. 207 (but contrast p. 783 for the highest rank of angels —'angels of the face'—in Tob. 12.15, the Dead Sea Scrolls [1QH 6.13] and other

is already true for Isa. 6.2). But the development of the doctrine of resurrection both in apocalyptic and in Pharisaism opened up the prospect of a possible attainment to the vision of God in a future life for which the biblical writers had left no room.[261]

What we find in the New Testament largely corresponds with this. Jn 1.18, 1 Jn 4.12 and 1 Tim. 6.16 are all unambiguous statements that no one has seen God in this life. But there are also three texts in addition to this beatitude which look for a vision of God in the eschatological future: 1 Cor. 13.12, Heb. 12.14 and 1 Jn 3.2,[262] and of these the two latter, like the beatitude, link it expressly with sanctification,[263] and have references to Christians as 'sons' (1 Jn 3.2 'children') of God in close proximity.[264] It is not necessarily to be assumed that these texts and the beatitude are wholly independent of one another; but it is unlikely that the dependence, if any, is on the side of Matthew.[265]

Matthew himself has left one indication that the later Jewish insistence on the divine transcendence could have been modified to some degree by his own emphasis on the Fatherhood of God. For the rabbinic tradition, as we have seen, even angels do not see God, and only the most exalted ones actually dwell in his presence.[266] But at Mt. 18.10 Jesus says that the guardian angels of the 'little ones' (meaning all disciples, but with particular reference, it would seem, to those disparaged by their fellow Christians[267]) 'continually see (βλέπουσιν) the face of my Father in heaven'. βλέπειν usually conveys ongoing sense-perception rather than vision;[268] and since in the court language of ancient

---

post-biblical Jewish literature); cf. Dupont, *Béatitudes*, III, pp. 561-62; Michaelis, 'ὁράω', p. 339.

261. The most explicit example of this (prior to the rabbinic literature) is at *4 Ezra* 7.87, 91, 98.

262. See also Rev. 22.4, where the 'slaves' of God are promised the sight of his face in the context of the heavenly worship previously depicted in ch. 4—a more explicitly 'cultic' understanding of their final state.

263. Heb. 12.14: ἁγιασμόν; 1 Jn 3.3: ἁγνίζει; cf. Michaelis, 'ὁράω', p. 366.

264. See Heb. 12.5-9; 1 Jn 3.1.

265. Heb. 12.14 may be a direct allusion to the Matthaean beatitude; so Green, 'Clement', p. 24. Michaelis ('ὁράω', p. 366) takes the same view of 1 Jn 3.3. In the case of 1 Cor. 13.12 such dependence is only possible if the *agape* hymn was not a part of the original letter but interpolated later before (or at) its publication.

266. Note 260 above.

267. See §1d above, and cf. Green, *Matthew*, pp. 159-60.

268. BAGD, s.v.

rulers 'to see the face of' means 'to be admitted to the presence of',[269] the expression need not mean more than that the angelic guardians of the 'little ones' belong to the most privileged order of the company of heaven—less a statement of the possibility of their seeing God than an indication of the preciousness of their charges. Nevertheless the possibility that some weakening of the tradition of absolute transcendence may have affected Matthew's exegesis cannot be entirely ruled out.[270]

Only a relatively small number of texts remained unaffected by the process of hermeneutic modification noted above. Among them are the following.

(1)   Gen. 32.31: καὶ ἐκάλεσεν Ἰακὼβ τὸ ὄνομα τοῦ τόπου ἐκείνου Εἶδος θεοῦ· εἶδον γὰρ θεὸν πρόσωπον πρὸς πρόσωπον, καὶ ἐσώθη μου ἡ ψυχή.

There is no evading the explicitness of this reference to 'seeing God', which is further emphasized by the translators' insistence on a Greek rendering of the name Peniel. It is on this occasion that Jacob is given his new name *Israel* (see v. 29),[271] and thus what is narrated of Jacob/Israel in this passage is promised to the pure in heart in Mt. 5.8. To make the transition from one to the other we need look no further than Ps. 72.1 (in which we have already found lexical associations with this beatitude[272]), which in its present form[273] runs: 'Truly God is good to

269. E.g. 2 Kgdms 14.24 (βλέπειν); Gen. 43.3; Exod. 10.28-29, where ὁρᾶν represents the same Hebrew word; cf. Dupont, *Béatitudes*, III, pp. 560-61.

270. So, e.g., Schniewind, *Matthäus*, p. 127; Michel, 'μικρός', p. 651 n. 29; Michaelis, 'ὁράω', p. 343; Thompson, *Advice*, p. 154; Légasse, *Enfant*, pp. 71-72.

271. Philo, being innocent of Hebrew, explains the meaning of the name 'Israel' as (ὁ) ὁρῶν (τὸν θεόν) (28 times in all, exclusive of related expressions). See J.W. Earp's Index of Names in *Philo*, X (Loeb Classical Library; London: Heinemann, 1962), p. 334 n. [a]. Though there are only two allusions to Gen. 32.23-33 in his surviving works (so Hanson, 'Treatment', p. 558; both missed by Michaelis, 'ὁράω', p. 336), a reference to this passage, with the meaning of the suppressed *Peniel* transferred to Israel, must lie behind Philo's strange etymology. This is interesting in view of the extended denotation that he gives to the name, remote though his allegorization is from Matthew's style of exegesis.

272. Above, §4a.

273. Graetz's proposal to read *lᵉyāšar'el* for *lᵉyiśra'el* (cf. W.O.E. Oesterley, *The Psalms* [London: SPCK, 1939], p. 342; cf. xi) gives a more straightforward parallelism with 'pure in heart', and is followed by RSV, NRSV, NEB, REB, and many

Israel, to those who are pure in heart' (RSV margin). Assuming what other passages have confirmed,[274] that Matthew was familiar with the Hebrew text as well as with the LXX, the identification leaps to the eye.

(2)   Isa. 6.1: ...I saw the Lord sitting upon a throne, high and lifted up... (v. 7) And I said: 'Woe is me! For I am lost; for I am a man of unclean lips, and I dwell in the midst of a people of unclean lips; for my eyes have seen the King, the Lord of hosts!' (RSV)

If exegesis of the preceding text by the accepted methods of the time establishes that the pure in heart are to see God, this one points up the ethical appropriateness of the promise. For an indication of what Matthew would have understood by Isaiah's expression 'unclean lips', we can compare his use (following Mark) of another Isaiah text, Isa. 29.13:

This people honours me with their lips (χείλεσιν),
but their heart (καρδία) is far from me (15.8).

It is the discrepancy between lips and heart that makes the lips unclean; cf. Ps. 14.3; 23.4; 31.2; 33.14 for the incompatibility of δόλος (deceit, insincerity) with the integrity of the God-fearing person.[275]

(3) For the promise of the vision of God in the future we have to turn to the Psalter. Here what were originally cultic statements, expressions of what the psalmist looked forward to experiencing in the worship of the temple, lie open to transformation by a Christian hermeneutic into descriptions of the state of final blessedness. The least altered of these passages is from Ps. 83, where a beatitude in v. 5:

Blessed are those who dwell in thy house,
ever singing thy praise!

(paired with another in v. 6) is followed (v. 8) by the promise:

...ὀφθήσεται ὁ θεὸς τῶν θεῶν ἐν Σιών.

commentators. The LXX's choice here of εὐθής as equivalent for the Hebrew *bar* might have been a reminiscence of this variant, but what it rendered was the present Hebrew text, which was thus established upwards of two centuries before Matthew.

274. See Chapter 3 §§2, 4; in this chapter §§1a, b, 4a above.

275. See n. 249 above.

Two other texts have been modified by the exegetical process mentioned above, so that the first half of the line, which originally spoke of 'seeing' God, is now understood to mean 'appearing before' him; but the second half, which speaks of the sight of his *glory*, remains intact:

Ps. 62.3: οὕτως ἐν τῷ ἁγίῳ ὤφθην σοι
τοῦ ἰδεῖν τὴν δύναμίν σου καὶ τὴν δόξαν σου.

Ps. 16.15: ἐγὼ δὲ ἐν δικαιοσύνῃ ὀφθήσομαι τῷ προσώπῳ σου,
χορτασθήσομαι ἐν τῷ ὀφθῆναι τὴν δόξαν σου.

I have already noted[276] the influence of the second of these on the wording of IV, and the implied connection between IV and VI. This is evidence that, whatever the hesitations of later Jewish exegesis, Matthew himself would not have distinguished sharply between the Psalmist's 'see the glory of God' and his own 'see God', and that on the basis not of a cultic but a transcendental understanding of the latter. The apodoses of the Beatitudes are all to find fulfilment in the final eschatological reign of God; both the satisfaction and the vision are to do with that kind of reality.[277]

c. *Persecution for Righteousness*

The final beatitude within the formal composition (5.10) is followed by a further beatitude, framed in the second person and with a parallel in Luke, outside it (5.11-12). Nearly all commentators treat the latter as the original tradition and the former as a generalizing summary constructed either by the Evangelist himself or by a hand immediately before him in the redactional process. Such a conclusion is hardly avoidable if the genetic method, which makes the question of sources the first to be put to any unit of a Gospel, is adhered to. But if the two beatitudes are examined first in relation to their context at the opening of the Sermon on the Mount, a different picture emerges. 5.10 is integral to the Beatitudes as a composition; coming at the end of the second quatrain, its mention of righteousness[278] corresponds formally to that in

276. Above, §3b.

277. Both aspects are touched on at Exod. 24.11, where the elders of Israel 'saw God, and ate and drank' (MT; LXX ὤφθησαν ἐν τῷ τόπῳ τοῦ θεοῦ). Cf. E.W. Nicholson, *God and His People* (Oxford: Clarendon Press, 1986), pp. 127-30. If Matthew could have recognized the original force of this, it might have contributed to the build-up of his own text.

278. The absence of the definite article in VIII is best explained in terms of the

IV, the final line of the first, and its apodosis, through the *inclusio* which it makes with I, rounds off the whole poem by bringing it back to the point at which it started. In itself it is a general statement about a category of persons: the kingdom is promised to those who have endured persecution (the force of the perfect participle should not be underplayed[279]) for righteousness—including, presumably, those who have died under it.[280] 5.11-12, as it stands in Matthew, is the first allusion outside the composition to what has been affirmed within it; it

word count of the strophes (see n. 9 to Chapter 2), rather than of any real distinction of meaning: e.g., Bonhoeffer's suggestion of 'a good cause' (see *The Cost of Discipleship* [trans. R.H. Fuller; London: SCM Press, 1962], p. 102; *Ethics* [trans. N. Horton-Smith; London: SCM Press, 1955], p. 192). Contra Betz, *Sermon on the Mount*, p. 142 n. 403, who thinks it should be supplied.

279. Dupont's argument (*Béatitudes*, III, p. 333 n. 5) that the force of the perfect participle is not readily distinguishable from that of the present is not convincing; it seems to be forced on him by his (widely shared) position that 5.10 is a generalizing summary of 5.11-12. If 5.10 is considered within the context of 5.3-10 (apart from which, as nearly all agree, it had no independent existence), it can be seen that it is grouped with the beatitudes of the second quatrain, which speak of qualities which abide and are rewarded, not (as do those of the first) of situations that will be reversed (see Chapter 8 §2 below). The state of *having endured* persecution faithfully (whether, from the standpoint of the implied speaker, in the past, the present or the pre-eschatological future) is one of these: 'ein bleibendes und notwendiges Merkmal der Junger' (Lohmeyer, *Matthäus*, p. 94); cf. Gnilka, *Matthäusevangelium*, I, p. 127; Luz, *Matthew*, I, pp. 241-42. Present consequences are not the same as present continuation (contra Davies and Allison, *Matthew*, I, p. 459; Betz, *Sermon on the Mount*, p. 146 n. 440); the French idiom to which Dupont appeals actually has its New Testament Greek counterpart in the use of the present tense at, e.g., 11.12. For the proper force of the perfect participle see B.M. Fanning, *Verbal Aspect in New Testament Greek* (Oxford: Clarendon Press, 1990), p. 416: 'a state or condition resulting from an anterior occurrence...it often emphasizes the *resulting state* and only implies the anterior occurrence. The sense comes through especially in instances of passive participles' (his emphasis). Mt. 5.10 is the first example cited. Contra S.E. Porter, *Verbal Aspect in the Greek of the New Testament with Reference to Tense and Mood* (SBG, 1; New York: Peter Lang, 1989), p. 396, whose suggested parallel (πεφορτισμένοι in 11.28) supports Fanning's account better than his own; it speaks of the condition of those who, having had burdens imposed on them at some point in time past (cf. 23.4), are weighed down by them in the present. For further New Testament examples cf. 1 Cor. 1.23 ('a Messiah who has suffered crucifixion'; contra NEB, REB); Rev. 5.6 ('a lamb with the marks of sacrifice upon him'; so REB).

280. See n. 284 below.

applies the teaching of this final beatitude to the situation of those whose persecution is in the present or still in the indefinite future.[281]

Something of the nature of the persecution of which this beatitude speaks can be deduced from these allusions elsewhere in the Gospel: in addition to 5.11-12, 10.17-23 (much of it, strikingly, transposed in Matthew's redaction from its original apocalyptic context in Mark); 23.34-36; 24.9.[282] The most significant feature of these is that the persecution of Christian missionaries (23.34a) is seen in direct continuity with the pre-Christian record of rejection and murder of Old Testament prophets (23.29-33),[283] and this will remain true of those facing present or future persecution (so 5.12: τοὺς προφήτας τοὺς πρὸ ὑμῶν). Matthew thus has in view persecution (not necessarily official or systematic) by Jews, which has in some cases involved death as well as harassment.[284] It will have had its beginnings in local response to Christian propaganda in Palestinian synagogues (hence the floggings of 10.19).[285] Whether that form of witness was still taking place in the communities for which Matthew wrote is questionable;[286] the expression *'their* synagogues'

281. Cf. de Diétrich, *St Matthew*, p. 31: '...the ninth Beatitude is actually a development of the eighth'.

282. See the discussion in Hare, *Persecution*, pp. 80-129. To a dispenser with Q Hare's conclusions often have more intrinsic weight than the redaction-critical arguments with which he supports them. Q imposes severe constraints on the scope of Matthew's authorial activity.

283. Cf. Hare, *Persecution*, pp. 121, 137-40.

284. This is not only required by the comparison with murdered Old Testament prophets (cf. 23.29-31, and the implications of the allegorized parable at 21.33-41, esp. v. 35; on this, Hare, *Persecution*, p. 139), but explicitly stated at 23.34b. Hare's elimination of σταυρώσετε there (*Persecution*, pp. 89-91; I accepted this too readily in *Matthew*, p. 193) would not affect this, even if justified (in fact it fails both on text-critical and rhythmical grounds and because crucifixion by Jews, though unthinkable as a judicial sentence, is not totally ruled out as mob justice, as certainly happened later during the Bar-Kokba rebellion. It does not take many atrocities to establish a tradition at the receiving end).

285. On these Hare, *Persecution*, pp. 43-46, 101-106, is illuminating.

286. Hare (*Persecution*, p. 127) thinks that it was a thing of the past by Matthew's time, but that the abandonment of the mission to Jews was still fairly recent; cf. Stanton, *Gospel*, pp. 113-42. L. Goppelt, *Apostolic and Post-Apostolic Times* (trans. R.A. Guelich; London: A. & C. Black, 1970), p. 121, concurs from evidence in the later rabbinic tradition. On the basis of this four phases of the mission to Jews as understood by this Gospel can be distinguished: (1) mission during the Galilaean ministry (the ostensible subject of ch. 10); (2) mission to (?Palestinian) Jews

which he so often repeats[287] indicates that the decisive break with Judaism has already taken place. But the offence and bitterness that have built up from it remain a reality wherever there is contact with 'the synagogue across the street'. Moreover Matthew's mind on this matter will owe something to personal experience gained in an earlier phase of the conflict, and his writing can be expected to reflect this as well as the present situation of his readership.[288] In the light of that the LXX wording of Ps. 39.10-11 could have had special significance for him:

εὐηγγελισάμην **δικαιοσύνην** ἐν ἐκκλησίᾳ μεγάλῃ·
ἰδοὺ τὰ χείλη μου οὐ μὴ κωλύσω·
κύριε, σὺ ἔγνως.
τὴν **δικαιοσύνην** σου οὐκ ἔκρυψα ἐν τῇ καρδίᾳ μου,
τὴν ἀλήθειάν σου καὶ τὸ σωτήριόν σου εἶπα,
οὐκ ἔκρυψα τὸ ἔλεός σου καὶ τὴν ἀλήθειάν σου ἀπὸ
συναγωγῆς πολλῆς.

The Hebrew of the final phrase means 'from the great assembly'.[289] A literal rendering of the LXX could be 'from many a synagogue'. Whatever the translators originally meant by their version,[290] it would, if the argument of Douglas Hare is well founded, have had resonances with the Evangelist's personal history.

between the resurrection and 70 CE (i.e., before the execution of judgment on the old Israel) (the real subject of ch. 10); (3) mission to Jews in the territory controlled or penetrated by the neo-Pharisaic Judaism of Jamnia after the events of 70 CE: seen with hindsight, in the light of the above interpretation of those events, to have been an error as well as a failure; (4) as a consequence of that realization, organized mission to Gentiles only. This does not however preclude continuing approaches to individual Jews (see n. 286 to Chapter 4, above), nor continuing harassment of Christians by Jews, the fruit of accumulated bitterness engendered during phases (2) and (3).

287. See n. 302 to Chapter 4.

288. One question which this raises is whether the Beatitudes poem was originally composed for its present position at the head of the Sermon on the Mount, or had, like the Lord's Prayer, an independent existence before its incorporation into it. This is reserved for my final chapter, Chapter 10.

289. So NEB; 'congregation' in earlier versions down to and including RSV.

290. The Hebrew phrase in v. 11 is identical with that at the beginning of v. 10, and it is unlikely that συναγώγη could have acquired its later technical sense by the time of the LXX translation of the Psalter.

I have already concluded[291] that in IV to 'hunger and thirst for righteousness' should be taken as meaning to 'long to know the will of God, so as to do it'. In VIII the 'righteousness' for which the missionaries have been persecuted can by analogy be defined as 'proclaiming the will of God to others, that they may do it'. Such proclamation can of course be as much a matter of lifestyle as of explicit preaching; hence the image of the city on a hill (5.14) and the instruction that disciples are not to hide their light (see further Chapter 8 §3 below). But at the same time part of the significance of the concluding words of 5.12 is that the persons addressed are invited to see themselves as standing in the prophetic line, and the function of prophets is proclamation by word of mouth. Furthermore, the expression in 5.11 which corresponds to ἕνεκεν δικαιοσύνης in 5.10 is ἕνεκεν ἐμοῦ; and at 28.20 the disciples are instructed to teach their converts ὅσα ἐνετειλάμην ὑμῖν. 'Righteousness' has therefore prophetic and christological as well as ethical associations; yet the reference is still, in VIII as in IV, to human behaviour. The two beatitudes come at it from different angles, but the meaning remains essentially the same in both.

At v. 15 (Heb. 14) of this psalm the Psalmist prays for the confusion of those who seek his life, and at v. 18 (Heb. 17) he speaks of himself as πτωχὸς καὶ πένης (Hebrew ʿānî wᵉ-ʿebyôn), an expression used in a number of other passages, especially in the Psalter, which speak of the oppression of the faithful remnant, as was noted above in my discussion of the background of I and III.[292] There the distinction between ʿānāw and ʿānî was found not to offer a valid basis for the understanding of that between the meek and the poor in spirit; but it does not follow that that distinction has had no other influence on the vocabulary of the Beatitudes. If, as we saw then, ʿānāw lies behind the poor in spirit, and if, as we see now, ʿānî lies behind the persecuted, I and VIII are clearly related in their lexical background as well as identical in their apodoses.

Moreover Ps. 36.14, one of the texts in question and from a psalm which is a major contributor to the Beatitudes, has πτωχὸν καὶ πένητα in parallelism with τοὺς εὐθεῖς τῇ καρδίᾳ. This association is present in Psalm 39 too; the verses quoted above are immediately preceded by this:

---

291. Above, §3b.
292. Above, §1.

τοῦ ποιῆσαι τὸ θέλημά σου, ὁ θεός μου, ἐβουλήθην
καὶ τὸν νόμον σου ἐν μέσῳ τῆς καρδίας μου (v. 9).

The first of these lines sums up what is meant by hunger and thirst for righteousness; the second implies that it is a matter of the 'law in the heart'.

These texts offer some justification for treating VI and VIII as a pair, even if there is less emphasis on the relation between them than on that between VIII and I. To go deeper, those who have faithfully endured persecution at the cost or risk of life are those who love God, according to the contemporary interpretation of the *Shema'*, with all their soul,[293] and thus make an appropriate counterpart for those who love him with all their heart—as well as for those who do so not *with* their strength (= wealth) but by letting go of it: the poor in spirit.

d. *The Promise of the Kingdom*

Something remains to be said of the meaning of the apodosis shared by I and VIII. Too much is made by some commentators of the apparent contrast between the present tense of this and the future of the intervening apodoses. The latter are all aspects of the final eschatological reign that lies on the far side of the coming judgment; 'kingdom' cannot mean that in these individual promises and something else in the summary of them. The whole composition consists of a series of variations on the theme of the 'poor';[294] the apodoses are similarly variations on the theme of the kingdom. The present tense in I and VIII must therefore be understood not of a present kingdom (except in so far as the final reign of God is already at work by anticipation), but of a present claim to the future kingdom. What the final judgment will confirm in the case of, e.g., the poor in spirit is true of them already; they have an authentic present claim to the future fulfilment.[295]

293. See Gerhardsson, *Testing*, pp. 75-76.
294. So, rightly, Betz, *Sermon on the Mount*, pp. 109-10.
295. See Davies and Allison, *Matthew*, I, pp. 446-47. ('a futuristic or proleptic present'); Catchpole, *Quest*, p. 86. For Luz, *Matthew*, I, p. 235 'the kingdom of heaven' (= 'the content of salvation') is future, but the promise of it is 'not spiritualized or moved to the beyond'. While this does justice to 5.5 (see §1b above), the final eschatological reign still lies on the far side of parousia, general resurrection and judgment. I see no justification for Catchpole's assertion that IV and VII imply a pre-eschatological fulfilment (*Quest*, p. 83). See respectively §3c and n. 180, above.

5. *Conclusion*

Finally, with reference to all four beatitudes of the 'right-hand column', it can be shown that the meanings that we have discovered for each of them occur repeatedly in the stanzas of Psalm 119 (118). The details are set out in Appendix C. Although I have accepted[296] the suggestion that Psalm 119 offers a formal model for the Beatitudes composition, these thematic parallels, as will be seen, have no corresponding formal arrangement, and direct verbal links with the LXX text are relatively infrequent. They indicate, nevertheless, that the content of this psalm was constantly present to the Evangelist's mind.

296. Chapter 2 above.

Chapter 8

THE SHAPE OF THE WHOLE POEM

1. *'Poor in Spirit' and 'Pure in Heart'*

Our examination has disclosed a complex web of relationships between the individual beatitudes, all ultimately stemming from that at the head of the list. The poor in spirit and the meek are variations on the theme of the *ʿnāwîm*, as are, less directly, those persecuted for righteousness. The merciful are the converse of the poor in spirit, and the peacemakers, correspondingly, of the meek. The penitential activity of mourners, humbling themselves before God, is an outward expression of the humility, with its awareness of sinfulness, which is central to the meaning of 'poor in spirit'. But the deprivation implicit in their fasting is only the negative aspect of that positive longing for God and the fulfilment of his will which is conveyed by the image of hunger and thirst for righteousness, and then spelled out in plain language in the beatitude on the pure in heart which is the real climax of the whole composition. We saw when examining the structure of the poem[1] that πτωχοὶ τῷ πνεύματι and καθαροὶ τῇ καρδίᾳ are expressions of the same grammatical type, both of them alliterative, and it is probably not accidental that the central idea behind each is expressed in the Psalter by a double beatitude—the former at Ps. 31.1-2, the latter at Ps. 118.1-2—and, furthermore, that each of these psalms concludes with the thought with which the other opens. Psalm 31, the penitential one, ends (v. 11):

> Be glad in the Lord and rejoice, O righteous.
> And shout for joy, all you upright in heart!

And Psalm 118, the paean on wholeness of heart, ends penitentially (v. 176):

---

1. Above, Chapter 2.

I have gone astray like a lost sheep;
seek thy servant, for I have not forgotten thy commandments.

The association of the two themes was clearly familiar at Qumran; the Hebrew equivalent of 'poor in spirit' at 1QM 14.7 is found in parallelism with 'the perfect of way'—an allusion, once more, to Ps. 118(119).1.[2]

Matthew however brings to it a special emphasis of his own. As we have seen,[3] the injunction not to accumulate treasure in 6.19 is capped by the remark 'where your treasure is, your heart will be also'; the gnomic saying in 6.24 about being slave to two masters is shown by its application 'you cannot serve God and mammon' to be an image of the heart divided by the evil *yēṣer*, and the rich young man of 19.16-22 is invited, if he wishes to be τέλειος, to dispose of his possessions.[4] It would seem that poverty in spirit, in the second of the two meanings that have been identified for it, is for this Evangelist a precondition of purity in heart.[5]

The tensive relationship between these two beatitudes can be compared to that between the tonic and the dominant in the chromatic scale.[6] I is the ground of the whole composition; in VI it rises to a climax, before returning, after a fashion, to where it started.[7] Together they strike the keynotes for the entire poem.

2.   Cf. Chapter 7 §4a, above.
3.   See Chapter 7 §4a.3, above.
4.   Chapter 7 §1e.3b.
5.   But not therefore 'synonymous' with it, as Betz in an unguarded comment implies (*Sermon on the Mount*, p. 136). He is nevertheless perceptive about the close relationship of the two qualities.
6.   The comparison (I hope it will be superfluous to insist) is offered by way of analogy, not allegory. The author is aware that the dominant is actually the *fifth* note of the scale.
7.   Betz however (*Sermon on the Mount*, p. 146) treats VIII as the climax of the composition, and persecution for the sake of righteousness as the 'highest' of the virtues (in contrast to poverty of spirit as the 'most elementary'). This, I suspect, has to do with the continuation of the theme in 5.11-12, his 'ninth' and 'tenth' beatitudes (though falling, as he admits, outside the formal composition closed by the *inclusio* of 5.10).

2. *The Overall Structure of the Beatitudes*

This can now be expressed diagrammatically (Fig. 8.1).

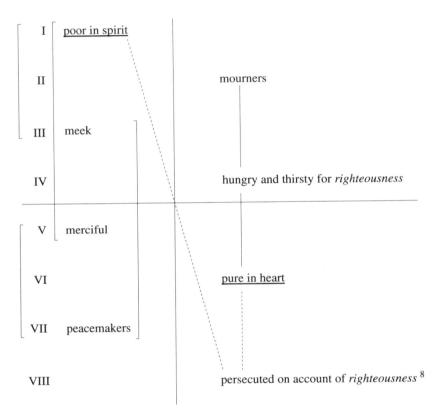

Figure 8.1. *The overall structure of the Beatitudes*

8.   Subtle and elaborate as this pattern is (and thus characteristic of much poetry), I cannot forbear to contrast it with the account of the Matthaean Beatitudes offered by Catchpole, *Quest*, pp. 16-18: a botched job containing four or five major unresolved tensions, explained (though hardly excused) by him as the product of 'editorial interference'. He seems to assume that (a) no 'blessedness' could attach, even paradoxically, to any condition experienced originally as unpleasant; (b) mourning (for a bereavement) or persecution (seen as ongoing) properly fall into this category. The havoc that these assumptions make with the integrity of the composition might have suggested a review of them.

We have so far concentrated mostly on the vertical lines within the left- and right-hand columns.[9] There is still something to be said about the 'horizontal' division between the two halves of the composition. It can be seen that the subjects of the first four, despite or even by virtue of their qualitative aspect, are in some sense conditions to be reversed, whereas those of the second four are positive qualities to be rewarded. Thus, obviously, the mourners, when comforted, will cease from their mourning; the hungry and thirsty, when satisfied, will hunger and thirst no more. But poverty also, in any sense, whether material or spiritual, literal or metaphorical, calls for relief; it is a positive quality only under the conditions of the present age, and cannot be thought of as continuing in those of the final eschatological reign. Meekness, similarly, implies an acceptance of present powerlessness;[10] the image of inheriting the earth cannot convey less than its reversal. Conversely, the merciful and the peacemakers stand, as we have seen,[11] for aspects of the *imitatio Dei*, as do the pure in heart if taken, as they rightly should be, as the equivalent of τέλειοι in 5.48 (itself modelled on Lev. 19.2). If the persecuted cannot be said to imitate God directly, their condition is nevertheless a form of the imitation of Christ, and the perfect tense moreover denotes not only a persecution that is over, or will be, before the time of its reward, but a state (that of *having endured* persecution) that will continue into the eschaton.[12] *A fortiori* this will be true of those qualities or dispositions that reflect the character of God himself.

This distinction between the two quatrains will be found significant when we come to consider the Lukan form of the Beatitudes.[13] The

9.   This aspect of the literary structure has been independently recognized by A. Kodjak, *A Structural Analysis of the Sermon on the Mount* (Religion and Reason, 34; Berlin: de Gruyter, 1986), pp. 41-74, esp. p. 58. His analysis is flawed by his insistence on including 5.11-12 in the composition, and he seems blithely unaware of the critical problems involved in treating the entire Sermon on the Mount as a transcript of Jesus' personal teaching. But his distinction of II, IV and VI as beatitudes of 'internal predominance' and III, V and VII as beatitudes of 'external predominance', with I and VIII straddling the two, comes very near to what my study has revealed. See further Chapter 10, below.

10.   See n. 169 to Chapter 7.

11.   Chapter 7 §2 above.

12.   See n. 279 to Chapter 7.

13.   Below, Chapter 9 §3b *ad fin*. The distinction is noted also by M.A. Powell, 'Matthew's Beatitudes: Reversals and Rewards of the Kingdom', *CBQ* 58 (1996), pp. 460-79.

close formal relationship between them also bears on a further question to which we now turn.

3. *The Beatitudes in Relation to the Rest of the Sermon on the Mount*

The Beatitudes occupy the same position in relation to the Sermon on the Mount as the Decalogue does in relation to the first instalment of the law given on Sinai (Exod. 20–23), and we have found that their meaning is taken up and developed at various points in the Sermon. Can we go further and discern a formal connection between the actual order of the contents of the latter and that which we find in the Beatitudes?

This was proposed in 1953 by Austin Farrer, whom Michael Goulder later claimed, perhaps over-modestly, to be 'following but amending'.[14] In fact the most substantial agreement between the two lies in their perception that the first application of a beatitude in the Sermon is that which takes up 5.10 at 5.11-12,[15] and that consequently, if there *is* any strict order in which the meaning of the Beatitudes is drawn out in the rest of the Sermon, it can only be the inverse of that of the Beatitudes themselves; that is, it is chiastic. In other respects the two proceed very differently, as their respective findings show. Farrer starts from an idiosyncratic analysis of the order of the Beatitudes: assuming the correctness of the western/Syrian inversion of the order of II and III,[16] and a pairing of VI and VII which could possibly (though he does not say so) claim the authority of the Letter to the Hebrews,[17] he arranges them in three pairs, with an additional line attached to the second and third: I-III, II-IV (V), VI-VII (VIII). Armed with this, he then proceeds to divide up the main body of the Sermon into three sections: 5.17-48; 6.1-18; 6.19–7.27. By ignoring the obvious break after 7.12 he has compounded the notorious but, as we have found,[18] by no means insuperable difficulty of discovering a coherent pattern in the material of 6.19–7.12. Consequently, while his correlation of the Beatitudes with the Sermon has a measure of plausibility down to 5.48, and even possi-

14. Farrer, *St Matthew and St Mark*, pp. 160-76; Goulder, *Midrash*, p. 252.
15. Cf. Hare, *Persecution*, pp. 130-32; W.J. Dumbrell, 'The Logic of the Rule of Law in Matthew v.1-20', *NovT* 23 (1981), pp. 1-31 (2).
16. See above, n. 2 to Chapter 2.
17. Heb. 12.14; see above, Chapter 7 §4b.
18. Above, Chapter 6, Chapter 7 §§1e, 2b.

bly as far as 6.18, thereafter it runs into the sand; he can only make sense of 6.19–7.5 by bringing in (in anticipation of Bornkamm) the Lord's Prayer, and of what remains by drawing on the content of Mk 6.30–8.21. This is really an admission of defeat for the enterprise as he first envisaged it.

Goulder,[19] on the other hand, begins with the Beatitudes as they stand, but deliberately refrains from any detailed analysis either of their structure or their meaning, in the hope that the latter will emerge from such correspondence as can be detected between them and the content of the remainder of the Sermon. The method (even if it can be acquitted of assuming what it seeks to establish) is an invitation to subjectivity and arbitrariness when strictly followed, as can be seen from some of his findings: for instance, 5.38–6.4 is held to be concerned with the merciful, by dint of ignoring both the content of 5.48 and the break between sections which follows it, to say nothing of the echo of VII at 5.45; while 6.19-34 is assigned to the meek by appeal to the total content of Psalm 36 from which III is quoted, as though that psalm had no associations for any of the other beatitudes. Only when he turns his attention to the poor in spirit (to make a connection with 7.7-11,[20] a point well taken) does he adequately consider the prehistory of the expression, and the contrast between this and what has gone before only serves to show up the poverty of his method with the others.

The details of the two attempts are as follows:

Farrer	Goulder[21]
VIII 5.11-20	VIII 5.11-20
VII/VI 5.21-48	VII 5.21-26
	VI 5.27-37
V 6.1-15	V 5.38–6.4
IV/II 6.16-18	IV 6.5-18
III/I 6.19-34	III 6.19-34
	II 7.1-6
	I 7.7-11

19. *Midrash*, pp. 255-68.
20. *Midrash*, pp. 267-68.
21. Dupont, who himself has no time for 'des jeux de ce genre' (*Béatitudes*, III, p. 316), nevertheless reproduces details of a similar attempt by F. Grawert, *Die*

A natural initial reaction to this disparity would be to wish a plague on both houses—to abandon the whole enterprise as unprofitable, not to say quixotic. Two points only suggest that something can possibly be salvaged from it: first, the shared starting point that the correspondence, if any, must be chiastic, and the broad agreement between them on the application of this at least as far as 5.37; and secondly, Goulder's argument connecting 7.7-11 with I. It is therefore still worth considering whether a fuller initial understanding of the meaning of individual beatitudes than Goulder's, and a more coherent account of the form of the composition than Farrer's, could yet produce the desired result. The following scheme is based on the two-quatrain analysis of the Beatitudes, with close relationship in form and meaning between the two quatrains, outlined above, and on a structural subdivision of the central section of the Sermon which is widely accepted, and assumes a chiastic alignment of the two as proposed by both Farrer and Goulder.

VIII/IV	5.11-20	+ VII (5.13)
VII/III	5.21-48	+ VI (5.27-37, 48)
VI/II	6.1-18	+ V (6.2-5, 9-15)
V/I	6.19–7.12	+ VI (6.19-24), IV (6.33, 7.7-11)
(IV	7.21, 24)	

Something needs to be said in justification of this. VIII, the beatitude on the persecuted, is taken up, as we have seen, in the subsidiary beatitude at 5.11-12. Most scholars see the section as running on to 5.16, and the series of sayings at 5.13-16 is to be understood as an injunction to disciples not to keep their heads down, not to avoid persecution by being so inconspicuous that they have no example and no message for the world at large.[22] 5.17-20, on the other hand, is not concerned with persecution as such, but with the 'greater righteousness' for which disciples must aim whether persecuted for it or not; whereas Farrer and Goulder want to continue the correspondence with VIII down to 5.20, the 'greater

---

Bergpredigt nach Matthäus auf ihre äussere und innere Einheit...untersucht (Marburg, 1900), p. 66 onwards, which coincides strikingly with Goulder's at the points where the latter's case is strongest, notably down to 5.37 and in 7.1-11.

22. There is thus no contradiction between these verses and the warnings of 6.1-18. The latter concern the practice of personal piety and its true reward, the former the public witness that is inseparable from mission, and the glorification that will result. Cf. Strecker, *Sermon on the Mount*, p. 101 n. 19.

righteousness' of 5.20 is in its immediate context more appropriately identified with that for which people hunger and thirst in IV.

At one point there is anticipation of the following section. Matthew's only identifiable source for 5.13 is Mk 9.50,[23] which concludes: 'have salt within [*or*, among] yourselves, and be at peace (εἰρηνεύετε) with one another'. This points to VII, and VII is the 'lead' for the next section.

In 5.21-48, the first antithesis (5.21-22) warns against aggression, while its subsidiaries (5.23-26) are concerned with peacemaking (VII); the final one (5.43-47) has an echo of 5.9b at 5.45 (VII again), while the penultimate one (5.38-43) is an example of III.[24] Between them lie that on adultery and lust (5.27-30), with its subsidiary on divorce (5.31-32),[25] and that on truthfulness and the avoidance of swearing (5.33-37),[26] both of which have to do with one aspect or another of VI. The command to be 'perfect' (5.48), which we have seen[27] to be equivalent to 'pure in heart' (VI), both defines the '*greater* righteousness' required at 5.20, sums up the message of the whole section, and at the same time

---

23. If Q is not assumed, Mk 9.50 is Matthew's only identifiable source for 5.13; the obscure Mk 9.49 ('salted with fire') may be responsible for Matthew's placing of 5.13 in the context of 5.11-12. Salt in the Old Testament has both sacrificial and covenantal associations (see Lev. 2.13; Num. 18.19; 2 Chron. 13.5), and O. Cullmann, 'Das Gleichnis vom Salz', in *Vorträge und Aufsätze (1925–62)* (Tübingen: J.C.B. Mohr, 1966), pp. 192-201, and R. Schnackenburg, *Schriften zur Neuen Testament* (Munich: Kösel, 1971), pp. 177-200, agree that in its Sermon context it concerns disciples' 'willingness to be offered' (references from Dumbrell, 'Logic', pp. 11-12). Cf. Gerhardsson, *Shema*, p. 60 (= *NTS* 19 [1972–73], p. 23), n. 1. That Matthew has dropped the explicit mention of peace in his version could not be due to any wish to suppress it (which would hardly be compatible with 5.9), but rather to the fact that it will be coming up in the following section.

24. J.H. Neyrey, *Honor and Shame in the Gospel of Matthew* (Louisville, KY: Westminster/John Knox Press, 1998), pp. 190-211, has recently argued that the antitheses are *all* directed against forms of aggressive behaviour; cf. Betz, *Sermon on the Mount*, p. 138. If he is right, then VII overarches this section in the same way that V overarches 6.19–7.12 (as argued in Chapter 7 §2c above).

25. Goulder, *Midrash*, p. 259, is hardly justified in treating sexual purity as the primary reference of VI (so also Freyne, *Galilee*, p. 73), but it is concerned with the divisive influence of the evil *yēṣer*, and sexuality falls within the scope of that.

26. Goulder, *Midrash*, p. 260, rightly connects this passage with Ps. 23.4 and the closely related Psalm 14, which underlie VI (see Chapter 7 §4a, above). As often, Matthew takes a more radical line than his sources.

27. Above, Chapter 7 §4a.

points forward to that of the section following.[28] As VI is, in an important sense, the 'key' beatitude, so 5.48 is a pivotal text in the Sermon on
the Mount.

6.1-18 is about worship and its essentially ethical character. τέλειος,
as we have seen,[29] has sacrificial overtones connected with the unblem-
ished quality of the offering; translated into ethical terms, this concerns
its inwardness and its freedom from ulterior motive. The threefold
instruction on almsgiving, prayer and fasting thus falls under the rubric
of VI; and the third item (which does not occupy that position in most
other lists[30]) is part of the meaning of II. And once more the 'lead'
theme of the following section (i.e. V) is anticipated: possibly (though
without emphasis) in 6.2-4 (ἐλεημοσύνην), certainly by the addition of
the Lord's Prayer (6.9-13), with explicit emphasis laid on the petition
requiring forgiveness of others (6.14-15).[31]

I have already argued[32] that the key to the section 6.19–7.12 is the
theme of mercy, first in the sense of generous and sacrificial almsgiving
(6.19-24), and secondly in that of refraining from judgment (7.1-6).
Each is an aspect of what is commended in V, and each is followed by
a poem setting out the corresponding aspect of I: 6.25-33 is an invitation to depend on God's goodness for the necessities of life and, as
6.34 emphasizes, to live in the present; and 7.7-11 encourages disciples
who know themselves to be under judgment to trust in his goodness for
their forgiveness and salvation (cf. 1.21) as they have already been
urged in 7.1-5 to believe the best of others.

At the same time 6.19-24 is also closely related to VI (undivided
heart, single eye, singleness of service).[33] VI is so central to Matthew's
ethic that its influence necessarily pervades the whole Sermon.[34] Again,
6.33 (seek God's kingdom and righteousness) picks up the theme of IV,

---

28. Luke's parallel at 6.36 retains this characteristic; cf. Green, 'Clement', pp.
8-9; contra Jacobson, *First Gospel*, p. 102.

29. See n. 234 to Chapter 7.

30. See now Betz, *Sermon on the Mount*, pp. 335-38. The sources cited include
Tob. 12.6-10; *Gos. Thom.* 6; *P. Oxy.* 654; *2 Clem.* 16.4; *Qoh. R.* 5.6 (quoted from
S.T. Lachs, *A Rabbinic Commentary on the New Testament: The Gospels of Mat-
thew, Mark and Luke* [Hoboken, NJ: Ktav, 1985], p. 112).

31. See Chapter 7 §2b, above.

32. Chapter 7 §2b-c, above.

33. See Chapter 7 §4a.3, above, and notes.

34. This is suggested by its climactic position in the formal structure (see above),

while ἀγαθὰ in 7.11 recalls Ps. 33.11; 106.9 among the contributors to the meaning of that beatitude; it points to that with which those hungry and thirsty for righteousness will finally be satisfied.

The three main sections of the Sermon proper have now been covered, and the double correspondence of the Beatitudes with individual items in them. But the Sermon itself is not quite complete, and as the correspondence began before the inception of its inner core at 5.17, so we should expect it to continue to some extent in the epilogue of 7.13-27. The latter, like the second half of each of the Five Discourses, is addressed directly to the Evangelist's contemporaries in the light of the approaching end, when the final eschatological reign will be established. Though the rewards of all the Beatitudes are eschatological in character, none makes the connection between present righteousness and future recompense as direct and explicit as does IV. It is thus appropriate from considerations of meaning as well as form that it is IV that seems to be echoed in 7.21 (doing the will of God is definitive of righteousness for Matthew) and in the heading (hearing and doing) of the final parable at 7.24-27.

and amply justified in the text of the Sermon; cf. Betz, *Sermon on the Mount,* p. 136: 'purity of heart is a virtue that underlies all ethical attitudes in the SM', contra Schnackenburg, 'Freidenstiften', p. 170 (see n. 230 to Chapter 7).

Part III
CONCLUSIONS

Chapter 9

SOURCES OR INFLUENCES?

It was argued in Chapter 1 §1 that while the question of literary sources should not be the first to be put to a text, especially a poetic one,[1] it would need nevertheless to be faced eventually;[2] and, again, that for anything beyond straight copying, unlikely and plagiaristic in poetry, it was better to speak of influences than of sources.[3] What we have learned from examination of the Beatitudes against their Old Testament background would appear to bear this out. The results are shown in tabular form (Table 9.1).

It will seen from this table that, except for the apodosis promising the kingdom in I and VIII, and the expression 'persecuted for righteousness' in the latter, every detail of the wording of the Beatitudes has its counterpart somewhere in the LXX text. This applies no less to the so-called Q beatitudes than to the rest; it is impossible to make any distinction on the basis of LXX provenance.

The distribution of the Old Testament parallels is interesting, and probably significant. Twice as many of them come from the prophets as from the Pentateuch, and twice as many again from the Psalter, the bulk of these being drawn from the same section of it as Psalm 36, i.e., broadly, the second half of the first Book. Of these Psalms 36 and 33 at least can be classified as 'wisdom' psalms, and the same can be said of most of those laid under contribution from outside that section: notably Psalms 72, 106,[4] 111, and above all 118. The 'wisdom' interest is reflected also in the parallels with Proverbs and Ben-Sira.

1.   Above, pp. 17-22.
2.   pp. 22-25.
3.   pp. 25-26.
4.   For the 'wisdom' background of this psalm see its final verse, and cf. Hos. 14.10.

Matthew, like some other New Testament writers,[5] seems to have reckoned the Psalter among the prophetic books;[6] and since he apparently knows nothing of any further subdivision of the scriptures beyond Torah and prophets, he may well have seen the prophetic strain as continuing in at least some of the books that the rabbis assigned to the Writings.[7] However that may be, the fact that he placed at the head of what he meant to be seen as the definitive messianic reinterpretation of Torah a composition that was overwhelmingly prophetic in inspiration should shed some light on his own understanding of his preferred expression 'law and prophets'.

The attempt (in the right-hand column) to find an Old Testament beatitude to correspond with each of Matthew's may seem at first sight a little far-fetched. Obviously they are not full parallels, since each is related either to protasis or apodosis, but, with a single minor exception (Ps. 83.6-8), not to both. Yet it should not be forgotten that Psalm 118, which provided the formal model for the whole composition, itself begins with a pair of such beatitudes. Only for VII has it not been possible to suggest one. Too much need not be made of the deficiency in view of such nearly contemporary comments as this from R. Akiba: 'Beloved are Israel, for they were called children of God; still greater was the love in that it was made known to them that they were called children of God'.[8]

Something further must still be said of the promise of the kingdom to the 'poor', in both I and VIII.[9] In Isa. 61.1 the prophet, anointed with the Spirit, has been sent to proclaim good news to the poor. Both for the historical Jesus and for the Evangelist the content of that good news is the imminent irruption of God's kingdom. Is that sufficient to account for the creation of this beatitude, and the placing of it at the head of the list, or was Matthew familiar with a traditional *verbum Domini*, whether in beatitude form or not, which offered the kingdom to the poor?

---

5. Lk. 24.44, though ostensibly distinguishing psalms from prophets, seems actually to bracket the two as counterpart to the 'law of Moses'. At Acts 2.30 David, who has just been quoted at length, is explicitly called a prophet. Jn 10.34, on the other hand, quotes Ps. 81.6 as from 'your law'.

6. On the prophetic attribution of 13.35 see n. 8 to Chapter 3.

7. See Orton's remarks on Ben Sira, *Scribe*, pp. 65-75.

8. See *Sifre* on Deut. 14.1; and cf. *Sifre* on Num. 6.26: 'he who practises peace is a child of the world to come'.

9. For the persecuted as a category of the poor see Chapter 7 §4c, above.

Table 9.1: *LXX Roots of Beatitudes*

	Base text	Protasis	Apodosis	Beatitude
I	Isa. 61.1. Πνεῦμα κυρίου ἐπ' ἐμέ, οὗ εἵνεκεν ἔχρισεν με· εὐαγγελίσασθαι πτωχοῖς ἀπέσταλκέν με, ἰάσασθαι τοὺς συντετριμμένους τῇ καρδίᾳ,...	Ps. 33.19. ἐγγὺς κύριος τοῖς συντετριμμένοις τὴν καρδίαν, | καὶ τοὺς ταπεινοὺς τῷ πνεύματι σώσει.		Ps. 31.1-2; Sir. 34(31).8[1]; Ps. 33.9 (cf. IV)
II	Isa. 61.2. παρακαλέσαι πάντας τοὺς πενθοῦντας	Jer. 38(31).21. ὁδὸν ἣν ἐπορεύθης ἀποστράφητι, παρθένος Ἰσραήλ, ἀποστράφητι εἰς τὰς πόλεις σου πενθοῦσα.	Jer. 38(31).15 ap. Mt. 2.18. Ραχὴλ κλαίουσα... καὶ οὐκ ἤθελεν παρακληθῆναι.... Isa. 49.10 οὐ πεινάσουσιν, | ...ἀλλ' ὁ ἐλεῶν αὐτοὺς παρακαλέσει.	Ps. 93.12[2]
III	Isa. 61.7. οὕτως τὴν γῆν ἐκ δευτέρας κληρονομήσουσιν, Ps. 36.11. οἱ δὲ πραεῖς κληρονομήσουσιν γῆν, | καὶ κατατρυφήσουσιν ἐπὶ πλήθει εἰρήνης.			Ps. 32.12
IV	Ps. 36.18. γινώσκει κύριος τὰς ὁδοὺς τῶν ἀμώμων, | καὶ ἡ κληρονομία αὐτῶν εἰς τὸν αἰῶνα ἔσται· | [19]οὐ καταισχυνθήσονται ἐν καιρῷ πονηρῷ, | καὶ ἐν ἡμέραις λιμοῦ χορτασθήσονται.	Jer. 38(31).25. ὅτι ἐμέθυσα πᾶσαν ψυχὴν διψῶσαν, καὶ πᾶσαν ψυχὴν πεινῶσαν ἐνέπλησα. Ps. 106.5. πεινῶντες καὶ διψῶντες, | ἡ ψυχὴ αὐτῶν ἐν αὐτοῖς ἐξέλιπεν. Deut. 8.3; Amos 8.11; Sir. 24.21; Ps. 41.3	Ps. 106.9 ὅτι ἐχόρτασεν ψυχὴν κενήν, | καὶ ψυχὴν πεινῶσαν ἐνέπλησεν ἀγαθῶν. Ps. 16.15. ἐγὼ δὲ ἐν δικαιοσύνῃ ὀφθήσομαι τῷ προσώπῳ σου, | χορτασθήσομαι ἐν τῷ ὀφθῆναι τὴν δόξαν σου.	Ps. 33.9

1. Cf. Mt. 19.21.
2. Cf. Jer. 38(31).18.

	Base text	Protasis	Apodosis	Beatitude
V	Ps. 36.21 ὁ δὲ δίκαιος οἰκτείρει καὶ διδοῖ. Ps. 36.26a ὅλην τὴν ἡμέραν ἐλεᾷ καὶ δανίζει,	Ps. 111.4. ἐλεήμων καὶ οἰκτίρμων καὶ δίκαιος. Hos. 6.6. ἔλεος θέλω ἢ θυσίαν,	Ps. 40.5. ἐγὼ εἶπα Κύριε, ἐλέησόν με· | ἴασαι τὴν ψυχήν μου, ὅτι ἥμαρτόν σοι. Ps. 50.3. Ἐλέησόν με, ὁ θεός, κατὰ τὸ μέγα ἔλεός σου.	Ps. 111.1; Ps. 40.1
		Prov. 17.5. ὁ δὲ ἐπισπλαγχνιζόμενος ἐλεηθήσεται.		Prov. 14.21
VI	Ps. 36.31. ὁ νόμος τοῦ θεοῦ αὐτοῦ ἐν καρδίᾳ αὐτοῦ, (cf. 14d τοὺς εὐθεῖς τῇ καρδίᾳ; 18.28 ἄμωμοι)	Ps. 23.4. ἀθῷος χερσὶν καὶ καθαρὸς τῇ καρδίᾳ. Ps. 72.1. Ὡς ἀγαθὸς τῷ Ἰσραὴλ ὁ θεός, τοῖς εὐθέσι τῇ καρδίᾳ Ps. 14.2; 39.9; Deut. 6.5	Gen. 32.31 καὶ ἐκάλεσεν Ἰακὼβ τὸ ὄνομα τοῦ τόπου ἐκείνου Εἶδος θεοῦ· εἶδον γὰρ θεὸν πρόσωπον πρὸς πρόσωπον... Isa. 6.1, 5; Ps. 16.15 (above)	Ps. 118.1-2 Ps. 83.6, 8
VII	Ps. 36.37 ὅτι ἐστὶν ἐγκατάλειμμα ἀνθρώπῳ εἰρηνικῷ. (cf. 11b)	Ps. 33.15. ζήτησον εἰρήνην καὶ δίωξον αὐτήν. Prov. 10.10. ὁ δὲ ἐλέγχων μετὰ παρρησίας εἰρηνοποιεῖ. Isa. 45.7. ἐγὼ κύριος ὁ θεός,...ὁ ποιῶν εἰρήνην	Hos. 2.1 κληθήσονται υἱοὶ θεοῦ ζῶντος. Deut. 14.1 1 Chron. 22.9.	
VIII	Ps. 36.39 σωτηρία δὲ τῶν δικαίων παρὰ κυρίου, | καὶ ὑπερασπιστὴς αὐτῶν ἐστιν ἐν καιρῷ θλίψεως³ (cf. 14c τοῦ καταβαλεῖν πτωχὸν καὶ πένητα.)	Ps. 33.20. πολλαὶ αἱ θλίψεις τῶν δικαίων, | καὶ ἐκ πασῶν αὐτῶν ῥύσεται αὐτούς. Ps. 39.10. εὐηγγελισάμην δικαιοσύνην ἐν ἐκκλησίᾳ μεγάλῃ· | ἰδοὺ τὰ χείλη μου οὐ μὴ κωλύσω. | κύριε, σὺ ἔγνως· | τὴν δικαιοσύνην σου οὐκ ἔκρυψα ἐν τῇ καρδίᾳ μου, | τὴν ἀλήθειάν σου καὶ τὸ σωτήριόν σου εἶπα· Ps. 39.18. ἐγὼ δὲ πτωχός καὶ πένης εἰμί, | βοηθός μου καὶ ὑπερασπιστής μου εἶ,...		Ps. 39.5

3. Cf. Mk 4.19 (// Mt. 13.21): γενομένης θλίψεως ἢ διωγμοῦ διὰ τὸν λόγον.

There are three texts that have a bearing on this question: *Gos. Thom.* 54 (cf. 68, 69a), Jas 2.5, and Lk. 6.20. We shall consider each of them in relation to Matthew, in that order; in the case of Luke this will extend to his whole Beatitudes/Woes complex.

1. *Gospel of Thomas 54*

Gos. Thom. 54: Blessed [are] the poor, for yours is the kingdom of heaven.

Against the pressures from one school of thought in the United States to treat the *Gospel of Thomas* as wholly independent of the Synoptic Gospels,[10] I am not alone in regarding this version of I as a conflation of the forms in Matthew and Luke;[11] the characteristic Matthaean expression 'kingdom of heaven'[12] gives it away. The impression is reinforced by the fact that the opening words of *Gos. Thom.* 69a are closely parallel to those of 5.10 (including the perfect participle[13]),[14]

10. E.g. H. Koester, *Introduction to the New Testament* (Philadelphia: Fortress Press, 1982), pp. 150-54; *idem*, 'Q and its Relatives', in Goehing *et al.* (eds.), *Gospel Origins*, pp. 49-63; J.H. Sieber, 'The Gospel of Thomas and the New Testament', in Goehing *et al.* (eds.), *Gospel Origins*, pp. 64-73; R. Cameron, *The Other Gospels: Non-Canonical Gospel Texts* (Guildford: Lutterworth, 1983), pp. 23-25; S.L. Davies, *The Gospel of Thomas and Christian Wisdom* (New York: Seabury, 1983); J.D. Crossan, *Four Other Gospels* (Philadelphia: Fortress Press, 1985); further literature in S.L. Davies, 'The Christology and Protology of the Gospel of Thomas', *JBL* 111 (1990), pp. 663-82. For opposed views see n. 124 to Chapter 4.

11. So also R.M. Grant, *The Secret Sayings of Jesus: The Gnostic Gospel of Thomas* (London: Collins, 1960), pp. 168-69; Strecker, 'Makarismen', p. 260 n. 1; Fitzmyer, *Luke*, p. 632; Goulder, *Luke*, p. 359; contra Koester, *Introduction*, p. 152; Cameron, *Other Gospels*, p. 24; Davies, *Thomas and Wisdom*, p. 3; Crossan, *Four Other Gospels*, p. 24. M.E. Boring, 'The Historical-Critical Method's "Criteria of Authenticity": Q and Thomas as a Test Case', *Semeia* 31 (1985), pp. 9-44 (25-27), is undecided. B.D. Chilton, 'The Gospel according to Thomas as a Source of Jesus' Teaching', in D. Wenham (ed.), *The Jesus Tradition Outside the Gospels* (GP, 5; Sheffield: JSOT Press, 1985), pp. 155-75, after appearing to endorse the view that *Gos. Thom.* 54 is a harmonization of the Matthaean and Lukan versions (pp. 157-58) concludes (p. 168) for independent transmission of an authentic saying of Jesus. The logic of this eludes me.

12. Found also in *Gos. Thom.* 20; elsewhere (see 57, 96, 99) 'the kingdom of my father' is preferred (cf. Mt. 13.43; 26.29 [both redactional]).

13. See Chapter 7 §4d, above, and n. 279 to Chapter 7.

14. They are followed by 'in their hearts', which suggests influence from Mt. 5.8; cf. Goulder, *Luke*, p. 359.

which adherents of and dispensers with Q are largely agreed in assigning to the Evangelist; and this, moreover, is preceded by v. 68, which conflates words from Mt. 5.11 and Lk. 6.22 in a similar way.[15]

I submit that this text offers no further case to answer.

2. *James 2.5*

Jas 2.5: οὐχ ὁ θεὸς ἐξελέξατο **τοὺς πτωχοὺς τῷ κόσμῳ** πλουσίους ἐν πίστει καὶ κληρονόμους τῆς βασιλείας ἧς ἐπηγγείλατο τοῖς ἀγαπῶσιν αὐτόν;

To those who see τῷ πνεύματι in Mt. 5.3 as Matthew's own gloss on an originally unqualified πτωχοί,[16] James' expression looks like an alternative gloss on the same original, and moreover one which retains and conveys its original sense. However, a comparison of this verse with 1 Cor. 1.27-28 makes it very difficult to resist the impression of influence from that letter.[17] The words ἐξελέξατο ὁ θεός occur three times in the verses cited, each time with a category of the unprivileged as their object (μωρά...ἀσθενῆ...ἀγενῆ), followed in each case by τοῦ κόσμου. In addition τοῖς ἀγαπῶσιν αὐτόν is found at 2.9 of the same letter;[18] βασιλείαν κληρονομεῖν at 6.9 and 15.50 (note also κατ᾽ ἐπαγγελίαν κληρονόμοι at Gal. 3.29). There is too much of this for coincidence; it

15. Cf. Boring, 'Test Case', pp. 26-27.

16. See Chapter 7 §1c, above.

17. Earlier commentators (Hort, Mayor, etc.) readily drew attention to this parallel, perhaps because they were sufficiently confident of the ascription of the letter to James of Jerusalem to be able to discount the possibility that its anti-Paulinist author might have drawn on an epistle of Paul himself. More recent commentaries have been noticeably more reticent. But the fact that James is resisting a debased Paulinism does not preclude familiarity with one or more letters of the apostle if he wrote at a time and place where these were already current. Rome is among the places of origin more recently suggested for James (see S.S. Marshall [S. Laws], 'The Character, Purpose and Setting of the Epistle of James' [BLitt dissertation, University of Oxford, 1968]; *The Epistle of James* [BNTC; London: A. & C. Black, 1980], pp. 24-26), and Rome knew both 1 Corinthians and Matthew before *1 Clement* was written; see, for the former, D.A. Hagner, *The Use of the Old and New Testaments in Clement of Rome* (NovTSup, 34; Leiden: E.J. Brill, 1973), pp. 195-209; for the latter Luz, *Matthew*, I, p. 93; O. Knoch, 'Kenntnis und Verwendung des Matthäus-Evangelium bei den apostolischen Vätern', in Schenke (ed.), *Studien*, pp. 157-77 (162-63); Green, 'Clement', *passim*.

18. Also Rom. 8.28. James has already used the expression at 1.12, where he associates it with the 'crown of life' found also at Rev. 2.10.

is evidence that alongside his protest against popular (and debased) Paulinism (2.14-26) the author was quite prepared to support his arguments with language drawn from the apostle himself.

On this view James' πτωχοὶ serve as a shorthand for the three classes of the unprivileged distinguished by Paul, and his τῷ κόσμῳ corresponds to the latter's τοῦ κόσμου. Why then the dative, in a document written in such admirable Greek style as the Letter of James?[19] As the *lectio difficilior* it is almost certain to be right, yet it has evidently caused problems for copyists.[20] It is a reasonable conjecture that James knew the beatitude in its Matthaean form, made the connection with Paul, and coined his own expression by analogy with Matthew's. Familiarity with the Lukan version,[21] or with a posited Q form underlying it, will not explain the additional words in James.

We have therefore to conclude that Jas 2.5 does not witness to an independent version of this beatitude.

3. *Luke 6.20*

Lk. 6.20: μακάριοι οἱ πτωχοί, ὅτι ὑμέτερα ἐστὶν ἡ βασιλεία τοῦ θεοῦ.

Whether Luke is an independent witness to a traditional promise to the poor is a question that demands examination of his version in its entirety; and on the answer to it will hang the validity of the main thesis of this book. If the Matthaean Beatitudes are, as I have been arguing, an organic whole, a structured poetic composition, and if the verbal influences on them from elsewhere are sufficiently explained by their author's familiarity with the LXX, then Luke's version can only be secondary, a radical scaling down of Matthew's. Is this account, which runs counter to the position of the overwhelming majority of New Testament scholars,[22] compatible with the evidence of Luke's text?

Where Matthew has eight beatitudes arranged in two quatrains, Luke has four beatitudes followed by four corresponding woes. His version has thus either been assimilated to or has itself given impetus to the four-beat rhythm that is discernible in the rest of the Sermon on the

19. Dibelius, *James*, pp. 334-38.

20. ἐν τῷ κόσμῳ (322 323 pc) is obviously an attempt to 'improve' the text of James as it stands; τοῦ κόσμου (A² C² P Ψ 'M' co) apparently recognizes the contact with 1 Cor. 1.27.

21. Suggested by Goulder, *Luke*, p. 358-59. But see n. 64 below.

22. See however Goulder, *Luke*, pp. 346-50.

Plain,[23] but for all that is structurally less of a departure from Matthew's than it will look if only his Beatitudes are considered. We shall return to this aspect of the matter. But it will be necessary first to examine separately the three components of the Lukan composition: the three shorter beatitudes (6.20-21), the expanded one (6.22-23), and the Woes (6.24-26). It will be convenient to take them in inverse order.

a. *Luke's Woes*

The main point at issue between scholars, which is clearly relevant to my own discussion, is whether these Woes came to Luke as tradition or were constructed by himself on the model of his Beatitudes. Most of the argument turns on the verbal overlap between Luke's Woes and Matthew's Beatitudes:

(1) The only Gospel parallel to the rare and unliterary sense in which ἀπέχειν[24] is used in Lk. 6.24 is Mt. 6.2, 5, 16—outside the Beatitudes but within the Sermon on the Mount.

(2) In the same verse παράκλησιν recalls παρακληθήσονται in Matthew's (but not Luke's) beatitude on the mourners.

(3) Lk. 6.25 adds πενθήσετε to κλαύσετε without any counterpart in the Lukan beatitude. πενθεῖν is the Matthaean equivalent of Luke's κλαίειν (Mt. 5.4//Lk. 6.21).

(4) In Lk. 6.26 ὑμᾶς καλῶς εἴπωσιν is formally parallel with ἐκβάλωσιν τὸ ὄνομα ὑμῶν ὡς πονηρὸν in 6.22. But the wording with which it materially corresponds is εἴπωσιν πᾶν πονηρὸν καθ᾽ ὑμῶν in Mt. 5.12.

(5) ψευδοπροφήτης, used in Lk. 6.26, is another word found elsewhere in the Sermon on the Mount (cf. 1.), at Mt. 7.15. In the New Testament it usually denotes an anticipated feature of the forthcoming eschatological tribulation,[25] but is sometimes used to identify contemporary figures as embodiments of this.[26] Mt. 7.15 is a case in point:[27]

.

---

23. See Green, 'Clement', pp. 8-10.
24. See M-M, pp. 57-58, s.v.
25. Mk 13.22; Rev. 16.13; 19.20; 20.10.
26. 1 Jn 4.1; by implication Rev. 2.20.
27. On this see Barth, in Bornkamm, Barth and Held, *Tradition*, pp. 73-75, cf. pp. 159-63. While his identification of the 'false prophets' as antinomian teachers has not found general acceptance, his linking of 7.15-23 with 13.36-43 and 24.9-14 is convincing. 7.22-23 is evidence of the activity of charismatic prophets in

Matthew found the word in the context of the eschatological discourse at Mk 13.22, and not only retained it in his own version at 24.22, but introduced it (at 24.11) into the previous (pre-final) stage of his eschatological programme which he identified with the situation of his own contemporary church.[28] 7.15 is what I have called 'throwback'[29] from this. Luke on the other hand has the word nowhere else in his Gospel, and his use of it to denote Old Testament figures is unparalleled in the New Testament, though it has its counterpart in his use of 'prophet' not only in 6.23 but elsewhere in his Gospel.[30] The opposition of 'prophets' and 'false prophets', though found of course in the LXX,[31] is, once more, unique to him in the New Testament. Thus whereas Matthew's usage is rooted in the situation of the contemporary church as well as in a synoptic *Vorlage*, Luke's is literary and verbal and therefore more likely to be secondary.

For those who retain the services of the Q hypothesis two alternative approaches to this evidence are possible. The first, while it can be called the majority opinion, is most systematically explored in the work of Heinz Schürmann.[32] It argues, on the grounds of vocabulary and content, that the Lukan Woes are actually pre-Lukan; though composed subsequently to the (original) Beatitudes, they could have had no independent existence apart from them, and they therefore reached Matthew as part of Q. Matthew's agreements with the Woes against the Lukan Beatitudes are thus attributable to first-hand knowledge of the former.

Let us then examine the implications of this line of argument for the details of the overlap noted above:

(1) Schürmann argues[33] that it was because Matthew read ἀπέχουσιν in his source for the Beatitudes that he was led to introduce the instruction of 6.2-6, 16-18 into the Sermon on the Mount.

Matthew's church(es). Cf. E. Cothenet, 'Les prophètes chrétiens dans l'Evangile selon saint Matthieu', in Didier (ed.), *L'Evangile*, pp. 281-308.

28. See nn. 269-70 to Chapter 4.

29. Note 177 to Chapter 4.

30. Whereas Mt. 5.12 is addressed to disciples as standing in the prophetic line, Luke has Peter in Acts 3.25 addressing his unconverted Jewish audience as 'sons of the prophets'. Cf. Lk. 1.79; 9.8, 19; 13.32.

31. E.g. Zech. 13.2, 4; Jer. 33(26).7-8; 34(27).9; 35(28).1; 36(29).1, 8.

32. *Untersuchungen*, pp. 303-307.

33. *Untersuchungen*, p. 306.

The difficulty here is that this kind of catchword connection at a distance is actually more characteristic of Luke than of Matthew, whose tendency is rather to use catchwords in contiguous sentences or paragraphs, and in parallel contexts to his sources, where these are identifiable.[34]

(2-3) While the association of πενθεῖν and κλαίειν is found, if rarely, in the LXX[35] and, taken by itself, does not have to be treated as evidence of redaction, the implication that the unusual expression παράκλησιν ἀπέχειν used of the rich is primary and παρακαλεῖσθαι used of the mourners in Mt. 5.4 is dependent on it is not, on the face of it, the most natural explanation of the parallel.[36] Further, the placing of II next to I in Matthew's version and the choice of wording in II are fully explicable in terms of the LXX inspiration of both in Isa. 61.1-2. To offer a source-critical account alongside an exegetical one is both superfluous and confusing.

(4) Here no difficulty arises. ἐκβάλωσιν...πονηρὸν will be simply LkR, while Matthew (on the assumptions of this account) represents the original text of Q.

(5) Here Schürmann maintains[37] that it was the presence of ψευδοπροφήταις in his Q *Vorlage* that was responsible both for Matthew's insertion of ψευδόμενοι in 5.11 and his introduction of false prophets at 7.15. The first of these suggestions attributes to Matthew a form of redaction based on sound alone which is not characteristic of him (and *is* significantly more characteristic of Luke[38]), while the second offers

---

34. Luke (it could in theory be a source, but that would only distance the problem by a single stage, and leave for attention the question why he left the material unaltered) uses catchword connections to bring together originally unconnected material at 11.33-36 (λύχνος), 16.9-13 (μαμωνᾶς), 16.16-18 (νόμος), and 17.22-30 (ἡμέρα/ἡμέραι). The result is in some instances embarrassingly lame or artificial. Matthew, on the other hand, extends the associations of words from his sources to produce a well-integrated text: cf. his expansion of Mk 9.42-48 at 18.1-14 (using two catchwords both found in Mk 9.42), his development of Mk 13.33-35 into the four parables of 24.43–25.30 (see Goulder, *Midrash*, pp. 4-5, 65, 436-42) and his development of Mk 6.31 into the poem at 11.28-30 (see Chapter 4 §7a, above).

35. 2 Esd. 11.4; 18.9 (= Neh. 1.4; 8.9).

36. Tuckett, 'Beatitudes', and Catchpole, *Quest*, p. 85, both see Matthew's wording as original here, and Luke's as (in the latter's words) an 'infelicitous echo' of it.

37. *Untersuchungen*, p. 306.

38. The most obvious instance is Acts 9.40, where the words Ταβιθά, ἀνάστηθι

yet another superfluous source-critical explanation for the presence of a word which is better accounted for by the redactional process outlined above. It also remains unclear on Schürmann's view why Luke's source's choice of the word to denote Old Testament figures should have encouraged Matthew to use it to denote contemporary (and to him sinister) ones.

The second of the two possible approaches to this problem is most fully represented, in recent study, by the work of Dupont.[39] In his view the Woes are Luke's own composition, based on nothing beyond the Beatitudes he found in Q.[40] They were therefore not independently known to Matthew, who had access only to Q. For this position, where the Woes agree with the Matthaean against the Lukan Beatitudes, it is Matthew's text that represents Q; the echoes of Isa. 61.1-2 that we find in Matthew were therefore already in Q and were suppressed by Luke.[41]

recall the Aramaic ταλιθα κουμ of Mk 5.43 (entirely omitted by Luke in his parallel at 8.54); contra M. Wilcox, 'ΤΑΛΙΘΑΚΟΥΜ in Mark 5.41', in Delobel (ed.), *LOGIA*, pp. 433-34. There is also a striking parallel (not previously noted as such, I think, though links between the two contexts have been), between Luke and the Johannine Apocalypse:

Rev. 9.1: εἶδον ἀστέρα ἐκ τοῦ οὐρανοῦ πεπτωκότα.
Lk. 10.18: ἐθεώρουν τὸν Σατανᾶν ὡς ἀστραπὴν ἐκ τοῦ οὐρανοῦ πεσόντα.

Behind Rev. 9.1 (which anticipates 12.7-9) lies Isa. 14.12; but the LXX of this, which does not have ἀστήρ, cannot be the common factor between the two New Testament texts. The alternative would appear to be Lukan knowledge of the Apocalypse (or of an intermediate source for Rev. 9.1, if such existed). Luke has a liking for ἀστραπή and its cognates; cf. 9.29; 11.36 (both LkR); 17.24 (//Mt. 24.27, but intensified).

39. *Béatitudes*, I, pp. 299-342.

40. Tuckett, 'Beatitudes', p. 196, argues against Lukan composition on grounds of vocabulary, claiming that ἀπέχειν, πλούσιος, ἐμπιμπλάναι can hardly come from him. The first of these I perceive as borrowed from Matthew (see below); for the second see Goulder, *Luke*, p. 807 (note the LkR conclusion at Lk. 18.23). The objection to the third lies in the compounding of the verb, the uncompounded form being well represented in Luke's vocabulary (cf. Goulder, *Luke*, p. 807). But he does compound verbs as a form of variation from his sources (e.g. 6.38//Mt. 7.2); this one is common in the LXX (a whole page in H-R), from which it finds its way into the Magnificat (1.53). For the latter as Lukan see below, and cf. Chapter 5 §4a above.

41. Dupont, *Béatitudes*, I, pp. 268-69, 309, 316.

This position offers a coherent and, on its own assumptions, consistent account of (2), (3) and (4), where the parallels to the Woes are within the Matthaean Beatitudes. The difficulties arise where the parallels are with passages elsewhere in the SM:

(1) Unless the parallel between Lk. 6.24 and Mt. 6.2, 5, 16 is dismissed as coincidence, it can only be explained by positing that Luke was familiar with the *Vorlage* of Mt. 6.2-6, 16-18. As the latter clearly derives from a Jewish-Christian milieu and is concerned with the piety allegedly associated with the (local?) synagogue,[42] it has to be asked how likely it is that Luke could have come across it as a piece of independent tradition, let alone drawn upon it for a rare unliterary word usage and nothing else.

(5) No explanation beyond sheer coincidence is advanced by Dupont, or indeed could be on his assumptions, for the occurrence of ψευδοπροφήτης in both versions, but in totally different contexts, of the Sermon, and with dissimilar connotations.

This second alternative thus offers a more satisfactory account of those parallels to the Woes which fall within Matthew's Beatitudes, but at the price of presuming a substantially 'Matthaean' content for Q. It is no more successful than its rival with the parallels that fall outside the Beatitudes but within the Sermon on the Mount, which, as a whole, Luke *ex hypothesi* could not have have known. This gives sufficient grounds for calling the hypothesis itself into question. If the parallels within the Beatitudes are best explained by positing a *Vorlage* not readily distinguishable from what we have in Matthew, why cannot parallels with texts elsewhere in the Sermon be explained on similar lines?

The impression left on a student of the subject who is not committed to the Q hypothesis by these diverse responses to the problem of

---

42. The threefold instruction contrasts true piety with that of the 'hypocrites' who do everything in order to be seen. These are evidently outside the Christian community, and the theme is picked up in the heavy criticism of 'scribes and Pharisees' at 23.5-7 (followed by the denunciation of them as 'hypocrites' at 23.13-33). 6.1-6, 16-18 is thus the product of a particular conflict situation in proximity to local neo-Pharisaic Judaism; it is not to be assumed that it would travel, except as part of a larger compilation such as we find in Matthew. Catchpole, *Quest*, p. 89, recognizes the impossibility of including it in Q, but opts for the alternative that the original of Lk. 6.24 was known to Matthew.

sources in the Lukan Woes is that they both deploy impressive resources of learning and ingenuity towards 'saving the appearances' of a theory which is essentially Ptolemaic, while the plain and straightforward Copernican solution—Luke's knowledge and use of Matthew—stares them in the face.

b. *Luke's Beatitudes*

What then of Luke's Beatitudes? Those who find in them a core of authentic dominical proclamation have mostly conceded that this can only apply to the first three; the fourth, which is distinguished from the others both by its greater length and detail and by being formulated, in both versions, in the second person, can only have originated in a community that was already experiencing persecution, for which there is no hard evidence in the lifetime of the historical Jesus. This lack of coherence with the other three, and the fact that Matthew has a parallel to it, corresponding in some detail, *outside* his verse structure, prompts the question: could it too have been adapted from Matthew?

A good *prima facie* case that it could is provided, quite unwittingly, by O.H. Steck.[43] Steck is one of many scholars whose response to outstanding problems which the Q hypothesis in its strong form fails to resolve is to postulate a Q which circulated in different recensions.[44] It is striking how close his reconstruction of Q^{Mt} for Mt. 5.11-12//Lk. 6.22-23 is to the text of Matthew (only πᾶν and ψευδόμενοι are missing from it), and at the same time how relatively little it differs from his basic text of Q (four particulars only: καὶ διώξωσιν [Mt. 5.11] and τοὺς πρὸ ὑμῶν [5.12] are treated as MtR; Luke's ἐποίουν τοῖς προφήταις [6.23b] is preferred to its counterpart in Matthew; and the singular οὐρανῷ [Luke 6.23a] likewise to Matthew's characteristic plural). Steck is undecided between ἕνεκεν ἐμοῦ (Matthew) and ἕνεκα τοῦ υἱοῦ τοῦ ἀνθρώπου (Luke).

This is an encouragement to go further and consider the possibility that the original text is what we have in Matthew. I take first the verbs in Mt. 5.11//Lk. 6.22:

---

43. Steck, *Israel*, pp. 20-27.

44. For these, and the methodological problems that they present, see Tuckett, *Q*, pp. 96-100; Neirynck, *Evangelica*, *II*, pp. 475-86; more briefly and polemically, Goulder, *Luke*, p. 10.

Matthew	Luke
	μισήσωσιν
ὀνειδίσωσιν	ἀφορίσωσιν
διώξωσιν	ὀνειδίσωσιν
εἴπωσιν πᾶν πονηρὸν καθ᾽ ὑμῶν	ἐκβάλωσιν τὸ ὄνομα ὑμῶν ὡς πονηρὸν

Luke has four verbs to Matthew's three, and this forms part of the four-beat rhythm to which attention has already been drawn. His μισήσωσιν is the odd verb out; it reappears at 6.27, where once again it has no parallel in the shorter (but not necessarily shortened) version of Matthew. ὀνειδίσωσιν alone is common to the two versions; its displacement in Luke's order is quite typical of his habit of variation with traditional texts. διώξωσιν has usually been taken to be MtR of Q; but it is less clear that Matthew, who never imports the word into a Markan context, is in the habit of introducing it redactionally than it is that Luke restricts its use to strictly delimited cases, of which general persecution of Christians is not one, and otherwise avoids it.[45] For Matthew, as noted above,[46] the word seems most at home in a missionary situation; two instances belong explicitly to this,[47] and the other four fit sufficiently into it.[48] Matthew 5.12 which speaks of the persecution of Old Testament prophets does so only to remind disciples that they stand in the prophetic succession (with the implication that they will be persecuted for speaking out); the themes are linked again at 23.29-36.[49] Luke's ἀφορίσωσιν, on the other hand, seems to reflect a situation of uneasy coexistence under the *pax Romana*, in which neither propa-

45. Luke has the word only at 11.49, which in his redaction concerns Old Testament prophets, 17.23 (irrelevant here), and 21.12, a prediction of events which for him already lay in the past (i.e., prior to the investment of Jerusalem at 21.20). He omits the cognate noun in his parallel to Mk 4.17 at 8.13 (noted by Boring, 'Test Case', p. 25 n. 28). Of 9 occurrences of διώκειν in Acts, 8 are concerned with the activities of Paul before his conversion; the exception (7.52) takes up once more the persecution of Old Testament prophets. It seems that he avoids any suggestion that persecution could be part of the present or immediate future experience of his implied reader.

46. Chapter 7 §4c, above.

47. 10.23; 23.34.

48. Those in this context, and 5.44.

49. The martyred prophets of 23.29-31 are clearly Old Testament figures; those of 23.34 are as clearly the post-resurrection emissaries of Jesus. 23.35 unites them in a single succession.

ganda within synagogues nor retaliation according to the prescriptions of the Torah is any longer a live option. Despite recent questioning of the date and effectiveness of the *birkāt ha' minîm*,[50] it is still tempting to see in Luke's ἐκβάλωσιν τὸ ὄνομα ὑμῶν ὡς πονηρὸν a reflection of its working, and even of the stage at which a specific mention of *nosrîm* was first included.[51] It might actually support the late date for Luke for which I have argued elsewhere.[52]

As to the possibility of Luke's having substituted ἕνεκα τοῦ υἱοῦ τοῦ ἀνθρώπου for Matthew's ἕνεκεν ἐμοῦ, it may be observed, first, that of three instances of ἕνεκεν ἐμοῦ that he finds in Mark, Luke eliminates the personal pronoun in two,[53] and, secondly, that although in these cases he does not substitute 'Son of man' for it, he gratuitously introduces the expression into two contexts, one of them Markan,[54] to denote the earthly Jesus. There is thus no valid objection to his having done the same here.

ψευδόμενοι in Mt. 5.11 is the consequence of Matthew's insistence in 5.10 on persecution being 'for righteousness'. Luke's emphasis is on the *name* of Christian as the ground of the ostracism, which makes the issue of false accusation pointless.[55]

Luke's χάρητε is to be connected with his introduction of the eschatological expression ἐν ἐκείνῃ τῇ ἡμέρᾳ: his readers are to rejoice when their time of trial comes (as part of the tribulation that will precede the end), whereas Matthew's, for whom it is part of the pre-final phase in

50. See Chapter 4 §8d, above, with nn. 246-48 to Chapter 4.

51. For arguments for taking the words in this sense see Goulder, *Luke*, pp. 351-52. If the allusion is really to the 'Test' Benediction and not simply to the name of Christian (cf. 1 Pet. 4.16), which Luke also knows (cf. Acts 11.26), it probably means that the word *nosrîm*, which is not found in all versions of the additional Benediction, was nevertheless current at the time and place at which Luke was writing.

52. See Green, 'Clement', pp. 24-25. Goulder's case can be argued more plausibly for the later date than for that assumed by him as part of his 'New Paradigm' (see *Luke*, p. 22).

53. Compare Lk. 9.24; 18.29; 21.12 with Mk 8.35; 10.29; 13.9.

54. 19.10; 22.48 (diffMk 14.45).

55. Matthew's insistence that there must be no grounds for just accusation is followed by 1 Pet. 2.11-12; 3.13-17 (3.14 virtually quotes Mt. 5.10). So, cautiously, Luz, *Matthew*, I, p. 93; contra Catchpole, *Quest*, p. 89. 1 Pet. 4.12-19 continues the theme, but associates the suffering explicitly with the name of Christian.

which they are already living,[56] are to continue to do so (χαίρετε) while it lasts. The substitution of σκιρτήσατε (a word conveying special excitement[57]) for Matthew's ἀγαλλιᾶσθε is generally put down to LkR, while the singular οὐρανῷ follows his normal practice. Luke rejects the implications of Matthew's τοὺς προφήτας τοὺς πρὸ ὑμῶν (see above); he sees analogy rather than continuity between Israel's treatment of prophets and Judaism's handling of Christians.[58] The phrase κατὰ τὰ αὐτά...ἐποίουν not only avoids the associations which διώκειν had for Matthew, but permits a more exact parallel with his own woe in 6.26.

There are thus no internal reasons why Lk. 6.22-23 cannot be regarded as Luke's own redaction of Mt. 5.11-12. This however is the least difficult part of the case to establish, since the two texts are directly parallel and Matthew's version falls outside his Beatitudes composition. The relationship of Luke's three remaining beatitudes to the totality of Matthew's composition is more complex. If the latter is his immediate source here, Luke has not redacted the full text, but excerpted from it and then altered the bearing of his excerpts. For him the poor, the hungry, the tearful are such in the literal and material sense of the words. This is indicated not only by the absence of the qualifying suffixes which the first two carry in Matthew's version, but by their juxtaposition, which both reinforces the 'material' interpretation and cuts across any direct allusion to Isa. 61.1-2 (which would demand the order poor–mourners).

If this makes difficulties for the case I am arguing, it also raises a dilemma for those who see these three beatitudes as representing Jesus' inaugural proclamation of the kingdom.[59] On that assumption, either the message was for the economically deprived, or it was an application of the earlier prophecy of Isaiah 61, intended for downtrodden Israel as a

56. See n. 270 to Chapter 4.

57. LXX at Ps. 113.4, 6; New Testament only Lk. 1.41, 44 and here. Cf. Catchpole, *Quest*, p. 92 n. 4.

58. Lk. 6.23 compares the lot of disciples with that of persecuted prophets, but here the continuity is on the side of the persecutors ('*their*' fathers). Luke never uses 'prophet' of the apostles, and his references to Christian prophets in Acts (11.28-29; 19.6; 21.9-11) are strictly functional.

59. E.g. R. Bultmann, *Theology of the New Testament* (trans. K. Grobel; London: SCM Press, 1952), I, pp. 195-96; H. Conzelmann, *Outline of the Theology of the New Testament* (trans. J. Bowden; London: SCM Press, 1969), p. 111; Dupont, *Béatitudes*, II, pp. 379-80; Percy, *Botschaft*, pp. 166-69.

whole; it could not do both jobs simultaneously. If it was the former, the beatitudes on the poor and the hungry hang together, and that on the tearful stands somewhat apart; if the 'prophetic' interpretation is right, the text alluded to associates the poor and the mourners, and the hungry are an afterthought, especially in the literal sense—and the word will hardly bear a non-literal meaning without qualification of some sort. Either way, the coherence of what are taken, on source-critical grounds, to be the four original beatitudes is further eroded; not only is the fourth plainly post-resurrection,[60] but two (varying with the position taken) rather than three indicate the posited content of Jesus' inaugural *kerygma*.

Whether it is possible or not to connect the Lukan series and sequence of Beatitudes with the authentic message of Jesus, there can be little question that, in conjunction with the Woes, it represents its author's own position. The theme of *peripeteia*,[61] to which the reader of the Gospel is introduced in the Magnificat (see 1.52-53) reappears here with an explicitly eschatological dimension, as it will again in the parable of Dives and Lazarus. The same conjunctions of vocabulary are found in all three: e.g., 1.53: πεινῶντας ἐνέπλησεν ἀγαθῶν |καὶ πλου-τοῦντας ἐξαπέστειλεν κενούς (cf. 6.21: πεινῶντες; 6.25: ἐμπεπλ-ησμένοι); 16.19-20: πλούσιος…πτωχός (cf. 6.20, 24); 16.21: χορτασ-θῆναι (cf. 6.21); 16.25: παρακαλεῖται (of the poor man); cf. 6.24 (of the rich). Both the juxtaposition of the hungry with the poor in Luke's Beatitudes and the diversion of the thought of comfort from the situation of the mourners/tearful to that of the rich in the Woes make clear that it is material poverty that he is primarily concerned about.[62] The direct contrast of tears and laughter in 6.21 was probably suggested by Eccl. 3.4: καιρὸς τοῦ κλαῦσαι καὶ καιρὸς τοῦ γελάσαι;[63] the wording of the corresponding woe at 6.25 with its addition of πενθήσετε to

60. Dupont, *Béatitudes*, II, pp. 281-84, cf. 380-81.

61. See York, *The Last*, esp. pp. 55-62; and, behind him, C.H. Dodd, *More New Testament Studies* (Manchester: Manchester University Press, 1968), pp. 1-10; cf. Dupont, *Béatitudes*, III, p. 186 n. 1.

62. There could be influence here from Isa. 49.10, where παρακαλεῖν is used of the relief of hunger (cf. Chapter 7 §3a *ad fin.*).

63. For Matthew's allusion to this text at 11.17, and Luke's redaction of it, see Chapter 4 §5 above, with n. 92 to Chapter 4. It offers a scriptural pair of opposites with which Luke would have been familiar (even if his narrative use of κλαίειν does not reflect it), and an apparent exception to the generally pejorative use of the word 'laugh' in the Old Testament; contra Tuckett, *Q*, pp. 224-25.

κλαύσετε may actually owe more to Jas 4.9 than to Mt. 5.4.[64] But that will be just a further example of Luke's 'habit of variation'.

Is it then possible that Luke imposed this interpretation on material excerpted from Matthew, and if he did, what motives can be offered for his proceeding in this apparently complicated way?

(1) Luke, as Cadbury in particular has shown,[65] would have worked under certain conventions about reproducing the work of previous writers. These did not permit him to lift the text of Matthew's Beatitudes completely unaltered; and the highly wrought composition that we have found the latter to be would hardly have lent itself to the minor verbal adjustments with which he usually contented himself in the case of, for instance, prose narrative. The alternative was to use the material selectively and to create a new composition from it. This is substantially what Morgenthaler (though without rejecting Q) has shown to be Luke's project in the Sermon on the Plain as a whole.[66]

(2) Matthew's Beatitudes stand at the head of the Sermon on the Mount, as a comprehensive list of the the dispositions and qualities proper to disciples, introducing a comprehensive account of what is required of them by the law of the New Covenant. The scope and

---

64. It is very possible that James also has Eccl. 3.4 in mind, since his theme in this section of his letter is the inappropriateness of euphoria to his readers' condition, and he speaks of both laughter and weeping. In v. 9b he requires a noun to contrast with γέλως, and κλαυθμός is relatively rare in Hellenistic usage apart from the translation Greek of the LXX; hence πένθος, and hence (together with the demands of rhythmical prose) the addition of πενθήσατε to κλαύσατε. The passage is self-contained and, given an understanding of basic rhetorical practice, needs no source beyond the Old Testament text to explain it. It could be said of Luke also that he needed no further exemplars than Eccl. 3.4 and Mt. 5.4. But there is no denying that the wording from James, if available to him, could have been of great assistance in arriving at his own. Jas 4.1 seems to have contributed to the cento of phrases at *1 Clem.* 46.5 (so Green, 'Clement', p. 12 n. 50; more cautiously, Hagner, *Use*, pp. 248-56); a Luke contemporary with Clement (Green, 'Clement', pp. 24-25) could have drawn on him too.

65. H.J. Cadbury, *The Making of Luke–Acts* (London: SPCK, 2nd edn, 1958), pp. 160-61; cf. H.J. Cadbury, F.J. Foakes-Jackson and K. Lake, 'The Greek and Jewish Traditions of Writing History', in F.J. Foakes-Jackson and K. Lake (eds.), *The Beginings of Christianity, Part 1* (London: Macmillan, 1972), II, pp. 7-30 (13): 'he must make a new work, recasting all in his own style by the method of paraphrase. *Verbatim copying of sources was not tolerated*' (my emphasis).

66. Morgenthaler, *Zeugnis*, I, pp. 81-84; *Quintilian*, pp. 260-70, esp. pp. 269-70.

length of the Sermon on the Plain are more modest,[67] and Luke could well have thought the Beatitudes as he found them in Matthew too grand in conception and scale to perform the same function for his own discourse.

(3) To summarize rather baldly: where Matthew's approach to the kingdom concentrates on the conduct and dispositions required from those who seek admittance to it, Luke's (especially if Acts is taken into account) is more concerned with the disconcerting success story of its progress; to characterize them by the defects of their qualities, Matthew's tendency is to moralism, Luke's to triumphalism. The latter trait can be detected very early on in the Gospel; the verses quoted above from the Magnificat (and others there) are the first examples, and the *peripeteia* arrangement of Beatitudes and Woes continues it. No less drastic handling of Matthew's Beatitudes would have yielded the desired result.

Luke's predilection for a four-beat rhythm in the Sermon on the Plain has already been noted; his four Beatitudes followed by four Woes set the tempo effectively. But we have previously recognized not only a 2×4 pattern in Matthew's version,[68] but a distinction of emphasis between the two quatrains: his first four beatitudes speak of conditions to be reversed, his second four of abiding dispositions to be rewarded.[69] Luke's project, which expressly contrasts the present (νῦν) with the eschatological future, can accommodate the first group but not the second. He has therefore concentrated on the first. The πραεῖς are eliminated as too nearly a repetition of the poor, as well as tending to the moralistic, and a replacement is needed; the persecuted of Mt. 5.10 could not be used as they stand, not only on account of their perfect participle (which could be altered[70]), but of Luke's avoidance of διώκειν,[71] and because Matthew's apodosis here duplicates that of the

67. 30 verses instead of 107. On Luke's general scaling down of discourses that he had before him in Matthew (and Mark!) see Green, 'Credibility', p. 135; Goulder, *Luke*, pp. 346-48; Sanders and Davies, *Studying*, p. 115. Luke could not have included the Matthaean material as he found it without either affecting the balance of his own more expressly narrative work or making the whole disproportionately long. Tuckett's reply to Goulder, *Q*, pp. 26-27, by a too narrow concentration on the latter's rhetoric, misses the real force of this objection.

68. Chapter 1, above.

69. In Chapter 8 §2, above. Franklin, *Luke*, p. 321, argues on similar lines.

70. As it has been at *Polycarp*, Phil., 2.3.

71. See n. 45 above.

beatitude on the poor. However, 5.11-12, with its present tense and its multiplication of verbs was ready to hand. Luke has evidently found it simpler to assimilate the three foregoing beatitudes to the formulation of 5.11-12 in the second person than to recast the latter entirely.[72]

My conclusion, therefore, is that Luke's Beatitudes took shape through reduction and redaction of Matthew's. Much still remains to be discovered about his purpose in writing in the way that he did, and in particular about his implied readership. But the hesitations that are proper to the consideration of these matters are no less in order when we are invited to reject the possibility of Luke's having known Matthew on the assumption that we can confidently say how he would have proceeded had he been familiar with it.[73] Our knowledge is in part.

The three texts that we have examined thus offer no firm evidence that a saying promising the kingdom to the poor, whether macarism or not, existed in the tradition behind the Evangelists. It would be going beyond the evidence to say categorically that there was none; to prove a negative is as difficult for historical investigation as it is in logic. But there is nothing in the existing texts that positively requires it, and the materials for an alternative account of the genesis of Beatitude I are present and available in Isa. 61.1, together with the fact, which no one doubts, that the core of Jesus' message concerned the kingdom of God.

---

72. Cf. Franklin, *Luke*, p. 321.
73. A major factor in the retention of the Q hypothesis; see Chapter 1 §2 above.

Chapter 10

THE POEM IN ITS SETTING

The Beatitudes stand at the head of the Sermon on the Mount as (it has been suggested[1]) the Decalogue stands at that of the first instalment of the Mosaic Law in Exodus. Whether or not the Ten Commandments functioned originally as a summary of the whole duty of the covenant people,[2] it would seem that they were treated that way in some quarters in the first century CE, and their content observed to fall into two halves, concerned with duty to God and duty to one's neighbour respectively,[3] which were sometimes identified with the two stone tablets that Moses brought down from Sinai.[4] If the formal parallel with the Beat-

1.   Originally by F. Delitzsch, *Neuen Untersuchungen über Entstehung und Anlage der kanonischen Evangelien. I. Das Matthäus-Evangelium* (Leipzig: Dörffling & Franke, 1853), p. 76, who argued for a count of ten Beatitudes to correspond with the Ten Commandments; cf. Bacon, *Studies*, p. 174; revived in another form by N. Walter, 'Die Bearbeitung der Seligpreisungen durch Matthäus', *SE* 4 (TU, 102; Berlin: Akademie, 1968), pp. 246-58 (256).

2.   Cf. R.E. Clements, *Exodus* (CBC; Cambridge: Cambridge University Press, 1972), p. 121: '[The Commandments] are not law in the sense of providing a description of particular offences, and the penalties to be imposed. Rather they provide a description of the fundamental aims of conduct which form the foundation on which more specific laws can be based.' There is no suggestion that they summarize the miscellaneous injunctions that follow.

3.   Thus Philo, *Spec. Leg.* 2.63, classifies them under two heads: duty to God, defined as εὐσεβεία and ὁσιότης, and duty to men, defined as φιλανθρωπία and δικαιοσύνη. Here Philo is not a witness, as some have suggested, to the early dissemination of the 'double commandment of love' (see below); he is referring back to his own analysis of the Decalogue on these lines in *Dec.* 50-52; cf. 106-21, where he includes the fifth commandment in the former category, it would seem in order to give him two sets of five.

4.   Exod. 32.15-19 already seems to imply that the Ten Commandments were inscribed on the tablets (so Nicholson, *God*, p. 145), but explanations of the number two and distribution of the content between them (e.g. Philo, *Dec.* 50) are clearly

itudes holds, it is reasonable to infer that these too have a summary function of some kind, whether of the content of the Sermon on the Mount or of the dispositions with which it is to be approached; and I have already suggested[5] a subtle chiastic correspondence between the sequence of the individual beatitudes and the items in the rest of the Sermon which take them up. There is however a more obvious and more directly scriptural summary of the law as taught by Jesus in this Gospel at a later point, in his reply to the Pharisee's baited question[6] at 22.36 concerning the 'great' commandment in it. His answer (following Mark, but with significant modifications[7]) combines Deut. 6.5 (the second

post-biblical. Walter ('Seligpreisungen') suggested that the two strophes of the Beatitudes were intended to recall the two tablets; but my findings on the arrangement of their content make this improbable (see below).

5.   Chapter 8 §3, above.

6.   Matthew has altered Mark's friendly encounter with a scribe (Mk 12.28-34; note especially vv. 32-34) to a hostile confrontation with a Pharisee; cf. πειράζων in 22.35. The question, on the face of it, is an invitation to elevate one precept above the rest, whereas for the Pharisees all are equally binding. Jesus' reply turns the question by understanding 'great' as 'fundamental to the meaning of all'.

7.   Many Q supporters argue for a second version shared with Lk. 10.25; cf. Gerhardsson, *Shema*, p. 214 (= R.G. Hamerton-Kelly and R. Scroggs (eds.), *Jews, Greeks and Christians* [Festschrift W.D. Davies; Leiden: E.J. Brill, 1976], p. 141); Tuckett, *Q*, pp. 416-18. J. Lambrecht, 'The Great Commandment Pericope in Q', in R.A. Piper (ed.), *The Gospel Behind the Gospels* (NovTSup, 75; Leiden: E.J. Brill, 1994), pp. 73-96, even argues for the posited Q version as the basic source for Mark's. Acceptance of Lukan familiarity with Matthew obviates the need for this. Matthew's alterations are all well within his own redactional range. For his restoration of the 'three-tone' form of Deut. 6.5//4 Kgdms 23.25 see Chapter 7 §1e.2, above. His substitution of μεγάλη for Mark's πρώτη removes the imputation of a serial order of importance to which the latter version was vulnerable; though πρώτη is retained in the sequel (but now as explained by μεγάλη), the admission of a 'second' precept now rests on its '*likeness*' to the first, conveyed by the word ἀγαπήσεις with which both begin (cf. Gerhardsson, *Shema*, pp. 207-12). In Mark the two head the list; in Matthew they are its *raison d'être*.

External evidence points to the Hellenistic Diaspora as the most likely soil for the original conjunction of the two love commandments. It is possible that Jesus' original answer quoted only the *Shema'* (see K. Berger, *Die Gesetzesauslegung Jesu* [WMANT, 40; Neukirchen: Neukirchener Verlag, 1972], p. 183), and that Mark's version was a natural consequence of the expansion of Christianity into the Hellenistic world. In that case Matthew's redaction may be affirming in respect of the double command approximately what Jesus had said of the *Shema'* alone. That

verse of the *Shema'*) with Lev. 19.18 and declares that the law and the prophets 'hang' on these (22.37-40).

The scholar who has done most to draw attention to the importance that the *Shema'* would have had for the first Christians as practising Jews is Birger Gerhardsson. In his monograph *The Testing of God's Son*,[8] and in a long stream of shorter essays in journals and *Festschriften*, now assembled in *The Shema in the New Testament*,[9] he has found evidence in the New Testament, especially in Matthew, of the influence of what became the standard interpretation of Deut. 6.5 in Jewish exegesis: to love God with one's whole (i.e. undivided) heart, with one's whole soul (i.e., at the cost, if required, of life itself) and with one's whole might (interpreted as one's material resources or 'substance').[10] The principal texts that, in his judgment, support this exegesis, in addition to 22.37-40, are the temptation of Jesus in Matthew's version[11] (with the resonances of it in his passion narrative[12]), the parable of the sower with its interpretation,[13] the remaining parables in Matthew 13 (without their interpretations),[14] and the instruction on true

---

Jesus also stressed, if separately, the importance of Lev. 19.18, and universalized its scope (cf. 5.43-44), is not in question.

8.   Published in 1966, as the first part of a work to be completed later. This is still awaited. Cf. Chapter 7 §§3a, b, with notes, above.

9.   I cite from this first where possible. Gerhardsson retains Stendahl's hypothesis of a Matthaean 'school', and on this basis urges the possibility of a core of material going back to Jesus himself. He regards the 'final redactor' of the Gospel as responsible for diluting its impact (including, possibly, the substitution of διάνοια for ἰσχύς at Mt. 22.37; cf. *Ethos*, p. 45; more cautiously, *Shema*, p. 29 n. 1).

10.   See above, Chapter 7 §1e.2, and n. 93 to Chapter 7.

11.   See *Testing*. Gerhardsson sticks to Q as Matthew's immediate source for this, but sees Matthew throughout as the original form of the tradition preserved there. What is missing here (as from most treatments that assume Q) is a satisfactory account of the relation of the pericope in Matthew (and Luke) to Mk 1.12-13, on which see Green, *Matthew*, pp. 66-67.

12.   27.39-43; cf. n. 48 below.

13.   *Shema*, pp. 24-52 (= *NTS* 14 [1967–68], pp. 165-93). Gerhardsson, while he accepts (a little reluctantly, it would seem) the priority of Mark to our present Matthew, regards the Matthaean version of the parable and its interpretation as more 'authentic', and its alterations of Mark as made on the basis of material previously available to the 'Matthew' tradition.

14.   *Shema*, pp. 53-74 (= *NTS* 19 [1972–73], pp. 16-37). Here he distinguishes the six added parables in Mt. 13.24-48 from the secondary interpretations of two of

and false piety in 6.1-6, 16-18 (with which he includes 6.19-21).[15]

The Beatitudes do not figure in this list. Gerhardsson nowhere recognizes in them an instance of what he has identified elsewhere in this Gospel as allusion to the *Shema'*. This investigation, however, has found reason to associate VI with loving with the heart[16] and VIII with loving with the soul,[17] and to see I as the counterpart, in a rather subtle and special sense,[18] to loving with one's resources. These three, as the formal analysis in Chapter 8 showed, are fundamental to the structure of the poem. But they do not account for its whole content, which is derived not from the *Shema'* alone, but from it as conjoined with Lev. 19.18. The beatitudes of the 'left-hand column' (III, V and VII) are essentially applications of the latter. I have found the πραεῖς of III to be 'humble before men' (as compared with the poor in spirit, who are 'humble before God'),[19] i.e. gentle, non-assertive, and non-violent (even under provocation: cf. 5.38-42).[20] With regard to V, Gerhardsson notes[21] that for Matthew, who uses the word ἀγαπᾶν only in quotation of or direct allusion to Deut. 6.5 and Lev. 19.18, ἐλεεῖν and its cognates are the preferred terms for conveying love of one's fellows.[22] With regard to VII, the virtual identification of peacemaking with love

---

them, and their author from the final redactor of the Gospel. But U. Luz, 'Von Taumelloch im Weizenfeld', in H. Frankemölle and K. Kertelge (eds.), *Von Urchristentum zu Jesus* (Festschrift J. Gnilka; Freiburg: Herder, 1983), pp. 154-71, has now argued convincingly that the parable of the tares was the work of the Evangelist, which makes any attempt to drive a wedge between them implausible.

15. *Shema*, pp. 75-83 (= H. Baltensweiler and B. Reicke (eds.), *Neues Testament und Geschichte* [Festschrift O. Cullmann; Tübingen: J.C.B. Mohr, 1972], pp. 69-77). This is the least impressive of his examples, since the intention of the passage, even without the interpolation of the Lord's Prayer, is not to discuss the pious practices in themselves, but only the unprofitability of performing them in order to make an impression. 6.19-21, as we have seen (Chapter 7 §1e.3, above), is better taken with what follows it.

16. Chapter 7 §4a, above.

17. Chapter 7 §4c, above.

18. Chapter 7 Sections 1e.2, 4c, above.

19. Above, Chapter 7 §1b.

20. See Chapter 7 §2d, above.

21. *Shema*, p. 220 (= *Jews, Greeks and Christians*, p. 147).

22. The meaning of the Hebrew *ḥesed* (frequently rendered by ἔλεος in the LXX, and by 'loving-kindness' in the earlier English versions) is closer to 'love' than to 'mercy', though the latter cannot of course be excluded.

of enemies at 5.43-47 has been noted above.[23] I have also argued that VII overarches the content of the antitheses of 5.21-48,[24] and that V contains the connecting theme of the much-disputed 6.19–7.11.[25] Moreover the Golden Rule at 7.12 (which seems to be the equivalent in its own context of Lev. 19.18 at 22.39) is clearly used to sum up everything that has been said since the previous reference to law and prophets at 5.17. This *inclusio* indicates, however, that the Sermon on the Mount is not framed between Beatitudes and Golden Rule, as it were between love of God and love of neighbour, but rather that the Beatitudes, standing at the head of the whole Sermon, embrace both. Possibly the final parable at 7.24-27, with its warning against hearing and not doing, is the counterpart to the veiled allusion to the *Shema'* ('Hear') in the Beatitudes.

Thus, though the Beatitudes poem is divided into two strophes, this horizontal division does not correspond to that in the Decalogue, which is a matter of content not form, serving to distinguish direct obligations towards God from those to one's neighbour.[26] The division in the Beatitudes which is significant for this question is the vertical one between the 'left-hand' column concerned with love of neighbour and the 'right-hand' column concerned with the love of God. Taken together they convey the inextricable involvement of the two love commandments in one another; not for nothing are they called 'like' (22.39). As Gerhardsson has put it, 'the coupling of the two commandments causes Deuteronomy 6.5, with its demands for totality..., to deepen and expand the commandments concerning the obligations to one's fellow man'.[27]

The Beatitudes, then, are a summary description of the character of the true disciple; they encapsulate both the kind of person the disciple will be seen to be if he or she faithfully follows the requirements of the Sermon on the Mount, and, conversely, the kind of person the disciple will need to be if he or she is to rise to its demands and to persevere in the right (and narrow) path (7.13-14). They spell out what is involved in obedience to the double commandment of love, on which 'hang all the law and the prophets', and this is now brought to bear on the new interpretation of Torah which is to 'fulfil law and prophets'. There is

---

23. Chapter 7 §2d.
24. See n. 24 to Chapter 8.
25. See Chapter 6, Chapter 7 §2b, Chapter 8 §3 above.
26. Cf. n. 3 above.
27. *Shema*, p. 213 (= *Jews, Greeks and Christians*, p. 140).

tension here between 'Torah' understood as embracing the whole revealed will of God,[28] for which Matthew's equivalent expression is not 'law' but 'righteousness',[29] and the overtones of its Greek equivalent νόμος which is more naturally understood as (and restricted to) the Mosaic law in the Pentateuch. It clearly underlies the conjunction of 'law and prophets' on which the Matthaean Jesus always insists. At one level that can simply denote the whole content of scripture, as did the developed rabbinic division of it into Law, Prophets and Writings (*Kethubîm*).[30] The latter however presupposed a fixed canon; and though belief in the existence of such a thing necessarily antedates full agreement about what it contains (as can be seen from the history of its Christian analogue), the fluidity of tolerated opinion about it in first-century Judaism (ranging from Sadducean restriction of it to the Pentateuch to the proliferation of writings admitted at Qumran) does not encourage us to limit the force of Matthew's expression to this. While its reference to 'the prophets' cannot be simply disconnected from the content of scripture, it is not just a ragbag for all of it that is not law, but expresses a principle of interpretation.[31] I have noted[32] among the scriptural contributors to the Beatitudes the great preponderance of texts from the prophetic books and the Psalter; the same is true, for instance, of 11.28-30,[33] another passage concerned with Jesus' (and/or Matthew's) attitude to the Christian disciple's practice of righteousness. His refusal to separate law and prophets is thus more than a literalistic appeal to the total content of holy writ; it means that the prophets are invoked for the new interpretation of Torah. This can be observed also outside the Sermon, particularly where the issue is the identification of the 'weightier matters of the law',[34] as with the quotation of Hos. 6.6 at 9.13 and 12.7 (the latter in the context of a dispute concerning the law's requirements) and the allusion to Mic. 6.8 underlying 23.23.[35] Nor is

28. Cf. Trilling, *Israel*, pp. 205-206.

29. See Chapter 7 §3b, and notes, above.

30. Cf. *Shema*, p. 208.

31. W. Zimmerli, *The Law and the Prophets* (trans. R.E. Clements; Oxford: Basil Blackwell, 1967), p. 10, sees theological significance in it, as opposed to mere classification of content.

32. Above, Chapter 9.

33. See Chapter 4 §7a, above.

34. For an interesting suggestion concerning these see *Shema*, p. 213.

35. Mic. 6.8 conveys the 'whole duty of man', in terms which sum up (although

the appeal necessarily limited to the official list of canonical prophets; that Matthew was not bound to the later Masoretic canon is clear from the way that he draws upon, and apparently ascribes authority to, Sirach.[36] Ben Sira's activity as a 'prophetic scribe' evidently did not die with him,[37] and Matthew himself sees the prophetic line as continuing until John the Baptist.[38] Did it even include for him the Golden Rule as prophetic comment on Lev. 19.18?[39]

The disciple is not greater than his master, and the Jesus who has come to fulfil law and prophets in himself teaches by example as well as by precept.[40] Hence, as has often been recognized,[41] the Beatitudes serve also as a portrait of Jesus himself. This can be spelled out in detail. Poverty of spirit, it was found,[42] has two basic meanings: the humility that identifies with the sinner, and a rejection of wealth and the security that goes with it. For the former, Jesus voluntarily shares with his people John's baptism of repentance 'to fulfil all righteousness' (3.15), and on their account accepts the challenge of a prolonged fast and testing (4.1-11); for the latter, he rejects the devil's offer, on terms, of 'the kingdoms of the world and their glory' (4.8-10), and declares to a would-be disciple that he has nowhere to lay his head (8.20). He calls

more clearly in the Hebrew than in the LXX) the essential message of the Beatitudes: righteousness, mercy and humility.

36. See n. 19 to Chapter 6.

37. See Orton, *Scribe*, pp. 69-75, for Sirach; pp. 77-133, for subsequent Jewish literature.

38. 11.9, 13; cf. Chapter 4 §4 above.

39. 19.19 (MtR of Mark) adds Lev. 19.18 to the list of commandments from the Decalogue that the rich young man is expected to keep—presumably not as a further individual requirement but as a compendium of them all (cf. Rom. 13.9-10). That concerned the Mosaic law. What follows (19.21) concerns the 'greater righteousness' that will fulfil law *and prophets* (NB τέλειος; cf. 5.48), which is expounded in the Sermon on the Mount and concluded with the Golden Rule. For the latter in early Judaism, for the famous pronouncement of Hillel, and for the apparently reductionist attempt of R. Simlai (third century CE) to bring the prophets to bear on the interpretation of the law, see Abrahams, *Studies*, I, pp. 21-25.

40. Cf. 11.29.

41. E.g. Schniewind, *Matthäus*, p. 45; P. Bonnard, *L'Evangile selon saint Matthieu* (Neuchâtel: Delachaux & Niestlé, 1963), p. 55; de Diétrich, *St Matthew*, p. 29; Strecker, 'Makarismen', p. 274 (= Didier [ed.], *L'Evangile*, p. 208); Zumstein, *Condition*, p. 294; Lambrecht, *Sermon*, p. 66; Davies and Allison, *Matthew*, I, p. 467.

42. Chapter 7 §1d-e, above.

himself πραΰς at 11.29, and the epithet is repeated in the formula quotation at 21.5, where his implied non-violence is linked with imagery associated with a ruler who comes in peace; hence, as becomes the Son of God, he is a peacemaker. Both the non-violent response to violence (III) and the refusal to intervene with the forces at his disposal (VII) are acted out in the scene of the arrest in the passion narrative (26.47-55), the former also (but in fulfilment of Isa. 53.7) in his silence before his accusers at 26.63; 27.12-14. His mercifulness is displayed in his healings and feedings of the multitudes and in his concern for the 'lost sheep' (9.36);[43] both of his appeals to Hos. 6.6 are protests against unmerciful judgment of those whom his love has reached;[44] and his own forgiveness of the paralytic (9.2) anticipates the shedding of his blood 'for the forgiveness of sins' (26.28). Jesus mourns for his people at 23.37-39 (II), and his fast in the wilderness is vicariously penitential; his refusal to terminate it prematurely (4.3-4) demonstrates that his hunger and thirst to do God's will (= righteousness) is stronger than his physical craving for food (IV).[45] His heart is thus preserved in wholeness (VI) from that which would have divided it.[46] The integrity which VI requires is also practised at 26.63-64, where Jesus' formally non-committal reply is to be taken as a rejection of the high priest's adjuration (as incompatible with his own teaching on swearing; cf. 5.33-36, and contrast the response of Peter at 26.72, 74),[47] and possibly at 27.34, where to accept the wine would have conflicted with his vow at 26.29. Finally, the entire passion narrative depicts Jesus as persecuted for righteousness (VIII); his innocence is acknowledged, with remorseful hindsight, by his betrayer (27.4), as it is by Pilate's dreaming wife (27.19), and finally by Pilate himself in passing sentence (27.24). The repetition of motifs from the temptation narrative in the crucifixion scene stamps the latter as the final testing of God's Son,[48] whom the elements (27.51)

---

43. Both in the summary of healings that introduces the first feeding narrative (14.14) and at the opening of the second (15.32) σπλαγχνίζεσθαι is used of Jesus, as it is in the healing of the two blind men at 20.34 (cf. also 9.36). Requests to him for healing regularly use the word ἐλεεῖν; cf. Held, in Bornkamm, Barth and Held, *Tradition*, pp. 221, 259, 263.

44. Cf. Held, in Bornkamm, Barth and Held, *Tradition*, pp. 257-58.

45. See Gerhardsson, *Testing*, pp. 41-47, and cf. Chapter 7 §3b, above.

46. See *Testing*, pp. 48-51, and Chapter 7 §4a, above.

47. So Barth, in Bornkamm, Barth and Held, *Tradition*, pp. 144-45.

48. See esp. 'Jesus, ausgeliefert und verlassen—nach dem Passiongericht des

and the executioners (27.54) recognize as such after he dies. The kingdom promised explicitly to the poor in spirit and to those who have endured persecution, and implied in the apodoses to the other beatitudes, is already his when he comes to deliver the great commission (28.18).[49]

The Beatitudes poem, although formally self-contained, is thus deeply involved thematically with the content and argument of the whole Gospel in a way that the composition that comes nearest to it in poetical elaboration, the Lord's Prayer, is not. We have seen how the latter is simply inserted at the mid-point of the Sermon, interrupting the sequence of the three aspects of piety, and not really linked to its immediate context by anything more than the mention of prayer.[50] I concluded that it had been composed originally for a quite different context, that of a church's liturgical worship, and that it was as a prayer in actual use that it found its place in the Sermon.[51] A liturgical origin has been proposed for the Beatitudes also,[52] and given the influence of the Psalter on both form and content this cannot be entirely ruled out. But the intensive involvement of the poem's themes with those of the Sermon and of the whole Gospel makes it difficult to believe that it could have been composed in total independence of the larger project. It gives a unique insight into what was in the Evangelist's mind when he undertook the enlargement of the Gospel of Mark into a comprehensive presentation of the Messiah in word and deed.

Matthäusevangelium', *Shema*, pp. 109-38 (127) (= *RB* 76 [1969], pp. 206-27 [221] [in French]): a powerful piece that repays close study.

49. See Chapter 4 §10, and notes, above.

50. Chapter 4 §2a, above. I have rejected Bornkamm's argument that the order of 6.19–7.12 is based on that of the Lord's Prayer; see n. 24 to Chapter 6.

51. Chapter 4 §2b, above.

52. Hengel, 'Bergpredigt', p. 356 (but assuming a pre-Matthaean form of the text which did not include 5.10).

Appendix A

THE LORD'S PRAYER IN LUKE (LUKE 11.2-4)

The account of the Matthaean Lord's Prayer offered in Chapter 4 §2 above has obvious implications for the status of the version found in Luke, and thus for the ultimate provenance of the Prayer. The purpose of that chapter was to offer examples of Matthew's verse composition and to examine their significance for the exegesis of his Gospel. The question of Luke's version was not directly relevant to that. But it has a wider bearing on the assumptions from which this study starts, and some response to it cannot fairly be avoided.

The conventional, and mainstream, view of its origins[1] sees the Lord's Prayer as in its essence a dominical creation, the tradition of which at some point in its transmission diverged into two distinct forms which lie behind those of Luke and Matthew respectively. Efforts have been made to locate this divergence back in the Aramaic-speaking stage of the tradition, but these have foundered on the presence in both versions of the rare word ἐπιούσιος;[2] the odds against this having been hit on by two translators independently are too heavy to allow much weight to a hypothesis that depends on it.

If then a single Greek version lies behind both forms, it is remarkable that although Luke's is the shorter by the omission of one of the three 'aspirations' and a verset of one of the three distich petitions, it is nevertheless, at the points at which the two run parallel but yet differ, in each case demonstrably further from the original.[3] The only seriously arguable exception to this is the opening address,

---

1. As represented by Lohmeyer, *Lord's Prayer*, pp. 15-17, 247-70; Manson, 'Lord's Prayer'; Jeremias, *Prayers*, pp. 82-104; Carmignac, *Recherches*; Schürmann, *Gebet*; Davies and Allison, *Matthew*, I, pp. 90-99; Luz, *Matthew*, I, pp. 369-72; Gerhardsson, *Shema*, p. 87, and others, and assumed in S.D. Anderson (ed.), *Documenta Q: Q 11.2b-4* (Leuven: Peeters, 1996). Betz, *Sermon on the Mount*, pp. 370-86, holds to dominical authorship at the oral stage (apparently in Greek) but maintains that 'there was never only *one original written* Lord's Prayer' (his emphasis).

2. M. Black, *An Aramaic Approach to the Synoptic Gospels and Acts* (Oxford: Clarendon Press, 3rd edn, 1967), pp. 203-207, argued that the word might have originated with one version and later in the course of transmission found its way across to the other (thus duplicating what was already there); but this suggestion has not made much headway.

3. See the evaluations in Anderson (ed.), *Q 11.2b-4*, pp. 135-36, 143-44, 154-55, 162-63, 169-70, 174, 176-77; cf. Gerhardsson, *Shema*, p. 87.

which has been widely taken as an indication of the *ipsissima vox* of Jesus;[4] yet it is at the same time used regularly by Luke in redactional passages in which Jesus addresses God: most notably at 22.42, where Mark in his parallel has ἀββα ὁ πατήρ, and Matthew's πάτερ μου corresponds to his πάτερ ἡμῶν in the Lord's Prayer, Luke's πάτερ is the same as in his version at 11.2.

The evidence of the wording is thus *prima facie* in favour of Luke's alteration either of Matthew or of a version closely resembling it. The question outstanding is why an author with the latter in front of him would *want* to alter it to something like Luke's, of which Goulder has said with justice that (by comparison with Matthew's) 'a bulldozer has been through the garden'.[5]

I do not find Goulder's own answer to this question[6] altogether persuasive, and I venture to offer an alternative which itself may not be very persuasive to those who, with Goulder, adhere to a date in the 80s for the composition of Luke, but can be argued more plausibly for one after 100 CE.[7]

The variant for the second clause in Lk. 11.2: ἐλθέτω τὸ πνεῦμά σου τὸ ἅγιον ἐφ᾽ ἡμᾶς καὶ καθαρισάτω ἡμᾶς is attested by codd. 700 and (in substance) 162; also by Gregory of Nyssa, Maximus the Confessor, and, in some form, by Marcion.[8] That is to say, it is both early and reputable enough not to have met with complete suppression. Though usually taken as an early variant from the original text, it was defended by A.R.C. Leaney[9] as the authentic reading not only of the Lukan but of the dominical Lord's Prayer. The latter conclusion was unconvincing even on its own assumptions, in view of the centrality of the kingdom of God to Jesus' message, and of the reticence of the early Gospel tradition about the Holy

---

4.   See Jeremias, *New Testament Theology*, I, pp. 61-68; *Prayers*, pp. 29-65; for the criticisms of Morton Smith and Vermes, see J.A. Fitzmyer, 'Abba and Jesus' Relation to God', in *A cause de l'Evangile* (Festschrift J. Dupont), pp. 15-38 (27-29).

5.   *Midrash*, p. 301.

6.   In a word, 'pithiness' (*Midrash*, p. 300). This gets some nuancing in his *Luke*, pp. 495-98: 'your will be done' is dropped to avoid any suggestion of fatalism (it is not clear why the clause in Matthew, which does not teach mere resignation, should have suggested this so strongly); and the exclusion of 'deliver us from (the) evil (one)' enables him to make a single expanded petition for 'the forgiveness and prevention of our sins'. This is not the most natural or obvious construction to put upon his version.

7.   See n. 52 to Chapter 9.

8.   See Lohmeyer, *Lord's Prayer*, pp. 261-65, and for documentation esp. Freudenberger, 'Zum Text', pp. 419-24. Marcion, if Tertullian got him right (cf. *Adv. Marc.* 4.26), conflated the variant with 'your kingdom come', the words which it supplants in the other witnesses.

Maximus presumably got the version from his reading of Gregory of Nyssa. Freudenberger traces the *canard* that has confused him in this connection with Maximus of Turin to Streeter, *Four Gospels*, p. 277; see 'Zum Text', p. 420 n. 3.

9.   A.R.C. Leaney, 'The Lukan Text of the Lord's Prayer (Lk. 11.2-4)', *NovT* 1 (1956), pp. 103-11; *The Gospel according to St Luke* (BNTC; London: A. & C. Black, 1958), pp. 59-68.

Spirit;[10] but as a clue to Luke's original text there is rather more to be said for it.[11] The logion (usually assigned to Q[12]) that follows the Prayer at 11.9-13 ends with the words 'if you, however niggardly you are, know how to give good gifts to your children, how much more shall your Father from heaven give *Holy Spirit* to those who ask him?' If the received text of 11.2 is right, there has been no previous reference to the Holy Spirit in this context, which, given the close juxtaposition and the clear evidence of Lukan redaction in 11.13,[13] is strange; with the variant, on the other hand, the connection is plain. The implication of the passage read thus is that the Spirit is not bestowed automatically on the children of God, but has first to be asked for by them; this is in line with the other evidence of Luke's theology of the matter, both in the Gospel and in Acts. In the Lukan baptism narrative (3.21-22) it is when Jesus has been baptized (aorist participle; presumably he has come up out of the water) and is *praying* that the Holy Spirit comes down upon him. In Acts, in addition to the event of Pentecost (2.1-13), which follows ten days of sustained prayer by the nucleus of the future Church (1.14), there are the two familiar, if much disputed, episodes, of Philip's converts at Caesarea on whom, though baptized by him, the Holy Spirit did not fall (i.e., the expected charismatic phenomena did not occur) until the apostles' hands had been laid on them with prayer (8.14-24), and of the twelve at Ephesus, baptized only with John's baptism, whom Paul rebaptized and laid hands on forthwith, producing the desired results (19.1-7). A number of different issues are evidently at work behind the various strands in these stories,[14] especially the former; but they must surely include, in the first instance, baptism failing to produce its proper sequel until supplemented by the prayers of the leaders of the Church, and in the second, one such leader not waiting for it to fail thus, but proceeding to the prayer without more ado.

The stories look as if they represent successive early stages in the development of Christian initiation practice towards the pattern that quite soon established itself west of the Aegean.[15] The first clear witness to that is Tertullian's tract *On Baptism*,

10.	See C.K. Barrett, *The Holy Spirit and the Gospel Tradition* (London: SPCK, 1947).

11.	For details of scholars who have held that the petition for the cleansing descent of the Holy Spirit is part of Luke's authentic text see I.H. Marshall, *The Gospel of Luke* (Exeter: Paternoster Press, 1978), p. 458; Anderson (ed.), *Q 11.2b-4*, pp. 4-8. Add van Tilborg, 'Form-Criticism', p. 100.

12.	But see n. 105 to Chapter 7.

13.	Besides the substitution of πνεῦμα ἅγιον for the thoroughly Septuagintal ἀγαθὰ (cf. Ps. 102.5; 106.9), ὁ πατὴρ <ὁ> ἐξ οὐρανοῦ is (whether ἐξ οὐρανοῦ is taken with πατὴρ or δώσει) a clumsy and uncharacteristically unidiomatic variation of Matthew's ὁ πατὴρ ὑμῶν ὁ ἐν τοῖς οὐρανοῖς, only explicable as a reaction to the wording of its source.

14.	E.g. control and supervision of Christian expansion in Judaea by the church of Jerusalem; recognition and regulation of prophets and itinerant charismatic missionaries by the official ministry of the local (or regional) church; the need to detect and unmask false prophets and other charlatans; and (Ephesus only) the terms on which members of fringe groups with a history overlapping at certain points that of Christianity could be admitted to Christian fellowship.

15.	A radically different order was characteristic of Syrian Christianity down to the

where baptism is followed, after a single anointing, by an imposition of hands 'by way of blessing, summoning and inviting the Holy Spirit'.[16] A similar sequence arguably, if more controversially, lies behind the rite in Hippolytus' *Apostolic Tradition*,[17] the structure of which in fact corresponds closely to the programme outlined at Acts 2.38.[18] How far back might this go? The outline in Justin's *First Apology* (61.1), though not explicit about a rite interposed between baptism itself and the neophytes' participation in the eucharist, mentions not only the prayers of the church but (apparently before them) prayers offered for the newly baptized,[19] which was as much as would have needed to be said at that point to a mixed readership. While Justin cannot be claimed as an unambiguous witness here,[20] his

---

fourth century: a single anointing followed by baptism, without any further ceremony before the eucharist. (For an up-to-date account of the evidence and implied theology see P.F. Bradshaw, *The Search for the Origins of Christian Worship* [London: SPCK, 1992], pp. 163-74). The assimilation of this in the later fourth century to western (and doubtless intermediate) practice by the addition of a post-baptismal chrismation for the sacramental bestowal of the Holy Spirit reflects further developments of western practice in which the latter rite had displaced the laying-on of hands.

16.   Tertullian, *Concerning Baptism*, 8 (ed. and trans. A. Souter; *Tertullian's Treatises Concerning Prayer, Concerning Baptism* (London: SPCK, 1919), pp. 55-56.

17.   Hippolytus, *Apostolic Tradition* 22 (ed. G. Dix; rev. H. Chadwick; *The Apostolic Tradition of St Hippolytus of Rome*; London: SPCK, 2nd rev. edn, 1968), p. 38. The problem here is that the introductory rubric directs the bishop to lay his hands on the candidates (i.e., individually) as he recites the prayer, whereas the present text of the latter speaks of them in the plural, indicating that it is being said once over them all. This development (doubtless due to pressure of numbers) may also account for the additional anointing on the head (not found in Tertullian) which follows the prayer and becomes the single point of sacramental contact with the bishop. This would make the present text of *Trad. Ap.* 22-23 a further stage in the development of the post-baptismal rite towards the form into which it settled at Rome (and that later exported to the Syrian east [n. 15 above]). All this tends to reduce the argument over the authentic text of the present form of the prayer (one witness, the usually reliable Verona Latin MS, omits the petition for a bestowal of the Holy Spirit at this point) to secondary importance.

18.   Renunciation of Satan: water-baptism: bestowal of the Holy Spirit. The content of the Hippolytan baptismal creed (*Trad. Ap.* 21.12-18; Dix, pp. 36-37) also has a distinctly Lukan ring to it.

19.   Justin's account, so far as it goes, is quite compatible with the rubrics of *Ap. Trad.* 21, 22 (Dix, pp. 38-39) at this point. Both accounts assume that baptism will take place at a distance from the place of assembly, to which the neophytes must return for their reception and the eucharist. Hippolytus's account implies that the bishop did not accompany the baptism party, but awaited its return with the rest of the church; obviously words and actions requiring his intervention would have to be reserved for that point. See E.C. Ratcliff, 'Justin Martyr on Confirmation', *Theology* 51 (1948), pp. 133-39, esp. pp. 137-38 (to be sharply distinguished from the attempts of other scholars at that time to foist additional ceremonies on Justin; contra Bradshaw, *Search*, p. 175 n. 48).

20.   A factor not usually considered is that Justin himself had been baptized not at

account clearly leaves room for a practice understood as essentially prayer (which is certainly true of the early Christian use of the imposition of hands), if the evidence should point to the development of such a practice before his time.[21]

In the Pauline churches, if Manson was right,[22] the initiates were expected, as a bare minimum, to express their sonship by invocation of God as *Abba*.[23] What would have been the reaction to a second- or third-generation candidate who failed to deliver what was expected? The practice of modern Pentecostal (and other charismatic) groups suggests a likely answer: a resort to fervent prayer that he or she might yet do so. Later still, as the failure became general, the prayer, accompanied by laying on of hands, became established as an invariable feature of the rite of initiation.[24] In this form however its purpose should be seen as inaugural rather than final. Tertullian at the conclusion of his treatise exhorts the neophytes, as they pass from the place of baptism (and imposition of hands) into that of the assembled church for the prayers that will precede the eucharist, to pray fervently for the special gifts of the Spirit;[25] and there is evidence for this as a continuing practice after his time.[26]

The wording of the Lord's Prayer, and particularly of this version of it, would have been more appropriately prayed by the neophytes themselves than prayed over them by the presiding minister. It is thus unlikely that it represents an early form of the latter's prayer as he laid on hands. But its appropriateness to the post-baptismal

Rome but somewhere in the east, and may therefore not have attached the same importance to certain innovations of the Roman rite as did their authors. See following note.

21. I have suggested elsewhere ('Matthew 28.19', pp. 136-37) that the evidence points to a major overhaul of the Roman rite of initiation not long before Justin wrote his *First Apology*.

22. T.W. Manson, 'Entry into Membership of the Early Church', *JTS* 48 (1947), pp. 25-31, and 'Baptism in the Church', *SJT* 2 (1949), pp. 391-403: 393 n. 3.

23. Rom. 8.15; Gal. 4.6. Manson thought that in the Pauline churches they did this *before* baptism, as a condition of receiving it. But his statement of the case for two radically divergent forms of baptism in the church of the New Testament relied too heavily on Dix's account of it (inversion of the order of confirmation and baptism), and failed to reckon with the improbability of the Syrian and Pauline traditions being found on the same side of the divide.

24. In the sense that its use was no longer *ad lib.*, not that content and practice did not undergo further development (cf. nn. 15, 17 above).

25. *Bapt.* 20; see the comments of K. McDonnell and G.T. Montague, *Christian Initiation and Baptism in the Holy Spirit* (Collegeville: Liturgical Press, 1991), pp. 98-99. The wording carries a clear allusion to Mt. 7.7//Lk. 11.9. There is nothing to distinguish the two Gospels as possible sources at this point, but Tertullian's choice of the word *charisma* strongly suggests that he has Luke in mind, in view of the latter's text at 11.13.

26. See F.J. Dölger, 'Das erste Gebet der Täufling in der Gemeinde der Bruder', in *idem*, *Antike und Christentum: Kultur- und religiongeschichtliche Studien* (Münster: Aschendorff, 2nd edn, 1974), I, pp. 142-55. Note in particular Cyprian, *Or.* 9, which points to the use of the Lord's Prayer (Matthew) by the newly baptized in the course of the rite of initiation. Cf. McDonnell and Montague, *Initiation*, p. 102 n. 31.

stage of the initiation process is not confined to the substituted petition; there are also other features of the Lukan Prayer for which this context is instructive. First, it goes without saying that it was only after their baptism that neophytes in this period were encouraged to address God as 'Father'. Secondly, extant primitive rites of Christian initiation begin almost universally with the renunciation of Satan;[27] the anointing which accompanied it from an early date (in some, particularly western, areas, with exorcized oil)[28] was treated as the final and decisive deliverance from his power. If, as I have argued, the Lukan prayer was for use at a later stage in the rite, after baptism itself, a petition for deliverance from the evil one would have been inappropriate at that point. Hence its omission from this version. Thirdly, the most natural interpretation of 'daily bread' in a liturgical setting is the sacramental one,[29] and Luke's alteration of Matthew's 'today', with its overtones of total dependence (and possibly of eschatological urgency),[30] to 'every day' may be compared with his account of the life of the first Christians in Acts 2.46, which records that their daily worship in the temple was balanced by the 'breaking of bread' at home. As applied to its narrative context this looks anachronistic.[31] But domestic communion on weekdays (from sacramental bread reserved at the Sunday eucharist) was a practice that began very early in western Christianity,[32] and it is not impossible that a Luke writing at the beginning of the second century is our earliest witness to it. Those on whom the cleansing Spirit comes can look forward to constant feeding with the Bread of life. Finally, the fact that the petition for forgive-

---

27. Hippolytus, *Trad. Ap.* 21.9 (Dix, p. 34) is our earliest witness (the silence of Tertullian is probably due to his decision to open his treatise with an extended account of the natural and biblical significance of water, from which he passes directly to the rite of baptism proper).

28. Hippolytus, *Trad. Ap.* 21.10; and the developed Roman rite, which speaks of the 'oil of catechumens'. For other areas see the diagram in McDonnell and Montague, *Initiation*, p. 238.

29. Luke may thus have given the first impetus to the interpretation of ἐπιούσιος as 'supersubstantial'—perhaps from sheer unfamiliarity with the word received from his source.

30. See Chapter 4 §2b.2, and notes, above.

31. Chilton, *Feast*, pp. 75-89, takes the historicity of this tradition seriously, connecting it with the 'Petrine circle' centred on Peter, James and John, to which he assigns a creative part in the development of the eucharist. In view however of the previous conflict between Jesus and the temple authorities and the part this had played in his death (*Feast*, pp. 65-66, 75), it is difficult to believe that his followers could have established such a symbiosis of temple and domestic worship before the deposition of Caiaphas in 36 CE (cf. n. 243 to Chapter 4). Chilton admits Lukan idealization here; possibly he underestimates the extent to which Luke also assimilates early liturgical practice to that of his own day, as seems probably to be the case in his account of John's baptism (cf. Green, 'Credibility', p. 145).

32. Cf. Justin, *Apol.* 1, 67.5 (for taking the reserved elements away from the place of celebration after the liturgy); Tertullian, *Ux.* 2.5; Hippolytus, *Trad. Ap.* 32 (Dix, pp. 38-39; see also Dix's note at pp. 84-85).

ness comes after that for daily bread implies that it is taken here to concern not the 'former sins'[33] which were remitted in baptism, but such as might be committed in the course of daily life after it.[34] The retention of the petition against temptation (or trial) which follows it bears this out.

Neither the claim that the petition for the cleansing Spirit is part of the original text of the Lukan Prayer nor the suggested association of it with the rite of baptism is new,[35] but a hypothesis which combines the two is a fresh development. Where previous arguments for the second of these positions have generally assumed post-Lukan modification of the Lukan version, mine is that all the variants noted above are due to direct adaptation of the Matthaean form for use by individual candidates in the rite of baptism. The evidence of characteristic Lukan phraseology, especially in 11.3,[36] favours the view that the adaptation was not borrowed from a church known to him, but was the work of Luke himself. The text now found in the majority of MSS is the product of partial assimilation to Matthew, probably after the retention of Luke's original form by Marcion had called its orthodoxy in question in various quarters.

I have shared over much of my life, and have an ongoing sympathy with, the reluctance of the majority to sever direct connection between any text of the Lord's Prayer and the *ipsissima vox* of Jesus. But to insist on this only throws a different problem into higher relief: if the disciple is not greater than his master, how is it that a disciple (the First Evangelist), as the whole praying tradition of Christendom has tacitly acknowledged, so signally improved on his Master's work? The question is not without its relevance for the Beatitudes also.

---

33. 2 Pet. 1.8; Justin, *Apol.* 1, 61.1; Hermas, *Man.* 4.3.3.

34. Recitation of the Lord's Prayer continued to be seen as a means of forgiveness of such sins as did not call for the imposition of public penance down to the time of Augustine (*Ep.* 265.8), if not later.

35. For the former see n. 11 above. Those who have argued for a baptismal explanation include Manson, 'Lord's Prayer', p. 106; Metzger, *Textual Commentary*, p. 132.

36. καθ' ἡμέραν is strongly characteristic of Luke (Matthew 1, Mark 1, Luke 5 [4 LkR], Acts 5); τὸ καθ' ἡμέραν unique to him in the New Testament (Lk. 11.3; 19.47; Acts 17.11). ἁμαρτία with ἀφιέναι or its cognates is also relatively commoner in the Lukan writings (Matthew 3, Mark 5, Luke 11 [6 LkR], Acts 5).

Appendix B

THE MAKING OF MATTHEW 11

The pivotal position of this chapter in the structure of the Gospel has been briefly noted above (by way of introduction to Chapter 4 §3). It recapitulates the essential significance of what has been disclosed since Jesus' proclamation of the kingdom (Mt. 4.17) succeeded that of John the Baptist (3.2): the messianic authority of Jesus as revealed in his teaching (cf. 7.29) and confirmed by his mighty acts (chs. 8–9); and it is at the same time the starting point for the story of the rejection of that authority by the people to whom it was originally proclaimed. (It is in ch. 12 that Matthew, whose redaction of Mark from 4.23 onwards has taken the form of selective rearrangement, first begins to follow its story in sequence, which continues now to the end of the earlier Gospel.) These two poles of the argument are expressed, respectively, in the passages with which the chapter opens and concludes. 11.5 looks back to a number of the mighty acts recounted in the preceding chapters, and implies that they are the fulfilment of messianic prophecy. The invitation to the easy yoke at 11.28-30 carries allusions to Old Testament prophetic texts which imply that its appeal is going to be rejected by mainstream Israel, and the beginning of this rejection is already signalled in the two pericopes immediately following (12.1-14), where the harshness of the Pharisees' application of the provisions of the Torah is implicitly contrasted with the unassertive gentleness which the poem has just claimed for Jesus.[1]

It is no accident that these two texts are, as regards poetic form, the most carefully crafted in the chapter (nor that another poem at the end of the Gospel [28.18-20] bears a striking formal correspondence to 11.28-30 at the end of its first half[2]). The chapter is, as it were, held in position by the two. This is an indication that they have been composed expressly for their present context. Both, moreover, are Mark-inspired: the miracles that Matthew has systematically arranged to form chs. 8–9 have all, with a single exception,[3] been excerpted from Mark; the work of selection and the concentration of the prophetic challenge that they present in a single poem at 11.5 may well have proceeded simultaneously. 11.28-30, as was

---

1.   See Chapter 4 §7a, above.
2.   See Chapter 4 §§7c, 10a, above.
3.   The centurion's boy (8.5-13), to whom there is no reference in 11.5.

argued above,[4] was developed out of reflection on Mk 6.31; removed from the latter's context in Mark, it serves as the final item of the response to the Baptist's question at 11.2.[5]

I have argued[6] that 11.16-19b, in the middle of the chapter, is also Mark-inspired, the product of reflection on the respective roles of John and Jesus in the light of Mk 2.15-20. John, it implies, is the prophet whose lifestyle is in line with his call to repentance, Jesus the messianic bridegroom in whose company the wedding guests cannot fast. Both, if for perversely contrary reasons, have met with rejection from their people.

This however is not now the sustained theme of the chapter as a whole. In the preceding pericope, 11.7-15, I have distinguished[7] an original short poem from a process of heavy redaction. Here the Markan influence is on the side of the redaction, and it introduces fresh aspects of Markan Christology. For the original poem John is not only a prophet but the last of the prophets; Jesus therefore, though in other respects a figure properly comparable with John, is not seen as a prophet. The redaction has reversed this. The role which makes John 'more than a prophet' is now that of the forerunner of the Messiah (11.10; cf. Mk 1.2), identified with Elijah *redivivus* (11.14; cf. Mk 1.6; 9.13); the distance between them is substantially increased, yet the designation of prophet is now common to both, since they are to share the traditional fate of prophets, rejection, persecution and violent death.[8] This is manifestly the Christology of Matthew's later chapters,[9] but the overall evidence of ch. 11 (possibly the first part of the Gospel to be drafted) suggests that he did not come to it all at once, even after he became familiar with Mark.

There is a further aporia on the other side of 11.16-19, in the denunciation of the unrepentant cities at 11.20-24. Nothing in the foregoing narrative has prepared the reader for this abrupt transition; there has so far been no account of any named town's reception of Jesus' miracles,[10] and two of the names, Chorazin and Bethsaida, are notoriously absent from the remainder of this Gospel (Chorazin from the rest of the New Testament also, apart from the parallel to this text at Lk. 10.13). Besides, the implication of the poem is that the appropriate response of those towns

4.   Chapter 4 §7a, above.
5.   See Chapter 4 §7a, above, for the LXX associations of δεῦτε in 11.28 and their echoes in the wording of 11.2.
6.   Above, Chapter 4 §5.
7.   Above, Chapter 4 §4; cf. Green, 'Matthew 11.7-15', pp. 459-61.
8.   See 5.11-12; 13.57 (//Mk 6.4); 23.29-33, 35, 37.
9.   See MtR of Mk at 14.4; 17.10-13; also the allegorical parable at 21.33-44 (//Mk 12.1-12. Cf. W. Trilling, 'Die Täufertradition bei Matthäus', *BZ* NS 2 (1959), pp. 271-89: 282-84; W. Wink, *John the Baptist in the Gospel Tradition* (SNTSMS, 7: Cambridge: Cambridge University Press, 1968), pp. 27-28.
10.   No places are named in Mt. 8–9, except Capernaum once (8.5; cf. n. 3 above). Matthew retains from Mark the anonymity of Jesus' πατρίς (13.54//Mk 6.1), and substitutes τὴν ἰδίαν πόλιν for Mark's 'Capernaum' at 9.1(//Mk 2.1). The challenge to Jesus in this chapter concerns the company he keeps (9.9-13), not the preceding miracle (9.2-8).

to the miracles performed in them would have been to repent; and although repentance is certainly an element in the message of Jesus as the Gospel presents it (cf. 4.17), the emphasis of this passage follows awkwardly on that of the one before it, in which the associations of repentance with prophetic preaching are concentrated on the figure of John.[11]

There is actually a much closer parallel to the content of 11.16-19 in the following chapter. 12.41-42 now belongs with the sign of Jonah (12.39-40), to which it has been linked by catchword connection. But that cannot be its original context, since the parallelism between the two figures to which it points, Jonah and Solomon, is integral to the whole, and the catchword link is with only one of them; what is called for is a context which does justice to both.[12] In its present position, following what has been said of the Son of man in 12.40, the referent of both 'greater than Jonah' and 'greater than Solomon' can only be Jesus himself; in the past proposals to refer the former to John[13] have always foundered on that rock. But to detach the text from its present context is to release it from its present exegetical constraints, with the possibility of identifying the prophet greater than Jonah as John, and the sage greater than Solomon as Jesus. Read that way, the lines make a natural sequel to 11.16-19; both texts are protests against the perversity of 'this generation' in its separate but parallel responses to John and Jesus. I suggest that in the original draft of the chapter 12.41-42 stood where 11.20-24 stands now.

This proposal allows a smooth transition to 11.28-30, and thus enhances the plausibility of my claim[14] that the latter originally stood on its own, and that 11.25-27 was added to it, rather than the other way round. Evidence has already been found in this text of a typological comparison and contrast with the figure of Solomon.[15] The sequence from the final words of 12.42, 'something greater than Solomon is here', to the invitation 'Come to me...' now leaps to the eye. It is

11. See Chapter 4 §5, above.

12. This is not offered by the parallel at Lk. 11.29-32, which inverts the two parts of the double logion and makes it the only explanation of the sign of Jonah, since the catchword connection still concerns only one member of it.

13. Originally by J.H. Michael, 'The Sign of John', *JTS* 21 (1920), pp. 146-59: 149-50; followed by Bacon, *Studies*, p. 383; C.H. Kraeling, *John the Baptist* (New York: Charles Scribner's Sons, 1951), p. 137; further (German) authorities in Jeremias, 'Ἰωνᾶς', p. 409 n. 21; cf. Percy, *Botschaft*, p. 238 n. 1. Q proponents who take Lk. 11.29-32 for original Q will naturally not allow that vv. 31-32 could have reached either Evangelist in a detached state. For their current approaches see Catchpole, *Quest*, pp. 244-47; Tuckett, *Q*, pp. 256-66. These presume a highly sophisticated process in the redaction of Q, more appropriate to a literary gospel; if Q was that, (1) *Gos. Thom.*, much canvassed in recent years as a parallel to Q and the answer to the problem of the latter's uniqueness (cf. J.M. Robinson and H. Koester, *Trajectories through Early Christianity* [Philadelphia: Fortress Press, 1971], *passim*) is, despite its title, nothing of the sort; (2) it is difficult to understand Q's failure to survive as Mark did. Catchpole's rejoinder (*Quest*, p. 54 n. 117) to Green, 'Matthew 12.22-50', pp. 167-68, thus does not fully dispose of this issue.

14. See Chapter 4 §§7a, b, above.

15. As in previous note.

further corroborated by the reference to 'something greater than the temple' at 12.6, which will make much better sense to the implied reader, if he or she has already seen that to 'something greater than Solomon', the builder of the temple.

The evidence then points to a first draft that consisted of 11.2-6; 11.7-9, 11a, 13;[16] 11.16-19b; 12.41-42; 11.28-30. These make a clearer and more intelligible arrangement, formally speaking, than the present form of the chapter. It begins with (1) the 'deeds of the Christ' as the fulfilment of messianic prophecy, followed by (2) John's role as the last and greatest of the prophets; (3) the rejection of both by 'this generation'; (4) what has been rejected with John: the prophetic call to repentance; (5) what has been rejected with Jesus: the overwhelming evidence of signs and wonders. The arrangement so far is characteristically chiastic. But because the comparison with Solomon covers not only the miracles of healing attributed to him in post-biblical tradition,[17] but also (and indeed primarily) the imparting of wisdom, it not only looks backwards to 11.2-5, but forwards to the invitation to the yoke at 11.28-30. Those convinced by the claims of the Messiah in deed are to become disciples of the Messiah in word.

This clear outline has been somewhat muddied by the redaction. 11.7-9 has been modified by the addition of matter conveying an alternative account of the relationship between John and Jesus and the sense in which John is 'more than a prophet'. 12.41-42 has been removed to another context where its original force could be neutralized, and replaced by 11.20-24, a piece evidently not written for its present position, yet bearing marks of Matthew's poetic style; the Evangelist, trained scribe that he is (13.52), has produced from his treasure, possibly at short notice, something old.[18] If this account of the process is convincing, it is probable that v. 19c was created in the course of the redaction.[19] What it means and how it relates to the rest of v. 19 have always been a *crux* for scholars, and the near-unanimity of Q adherents that Luke's τέκνων was the reading of the Q exemplar is readily understood.[20] But it is not therefore to be followed. All reference to a 'wisdom' understanding of the 'deeds of the Christ' has disappeared with the displacement of 12.41-42; 11.19c is a rather half-hearted attempt to compensate for the omission, and to restore continuity between 11.2 and the conclusion of the chapter.[21]

Finally, the addition of 11.25-27 to 11.28-30 has expanded what was originally, in some sense,[22] a 'Wisdom' Christology into a 'Son of God' Christology. The

---

16. In the form suggested in Chapter 4 §4, above; cf. Green, 'Matthew 11.7-15', pp. 460-61.

17. See n. 73 to Chapter 3.

18. See Chapter 4 §§6 and 9a (and notes), above.

19. Some Q scholars, from their own standpoint, regard the words as secondary addition; see Tuckett, *Q*, pp. 177-78.

20. If Q is assumed, τὰ ἔργα τοῦ Χριστοῦ in Mt. 11.2 is MtR; without it to refer back to, the reading ἔργων has no point.

21. See Chapter 4 §7a, above, for the 'works of the Lord' in LXX texts behind 11.28.

22. That it is a limited sense is argued in Chapter 4 §7a, above.

thanksgiving in 11.25-26, while formally modelled on the opening of Sirach 51, is addressed by Jesus as Son to the Father; the opening phrase of 11.27, which echoes the wording of the final commission at 28.18 (and not the other way round),[23] does so in the light of the account of the Father–Son relationship which follows and which, as we have already seen,[24] takes up Matthew's own redaction of the Markan baptism narrative.

If then a motive is sought for the final redaction of this chapter, it is to be found in the Evangelist's developing Christology. The passages that I have assigned to the original draft show John the Baptist in a decidedly favourable light: though he is the last of the prophets and Jesus the one who fulfils their prophecies, he is nevertheless accounted worthy to be spoken of in tandem with Jesus, as if his preaching of repentance and Jesus' announcement of the imminent blessings of the kingdom formed a single package. These are the most positive statements about John in the entire New Testament,[25] and suggest that their author's original way in to Christianity was through the Baptist movement.[26] Whether or not this was the case, the development of his Christology was by no means complete when he made his first draft; and although there are clear signs that he already had Mark in his hands as he made it, the effects upon him of his reflection on its contents were not released all at once, even to him. But the end product, on the evidence of 11.25-27 in particular, is fully in line with the Markan position as disclosed by that Evangelist to his assumed readers (if not fully to the actors in his story until Mk 14.62).[27]

11.25-26 also conveys, along with its more explicit statement of Jesus' Sonship, the thought that this can only be known by revelation, and that the revelation has been withheld from the official teachers of Israel (the 'wise and prudent') and given instead to the uninstructed (νήπιοι).[28] 11.28-30 already challenges, in anticipation of 23.3-4, the oppressive demands made by the Pharisaic scribes in their application of the law, but the latter text is introduced by 23.2, which acknowledges their authority to teach despite their abuse of it. Here, however, in what I argue is a later redactional addition to this chapter, there is a hint of a more decisive repudiation of the teaching authority of the old Israel as a way to salvation, which will be taken up in the response to Peter's confession at 16.17-19.[29]

Those who have followed me so far may nevertheless want to suggest the hand of a 'redactor' of this chapter other than its original (and principal) author. The methodology adopted by some commentators[30] leaves them with no alternative to

---

23. Chapter 4 §7c, above.

24. See Chapter 4 §7c, above, and cf. on 12.18, Chapter 3 §4, above.

25. Similarly (though from different critical assumptions), Wink, *Baptist*, p. 35.

26. See Chapter 4 §5, above.

27. Cf. n. 40 to Chapter 3.

28. See Chapter 4 §7b, above, and nn. 161, 162 to Chapter 4.

29. 16.17 echoes 11.25, 27. See Chapter 4 §§8d-e, above, on the implications of 16.17-19 for the supersession of the authority of the old Israel.

30. Notably Strecker, *Weg* (see n. 42 to Chapter 2); Gerhardsson (nn. 6, 10, 11 to Chapter 10).

such a move; but it inhibits the recognition of creativity in the final form of the text (to say nothing of the difficulty of maintaining objectivity in its application). The redactional modifications of this chapter that my analysis has disclosed all carry the argument further in a direction in which it was already moving, while the presence of verse composition, in however modest a form, in the added material still favours, as has already been argued,[31] the case for a single author. A diachronic approach to the question of his theological (and ecclesial) outlook gives most promise of understanding his work.

31. See Chapter 5 above.

Appendix C

PSALM 119 AND THE BEATITUDES

Prominent among the meanings established above for the beatitudes of the 'right-hand column' (II, IV, VI, VIII) are the following:

II: a penitential stance and practice, whether in repentance for one's own sins or in sorrow for those of one's people;

IV: a longing, expressed with the basic physical image of hunger and thirst, to know and do the will of God, which is identified with righteousness;

VI: fulfilment of the command in the *Shema'* to love God with one's whole heart, otherwise expressed as being 'perfect' or blameless. Its antithesis is double-mindedness, hypocrisy or deceit;

VIII: the persecution that the practice of, and witness to, righteousness attracts, and the reward promised for enduring it.

There are counterparts to these themes all over Psalm 119; some of them are to be found in every stanza. The incidence is as follows:

Aleph	1-2, 7:	VI
	3-6:	IV
Beth	9-11:	VI
	12-16	IV
Gimel	18-20, 24:	IV
	21-23:	VIII
Daleth	25-29:	II
	30-31:	IV
	32:	VI
He	33-34, 36-37:	VI
	35, 40:	IV
Waw	42, 46:	VIII
	43-45, 47-48:	IV
Zayin	50, 52-53:	II
	51:	VIII
	54-56:	IV

Heth	57, 60, 62:	IV
	58:	VI
	59:	II
	61:	VIII
Teth	67:	II (or VIII)[1]
	69-71:	VIII
	72:	IV
Yod	73:	IV
	75-77:	II
	78:	VIII
	80:	VI
Kaph	81:	IV
	82-83, 88:	II
	84-87:	VIII
Lamedh	92:	II (or VIII)[2]
	93-94:	IV
	95:	VIII
	96:	VI
Mem	97-104:	IV
Nun	105-106, 111:	IV
	107:	II (or VIII)[3]
	109-10:	VIII
	112:	VI
Samekh	113:	VI[4]/IV
	115:	(VIII)/IV
	117:	IV
	118:	VI[5]
	120:	II
Ayin	121-22:	VIII
	123-25, 127-28:	IV
	126:	II
	128b:	VI[6]

1.   It is not always clear what the source of the psalmist's affliction is: oppression by others, or his sense of failure (by himself or others) to rise to the demands of God's law.

2.   See note 1.

3.   See note 1.

4.   The Hebrew here has *sēʿᵃphîm*, 'half-hearted'; cf. Chapter 7, §4a.3 above.

5.   See Chapter 7 §4a.2, above, on deceit in relation to VI.

6.   See note 5.

Pe	129, 131, 135:	IV
	134:	VIII
	136:	II
Ṣade	137-38, 140, 142, 143b, 144a:	IV
	139a, 143a, 144b:	II
	139b:	VIII
Qoph	145a:	VI
	145b-48, 151-52:	IV
	150:	VIII
Resh	153-58:	VIII
	159-60:	IV
Sin	161:	VIII
	162, 164, 167-68:	IV
	163a:	VI
Taw	171-72, 174:	IV
	175-76:	II[7]

There is thus a counterpart to IV in every stanza, and to II, VI, or VIII in approximately half of them. The order in which they appear is haphazard; no attempt is made at a formal arrangement, apart from the double beatitude in vv. 1-2, with its echo in the corresponding verses of the following stanza. The psalmist's formal ingenuity is concentrated on maintaining his acrostic pattern, and, it would seem, exhausted by it. Nevertheless it is hardly coincidence that it is these reiterated themes that reappear, in subtle formal relation to one another, in Matthew's compressed composition.

There is nothing to correspond to this in the 'left-hand column', with the exception of I which, as the heading of the whole composition,[8] relates to both sides of it. Among the strands that I have distinguished in the meaning of 'poverty of spirit' are (1) readiness to let go of wealth for the sake of the kingdom: cf. Ps. 119.14, 36, 72, 127,[9] 162; (2) humility, clearly related to the 'littleness' expected of disciples in 18.1-6, and to the νήπιοι of 11.25-26: cf. Ps. 119.130, 141, and especially 97-100 which conveys in a nutshell the significance of 11.25-26[10]; (3) awareness of sinfulness: cf. Ps. 119.176.[11]

There is enough evidence here to justify the conclusion that Psalm 119 offered the Evangelist not only a formal model but an inspirational source for his own work.

---

7.   But cf. n. 8, below, on I.
8.   See Chapter 8, above.
9.   Cf. Ps. 19.11a, and v. 103 above with Ps. 19.11b.
10.   See n. 163 to Chapter 4.
11.   Cf. Chapter 8 above.

BIBLIOGRAPHY

A cause de l'Evangile (Festschrift J. Dupont; Paris: Gabalda, 1985).

Abrahams, I., *Studies in Pharisaism and the Gospels* (Cambridge: Cambridge University Press, I, 1917, II, 1924).

Ackroyd, P.R., *The Chronicler and his Age* (JSOTSup, 101; Sheffield: JSOT Press, 1991).

Aland, K., *Synopsis Quattuor Evangeliorum* (Stuttgart: Württemburgischer Bibelanstalt, 2nd edn, 1979).

Alexander, L.C.A., *The Preface to Luke's Gospel* (SNTSMS, 78; Cambridge: Cambridge University Press, 1993).

Allison, D.C., 'The Structure of the Sermon on the Mount', *JBL* 106 (1987), pp. 423-45.

—'The Eye is the Lamp of the Body (Matthew 6.22-23: Luke 11.34-36)', *NTS* 37 (1987), pp. 61-83.

—*The New Moses: A Matthean Typology* (Edinburgh: T. & T. Clark, 1993).

Alt, A., *Kleine Schriften* (Munich: Beck, 1953).

Alter, R., *The Art of Biblical Poetry* (New York: Basic Books; London: George Allen & Unwin, 1985).

—*The World of Biblical Literature* (New York: Basic Books; London: SPCK, 1992).

Amstutz, J., ΑΠΛΟΤΗΣ (Theophaneia, 19; Bonn: Peter Hanstein, 1968).

Anderson, S.D. (ed.), *Documenta Q: Q 11.2b-4* (Leuven: Peeters, 1996).

Arens, E., *The* ΗΛΘΟΝ *Sayings in the Synoptic Tradition* (OBO, 10; Fribourg: Presses Universitaires; Göttingen: Vandenhoeck & Ruprecht, 1976).

Arvedson, T., *Das Mysterium Christi* (Uppsala: Lundquist, 1937).

Ashton, J., *Studying John* (Oxford: Clarendon Press, 1994).

Auffret, P., 'Essai sur la structure littéraire des Psaumes CXI et CXII', *VT* 30 (1980), pp. 257-79.

Bacon, B.W., *Studies in Matthew* (London: Constable, 1930).

Baker, F., *Representative Verse of Charles Wesley* (London: Epworth Press, 1962).

—*Charles Wesley's Verse* (London: Epworth Press, 1989).

Baltesweiler, H., *Die Ehe im Neuen Testament* (Zürich: Zwingli, 1967).

Baltesweiler, H. and B. Reicke (eds.), *Neues Testament und Geschichte* (Festschrift O. Cullmann; Tübingen: J.C.B. Mohr, 1972).

Bammel, E., 'πτωχός', *TDNT*, VI, pp. 885-902.

Barrett, C.K., *The Holy Spirit and the Gospel Tradition* (London: SPCK, 1947).

—'The Interpretation of the Old Testament in the New', *CHB*, I, pp. 377-411.

—'The Place of John and the Synoptics within the Early History of Christian Thought', in Denaux (ed.), *John and the Synoptics*, pp. 63-75.

Barth, G., 'Matthew's Understanding of the Law', in Bornkamm, Barth and Held, *Tradition*, pp. 58-164.

Barton, J., *The Spirit and the Letter* (London: SPCK, 1997).

Bauer, B., *The Structure of Matthew's Gospel* (JSNTSup, 31; Sheffield: JSOT Press, 1988).

Beare, F.W., *The Earliest Records of Jesus* (Oxford: Basil Blackwell, 1964).

—*The Gospel according to Matthew* (Oxford: Basil Blackwell, 1981).

Benoit, P., 'L'enfance de Jean-Baptiste selon Luc', *NTS* 3 (1956–57), pp. 169-94.

Berger, K., *Die Gesetzesauslegung Jesu* (WMANT, 40; Neukirchen: Neukirchener Verlag, 1972).

Berlin, A., *The Dynamics of Hebrew Parallelism* (Bloomington, IN: Indiana University Press, 1985).

Betz, H.D., 'The Logion of the Easy Yoke and of Rest', *JBL* 86 (1967), pp. 10-24.

—*Essays on the Sermon on the Mount* (Philadelphia: Fortress Press, 1985).

—*The Sermon on the Mount* (Hermeneia: Minneapolis: Fortress Press, 1995).

Birkeland, H., *'Ani und 'anaw in der Psalmen* (Skriften utgitt av Det Norske Videnskaps-Akademie i Oslo, II. Hist.-Filos. Klasse 1932, No. 4; Oslo: Dybwad, 1933).

—*Der Feinde des Individuums in der israelitischen Psalmenliteratur* (Oslo: Grondahl, 1933).

Bishop, E.F.F., *Jesus of Palestine* (London: Lutterworth, 1955).

Black, M., *An Aramaic Approach to the Synoptic Gospels and Acts* (Oxford: Clarendon Press, 3rd edn, 1967).

—'The Christological Use of the Old Testament in the New Testament', *NTS* 18 (1971–72), pp. 1-14.

—'The Doxology to the *Pater Noster*, with a Note on Matthew 6.13b', in P.R. Davies and R.T. White (eds.), *A Tribute to Geza Vermes* (JSOTSup, 100; Sheffield: JSOT Press, 1990), pp. 327-38.

Bloch, R., 'Midrash', in W.S. Green (ed.), *Approaches to Ancient Judaism* (BJS, 1; Missoula, MT: Scholars Press, 1978), pp. 29-50.

Böhl, F., 'Die Demut (*'nwh*) als höchste der Tugenden: Bemerkungen zu Mt 5,3.5', *BZ* NS 20 (1976), pp. 217-23.

Bonhoeffer, D., *Ethics* (trans. N. Horton-Smith; London: SCM Press, 1955).

—*The Cost of Discipleship* (trans. R.H. Fuller; London: SCM Press, 1962).

Bonnard, P., *L'Evangile selon saint Matthieu* (Neuchâtel: Delachaux & Niestlé, 1963).

Boring, M.E., 'The Historical-Critical Method's "Criteria of Authenticity": Q and Thomas as a Test Case', *Semeia* 31 (1985), pp. 9-44.

—'The Beelzebul Pericope', in Van Segbroeck *et al.* (eds.), *The Four Gospels 1992*, pp. 587-619.

Bornkamm, G., 'End-Expectation and Church in Matthew', in Bornkamm, Barth and Held, *Tradition*, pp. 15-51.

—'Der Aufbau der Bergpredigt', *NTS* 24 (1977–78), pp. 419-31.

—'The Authority to Bind and Loose in Matthew's Gospel', in Stanton (ed.), *Interpretation*, pp. 101-14.

Bornkamm, G., G. Barth and H.J. Held, *Tradition and Interpretation in Matthew* (trans. P. Scott; London: SCM Press, 1963).

Bousset, W., *Kyrios Christos* (Göttingen: Vandenhoeck & Ruprecht, 2nd edn, 1921).

Box, G.H., *St Matthew* (Century Bible; Edinburgh: T.C. & E.C. Jack, 1926).

Bradshaw, P.F., *The Search for the Origins of Christian Worship* (London: SPCK, 1992).

Braun, H., 'Qumran and the New Testament', *TRu* NS 33 (1963), pp. 91-234.

Broer, I., *Die Seligpreisungen der Bergpredigt* (BBB, 61; Bonn: Peter Hanstein, 1985).

Brooke, G.J. 'The Wisdom of Matthew's Beatitudes', *ScrB* 19 (1989), pp. 35-41.

Brooks, C., *The Well-Wrought Urn* (New York: Reynal & Hitchcock, 1947).

Brooks, S.H., *Matthew's Community* (JSNTSup, 16; Sheffield: JSOT Press, 1987).

Brown, R.E., *The Gospel according to John* (AB, 29; New York: Doubleday; London: Chapman, 1971).

—*The Birth of the Messiah* (London: Chapman, 2nd edn, 1993).

Brown, R.E., K.P. Donfried, and J. Reumann, *Peter in the New Testament* (Minneapolis: Augsburg; New York: Paulist Press, 1963).

Brown, R.E., J.A. Fitzmyer, and R.E. Murphy (eds.), *The New Jerome Bible Commentary* (London: Geoffrey Chapman, 1989).

Büchsel, F., 'δέω', *TDNT* II, pp. 60-61.

Bultmann, R., *Theology of the New Testament* (trans. K. Grobel; London: SCM Press, 1952).

—*The History of the Synoptic Tradition* (trans. J. Marsh; Oxford: Basil Blackwell, 1963).

—'γινώσκω, ἐπιγινώσκω κτλ.', *TDNT*, I, pp. 689-719.

—'ἔλεος κτλ.', *TDNT*, II, pp. 477-87.

—'πένθος, πενθέω', *TDNT*, VI, pp. 40-43.

Burchard, C., 'Versuch, das Thema der Bergpredigt zu finden', in G. Strecker (ed.), *Jesus Christus in Historie und Theologie* (Festschrift H. Conzelmann; Tübingen: J.C.B. Mohr, 1975), pp. 409-32.

Burnett, F.W., *The Testament of Jesus–Sophia* (Washington, DC: Catholic University of America Presss, 1981).

Burney, C.F., *The Poetry of Our Lord* (Oxford: Clarendon Press, 1925).

Bussmann, W., *Synoptische Studien*. II. *Zur Redenquelle* (Halle: Waisenhause, 1929).

Butler, B.C., *The Originality of St Matthew* (Cambridge: Cambridge University Press, 1951).

Butt, J. (ed.), *The Poems of Alexander Pope* (Oxford Paperbacks; London: Oxford University Press, 1965).

Cadbury, H.J., *The Making of Luke–Acts* (London: SPCK, 2nd edn, 1958).

—'Four Features of Lucan Style', in L.E. Keck and J.L. Martyn (eds.), *Studies in Luke–Acts* (London: SPCK, 1968), pp. 89-101.

Cadbury, H.J., F.J. Foakes-Jackson and K. Lake, 'The Greek and Jewish Traditions of Writing History', in F.J. Foakes-Jackson and K. Lake (eds.), *The Beginnings of Christianity, Part I* (London: Macmillan, 1922), II, pp. 7-30.

Cameron, R. (ed.), *The Other Gospels: Non-Canonical Gospel Texts* (Guildford: Lutterworth, 1983).

Camery-Hoggatt, J., *Irony in Mark's Gospel* (SNTSMS, 72; Cambridge: Cambridge University Press, 1992).

Campenhausen, H.Fr. von, *Tradition and Life in the Early Church* (trans. A.V. Littledale; London: Collins, 1968).

—*Ecclesiastical Authority and Spiritual Power in the Church of the First Three Centuries* (trans. J.A. Baker; London: A. & C. Black, 1969).

Cangh, J.M. van, 'La Bible de Matthieu: les citations d'accomplissement', *RTL* 6 (1975), pp. 205-11.

Caragounis, C., *Peter and the Rock* (BZNW, 58; Berlin: de Gruyter, 1990).

Cargal, T.B., ' "His blood be on us and on our children": A Matthean Double Entendre?', *NTS* 37 (1991), pp. 101-12.

Carlston, C.E., 'Betz on the Sermon on the Mount', *CBQ* 50 (1988), pp. 47-57.

Carmignac, J., *Recherches sur le Nôtre Père* (Paris: Letouzeys & Ané, 1969).

Carr, D.A., and H.G.M. Williamson (eds.), *It is Written* (Festschrift B. Lindars; Cambridge: Cambridge University Press, 1988).

Carrington, P., *According to Mark* (Cambridge: Cambridge University Press, 1960).

Catchpole, D.R., *The Quest for Q* (Edinburgh: T. & T. Clark, 1993).

Cerfaux, L., *Recueil Lucien Cerfaux* III (Gembloux: Ducoulot, 1962).

Charette, B., *The Theme of Recompense in Matthew's Gospel* (JSNTSup, 79; Sheffield: JSOT Press, 1992).

—'To Proclaim Liberty to the Captives', *NTS* 38 (1992), pp. 290-97.

Chilton, B.D., 'The Gospel according to Thomas as a Source of Jesus' Teaching', in D. Wenham (ed.), *The Jesus Tradition Outside the Gospels* (GP, 5; Sheffield: JSOT Press, 1985).

—*Targumic Approaches to the Gospels* (Lanham, MD: University Press of America, 1986).

—*A Feast of Meanings* (Leiden: E.J. Brill, 1994).

Chilton, B.D., and C.A. Evans (eds.), *Studying the Historical Jesus* (Leiden: E.J. Brill, 1994).

Christ, F., *Jesus–Sophia* (Zürich: Zwingli, 1970).

Church of England Liturgical Commission [A.M. Farrer], *Modern Liturgical Texts* (London: SPCK, 1968).

Clements, R.E., *Exodus* (CBC; Cambridge: Cambridge University Press, 1972).

Cobb, W.H., *A Criticism of Systems of Hebrew Metre* (Oxford: Clarendon Press, 1905).

Collins, T., *Line-Forms in Hebrew Poetry* (Rome: Pontifical Biblical Institute, 1978).

Conybeare, F.C., 'The Eusebian Form of the Text Matth. 28,19', *ZNW* 2 (1901), pp. 275-88.

Conzelmann, H., *Outline of the Theology of the New Testament* (trans. J. Bowden; London: SCM Press, 1969).

—'χάρις κτλ.', C-E *TDNT*, IX, pp. 387-415.

Cope, O.L., *Matthew: A Scribe Trained for the Kingdom of Heaven* (CBQMS, 5; Washington, DC: Catholic Biblical Association, 1976).

Cothenet, E., 'Les prophètes chrétiens dans l'Evangile selon saint Matthieu', in Didier (ed.), *L'Evangile*, pp. 281-308.

—'La baptême selon saint Matthieu', *SNTU*(L) 9 (1984), pp. 79-94.

Cotter, W.J., 'The Parable of the Children in the Market Place', *NovT* 29 (1987), pp. 289-304.

Creed, J.M., *The Gospel according to St Luke* (London: Macmillan, 1930).

Crosby, M.H., *House of Disciples: Church, Economics and Justice in Matthew* (Maryknoll, NY: Orbis Books, 1987).

Crossan, J.D., *Four Other Gospels* (Philadelphia: Fortress Press, 1985).

Culler, J. (ed.), *On Puns* (Oxford: Basil Blackwell, 1973).

Culley, R.C., 'Metrical Analysis of Early Hebrew Poetry', in J.W. Wevers and D.B. Redford (eds.), *Essays on the Early Semitic World* (Toronto: Toronto University Press, 1970).

Cullmann, O., *The Christology of the New Testament* (trans. S.C. Guthrie and C.A.M. Hall; London: SCM Press, 1959).

—*Peter: Disciple, Apostle, Martyr* (trans. F.V. Filson; London: SCM Press, 1962).

—*Vorträge und Aufsätze (1925–62)* (Tübingen: J.C.B. Mohr, 1966).

—'πέτρα, Πέτρος, Κηφας', *TDNT*, VI, pp. 95-112.

Dahl, N.A., 'The Passion Narrative in Matthew', in Stanton (ed.), *Interpretation*, pp. 42-55.

Davies, S.L., *The Gospel of Thomas and Christian Wisdom* (New York: Seabury, 1983).

—'The Christology and Protology of the Gospel of Thomas', *JBL* 111 (1990), pp. 663-82.

Davies, W.D., *Paul and Rabbinic Judaism* (London: SPCK, 1948).

—*Christian Origins and Judaism* (London: Darton, Longman & Todd, 1962).

—*The Setting of the Sermon on the Mount* (Cambridge: Cambridge University Press, 1963).

—*The Gospel and the Land* (Berkeley: University of California Press, 1974).

Davies, W.D., and D.C. Allison, *Matthew* (ICC; Edinburgh: T. & T. Clark, I, 1988; II, 1991; III, 1997.

—'Matt 28.16-20: Texts Behind the Text', *RHPR* 72 (1992), pp. 89-98.

Degenhardt, H.J., *Lukas: Evangelist der Armen* (Stuttgart: Katholisches Bibelwerk, 1965).

Delitzsch, F., *Neuen Untersuchungen über Entstehung und Anlage der kanonischen Evangelien. I. Das Matthäus-Evangelium* (Leipzig: Dörffling & Franke, 1853).

Delling, G., 'τέλειος', *TDNT*, VIII, pp. 67-78.

Delobel, J. (ed.), *LOGIA: Les Paroles de Jesus* (BETL, 59; Leuven: Peeters, 1982).

Denaux, A., 'The Q-Logion Mt 11,27/Lk 10,22 and the Gospel of John', in *idem* (ed.), *John and the Synoptics* (BETL, 101; Leuven: Peeters, 1992).

Derrett, J.D.M., *Law in the New Testament* (London: Darton, Longman & Todd, 1970).

Descamps, A., *Les justes et la justice dans les Evangiles et le christianisme primitif* (Gembloux: Ducoulot, 1950).

—'Rédaction et Christologie dans le récit matthéen de la Passion', in Didier (ed.), *L'Evangile*, pp. 359-415.

Deutsch, C., *Hidden Wisdom and the Easy Yoke* (JSNTSup, 18; Sheffield: JSOT Press, 1987).

Devisch, M., 'Le Document Q, source de Matthieu: Problématique actuelle', in Didier (ed.), *L'Evangile*, pp. 72-97.

Dibelius, M., *Die urchristliche Überlieferung von Johannes der Täufer untersucht* (Göttingen: Vandenhoeck & Ruprecht, 1911).

—*From Tradition to Gospel* (trans. B.L. Woolf; London: Ivor Nicholson & Watson, 1934).

—*The Pastoral Epistles* (ed. H. Conzelmann; Hermeneia; Philadelphia: Fortress Press, 1972).

—*James* (ed. H. Greeven; Hermeneia; Philadelphia: Fortress Press, 1976).

Didier, M. (ed.), *L'Evangile selon Matthieu: Redaction et théologie* (BETL, 29; Gembloux: Ducoulot, 1972).

Diétrich, S. de, *St Matthew* (Layman's Bible Commentaries; London: SCM Press, 1961).

Di Lella, A.A., 'The Structure and Composition of the Matthean Beatitudes', in Horgan and Kobielski (eds.), *To Touch the Text*, pp. 237-42.

Dinkler, E., 'Jesu Wort von Kreuztragen', in W. Eltester (ed.), *Neutestamentliche Studien* (Festschrift R. Bultmann; BZNW, 21; Berlin: Alfred Töpelmann, 1954), pp. 110-29.

Dix, G. (ed.), *The Apostolic Tradition of St Hippolytus of Rome* (rev. H. Chadwick; London: SPCK, 2nd rev. edn, 1968).

Dodd, C.H., *The Bible and the Greeks* (London: Hodder & Stoughton, 1935).

—*According to the Scriptures* (London: Nisbet, 1952).

—*More New Testament Studies* (Manchester: Manchester University Press, 1968).

Dölger, F.J., *Antike und Christentum: Kultur- und religionsgeschichtliche Studien* (Münster: Aschendorff, 2nd edn, 1974).

Donaldson, T.L., *Jesus on the Mountain* (JSNTSup, 8; Sheffield: JSOT Press, 1985).

Downing, F.G., 'Redaction Criticism: Josephus' *Antiquities* and the Synoptic Gospels', *JSNT* 8 (1980), pp. 46-65 [= I]; 9 (1981), pp. 29-48 [= II].

—'A Paradigm Perplex: Luke, Matthew and Mark', *NTS* 38 (1992), pp. 15-36.

Draisma, S. (ed.), *Intertextuality in Biblical Writings* (Festschrift B.M.F. van Iersel; Kampen: Kok, 1989).

Drury, J., *Tradition and Design in Luke's Gospel* (London: Darton, Longman & Todd, 1976).

—*The Parables of the Gospels* (London: SPCK, 1985).

Dugmore, C.W., *The Influence of the Synagogue on the Divine Office* (London: Faith Press, 2nd edn, 1964).

Duke, P., *Irony in the Fourth Gospel* (Atlanta: John Knox Press, 1985).

Duling, D.C., 'Solomon, Exorcism and the Son of David', *HTR* 68 (1975), pp. 235-53.

—'The Therapeutic Son of David', *NTS* 24 (1977–78), pp. 392-419.

Dumbrell, W.J., 'The Logic of the Rule of Law in Matthew v.1-20', *NovT* 23 (1981), pp. 1-31.

Dungan, D.L. 'Mark: the Abridgement of Matthew and Luke', in D.G. Buttrick (ed.), *Jesus and Man's Hope* (Pittsburgh: Pittsburgh Theological Seminary, 1970), pp. 51-77.

Dungan, D.L. (ed.), *The Interrelations of the Gospels* (BETL, 95; Leuven: Peeters, 1990).

Dunn, J.D.G., *Christology in the Making* (London: SCM Press, 1980).

Dupont, J., 'Vous n'aurez pas achevé les villes d'Israel avant que le Fils d'homme ne vienne', *NovT* 2 (1959), pp. 228-44.

—*Mariage et divorce dans l'Evangile* (Bruges: Abbaye Saint-André, 1959).

—'Les πτωχοὶ τῷ πνεύματι et les *'nwy rwh* de Qumran', in J. Blinzler, O. Kuss and F. Müssner (eds.), *Neutestamentliche Aufsätze* (Festschrift J. Schmid; Regensburg: Regensburger, 1963), pp. 53-64.

—*Les Béatitudes* (Paris: Gabalda, I-II 1969, III 1973)

Earp, J.W., Indices to *Philo* (Loeb Classical Library; London: Heinemann), X, 1962, pp. 189-520.

Easthope, A., *Poetry as Discourse* (London: Methuen, 1983).

Edwards, R.A., *A Theology of Q* (Philadelphia: Fortress Press, 1976).

—'Matthew's Use of Q in Chapter 11', in Delobel (ed.), *LOGIA*, pp. 257-75.

Ehrhardt, A.A.T., *The Framework of the New Testament Stories* (Manchester: Manchester University Press, 1964).

Eichrodt, W., *Theology of the Old Testament* (trans. J.A. Baker; London: SCM Press, 1957).

Elliott, J.H., 'The Evil Eye and the Sermon on the Mount: Contours of a Pervasive Belief in Social Scientific Perspective', *BibInt* 11 (1994), pp. 51-84.

Elliott, J.K., 'Jerusalem in Acts and in the Gospels', *NTS* 23 (1976–77), pp. 462-69.

Ellis, P.F., *Matthew: His Mind and his Message* (Collegeville, MN: Liturgical Press, 1974).

Emerton, J.A., 'Binding and Loosing: Forgiving and Retaining', *JTS* NS 13 (1963), pp. 325-31.

Empson, W., *Seven Types of Ambiguity* (London: Chatto, 2nd edn, 1947).

Enslin, M.S., *Christian Beginnings* (New York: Charles Scribner's Sons, 1938).

Erlich, V., *Russian Formalism* (The Hague: Mouton, 2nd edn, 1965).

—'Roman Jakobson: Grammar of Poetry and Poetry of Grammar', in S. Chatman (ed,), *Approaches to Poetics* (New York: Columbia University Press, 1973).

Ernst, C., *Multiple Echo* (London: Darton, Longman & Todd, 1979).

Evans, C.A., 'Jesus in the Agrapha and Apocryphal Gospels', in Chilton and Evans (eds.), *Historical Jesus*, pp. 526-32.

Evans, C.F., *Saint Luke* (TPI; London: SCM Press, 1990).

Fanning, B.M., *Verbal Aspect in New Testament Greek* (Oxford: Clarendon Press, 1990).

Farmer, W.R., *The Synoptic Problem* (London: Collier-Macmillan, 1964).

—'The Statement of the [Two Gospel] Hypothesis', in Dungan (ed.), *Interrelations*, pp. 125-56.

—*The Last Twelve Verses of Mark* (SNTSMS, 25; Cambridge: Cambridge University Press, 1974).

Farrer, A.M., *A Study in St Mark* (Westminster: Dacre Press, 1951).

—'On Dispensing with Q', in D.E. Nineham (ed.), *Studies in the Gospels (In Memoriam R.H. Lightfoot)* (Oxford: Basil Blackwell, 1955).

—*St Matthew and St Mark* (London: A. & C. Black, 1954).

Farris, S., *The Hymns of Luke's Infancy Narratives* (JSNTSup, 9; Sheffield: JSOT Press, 1985).

Fenton, J.C., *The Gospel of St Matthew* (Pelican Gospel Commentaries; Harmondsworth: Penguin Books, 1963).

Filson, F.V., 'How Much of the New Testament is Poetry?', *JBL* 67 (1948), pp. 125-34.

Fitzgerald, A., 'Hebrew Poetry', in R.E. Brown, J.A. Fitzmyer and R.E. Murphy (eds.), *The New Jerome Bible Commentary* (London: Geoffrey Chapman, 1989).

Fitzmyer, J.A., 'David, "Being Therefore a Prophet" (Acts 2.30)', *CBQ* 34 (1972), pp. 332-39.

—'Aramaic *Kepha* and Peter's Name in the New Testament', in *To Advance the Gospel* (New York: Crossroad, 1981), pp. 114-24.

—*The Gospel according to Luke* (AB, 28; New York: Doubleday; London: Chapman, 1981).

—'Abba and Jesus' Relation to God', in *A cause de l'Evangile* (Festschrift J. Dupont), pp. 15-38.

Foerster, W., 'διάβολος', C-D *TDNT*, II, pp. 75-81.

—'εἰρήνη κτλ.', *TDNT*, II, pp. 400-20.

—'Σατανᾶς', *TDNT*, VII, pp. 1-63.

Fohrer, G., *Das Buch Jesaja* (Zurich: Zwingli, 1960).

—'υἱός', B-C.1a, *TDNT*, VIII, pp. 340-55.

Follis, E.R. (ed.), *Directions in Hebrew Poetry* (JSOTSup, 40; Sheffield: JSOT Press, 1987).

Frankemölle, H., 'Die Makarismen (Mt 5,1-12; Lk 6,20-23): Motive und Umfang der redaktionelle Komposition', *BZ* NS 15 (1971), pp. 52-75.

—*Jahwebund und Kirche Christi* (NTAbh NS, 10; Münster: Aschendorff, 1973).

—*Biblische Handlungserweisungen* (Mainz: Grünewald, 1983).

Franklin, E., *Luke, Interpreter of Paul, Critic of Matthew* (JSNTSup, 92; Sheffield: JSOT Press, 1993).

Freedman, D.N., *Poetry, Prophecy and Pottery* (Winona Lake, IN: Eisenbrauns, 1980).

—'Another Look at Biblical Hebrew Poetry', in Follis (ed.), *Directions*, pp. 11-27.

Freudenberger, R., 'Zum Text der zweiten Vaterunserbitte', *NTS* 15 (1968–69), pp. 419-32.

Freyne, S., *Galilee, Jesus and the Gospels* (Dublin: Gill & Macmillan, 1988).

Friedrich, G., 'Die formale Struktur von Mt 28,18-20', *ZTK* 80 (1983), pp. 137-83.

Fussell, P., *Poetic Metre and Poetic Form* (New York: Oxford University Press, 1965).

Gaechter, P., *Das Matthäus-Evangelium* (Innsbruck: Tyrolia, 1962).

Gale, H.M., 'A Suggestion Concerning Matthew 16', *JBL* 60 (1941–42), pp. 255-60.

Garland, D.E., *The Intention of Matthew 23* (NovTSup, 52; Leiden: E.J. Brill, 1979).

Gärtner, B., 'The Habakkuk Commentary and the Gospel of Matthew', *ST* 8 (1954), pp. 1-24.

Gench, F.T., 'Wisdom Christology in the Gospel of Matthew' (PhD dissertation, Union Theological Seminary, Virginia, 1988).

Gerhardsson, B., *The Testing of God's Son* (trans. J. Toy; ConBNT, 2.1; Lund: C.W.K. Gleerup, 1966).

—'Jésus livré et abandonné d'après la passion selon saint Mattieu', *RB* 76 (1969), pp. 206-27.

—*The Ethos of the Bible* (trans. S. Westerholm; London: Darton, Longman & Todd, 1982).

—*The Shema in the New Testament* (Lund: Novapress, 1996).

Giesen, H., *Christliche Handeln* (Frankfurt: Peter Lang, 1982).

Gignac, F.T., 'Phonological Phenomena in the Greek Papyri Significant for the Text and Language of the New Testament', in Horgan and Kobielski (eds.), *To Touch the Text*, pp. 33-46.

Glasson, T.F., *The Second Advent* (London: Epworth Press, 1947).

Gnilka, J., 'Die Kirche des Matthäus und die Gemeinde von Qumran', *BZ* NS 7 (1963), pp. 43-63.

—*Das Matthäusevangelium* (HTKNT, 1.1, 1.2; Munich: Kösel, I 1986, II 1988).

Goehing, J.E. *et al.* (eds.), *Gospel Origins and Christian Beginnings* (Festschrift J.M. Robinson; Sonoma, CA: Polebridge Press, 1990).

Goppelt, L., *Apostolic and Post-Apostolic Times* (trans. R.A. Guelich; London: A. & C. Black, 1970).

Goulder, M.D., 'The Composition of the Lord's Prayer', *JTS* NS 14 (1963), pp. 32-45.

—*Midrash and Lection in Matthew* (London: SPCK, 1974).

—'Farrer on Q', *Theology* 88 (1980), pp. 190-95.

—'The Order of a Crank', in Tuckett (ed.), *Synoptic Studies*, pp. 111-30.

—*Luke: A New Paradigm* (JSNTSup, 20; Sheffield: JSOT Press, 1989).

—'Luke's Compositional Options', *NTS* 39 (1993), pp. 150-52.

—'Is Q a Juggernaut?', *JBL* 115 (1996), pp. 667-81.

Goulder, M.D., and M.L. Sanderson, 'St Luke's Genesis', *JTS* NS 8 (1957), pp. 12-30.

Graham, A.C., *Poems of the Late Ta'ng* (Penguin Classics; Harmondsworth: Penguin Books, 1968).

Grant, R.M., *The Secret Sayings of Jesus: The Gnostic Gospel of Thomas* (London: Collins, 1960).

Green, H.B., 'The Command to Baptize and Other Matthaean Interpolations', *SE* 4 (TU, 102; Berlin: Akademie Verlag, 1968), pp. 60-63.

—*The Gospel According to Matthew* (New Clarendon Bible; Oxford: Oxford University Press, 1975).

—'Solomon the Son of David in Matthaean Typology', *SE* 7 (TU, 126; Berlin: Akademie Verlag, 1982), pp. 227-30.

—'The Credibility of Luke's Transformation of Matthew', in Tuckett (ed.), *Synoptic Studies*, pp. 138-57.

—'Matthew 12.22-50: An Alternative to Matthaean Conflation', in *Synoptic Studies*, pp. 158-76.

—'Matthew, Clement and Luke', *JTS* NS 40 (1989), pp. 1-25.

—'Matthew 28.19, Eusebius and the *Lex Orandi*', in R. Williams (ed.), *The Making of Orthodoxy* (Festschrift H. Chadwick; Cambridge: Cambridge University Press, 1989), pp. 124-40.

—Review of Bauer, *Structure*, *JTS* NS 41 (1990), pp. 175-78.

—'Mattthew 11.7-15: Redaction or Self-Redaction?', in C. Focant (ed.), *The Synoptic*

    Gospels: Source Criticism and the New Literary Criticism (BETL, 110; Leuven: Peeters, 1993), pp. 459-66.

—Review of Stanton, *Gospel, NovT* 37 (1995), pp. 95-97.

Green, S.W., *The Least of My Brothers (Matthew 25:31-46): A History of Interpretation* (SBLDS, 114; Atlanta: Scholars Press, 1989).

Grindel, J., 'Matthew 12.15-21', *CBQ* 29 (1967), pp. 110-15.

Grundmann, W., 'ταπεινός κτλ.', *TDNT*, VIII, pp. 1-26.

—*Das Evangelium nach Matthäus* (Berlin: Evangelische Verlagsanstalt, 1968).

Guelich, R.A., 'The Matthean Beatitudes: "Entrance Requirements" or "Eschatological Blessings", *JBL* 95 (1976), pp. 415-34.

—*The Sermon on the Mount* (Waco, TX: Word Books, 1982).

Gundry, R.H., *The Use of the Old Testament in St Matthew's Gospel* (NovTSup, 18; Leiden: E.J. Brill, 1967).

—*Matthew: A Commentary on his Literary and Theological Art* (Grand Rapids: Eerdmans, 1982).

Haenchen, E., 'Matthäus 23', *ZTK* 48 (1951), pp. 38-63.

Hagner, D.A., *The Use of the Old and New Testaments in Clement of Rome* (NovTSup, 34; Leiden: E.J. Brill, 1973).

—*Matthew* (WBC; Dallas: Word Books, 1993–95).

Hahn, F., *Mission in the New Testament* (SBT, 47; London: SCM Press, 1965).

—*The Titles of Jesus in Christology* (trans. H. Knight and G. Ogg; London: Lutterworth, 1969).

Hamerton-Kelly, R.G., *Pre-Existence, Wisdom and the Son of Man* (SNTSMS, 21; Cambridge: Cambridge University Press, 1973).

Hamerton-Kelly, R.G., and R. Scroggs (eds.), *Jews, Greeks and Christians* (Festschrift W.D. Davies; Leiden: E.J. Brill, 1976).

Hanson, A.T., 'The Treatment in the LXX of the Theme of Seeing God', in G.J. Brooke and B. Lindars (eds.), *Septuagint, Scrolls and Cognate Writings* (SBLSCS, 33; Atlanta: Scholars Press, 1992).

Harder, G., 'πονηρός', *TDNT*, VI, pp. 546-62.

Hare, D.R.A., *The Theme of Jewish Persecution of Christians in the Gospel of Matthew* (SNTSMS, 6; Cambridge: Cambridge University Press, 1967).

Hare, D.R.A., and D.J. Harrington, ' "Make Disciples of All Nations" ', *CBQ* 37 (1975), pp. 350-69.

Harnack, A., *Luke the Physician* (trans. J.R. Wilkinson; London: Williams & Norgate, 1907).

—*Sayings of Jesus* (trans. J.R. Wilkinson; London: Williams & Norgate, 1908).

Hartman, L., 'Scriptural Exegesis and the Problem of Communication', in Didier (ed.), *L'Evangile*, pp. 131-52.

Hauck, F., 'καταβολή', *TDNT* III, p. 620-21.

Hauck, F., and S. Schulz, 'πραΰς κτλ.', *TDNT*, VI, pp. 647-51.

Hawkes, T., *Structuralism and Semiotics* (London: Methuen, 1977).

Heaney, S., *The Redress of Poetry* (London: Faber & Faber, 1995).

Held, H.J., 'Matthew as Interpreter of the Miracle Stories', in Bornkamm, Barth and Held, *Tradition*, pp. 165-299.

Hengel, M., 'Zur matthäischen Bergpredigt und ihrem judischen Hintergrund', *TRu* NS 52 (1987), pp. 327-400.

—*The Zealots* (trans. D. Smith; Edinburgh: T. & T. Clark, 1989).

318   *Matthew, Poet of the Beatitudes*

Herntrich, V., 'κρίνω κτλ.', B, *TDNT*, III, pp. 923-30.

Herrenbrück, F., *Jesus und die Zöllner* (WUNT, 2.41; Tübingen: J.C.B. Mohr, 1990).

Hirsch, E., *Die Frühgeschichte des Evangeliums* (Tübingen: J.C.B. Mohr, 1941).

Hoffmann, P., 'Die Offenbarung des Sohnes', *Kairos* NS 12 (1970), pp. 270-88.

—*Studien zur Theologie der Logienquelle* (NTAbh NS 8; Münster: Aschendorff, 1972).

—'Der Petrus-Primat im Matthäusevangelium', in J. Gnilka (ed.), *Neues Testament und Kirche* (Festschrift R. Schnackenburg; Freiburg: Herder, 1974), pp. 94-114.

Hoffmann, P. (ed.), *Orientierung an Jesus: Theologie der Synoptiker* (Festschrift J. Schmid; Freiburg: Herder, 1973).

Horgan, M.P., and P.J. Kobielski, 'The Hodayot (1QH) and New Testament Poetry', in Horgan and Kobielski, *To Touch the Text*, pp. 179-93.

Horgan, M.P., and P.J. Kobielski (eds.), *To Touch the Text* (Festschrift J.A. Fitzmyer; New York: Crossroad, 1989).

Howell, D.B., *Matthew's Inclusive Story* (JSNTSup, 42; Sheffield: JSOT Press, 1992).

Hrushovski, B., 'Prosody, Hebrew', in *Encyclopedia Judaica* (New York: Macmillan, 1973), XIII, pp. 1195-1212.

Hubbard, B.J., *The Matthean Redaction of a Primitive Apostolic Commissioning* (SBLDS, 19; Missoula, MT: Scholars Press, 1974).

Huck, F., and H. Greeven, *Synopsis der drei ersten Evangelien* (Tübingen: J.C.B. Mohr, 1981).

Hummel, R., *Die Auseinandersetzung zwischen Kirche und Judentum im Matthäusevangelium* (Munich: Chr. Kaiser Verlag, 1967).

Hunter, A.M., *Design for Life* (London: SCM Press, 1953).

—'Crux Criticorum—Matt. xi.25-309: A Reappraisal', *NTS* 8 (1961–62), pp. 241-49.

Iersel, B.M.F. van, *Der Sohn in den synoptischen Jesusworten* (NovTSup, 3; Leiden: E.J. Brill, 1961).

Irigoin, J., 'La composition rhythmique des cantiques de Luc', *RB* 98 (1991), pp. 5-50.

Jacob, G., 'Die Proklamation der messianische Gemeinde: Zur Auslegung der Makarismen in der Bergpredigt', *ThV* 12 (1981), pp. 47-75.

Jacobson, A.D., 'The Literary Unity of Q', *JBL* 101 (1982), pp. 365-89.

—*The First Gospel: An Introduction to Q* (Sonoma, CA: Polebridge Press, 1992).

Jakobson, R., 'Closing Statement: Linguistics and Poetics', in Sebeok (ed.), *Style in Language*, pp. 350-77.

Japhet, S., *The Ideology of the Book of Chronicles and its Place in Biblical Thought* (Frankfurt: Lang, 1987).

Jasper, R.C.D., *The Development of the Anglican Liturgy: 1662-1980* (London: SPCK, 1989).

Jeremias, J., 'Golgotha und die heilige Felse', in *Angelos* 2 (Leipzig: Pfeiffer, 1926), pp. 74-128.

—'Zu Gedankenführung in den paulinischen Briefen', in J.W. Sevenster and W.C. Van Unnik (eds.), *Studia Paulina in honorem J. de Zwaan* (Haarlem: Bohn, 1953), pp. 146-54.

—*Jesus' Promise to the Nations* (trans. S.H. Hooke; SBT, 24; London: SCM Press, 1958).

—*The Parables of Jesus* (trans. S.H. Hooke; London: SCM Press, 1963).

—*The Prayers of Jesus* (SBT, 2.6; London: SCM Press, 1967).

—*New Testament Theology*, I (trans. J. Marsh; London: SCM Press, 1971).

—'ᾅδης', *TDNT*, I, pp. 146-49.

—' Ἰωνᾶς', *TDNT*, III, pp. 406-10.

—'κλείς', *TDNT*, III, pp. 744-53.

—'λίθος', *TDNT*, IV, pp. 269-80.

—'παῖς θεοῦ', B-D, *TDNT*, V, pp. 677-717.

—'πύλη', *TDNT*, VI, pp. 921-28.

Johnson, A.R., *The Vitality of the Individual in the Thought of Ancient Israel* (Cardiff: University of Wales Press, 1949).

Johnson, M.D., *The Purpose of the Biblical Genealogies* (SNTSMS, 8; Cambridge: Cambridge University Press, 2nd edn, 1988).

—'Reflections on a Wisdom Approach to Matthew's Christology', *CBQ* 36 (1974), pp. 44-64.

Jones, D.R., 'The Background and Character of the Lukan Psalms', *JTS* NS 19 (1968), pp. 19-50.

Jonge, M. de, 'The Earliest Christian Use of *Christos*', *NTS* 32 (1986), pp. 321-43.

Kähler, C., 'Zur Form- und Traditionsgeschichte von Matt. xvi.17-19', *NTS* 23 (1977), pp. 36-58.

Kahmann, J., 'Die Verheissung an Petrus', in Didier (ed.), *L'Evangile*, pp. 261-80.

Keck, L.E., 'The Poor among the Saints in the New Testament', *ZNW* 56 (1965), pp. 100-29.

Kennedy, G.A., *New Testament Interpretation through Rhetorical Criticism* (Chapel Hill: University of North Carolina Press, 1984).

Kilpatrick, G.D., *The Origins of the Gospel according to St Matthew* (Oxford: Clarendon Press, 1947).

Kimelman, R., 'Birkat ha-Minim and the Lack of Evidence for an Anti-Christian Prayer in Late Antiquity', in Sanders *et al.* (eds.), *Essays in Jewish and Christian Self-Definition*, II, pp. 226-44.

Kingsbury, J.D., 'The Composition and Christology of Matt 28.16-20', *JBL* 93 (1974), pp. 573-84.

—*Matthew: Structure, Christology, Kingdom* (London: SPCK, 1975).

—'The Figure of Peter in Matthew's Gospel as a Theological Problem', *JBL* 98 (1979), pp. 67-83.

Klausner, J., *Jesus of Nazareth* (trans. H. Danby; London: George Allen & Unwin, 1925).

Klein, S., 'Neue Beiträge zur Geschichte und Geographie Galiläas', *Palästina-Studien* (Vienna) 1 (1923).

Kloppenborg, J.S., *The Formation of Q* (Philadelphia: Fortress Press, 1987).

—*Q Parallels* (Sonoma, CA: Polebridge Press, 1988).

—'Theological Stakes in the Synoptic Problem', in Van Segbroeck *et al.* (eds.), *Four Gospels 1992*, pp. 93-120.

Knoch, O., 'Kenntnis und Verwendung des Matthäus-Evangelium bei den apostolischen Vätern', in Schenke (ed.), *Studien*, pp. 157-77.

Knowles, M., *Jeremiah in Matthew's Gospel* (JSNTSup, 68; Sheffield: JSOT Press, 1993).

Kodjak, A., *A Structural Analysis of the Sermon on the Mount* (Religion and Reason, 34; Berlin: de Gruyter, 1986).

Koester, H., *Introduction to the New Testament* (Philadelphia: Fortress Press, 1982).

Kospel, M.C.N., and J.C. de Moor, 'Fundamentals of Ugaritic and Hebrew Poetry', in van der Meer and de Moor (eds.), *Structural Analysis*, pp. 1-62.

Kraeling, C.H., *John the Baptist* (New York: Charles Scribner's Sons, 1951).

Kraft, R.A., 'Eis Nikos = Permanently/Succesfully: 1 Cor 15.54, Matt. 12.21', in *Septuagintal Lexicography 1* (SBLSCS, 1; Missoula, MT: Scholars Press, 1972), pp. 153-56.

Krentz, E., 'The Extent of Matthew's Prologue: Towards the Structure of the First Gospel', *JBL* 83 (1964), pp. 409-15.

Kretschmar, G., 'Ein Beitrag zur Frage der Ursprung frühchristlicher Askese', *ZTK* 61 (1964), pp. 27-67.

Kristeva, J., Σημειωτικὴ: *Recherches pour une sémanalyse* (Paris: Seuil, 1962).

Kruijf, T. de, *Der Sohn des Lebendiges Gottes* (AnBib, 14; Rome: Pontifical Biblical Institute, 1962).

Kugel, J.L., *The Idea of Biblical Poetry: Parallelism and its History* (New Haven: Yale University Press, 1981).

Kuhn, K.G., *Achtzehngebet und Vaterunser und der Reim* (WUNT, 1; Göttingen: Vandenhoeck & Ruprecht, 1961).

Kuhn, T.S., *The Structure of Scientific Revolutions* (Chicago: University of Chicago Press, 2nd edn, 1970).

Kümmel, W.G., *Introduction to the New Testament* (London: SCM Press, 1975).

Kürzinger, J., 'Zur Komposition der Bergpredigt', *Bib* 40 (1959), pp. 569-89.

Kynes, W.L., *A Christology of Solidarity: Jesus as Representative of his People in Matthew* (Lanham, MD: University Press of America, 1991).

Lachs, S.T., *A Rabbinic Commentary on the New Testament* (Hoboken, NJ: Ktav, 1985).

Lagrange, M.J., *Evangile selon saint Matthieu* (Paris: J. Gabalda, 1923).

Lambrecht, J., *The Sermon on the Mount: Proclamation and Exhortation* (Wilmington, DE: Michael Glazier, 1985).

—'The Great Commandment Pericope in Q', in R.A. Piper (ed.), *The Gospel Behind the Gospels* (NovTSup, 75; Leiden: E.J. Brill, 1994), pp. 73-96.

Lampe, P., 'Das Spiel mit dem Petrus-Namen—Matt 16.18', *NTS* 25 (1979), pp. 227-45.

Landy, F., 'In Defence of Jakobson', *JBL* 111 (1992), pp. 105-13.

Lange, J., *Das Erscheinen der Auferstandenen* (FB, 12; Würzburg: Echter, 1973).

Laws, S., *The Epistle of James* (BNTC; London: A. & C. Black, 1980).

Leaney, A.R.C., 'The Lucan Text of the Lord's Prayer', *NovT* 1 (1956), pp. 103-11.

—*The Gospel According to St Luke* (BNTC; London: A. & C. Black, 1958).

Ledogar, R.J., *Acknowledgement: Praise-Verbs in the Early Anaphoras* (Rome: Herder, 1968).

Légasse, S., *Jésus et l'enfant* (Paris: Gabalda, 1969).

—*Les Pauvres en Esprit* (LD, 78; Paris: Cerf, 1974).

Leivestad, R., 'ΤΑΠΕΙΝΟΣ-ΤΑΠΕΙΝΟΦΡΩΝ', *NovT* 8 (1966), pp. 36-47.

Lightfoot, R.H., *Locality and Doctrine in the Gospels* (London: Hodder & Stoughton, 1938).

Lindars, B., *New Testament Apologetic* (London: SCM Press, 1961).

Lindblom, J., *A Study on the Immanuel Section in Isaiah* (Scripta Minora 1757-58:4; Lund: C.W.K. Gleerup, 1958).

Linnemann, E., *Parables of Jesus* (trans. J. Sturdy; London: SPCK, 1966).

—'Der (wiedergefundene) Markusschluss', *ZTK* 66 (1969), pp. 255-87.

Linton, O., 'The Parable of the Children's Game', *NTS* 22 (1975–76), pp. 159-79.

Lohmeyer, E., *Kyrios Jesus: Eine Untersuchung zu Phil. 2,5-11* (Sitzungsberichte der Heidelberger Akademie der Wissenschaft, Phil.-hist Klasse, Jahr. 1927–28, 4 Abh.; Heidelberg: Winter, 1928).

—*Die Briefe an die Philipper, an die Kolosser und an Philemon* (KEKNT; Göttingen: Vandenhoeck & Ruprecht, 1930).

—'Mir ist gegeben alle Gewalt!', in W. Schmauch (ed.), *In Memoriam Ernst Lohmeyer* (Stuttgart: Evangelisches Verlagswerk, 1951), pp. 22-49.

—*Das Evangelium des Matthäus* (ed. W. Schmauch; KEKNT; Göttingen: Vandenhoeck & Ruprecht, 1956).

—*The Lord's Prayer* (trans. J. Bowden; London: Collins, 1965).

Lohse, E., *Colossians and Philemon* (Hermeneia; Philadelphia: Fortress Press, 1971).

Loisy, A., *Les Evangiles synoptiques*, I (Ceffonds: published privately, 1907).

Lowther Clarke, W.K., *New Testament Problems* (London: SPCK, 1929).

Lührmann, D., *Die Redaktion der Logienquelle* (WMANT, 3; Neukirchen–Vluyn: Neukirchener Verlag, 1969).

—'Liebet Eure Feinde', *ZTK* 69 (1972), pp. 412-38.

Luz, U., 'Die Bergpredigt im Spiegel ihre Wirkungsgeschichte', in J. Moltmann (ed.), *Nachfolge und Bergpredigt* (Munich: Chr. Kaiser Verlag, 1981), pp. 37-72.

—'Von Taumelloch im Weizenfeld', in H. Frankemölle and K. Kertelge (eds.), *Von Urchristentum zu Jesus* (Festschrift J. Gnilka; Freiburg: Herder, 1983), pp. 154-71.

—*Matthew 1–7* (trans. W.C. Linss; Edinburgh: T. & T. Clark, 1989) (= *Matthew*, I).

—*Das Evangelium nach Matthäus*. II. *Mt 8–17* (EKKNT, 1.2; Zürich: Benziger Verlag; Neukirchen–Vluyn: Neukirchener Verlag, 1989) (= *Matthew*, II).

—'Das Primatwort Matthäus 16.17-19 als wirkungsgeschichtlicher Sicht', *NTS* 37 (1991), pp. 415-33.

Maas, P., *Greek Metre* (Oxford: Clarendon Press, 1962).

McDonnell, K., and G.T. Montague, *Christian Initiation and Baptism in the Holy Spirit* (Collegeville, MN: Liturgical Press, 1991).

McKelvey, R.J., *The New Temple* (Oxford: Clarendon Press, 1969).

McNeile, A.H., *The Gospel according to St Matthew* (London: Macmillan, 1915).

Maier, J., *Die Texte vom Toten Meer* (Basel: Reinhardt, 1960).

Malina, B.J., 'The Literary Structure and Form of Matt xxviii.16-20', *NTS* 17 (1970–71), pp. 87-103.

Manson, T.W., 'Entry into Membership of the Early Church', *JTS* 48 (1947), pp. 25-31.

—'Baptism in the Church', *SJT* 2 (1949), pp. 391-403.

—*The Sayings of Jesus* (London: SCM Press, 1949).

—'The Lord's Prayer', *BJRL* 38 (1955–56), pp. 99-113, 436-48.

—*Ethics and the Gospel* (London: SCM Press, 1961).

Marshall, I.H., *The Gospel of Luke* (Exeter: Paternoster Press, 1978).

Marshall, S.S., 'The Character, Purpose and Setting of the Epistle of James' (BLitt dissertation, University of Oxford, 1968). [see also S. Laws]

Martin, R.P., *Carmen Christi* (SNTSMS, 4; Cambridge: Cambridge University Press, 1967).

Marxsen, W., *Introduction to the New Testament* (trans. G. Buswell; Oxford: Basil Blackwell, 1968).

—*Mark the Evangelist* (trans. R. Harrisville *et al.*; Nashville: Abingdon Press, 1969).

Mead, G.R.S. (ed.), *Pistis Sophia* (London: J.M. Watkins, 1921).

Mealand, D.L., *Poverty and Expectation in the Gospels* (London: SPCK, 1977).

Meer, W. van der, and J.C. de Moor (eds.), *The Structural Analysis of Biblical and Canaanite Poetry* (JSOTSup, 74; Sheffield: JSOT Press, 1988).

Meier, J.P., *Law and History in Matthew's Gospel* (AnBib, 71; Rome: Pontifical Biblical Institute, 1976).

—'Two Disputed Questions in Matthew 28.16-20', *JBL* 96 (1977), pp. 407-24.

—'Nations or Gentiles in Matthew 28.19?', *CBQ* 39 (1977), pp. 94-102.

—*The Vision of Matthew* (New York: Crossroad, 1979).

—'John the Baptist in Matthew's Gospel', *JBL* 99 (1980), pp. 383-405.

—*A Marginal Jew*, I (New York: Doubleday, 1991).

Menken, M.J.J., 'The References to Jeremiah in the Gospel according to Matthew', *ETL* 60 (1984), pp. 5-24.

—'The Quotations from Zech 9,9 in Mt 21,5 and in John 12,15', in Denaux (ed.), *John and the Synoptics*, pp. 571-78.

Metzger, B.M., *A Textual Commentary on the Greek New Testament* (London: United Bible Societies, 2nd edn, 1994).

Meyer, M.W., 'The Youth in Secret Mark and the Beloved Disciple in John', in J.E. Goehing *et al.* (eds.), *Gospel Origins and Christian Beginings* (Festschrift J.M. Robinson; Sonoma, CA: Polebridge Press, 1990), pp. 94-105.

Michael, J.H., 'The Sign of John', *JTS* 21 (1920), pp. 146-59.

Michaelis, C. 'Die π-Alliteration der Subjektsworte der ersten 4 Seligpreisungen in Mt. v 3-6 und ihre Bedeutung für den Aufbau der Seligpreisungen bei Mt., Lk. und in Q', *NovT* 10 (1968), pp. 148-61.

Michaelis, W., 'ὁράω κτλ.', *TDNT*, V, pp. 315-82.

Michel, O., 'The Conclusion of Matthew's Gospel', in Stanton (ed.), *Interpretation*, pp. 30-41.

—'μικρός', *TDNT*, IV, pp. 648-61.

—'οἶκος κτλ.', *TDNT*, V, pp. 119-59.

—'ὁμολογέω, ἐξομολογέω κτλ.', *TDNT*, V, pp. 199-220.

Moffatt, J., *A New Translation of the Old Testament* (London: Hodder & Stoughton, 1920).

Montgomery, J.A., 'Hebrew *ḥesed* and Greek *charis*', *HTR* 32 (1939), pp. 97-102.

Moor, J.C. de, 'The Reconstruction of the Aramaic Original of the Lord's Prayer', in van der Meer and de Moor (eds.), *Structural Analysis*, pp. 397-422.

Moore, G.F., *Judaism* (Cambridge, MA: Harvard University Press, 1927).

Morgenthaler, R., *Die lukanische Geschichtesschreibung als Zeugnis* (Zürich: Zwingli, 1948).

—*Statistische Synopse* (Zürich: Gotthelf, 1971).

—*Lukas und Quintilian* (Zürich: Gotthelf, 1993).

Neirynck, F., *The Minor Agreements of Matthew and Luke against Mark* (BETL, 37; Leuven: Peeters, 1974).

—*Evangelica*, I (BETL, 60; Leuven: Peeters, 1982); II (BETL, 99; Leuven: Peeters, 1991).

—'John and the Synoptics 1975–90', in Denaux (ed.), *John and the Synoptics*, pp. 3-62.

Neuhäusler, E., *Anspruch und Antwort Gottes* (Dusseldorf: Patmos, 1962).

Neusner, J., *A Life of Rabban Yohanan ben Zakkai* (Leiden: E.J. Brill, 1962).

—*The Development of a Legend* (Leiden: E.J. Brill, 1970).

Newton, M., *The Concept of Purity at Qumran and in the Letters of Paul* (SNTSMS, 53; Cambridge: Cambridge University Press, 1985).

Neyrey, J.H., 'The Thematic Use of Isaiah 42.1-4 in Matthew 12', *Bib* 63 (1982), pp. 457-73.

—*Honor and Shame in the Gospel of Matthew* (Louisville, KY: Westminster/John Knox Press, 1998).

Nickelsburg, G.W.E., 'Enoch, Levi and Peter: Recipients of Revelation in Upper Galilee', *JBL* 100 (1981), pp. 575-600.

Nicholson, E.W., *God and His People* (Oxford: Clarendon Press, 1986).

Nolan, B.M., *The Royal Son of God* (OBO, 23; Fribourg: Presses Universitaires; Göttingen: Vandenhoeck & Ruprecht, 1979).

Norden, E., *Agnostos Theos* (Leipzig: Teubner, 1913).

Noth, M., *The Chronicler's History* (JSOTSup, 50; Sheffield: JSOT Press, 1987).

Orchard, J.B., *Matthew, Luke and Mark* (Manchester: Koinonia, 1976).

—*A Synopsis of the Four Gospels Arranged according to the Two Gospel Hypothesis* (Edinburgh: T. & T. Clark, 1986).

Orton, D.E., *The Understanding Scribe* (JSNTSup, 25; Sheffield: JSOT Press, 1989).

Palmer, L.R., *The Greek Language* (London: Faber & Faber, 1980).

Pamment, M., 'The Kingdom of God according to the First Gospel', *NTS* 27 (1981), pp. 211-32.

Percy, E., *Die Botschaft Jesu* (Lund: C.W.K. Gleerup, 1953).

Perrin, N., *Rediscovering the Teaching of Jesus* (London: SCM Press, 1967).

Pesch, R., *Naherwartung* (Dusseldorf: Patmos, 1968).

—'The Position and Significance of Peter in the New Testament', *Concilium* 4.7 (1971), pp. 21-35.

Pesch, W., 'Zur Exegese von Mt 6,19-20/Lk 12,27-34', *Bib* 41 (1960), pp. 356-78.

—*Matthäus der Seelsorger* (SBS, 2; Stuttgart: Katholisches Bibelwerk, 1966).

—'Theologische Aussagen der Redaktion von Matthäus', in Hoffmann (ed.), *Orientierung an Jesus*, pp. 286-99.

Pettem, M., 'Luke's Great Omission and his View of the Law', *NTS* 42 (1996), pp. 35-54.

Phillips, C. (ed.), *Gerard Manley Hopkins* (The Oxford Authors: Oxford: Oxford University Press, 1986).

Piper, J., *Love Your Enemies* (SNTSMS, 38; Cambridge: Cambridge University Press, 1979).

Polag, A.P., *Die Christologie der Logienquelle* (Neukirchen–Vluyn: Neukirchener Verlag, 1977).

—*Fragmenta Q: Textheft zur Logienquelle* (Neukirchen–Vluyn: Neukirchener Verlag, 1979).

Porter, S.E., *Verbal Aspect in the Greek of the New Testament with Reference to Tense and Mood* (SBG, 1; New York: Peter Lang, 1989).

Powell, M.A., 'Matthew's Beatitudes: Reversals and Rewards of the Kingdom', *CBQ* 58 (1996), pp. 460-79.

Przybylski, J., *Righteousness in Matthew and his World of Thought* (SNTSMS, 41; Cambridge: Cambridge University Press, 1980).

Puech, E., '4Q425 et la pericope des Béatitudes en Ben-Sira et Matthieu', *RB* 98 (1991), pp. 80-106.

Quell, B., 'πατήρ', B, *TDNT*, V, pp. 959-74.

Rad, G. von, *Old Testament Theology* (trans. D.M.G. Stalker; Edinburgh: Oliver & Boyd, 1962).

Rahlfs, A., *Septuaginta* (Stuttgart: Württemburgische Bibelanstalt, 6th edn, 1952).

—'Über Theodotion-Lesarten im Neuen Testament und Aquila-Lesarten bei Justin', *ZNW* 20 (1921) pp. 182-89.

Ratcliff, E.C., 'Justin Martyr on Confirmation', *Theology* 51 (1948), pp. 133-39.

Ravens, D.A.S., *Luke and the Restoration of Israel* (JSNTSup, 119; Sheffield: Sheffield Academic Press, 1995).

Rengstorf, K.H., 'ἀπόστολος', *TDNT*, I, pp. 407-77.

—'Old and New Testament Traces of the Judaean Royal Ritual', *NovT* 5 (1962), pp. 229-44.

Riesner, R., 'Der Aufbau der Reden im Matthäus-Evangelium', *Theologische Beiträge* 9 (1978), pp. 173-76.

Rist, M., 'Is Matt. 11.25-30 a Primitive Baptismal Hymn?', *JR* 15 (1935), pp. 63-77.

Robinson, J.A.T., *Jesus and his Coming* (London: SCM Press, 1957).

—*Twelve More New Testament Studies* (London: SCM Press, 1984).

Robinson, J.M., 'Die Hodajot-Formel in Gebet und Hymnus des Frühchristentums', in W. Eltester and F.H. Kettler (eds.), *APOPHORETA* (Festschrift E. Haenchen; Berlin: Alfred Töpelmann, 1964), pp. 194-235.

—'Jesus as Son of Man and Sophia: Wisdom Tradition and the Gospels', in R.L. Wilken (ed.), *Aspects of Wisdom in Judaism and Early Christianity* (CSJCA, 1; Notre Dame: University of Notre Dame Press, 1975), pp. 9-11.

—'The Sayings Gospel Q', in Van Segbroeck *et al.* (eds.), *Four Gospels 1992*, pp. 361-88.

Robinson, J.M., and H. Koester, *Trajectories through Early Christianity* (Philadelphia: Fortress Press, 1971).

Rolland, P., 'From the Genesis to the End of the World: The Plan of Matthew's Gospel', *BTB* 2 (1972), pp. 135-76.

Ropes, J.H., *The Synoptic Gospels* (Cambridge, MA: Harvard University Press, 1934; Oxford: Basil Blackwell, 2nd edn, 1963).

Rothfuchs, W., *Die Erfüllungszitäte des Matthäus-Evangelium* (BWANT, 88; Stuttgart: W. Kohlhammer, 1969).

Sabourin, C., 'Why is God Called "Perfect" in Mt 5,48?', *BZ* NS 24 (1980), pp. 266-68.

Sabugal, S., 'La redaccion mateana del Padrenuestro (Mt 6,9-13)', *EstE* 68 (1983), pp. 307-29.

Sand, A., *Das Gesetz und die Propheten* (BU, 11; Regensburg: Regensburger, 1974).

—*Das Matthäusevangelium* (Regensburg: Regensburger, 1986).

Sanders, E.P., *Paul and Palestinian Judaism* (London: SCM Press, 1977).

Sanders, E.P., and M. Davies, *Studying the Synoptic Gospels* (London: SCM Press, 1992).

Sanders, E.P. *et al.* (eds.), *Essays in Jewish and Christian Self-Definition*, II (London: SCM Press, 1981).

Sanders, J.T., *The Christological Hymns of the New Testament* (SNTSMS, 15; Cambridge: Cambridge University Press, 1971).

Saussure, F. de, *Course in General Linguistics* (trans. W. Baskin; New York: The Philosophical Library, 1959; London: Fontana, 1974).

Schaberg, J., *The Father, the Son and the Holy Spirit: The Triadic Phrase in Matthew 28.19b* (SBLDS, 61; Chico, CA: Scholars Press, 1982).

Schechter, S., *Some Aspects of Rabbinic Theology* (London: A. & C. Black, 1909).

Schenke, L. (ed.), *Studien zur Matthäusevangelium* (Festschrift W. Pesch; SBS; Stuttgart: Katholisches Bibelwerk, 1988).

Schiffman, L.H., 'At the Crossroads: Tannaitic Perspectives on the Jewish-Christian Schism, in Sanders *et al.* (eds.), *Essays in Jewish and Christian Self-Definition*, pp. 15-56.

Schlatter, A., *Der Evangelist Matthäus* (Stuttgart: Calwer Verlag, 1929).

Schlosser, J. 'Marc 11,25, tradition et redaction', in *A cause de l'Evangile* (Festschrift J. Dupont), pp. 277-300.

Schmidt, K.L., 'ἐκκλησία', *TDNT*, III, pp. 501-36.

Schmidt, T.E., *Hostility to Wealth in the Synoptic Gospels* (JSNTSup, 15; Sheffield: JSOT Press, 1987).

Schnackenburg, R., *Christliche Existenz* (Munich: Kösel, 1967).

—*Schriften zur Neuen Testament* (Munich: Kösel, 1971).

—'Die Seligpreisung der Friedenstiften (Mt 5,9)', *BZ* NS 26 (1982), pp. 161-79.

Schneider, G., 'Das Vaterunser des Matthäus', in *A cause de l'Evangile* (Festschrift J. Dupont), pp. 57-90.

—'Im Himmel—auf Erde: Ein Perspektiv matthäischer Theologie', in Schenke (ed.), *Studien*, pp. 285-97.

Schniewind, J., 'Zur Synoptischer-Exegeser', *TRu* NS 2 (1930), pp. 129-205.

—*Das Evangelium nach Matthäus* (NTD; Göttingen: Vandenhoeck & Ruprecht, 1936).

Schökel, L.A., *A Manual of Hebrew Poetics* (Rome: Pontifical Biblical Institute, 1987).

Schönle, V., *Johannes, Jesus und die Juden* (Frankfurt: Peter Lang, 1982).

Schottroff, L., and W. Stegemann, *Jesus von Nazareth—Hoffnung der Armen* (Stuttgart: Kohlhammer, 3rd edn, 1990).

Schrage, W., *Das Verhältnis des Thomas-Evangelium zur synoptischen Tradition* (BZNW, 29; Berlin: Alfred Töpelmann, 1964).

Schrenk, G., 'δικαιοσύνη', *TDNT*, II, pp. 192-225.

Schubert, K., 'The Sermon on the Mount', in K. Stendahl (ed.), *The Scrolls and the New Testament* (London: SPCK, 1958), pp. 118-28.

Schulz, S., *Q: Die Spruchquelle der Evangelisten* (Zürich: Theologischer Verlag, 1972).

Schürer, E., *The History of the Jewish People* (trans. and rev. G. Vermes, F. Millar and M. Goodman; Edinburgh: T. & T. Clark, 1973–87).

Schürmann, H., *Traditionsgeschichtliche Untersuchungen zu den synoptischen Evangelien* (Dusseldorf: Patmos, 1968).

—*Das Lukasevangelium* (Freiburg: Herder, 1969).

—*Das Gebet des Herrn* (Freiburg: Herder, 1981).

Schwarz, G., 'Matthäus vi.9-13/Lukas xi.2-4: Emendation und Rückübersetzung', *NTS* 15 (1968–69), pp. 233-47.

Schweizer, E., 'πνεῦμα, πνευματικός', D-E, *TDNT*, VI, pp. 389-455.

—'υἱός', D, *TDNT*, VIII, pp. 363-92.

—*The Good News according to Matthew* (trans. D.E. Green; London: SPCK, 1976).

Scroggs, R., 'Eschatological Existence in Matthew and Paul', in J. Marcus and M.L. Soards (eds.), *Apocalyptic and the New Testament* (Festschrift J.L. Martyn; JSNTSup, 24; Sheffield: JSOT Press, 1989), pp. 125-46.

Sebeok, T.A. (ed.), *Style in Language* (Cambridge, MA: MIT Press, 1960).

Simons, E., *Hat der dritte Evangelist den kanonischen Matthäus benutzt?* (Bonn: Strauss, 1880).

Singer, S. (ed.), *The Authorised Daily Prayer Book* (London: Eyre & Spottiswoode, 1962).

Smit Sibinga, J., 'Eine literarische Technik im Matthäusevangelium', in Didier (ed.), *L'Evangile*, pp. 99-105.

Smith, M., *Clement of Alexandria and a Secret Gospel of Mark* (Cambridge, MA: Harvard University Press, 1973).

—*The Secret Gospel* (London: Gollancz, 1974).

Soares Prabhu, G.M., *The Formula Quotations in the Infancy Narrative of Matthew* (AnBib, 67; Rome: Pontifical Biblical Institute, 1976).

Soiron, T., *Die Bergpredigt Jesu* (Freiburg: Herder, 1941).

Souter, A. (ed. and trans.), *Tertullian's Treatises: Concerning Prayer; Concerning Baptism* (London: SPCK, 1919).

Standaert, B., 'Crying "Abba" and Saying "Our Father" ', in Draisma (ed.), *Intertextuality*, pp. 141-58.

Stankiewicz, E., 'Linguistics and the Study of Poetic Language', in Sebeok (ed.), *Style in Language*, pp. 69-87.

Stanton, G.N., *A Gospel for a New People: Studies in Matthew* (Edinburgh: T. & T. Clark, 1992).

Stanton, G.N. (ed.), *The Interpretation of Matthew* (London: SPCK, 2nd edn, 1995).

Staudinger, F., 'ἐλεημοσύνη', *EDNT*, I, pp. 428-29.

Steck, O.H., *Israel und das gewaltsame Geschick der Propheten* (WMANT, 23; Neukirchen–Vluyn: Neukirchener Verlag, 1967).

Stendahl, K., 'Matthew', in M. Black and H.H. Rowley (eds.), *Peake's Commentary on the Bible* (London: Nelson, 1962), pp. 769-98.

—*The School of St Matthew* (Philadelphia: Fortress Press, 2nd edn, 1968).

Stibbe, M.W.G., *John as Storyteller* (SNTSMS, 73; Cambridge: Cambridge University Press, 1992).

Strecker, G., *Der Weg der Gerechtigkeit* (FRLANT, 82; Göttingen: Vandenhoeck & Ruprecht, 1962).

—'Die Makarismen der Bergpredigt', *NTS* 17 (1971), pp. 255-75 [= 'Les macarismes du discours sur le montagne', in Didier (ed.), *L'Evangile*, pp. 185-208].

—*The Sermon on the Mount* (trans. O.C. Dean; Edinburgh: T. & T. Clark, 1989).

Streeter, B.H., *The Four Gospels* (London: Macmillan, 1924).

—*The Primitive Church* (London: Macmillan, 1929).

Stuhlmacher, P., *Gerechtigkeit Gottes bei Paulus* (FRLANT, 87; Göttingen: Vandenhoeck & Ruprecht, 1966).

Styler, G.M., 'The Priority of Mark', Excursus IV to C.F.D. Moule, *The Birth of the New Testament* (London: A. & C. Black, 1962), pp. 225-32.

Suggs, M.J., *Wisdom, Christology and Law in Matthew's Gospel* (Cambridge, MA: Harvard University Press, 1970).

Syreeni, K., 'Separation and Identity: Aspects of the Symbolic World of Matthew 6.1-18', *NTS* 40 (1994), pp. 522-47.

Tannehill, R.C., 'The Magnificat as a Poem', *JBL* 93 (1974), pp. 263-75.

—*The Narrative Unity of Luke–Acts*, I (Philadelphia: Fortress Press, 1986).

Taylor, V., 'The Order of Q', *JTS* NS 4 (1953), pp. 27-31.

—'The Original Order of Q', in A.J.B. Higgins (ed.), *New Testament Essays (in memoriam T.W. Manson)* (Manchester: Manchester University Press, 1959), pp. 240-69.

Thackeray, H.St J., 'Rhythm in the Book of Wisdom', *JTS* 6 (1905), pp. 232-37.

Thompson, W.G., *Matthew's Advice to a Divided Community* (AnBib, 44; Rome: Pontifical Biblical Institute, 1970).

Thrall, M.E., *II Corinthians* (ICC; 2 vols.; Edinburgh: T. & T. Clark, 1994, 2000).

Tilborg, S. van, 'Form-Criticism of the Lord's Prayer', *NovT* 14 (1972), pp. 94-105.

—*The Jewish Leaders in Matthew* (Leiden: E.J. Brill, 1972).

—*The Sermon on the Mount as an Ideological Intervention* (Assen: Van Gorcum, 1986).

Torrey, C.C., *Documents of the Primitive Church* (New York: Harper, 1941).

Traub, H., 'οὐρανός', C-E, *TDNT*, V, pp. 509-36.

Trilling, W., 'Die Täufertradition bei Matthäus', *BZ* NS 2 (1959), pp. 271-89.

—*Das Wahre Israel* (Munich: Kösel, 1964).

—*Christusverkundigung in den synoptischen Evangelien* (Munich: Kösel, 1969).

Tuckett, C.M., *The Revival of the Griesbach Hypothesis* (SNTSMS, 44; Cambridge: Cambridge University Press, 1983).

—'The Beatitudes: A Source-Critical Study. With a Reply by M.D. Goulder', *NovT* 25 (1983), pp. 193-215.

—'"Thomas" and the Synoptics', *NovT* 30 (1988), pp. 132-57.

—*Q and the History of Early Christianity* (Edinburgh: T. & T. Clark, 1996).

Tuckett, C.M. (ed.), *Synoptic Studies* (JSNTSup, 8; Sheffield: JSOT Press, 1985).

Van Segbroeck, F., 'Les citations d'accomplissement dans l'Evangile selon Matthieu d'après trois ouvrages récents', in Didier (ed.), *L'Evangile*, pp. 107-30.

Van Segbroeck, F., *et al.* (eds.), *The Four Gospels 1992* (Festschrift F. Neirynck; BETL, 100; Leuven: Peeters, 1992).

Vermes, G., 'Bible and Midrash: Early Old Testament Exegesis', in *CHB* I, pp. 199-231.

—'The Targumic Versions of Genesis IV.3-16', in *Post-Biblical Jewish Studies* (Leiden: E.J. Brill, 1975), pp. 92-128.

—*The Dead Sea Scrolls in English* (Harmondsworth: Penguin Books, 4th edn, 1995).

Via, D.O., *Self-Deception and Wholeness in Paul and Matthew* (Philadelphia: Fortress Press, 1990).

Vielhauer, P., *Aufsätze zum Neuen Testament* (Munich: Chr. Kaiser Verlag, 1965).

Viviano, B.T., *Study as Worship: Aboth and the New Testament* (SJLA, 26; Leiden: E.J. Brill, 1978).

Vögtle, A., *Das Evangelium und die Evangelien* (Dusseldorf: Patmos, 1971).

Vouga, L., 'La séconde passion de Jérémie', *LumV* 32 (1983), pp. 71-82.

Walter, N., 'Die Bearbeitung der Seligpreisungen durch Matthäus', *SE* 4 (TU, 102; Berlin: Akademie Verlag, 1968), pp. 246-58.

Watson, W.G.E., *Classical Hebrew Poetry* (JSOTSup, 26; Sheffield: JSOT Press, 1984).

—*Traditional Techniques in Hebrew Poetry* (JSOTSup, 170; Sheffield: Sheffield Academic Press, 1994).

Weiss, J., 'Das Logion Mt 11,25-30', in *idem* (ed.), *Neutestamentliche Studien* (Festschrift G. Henrici; Leipzig: J.C. Hinrichs, 1914), pp. 120-30.

Wenham, J.W., *Redating Matthew, Mark and Luke* (London: Hodder & Stoughton, 1991).

Wilckens, U., 'σοφία κτλ.', C-F, *TDNT*, VII, pp. 496-526.

Wilcox, M., 'Peter and the Rock: A Fresh Look at Matt 16.17-19', *NTS* 22 (1975–76), pp. 75-88.

—'ΤΑΛΙΘΑΚΟΥΜ in Mark 5.41', in Delobel (ed.), *LOGIA*, pp. 469-76.

Wilken, W., 'Zur Frage der literarische Beziehung zwischen Matthäus und Lukas', *NovT* 8 (1966), pp. 48-57.

Willes, J.T., 'Alternating A B A' B' Parallelism in Old Testament Psalms and Prophetic Literature', in Follis (ed.), *Directions*, pp. 49-76.

Windisch, H., 'Friedensbringer–Gottessöhne', *ZNW* 24 (1925), pp. 240-60.

Wink, W., *John the Baptist in the Gospel Tradition* (SNTSMS, 7; Cambridge: Cambridge University Press, 1968).

Winter, P., 'Magnificat and Benedictus—Maccabaean Psalms?', *BJRL* 37 (1955), pp. 328-47.

—'Matthew xi 27 and Luke x 22 from the First to the Fifth Century: Reflections on the Development of the Text', *NovT* 1 (1956), pp. 112-48.

Wright, N.T., *The Climax of the Covenant* (Edinburgh: T. & T. Clark, 1991).

York, J.O., *The Last Shall be First: The Rhetoric of Reversal in Luke* (JSNTSup, 46; Sheffield: JSOT Press, 1991).

Ziegler, J., *Isaias* (Septuaginta auctoritate Societatis Litterarum Gottingensis, XIV; Göttingen: Vandenhoeck & Ruprecht, 1939).

—*Jeremias* (Septuaginta auctoritate Societatis Litterarum Gottingensis, XV; Göttingen: Vandenhoeck & Ruprecht, 1957).

Ziesler, J.A., *The Meaning of Righteousness in Paul* (SNTSMS, 20; Cambridge: Cambridge University Press, 1972).

Zimmerli, W., *The Law and the Prophets* (trans. R.E. Clements; Oxford: Basil Blackwell, 1967).

—'Zwillingpsalmen', in , *Wort, Lied und Gottesspruch* (Festschrift J. Ziegler) (Würzburg: Echter Verlag, 1972).

Zumstein, J., *La condition du croyant dans l'Evangile selon Matthieu* (OBO, 16; Fribourg: Presses Universitaires; Göttingen: Vandenhoeck & Ruprecht, 1977).

INDEXES

INDEX OF REFERENCES

OLD TESTAMENT

APOCRYPHA

JOURNAL FOR THE STUDY OF THE NEW TESTAMENT
SUPPLEMENT SERIES